MUTUAL SECURITY

Mutual Security

A New Approach to Soviet-American Relations

Edited by
Richard Smoke and Andrei Kortunov

With Prefaces by
Cyrus Vance and Georgiy Arbatov

A Joint Study by
the Center for Foreign Policy Development
at Brown University
and
the Institute for the USA and Canada
of the Soviet Academy of Sciences

ST. MARTIN'S PRESS
New York

First published in the United States of America

Printed in the United States of America

ISBN 0-312-04804-1 cloth
ISBN 0-312-05036-4 paper

Library of Congress Cataloging-in-Publication Data
Mutual Security : a new approach to Soviet-American relations / edited by Richard
    Smoke and Andrei Kortunov; with prefaces by Cyrus Vance and Georgiy Arbatov.
        p. cm.
    "A joint study by the Center for Foreign Policy Development at Brown University
and the Institute for the U.S.A. and Canada of the Soviet Academy of Sciences."
    ISBN 0-312-04804-1. — ISBN 0-312-05036-4 (pbk.)
    1. United Statea — Foreign relations — Soviet Union. 2. Soviet Union — Foreign
relations — United States. 3. United States — Foreign relations — 1989- 4. Soviet
Union — Foreign relations — 1985-
I. Smoke, Richard. II Kortunov, A.V. III. Brown University. Center for Foreign
Policy Development. IV. Institut Soedinennykh Shtatov Ameriki i Kanady
(Akademiia Nauk SSSR)
E183.8.S65M88   1991
327.73047 — dc20   90-8618
                                                CIP

Contents

Preface, *by Cyrus R. Vance*   vii

Preface, *by Georgiy A. Arbatov*   xiii

Editors' Foreword   xxiv

I. Working Group on Principles and Criteria   1

1. Joint Introduction to Mutual Security, *by Viktor Kremenyuk and Richard Smoke*   3

2. Interdependence: A Perspective on Mutual Security, *by Mikhail Bezrukov and Andrei Kortunov*   10

3. U.S.-Soviet Relations: Evolution and Prospects, *by Alexander George*   19

4. Domestic Preconditions for the Transition to Mutual Security: A Soviet Perspective, *by Petr Gladkov*   42

5. A Theory of Mutual Security, *by Richard Smoke*   59

II. Working Group on Europe   113

6. Joint Statement, *by the Working Group on Europe*   115

7. A Soviet-American Dialogue on Eastern Europe, *by William Luers*   118

8. Eastern Europe and International Stability, *by Yuriy Davydov*   127

9. Implications for Western Policy, *by Mark Kramer*   137

10. The Common European Home and Mutual Security, *by Mikhail Bezrukov and Yuriy Davydov*   152

11. The German Question: A Mutual Security Approach, *by Francis Meehan*   161

12. The German Question and its International Dimensions, *by Mikhail Kozhokin*   166

III. Working Group on the Persian Gulf   171

13. Toward Mutual Threat Reduction in the Persian Gulf, *by Jo-Anne Hart, Harold Saunders and Andrei Shumikhin*   173

IV. Working Group on the North Pacific   193

14. Joint Statement, *by the Working Group on the North Pacific*   195

15. International Security in the Asia-Pacific Region: Confrontation or Balance of Interests?, *by Aleksis Bogaturov, Vladimir Lukin and Mikhail Nossov*   200

16. Creating a More Stable Security Structure in the Asia-Pacific Region, *by Donald Zagoria*   212

17. The Korean Problem and Possible Forms of Soviet-American Interaction, *by Aleksis Bogaturov, Mikhail Nossov, and Konstantine Pleshakov*   222

18. The United States, the Soviet Union and Korea: Beyond Confrontation, *by Alan Romberg*   233

V. Working Group on Nuclear and Conventional Arms Reductions   247

19. Fundamental Deterrence and Mutual Security Beyond START, *by Jan Kalicki, Fred Chernoff, Eric Mlyn, Sergei Fedorenko, Andrei Kortunov and Aleksandr Pisarev*   249

20. Mutual Security and Arms Reductions in Europe, *by P. Terrence Hopmann*   269

21. The Problems of Developing Stable Non-Offensive Structures for General-Purpose Forces and Conventional Arms in Europe, *by Aleksandr Konovalov*   288

22. Translating the Lessons and Methods of Nuclear Arms Control to the Conventional Arena, *by Stephen Fought*   317

VI. Working Group on Future Scenarios and Conclusion   335

23. The End of the Consensus That Never Was: The Future of Soviet-American Relations as Viewed by the Soviet Public, *by Andrei Melvil and Aleksandr Nikitin*   337

24. Mutual Security and U.S. Public Opinion, *by Mark Lindeman*   356

25. Conclusion: Mutual Security and the Future, *by Sergei Plekhanov and Howard Swearer*   371

Appendices   381

The Contributors   382
Members of the Working Groups   386
Chronology of Major Meetings   389
The Center for Foreign Policy Development   391
The Institute for the USA and Canada   393

Preface

CYRUS R. VANCE

Mutual security is a simple and basic idea. Mutual security between two nations or alliances simply means that each of them seeks to gain security along with the other. The two thus grow more secure together. This is a basic difference from the other, more familiar, approach where each side seeks its own security at the expense of the other.

Mutual security, if carried out to its full implications, is also a radical idea in some respects. For instance it requires abandoning the traditional notion of "victory." Victory used to mean defeating, even crushing, the other side. In a hot shooting war — or in a Cold War — victory for one side meant that it kept pushing ahead until the other side went down. But mutual security must exclude that idea of victory. We now live in the nuclear age. If the other side is pushed to the wall, it will hurl the nuclear thunderbolts upon its enemy and thus upon us all. Then there is no "winner," no victory for anyone.

In a world of mutual security, "victory" means something radically different. It means successfully defending oneself while allowing the other side to successfully defend itself too. In the long run, victory means growing more secure in what is rightly one's own — while leaving the other side also to grow more secure in what is rightly its own.

Cyrus R. Vance was Secretary of State of the United States from 1977 to 1980. Earlier he served as Secretary of the Army, as Deputy Secretary of Defense, and several times as a special representative of the President in diplomatic negotiations. He is a member of the Board of Directors or Trustees of numerous organizations in the United States, including the Board of Advisors of the Center for Foreign Policy Development at Brown University.

In some general way the idea of mutual security has been gradually developing in the mind of humanity for decades. It was put into words and brought to the world's attention in a work in which I was privileged to be involved, along with Georgiy Arbatov and many others, in the early 1980s. Olaf Palme, the late Prime Minister of Sweden, invited some sixteen of us to join with him in a commission that would rethink deeply the problem of finding security in the nuclear age. The Palme Commission consisted of representatives from the West, from the Soviet bloc, and from many unaligned countries. Academician Arbatov was the representative from the USSR. I was the representative from the United States. The Commission's report was entitled *Common Security*; it was published worldwide in several languages; and it advanced the viewpoint that I have just sketched.

Since then, many specialists have devoted efforts to developing this viewpoint. Work on it has been done in Western and Eastern Europe, in the USSR, in the United States, and in various neutral countries. In 1985, Mikhail Gorbachev became General Secretary in the USSR; Georgiy Arbatov was one of his advisers. Georgiy deserves much credit, and the world's thanks, for having made a point of bringing to Gorbachev's attention the Palme Commission's work and the philosophy that we had advanced. In 1986 the Soviet Union officially announced its acceptance and its advocacy of the viewpoint of common security — or as it is more often called now, mutual security. Ever since, the Soviet Union has been proclaiming that this is the best approach by which East and West can find security in the nuclear age.

I wish I could say that the U.S. government accepted the mutual security viewpoint with equal speed. Regrettably it did not, although it did not reject mutual security either. For some years the attitude in Washington, D.C. appears to have been one of waiting, to discover what this idea might mean in practice.

For anyone who might feel critical of Washington for this, I might add that there are particular reasons why the United States, of all countries, might not be instantly receptive to such a philosophy. The military history of the United States is unique among great modern nations. In all its history, the United States of America has never lost a war — save one, and even then the enemy remained 12,000 miles away. Most of America's victories have been crushing, in fact absolute. Psychologically and culturally, it is not easy for a nation that has lived such a history to embrace a new philosophy that demands giving up victory.

Even so, the world is changing. Of late it has been changing with blazing speed before our astonished eyes. In response, the Secretary of State of the United States gave speeches in the autumn of 1989 in which he said that the search for "mutual advantage" would be a new principle for the U.S. in its policy toward the Soviet Union. There is hardly a hairsbreadth distance between mutual advantage and mutual security. Indeed, since security is the most important goal of foreign policy, mutual security should be the most important element in a policy of mutual advantage.

Meanwhile, much work has been needed in developing the practical meaning and implications of mutual security. The idea may be simple in its essence, but its concrete applications are anything but simple. East and West, Russia and America, have developed over four decades an enormously intricate web of conflicts, as well as some cooperation. There are colossal nuclear forces facing each other across the globe, huge military forces facing each other in Europe and elsewhere, and legions of representatives jockeying with each other in the Third World. Disentangling and gently disengaging this web of conflicts is no easy task. Much thought, much care, and many frank discussions are required.

It was the awareness of this challenge that led to this book. In 1987, the Center for Foreign Policy Development at Brown University and the Institute for the USA and Canada of the Soviet Academy of Sciences launched a joint project to study the problems of developing mutual security. It was the first substantial, joint project by Soviet and American institutions specializing in foreign affairs that was focused specifically on the problem of mutual security. The two organizations should be commended, not only for having recognized the central importance of the mutual security approach, but especially for having accepted the special challenges of carrying out their research jointly. They understood that one side cannot unilaterally tell the other what mutual security means in practice. The very concept demands joint thinking, joint study, and joint development of practical solutions.

The two organizations also recognized that mutual security must be understood and approached broadly. Regrettably, there has been a tendency in some quarters to think that "mutual security" merely means arms control. Arms control is indeed part of it, but it is only one part. In their competition with each other the United States and Soviet Union have tried for decades to advance their security by many instruments besides arms, and have taken actions "for their national security" all around the world. As this book stresses, mutual security is a general approach to problems of national security. It applies to regional and political problems as well as to military ones.

The Brown Center and the Institute for the USA and Canada are planning to continue their work on mutual security. This book represents the chief written products of their research through the end of 1989. I hope it will be read and pondered widely. To what it offers, I would like to add one further theme of my own.

*

Mutual security between two nations or alliances that have been foes, and could conceivably be adversaries again, is vitally important for reasons that may go beyond what is obvious. There is a longer-term as well as a short-term significance in the development of mutual security.

Of course it is true that in the short run, the two can succeed in becoming more secure, and more at peace with each other, by seeking and finding ways to become more secure *together*. A joint search for ways mutually to reduce their explicit and implicit threats against each other, which is the topic to which much of this book is addressed, is the clear and absolutely essential first step. In the absence of a steadily developing process of "mutual threat reduction" (as it is termed in this study) neither side can possibly move on toward any greater form of security, nor would either particularly want to. Someone who feels threatened by someone else can cooperate with them only in the most limited ways. A continually progressive reduction of mutual threats, then, is the essential first step in the development of true mutual security.

However it is only the first step. A deeper and more lasting security, and a deeper and more lasting meaning of "mutual security," comes with the development over time of an entirely different relationship. Two nations who have achieved this more complete form of mutual security have left behind anything that involves threat or even the possibility of threat. They have brought themselves into alignment with each other in a more fundamental way that makes "threat," at least in any serious sense of the term, unthinkable.

In our time, a good example is the relationship that has developed among the West European nations. And for a long time, another important example has been the relationship between the United States and Canada. In each of these relationships it almost never would even occur to people to describe their relations as one of "mutual security"; and that is the proof that this deeper and more lasting form of it has been achieved. The nations of Western Europe simply do not make threats against each other any more, in the sense of "threat" normally used by specialists on security and foreign policy. Neither do Canada and the United States. The reason is not that it would be literally impossible to do so. The reason is that for everyone involved, it has become unthinkable to do so. There is something almost shocking in the idea.

It is sometimes thought that this kind of deeply secure relationship between nations can be achieved only when they have come together in the face of some common, outside threat. It is true that this is one way that such a relationship can form. No doubt the nations of Western Europe have developed such a relationship among themselves in recent decades at least in substantial measure because they felt themselves threatened by a common foe.

However it is not true that this kind of relationship can *only* be formed by uniting against some third party. The proof of this is the relationship between the United States and Canada. These two great nations, who even fought one another in a war once (the War of 1812), came together thereafter for reasons that had nothing to do with facing some common enemy. There was none. They came together, into a relationship that could certainly be called one of "mutual security" in the most profound sense of the term, for entirely other reasons. They simply found, decade after decade, that they had a great deal that united them, and that each of them could best achieve what it wanted and needed by maintaining and deepening a relationship characterized by great cooperation, harmony and trust. The famous three-thousand-mile open border, which has remained unfenced and unguarded for a very long time now, is merely the most obvious and tangible expression of a relationship in which any question — or even awareness — of "security" *against* each other simply doesn't arise.

"Mutual security" in this profound sense, then, is not merely some ideal we may imagine. We know from this case and others that it can actually be created.

The most important property of such a relationship, once it is fully formed, is that it is permanent. (At any rate it is permanent insofar as anything in international affairs may be said to be permanent.) Relations between the two do not revert back, at some later time, to the more common kind of relations among nations, characterized by suspicion and even by a possibility of hostility. Rather this form of harmony between the two countries continues on. It continues, even weathering small storms that may arise between them resulting from some misunderstanding or even some minor real conflict of interests. It would be true, but does not quite catch the essence, to say that this relationship is "irreversible." It would be more deeply true to say that the relationship has been transformed in kind.

Such a relationship is able to continue permanently, because once it is created it contains within it the means for resolving small conflicts. Very likely, strong mechanisms will already exist for consultations and discussions between the two, in which their points of view can be aired and mutually understood and some compromise reached. But if adequate mechanisms do not yet exist when a dispute appears, they will instantly be created by the two sides, of whatever kinds may be needed to resolve the dispute. Until it is resolved, mechanisms will go on being created, up to and including extraordinary means if necessary, such as the creation of high-level joint commissions made up of some of the most senior and respected citizens from each side.

Such is the relationship that now exists among the West European nations and that has long existed between Canada and the United States. This is mutual security in the deepest and the final sense of the term. With the passage of time, we may hope that this kind of relationship can be formed between other nations and groups of nations as well. We may indeed hope that in time conditions may emerge that may make it possible for such a relationship to develop between East and West.

By all means then, let us proceed over the coming years, as this book recommends, with the process of mutual reductions in the threats between East and West. Let us carry out that task as thoroughly as we can, as carefully as we can, and as rapidly as we can consistent with care. But let us not imagine that mutual security will then have been fully achieved. Threats that have been reduced, even greatly, can be increased again later unless something more fundamental is done as well.

What reducing and eliminating threats *can* do is create a new situation for all parties involved; and that new situation in turn may enable us, if we are wise, to move on to important additional steps. In this fashion we may move forward, acting prudently but steadily to approach the day when the final form of mutual security may become feasible.

A new century is rapidly approaching, beckoning us toward a more hopeful future. Let us, on both sides, be wise enough to take the steps that will make it a future of mutual security, in ever more complete ways, not only for East and West but also for more and more of the Earth's nations.

Preface

GEORGIY A. ARBATOV

The problem of security is as old as the world. And, at the same time, every historical era gives new content to this concept. And each time an intense struggle precedes the new understanding of security.

If you take a look at the past, at the sources of human civilization, you can easily become convinced that ideas about security have changed in the sense that they have become more inclusive. This is evidently an important criterion of social progress.

During barbarian times security was understood as essentially the security of one human being in the endless "war of all against all." It did not extend even to the closest relatives. Human egotism achieved its absolute, since only under these conditions could survival be guaranteed. The Greek myth of Chronos devouring his children is probably an echo from these ancient, archaic times.

As the first signs of human civilization appeared, the security of a particular individual expanded to mean the security of a family or clan. A person no longer thought only of his own survival, but also of assuring the security of those close to him, and was even ready to sacrifice himself for the survival of the community. The concept of "self-sacrifice" emerged. It is hardly necessary to prove how important an advance this extension became, since it signified the rise of morality

Georgiy A. Arbatov is an Academician of the Soviet Academy of Sciences, a member of the Congress of Peoples' Deputies, and a member of the Central Committee of the Communist Party of the Soviet Union. He has been Director of the Institute for the USA and Canada since its founding in 1968. His many books and articles on Soviet-American relations and international affairs include The Soviet Viewpoint, *published in New York in 1981.*

as a social category (perhaps a limited morality, only for "one's own," but morality nonetheless).

Then there was another step forward — security overstepped the borders of family ties. In ancient Greece it was a citizen's duty (the very concept of citizenship appeared) to assure the security of the city, of the *polis*. Sacrifice became necessary in the name of distant, unknown persons, and not just in the name of those close to one. The concept of motherland appeared. Then mankind made yet another jump — security began to be formulated as the security of a people, of a nation.

Even examples taken from the Bible before the Jews became one people led by Moses, suggest that they passed through several stages of individual insecurity when a brother posed a threat to a brother (Cain and Abel) and a father (Abraham, Noah) to his son or sons. It was a threat to their survival from the Pharaoh which turned the Jews into one people united against an external threat. More generally, threats to survival of a group of people united by language and common territory, and usually by religion, caused them to live together in a certain form of social organization (a state or city) united against the outside threat.

This process was paralleled by empire-building. It would be a mistake to see in empires only one aspect: the domination of the center over the periphery. Empires also took responsibility for the security of their whole territory, and thus contributed to such processes as trade and communication, exchange of goods, services, knowledge and culture. The traditional state or city-state tended to isolate itself from the outer world, mainly for security reasons. In this respect, empires were a forceful but useful way of incorporating such isolated communities into larger entities, living together in peace and security. Naturally this did not mean that external threats disappeared. Always there were contestants, challengers who would attack empires. Thus human history, while being a stage for endless wars and forays, also witnessed imperial duels: Babylon and Assyria, Rome and Carthage, Charlemagne's Empire and the Arabs, the Holy Roman Empire and the Ottomans, the Russian Empire and the Tartars, and so on. What Thomas Hobbes called "the war of all against all" never really ceased and security was never durable.

Different societies sought security by different methods, or models: by expansion of their borders (many examples of empire-building), by strengthening their borders with walls or other defenses (e.g., the Great Wall of China), by using natural obstacles (e.g., Britain shielded by the English Channel), or by a combination of political and natural factors (e.g., the United States, isolated for a long time). Nonetheless it was essentially an insecure world, made up of separate nations that based their security policies on their own efforts, and only partly on collective arrangements such as coalitions and alliances, which were not trusted in the long run. The motto "nations do not have permanent alliances, only permanent interests" was the governing principle.

The principles of some permanent, collective security arrangement introduced by the Vienna Congress in 1815 were to a large extent innovative, but still very embryonic. These principles tried to combine both national efforts in military security and collective diplomatic arrangements. The effort to safeguard the status quo became a victim of rising nationalism, first in Italy and then in Germany. The security system introduced by the Vienna Congress could not resist the intensifying nationalism and finally was destroyed by it. Attempts to supplant it with a security system based on alliances and the balance of power principle only precipitated World War I. The League of Nations, seen as an attempt to create a new European security system after that war, also proved ineffective because it became a system for the containment of Germany, through various loose measures.

The bloc principle of assuring security reached its apotheosis in the second half of our century — the world became a bipolar one, where the black-and-white opposition of East and West achieved unprecedented dimensions.

However, the headlong expansion of the principle of security has also led to increased fragility in its practical application. The bipolar world of the last few decades turned out to be extremely unstable, far less stable than the multipolar "balance of forces" which preceded it. This was recognized quite a long time ago, when young and newly liberated states first formed the Non-aligned Movement which, among its other purposes, was called upon to somehow stabilize the bipolar international system. In a bipolar world the principle of security came increasingly into conflict with the principle of freedom of choice. The "younger" partners in alliances more and more resembled mute puppets. And the lessening of international tension now taking place is destroying the accustomed structure of bipolar confrontation before our very eyes.

What are we returning to? To national security? But this can hardly be viewed as an acceptable solution. After all, the system of national security, the so-called "war of all against all" on the state level, engendered numerous wars and clashes. But attempts to preserve the bloc system of security would not be likely to succeed — it would necessitate freezing the entire structure of international relations in the "cold war" era. We should probably go forward, not back, and more from the security of blocs to the security of mankind, but not return to national security.

Here, international organizations, and primarily the United Nations, can play a tremendous role. The paradox and, if you prefer, the tragedy of the U.N. during the first forty years of its existence, is that an organization universal in its nature cannot act successfully in a world split into two opposing blocs. The world schism paralyzed many U.N. bodies and mechanisms, had a tangential bearing on its bureaucratization and sometimes forced it to deal with secondary, local matters. The U.N. requires a universality of ideas about security, a concept of general security common to all mankind, which for a number of reasons was not created immediately after World War II but which is beginning to take shape today before our eyes.

On the other hand, the development of civilization is also demonstrating an enrichment in the content of the concept of security. Security initially presupposed only a guarantee of the physical survival of a person, clan or nation. Accordingly, it referred primarily to the military sphere. When people's lives were threatened, everything else was strictly secondary and insignificant.

However, as civilization developed, security began to be interpreted in a broader context. After all, threats to the security of a complex social mechanism, for a relatively high level of civilization, can be political, economic and even spiritual, not just military. The security of a state may be undermined simply by cutting it off from vitally important sources of raw materials, by closing basic trade routes or isolating it politically. A new religion or ideology that shatters traditional life structures and customary value systems can also present a threat to security. Later, ecological dimensions to security, information security, and other similar factors appeared.

"Peace is not simply the absence of war," Spinoza emphasized in his day. In our times security is not simply the absence of immediate threats to the existence of the human community. Moreover, security can no longer be restricted to the securing of conditions for the functioning of society. Security is also the presence of guarantees for its economic, social and spiritual development. And there is in this rather widely accepted understanding of security a reflection of the progress achieved by mankind.

Thus, an evolution in the concept of security has occurred in two directions: in the direction of broadening the subject of security (person-family-clan-city-nation-bloc-mankind) and enriching its content (survival-functioning-development). This logic requires all of us to take a look at problems related to security.

Interpretation of new problems can be neither easy nor rapid. The subject, after all, concerns the most important questions of policy. Any progress here is achieved with colossal effort. One can understand the conservatives, who are in no hurry to reject traditional concepts: Any haste, mistake or error can be exceedingly costly. But to understand them is not necessarily to agree with them. Stubborn adherence to old approaches can be even more costly to mankind.

As for the Soviet Union, we have already paid dearly for a stubborn effort to preserve unchanged the traditional concepts of security. Until very recently, until the advent of perestroika and new political thinking, attempts were made to treat the problem of security as a strictly military one. Any other threats were somehow considered not serious, something that could be left to future generations. The results of this are generally recognized: having created a colossal "safety margin" in the military sphere, the USSR began to lag further and further behind developed countries in non-military areas, where planning was guided by the residual principle.

Did this harm our security? Undoubtedly, if, of course, you understand security in the broad sense which I spoke of earlier. Today we are attempting — not always consistently and not always successfully — to correct the situation, to approach the problem of security overall, giving consideration to its political, economic and humanitarian dimensions, as well as the military ones.

At the same time, the Soviet Union made the principle of national security an absolute one for many decades. We were among the most irreconcilable defenders of sovereignty, against any interference by certain countries in the affairs of others. I well remember how, in the postwar years, we assailed the idea of a world government, portraying plans for creating it as virtually a "world conspiracy." And shouldn't one view the campaign of the fight against cosmopolitanism in the early 1950s as an ugly manifestation of the striving toward absolute sovereignty?

I should stipulate at once: both of these particular features of Soviet thinking in the field of security were provoked by well-known objective causes. One should not discount the hostile external encirclement of the only socialist state during the interwar period, the country's economic isolation and the West's real attempts to interfere in our domestic affairs, to influence internal processes in the Soviet Union. And the national trauma of the Second World War, which is still imprinted on the memory of society, also had a profound influence on the attitude toward security.

But at the same time one cannot avoid seeing that, in our zealous worship of the idols of sovereignty and military security, we forgot the principles of that new society which we were trying to build in our country.

After all, even Marx wrote about a system of economic mutual interdependence which would be the inevitable result of the growth of large-scale machine production, of newer and newer restraints on "absolute sovereignty." And Lenin emphasized that the interests of mankind, the interests of social development, must be placed above the interests of individual social groups, including the working class. Socialism is in essence international, planetary in scope; it is organically incompatible with any form of national narrowness or state exclusivity.

Now we are trying to return to our primary sources in this and in many other questions. Naturally, with the understanding that we are running up against many new problems which were unknown to Marx and Lenin. For example, nuclear weapons. Or the ecological crisis, the shortage of fuel and energy resources, and the spread of AIDS.

However, new problems only confirm the old Marxist thesis that in the future we must move forward together, with the entire human community, and not in individual countries or social groups. And we must move forward simultaneously in all areas: political, military, economic and humanitarian. Otherwise even very important "breakthroughs" may prove inadequate.

For example, can we speak of assuring the military security needed by the world when the economic gulf between North and South is widening? The answer to this question is obvious: absolutely not. Economic backwardness leads to economic instability. Instability has political extremism as a consequence, and extremism turns into regional conflicts, wars, crises and terrorism. In our time, questions of security cannot be separated from questions of development.

It is equally inappropriate today to talk about regional security. For example, it is very difficult to imagine that Europe or North America will be islands of stability in a stormy sea of conflicts and contradictions. The times of a "shining city on a hill" have passed; the idea of isolationism — even a regional or continental isolationism — has conclusively become obsolete. And if we want to survive we must act together. There is no other way.

This new understanding of the problems of security is coming into its own with great difficulty; it has not yet led to a transformation of the world. But something very important has occurred in recent years. For the first time in many years a real alternative, the promise of something better than what we had after the Second World War, has appeared in the modern world, in the international relations of today. Of course, only life, political practice, will show how real is this promise, this alternative.

But I would like to believe (and I do believe) that the triumph of the new approach to security is possible and even inevitable — if only we do not commit a fatal stupidity which would prevent mankind from surviving until the day of its triumph. My optimism is not based solely on the certainty that the old way would sooner or later have led to catastrophe, so that it would have been a fatal mistake, a delusion, to have followed it. That would be an argument in a debate, but not a guarantee against misfortune. History supplies many examples of the most terrible mistakes being made by whole nations and states, and not only by individuals.

But I feel a certain optimism in this respect. It is based on the realism of the new concept of security, on the fact that its main premises have been drawn from real life, that it does not require the impossible of anyone and, specifically, does not require anyone to disregard or forget about his vital interests.

One of the new realities of international relations is that war has become a luxury which none of us can allow ourselves any longer, that to wage war is now prohibited. This has already become generally recognized with respect to nuclear war — that one cannot win it and must not wage it has been officially agreed on the very highest political levels. In general, it is recognized that in Europe non-nuclear war is also unthinkable because of the catastrophic consequences for the very existence of the continent: there are more than two hundred nuclear power plants in Europe, and that means more than two hundred potential Chernobyls. The continent is literally interlaced with chemical enterprises and warehouses of toxic substances. Unimaginable quantities of fuel, kerosene and other kinds of liquid fuels are stored. It's not easy to live on such a powder keg. And to wage war is absolutely out of the question.

Moreover, the historical experience of the past decades has revealed yet another truth to those who can and wish to face it: it is no longer possible to achieve rational political goals — at least not in conflicts exceeding Grenada and the Falkland Islands in scale — with the help of military means. In other words, as the risk associated with war grew, the return, the "reward," diminished in parallel fashion. Conceivable motives for war also simultaneously decreased in value. The myth of "lebensraum" disappeared (after all, the countries which were most successful after the war — Japan and the FRG — had never been so limited geographically, which perhaps even forced them to make better use of other advantages offered by modern civilization). Influence on other countries gained by military force invariably proved to be transitory. And, upon inspection, the ideological fruits of victory increasingly turned out to be illusory.

It is increasingly obvious that the real interests of states and their military power have lost direct mutual connection. Therefore a proposal to exclude the use and the threat of use of military force from the foreign policy arsenal no longer seems so naive today. And tomorrow, one can imagine that it will be accepted as the only realistic proposal. It is the cornerstone of new political thinking.

Equally so is the recognition that every country, every people, has the right to its own social, economic, political and ideological choice. Even if you do not agree with it. Even if it sickens you and contradicts your convictions and values. This principle, of the recognition of choice of every country, embodies one of the principal norms of political morality today. It also can and must become a law in the international conduct of states. Again, all modern history demonstrates that this is not just a matter of good will, but of realism — attempts to somehow impose one's will on another by force have, in the final analysis, turned out to be both unsuccessful and very costly.

Yet another new and very important reality: in all countries, both large and small, rich and poor, developed and developing, the most important priorities are turning out to be domestic ones, primarily economic concerns (here all countries — the USSR, U.S., Western Europe, China and Finland — are in the same boat, despite the variety in their characters and the acuteness of their problems). Since this is the case, the main task of foreign policy becomes the creation of the most favorable external conditions for solving domestic problems, for the economic, social and spiritual progress of one's country. It means that the time of empires is receding into the past. It means that military rivalry, like imperial ambitions, is not simply fruitless, it is harmful. Finally, it means that mutually advantageous economic, scientific-technical and cultural cooperation is becoming a necessity.

One special characteristic of the modern world is its growing variety. We had to reject some old concepts to arrive at an understanding of this fact. In particular, we assumed for a long time that the modern world was distinctly divided into two systems, the capitalist and socialist. We thought that they were engaged in an irreconcilable struggle which would determine world development. It seemed to us that mankind was moving in the direction of ever greater unification and standardization, that the development of socialism would be determined by some kind of almost comprehensive "general conformity to laws," that historical laws would inevitably wipe out capitalist development, national distinctions and the particular cultural features of different peoples.

In fact, the opposite is happening. The socialist countries are developing along their own paths, Cuba is fundamentally different from Hungary, and Vietnam from China. Both political systems and economic "models" of diversification are diverging. Greater and greater diversity is observable in the West as well, especially if you compare it with the industrialized East — Japan, South Korea, etc. Most important is that an understanding of the interdependence of the world, the interdependence of societies and states, be they socialist or capitalist, has replaced the idea of inexorable and irreconcilable confrontation. The case of Eastern Europe is especially revealing in this connection. Putting aside the cold war logic, the West has clearly demonstrated its desire to participate positively and actively in preserving stability in the region.

Furthermore, we understood how complex international relations have become. Earlier, world politics were determined by the interaction of a few — sometimes two — great powers, which created powerful military and political alliances around themselves. Today small and medium-sized states, neutral and non-aligned countries, are taking an increasingly active role in solving international problems. Moreover, most of these countries are young and in the process of establishing their own state and society. Their internal instability leads to frequent changes in foreign policy orientation, to constant international re-groupings on both the regional and global levels. This fact lends a new importance to a multilateral diplomacy which is capable of reconciling the divergent interests of the numerous participants in world politics.

And, finally, global problems — both those that directly or indirectly affect all mankind and those that can only be solved by the united efforts of all countries — are acquiring increasingly greater importance in international relations. Among such problems are the acute deterioration in the ecological situation revealed by the shortage of fuel and power resources, problems of food production and the gap between industrially developed countries and the "third world." The further aggravation of these problems may threaten the future of all mankind and lead to unpredictable social and political consequences.

I have often thought: What, after all, is the most important, the main thing, that the Soviet Union has done in recent years in the field of international relations? Bold unilateral initiatives for the reduction of conventional weapons and armed forces in Europe, or the eighteen-month-long moratorium on nuclear explosions? Withdrawal of its forces from Afghanistan or agreement to the most far-reaching measures of confidence building and inspection? Or, perhaps, the new approach to the United Nations, a new style in international intercourse, bold ideas for the future, such as the idea of a non-nuclear, non-violent world? Or the honest attitude toward oneself, including one's own mistakes? Or, finally, perestroika — internal changes, the process of renewal which has unfolded in the Soviet Union?

And I come to the conclusion that it is hard to single out one element. Most likely, one should speak of a cumulative effect which has vitally transformed the entire image of the Soviet Union over a very short period of time, wiping out the "image of the enemy." And this, perhaps, holds the promise that a whole epoch in international relations is receding into the past.

In a polemic with a very conservative American journalist on the pages of *The New York Times*, I once wrote: We are doing something really terrible to you — we are depriving you of an enemy. Maybe in form this was said half-jokingly, but in essence I meant something of the utmost gravity.

In the first place, about what I just said — that perestroika, glasnost, new political thinking and the foreign political initiatives of the Soviet Union are really destroying the habitual image of the enemy, the image of an "evil empire." In the last few years the world, the West, have seen an entirely new and unprecedented Soviet Union — a dynamic, searching, society, free from messianic self-satisfaction, engaged in profound internal transformations and ready for new and unorthodox approaches to the solution of military and foreign policy problems. I'm not referring to the intellectual level of Soviet politics, which has improved rapidly before our very eyes — I would like to hope that very soon this will pull other countries up to the very highest grades in new political thinking (this is a sincere wish on my part: We need partners in politics, not losers in intellectual argument or propaganda, to achieve the goal we have set ourselves).

And, in the second place, I had in mind the fact that erosion of the "Soviet threat" is a change of truly historic importance. After all, the entire postwar international system was built on the existence of an enemy, on the existence of an "evil empire." The military-political alliances and ideological crusades, military and political doctrines, military programs and military expenditures of the last forty-plus years, the role of the United States in the world, the placement of forces and relationships of powers in Europe were all — like pieces of meat for shishkebab — strung on the single skewer of the "Soviet threat," were based on and justified by the existence of an enemy. And when the "image of the enemy" is erased, falls apart, begins, like the cat's smile in the famous English fairy tale, to dissolve in the air, then the entire international system which arose after the war is naturally threatened.

Isn't this the worst thing that could happen to the traditional type of Western politicians, those who grew up and were shaped under "cold war" conditions and who are simply unable to see the world in other dimensions and concepts?

The ending of the "cold war" — and I sincerely believe that we are approaching the end of this far from the best of epochs in the history of mankind — also poses, on an entirely different plane, the question of the further fate of Soviet-American relations. For decades we have been observing each other closely, were bound fast to each other and were in a certain sense each other's prisoners. Now both the USSR and U.S. are again becoming free — free to make independent decisions, irrespective of the other's decisions. How will they make use of this freedom? And what will this independence mean for their relations in the future?

On our side there is as yet no single answer. One view is that we relate to America mainly in matters of security, prevention of nuclear war and disarmament, and that when these problems are solved or, in any case, when they are reduced to "manageable" proportions, our bilateral relations will be far less important to us both than they are today. Western Europe, and even East Asia, are closer to us economically, geographically and historically. Also, Americans do not have very many "positive" stimuli to develop relations with the Soviet Union. It is presumed that in this case both sides will act like spouses who are fed up with each other, who have finally obtained a divorce and hurry to use their newly acquired freedom to search for new partners. Other countries would gain from the new orientation of the two "superpowers" and would no longer feel themselves relegated to the background of world politics.

A second view is that, even after achieving very important breakthroughs in the field of disarmament and strengthening security, the Soviet Union and the United States will remain, if one may so express it, "natural partners." They are brought closer by the very size of both states, by some psychological characteristics in their national characters, by growing pressure from new "power centers," and by many common economic, social and cultural problems. Solving the problems of security will only shift Soviet-American relations into some new dimension and open up opportunities for cooperation that we do not even suspect exist today.

Evidently there is some justification for both of these views. On the one hand, the downfall of bipolarity in the modern world and the achievement of a more harmonious system of foreign policy priorities are bound to reduce the significance of Soviet-American relations to a certain extent. On the other hand, a posture of "courteous neglect" of each other is hardly likely to suit us in the complex and contradictory world of the future, if only because, without positive "linkage," our relations could very easily slide back to a renewal of confrontation.

A particular feature of new political thinking is the rejection of all kinds of isolationism, whether in politics, economics or the spiritual sphere. We are also trying to be as open as possible in relations with the United States. As far as perestroika is concerned, in my opinion it is not only a national policy, but an international cause common to all mankind, both in the sense that its defeat would not be a defeat for us alone and in the sense that, should it be successful, its fruits will be enjoyed by other countries as well as by the Soviet Union.

Editors' Foreword

This book is a product of a study, stretching over nearly two years, by a unique group of American and Soviet specialists working together. The study was conducted by the Center for Foreign Policy Development at Brown University in the U.S., and by the Institute for the USA and Canada of the Soviet Academy of Sciences. On both sides, specialists from outside these two institutions also joined in the project. In all, some forty specialists on many aspects of policy contributed to the study.

To the maximum extent possible, research was conducted by Soviet and American specialists working together. When they could not meet together in person, they exchanged draft papers, memoranda and commentaries frequently. Every effort was made to ensure the maximum possible communication between the two sides and among individuals. The fact — highly unusual at the time of this writing — that the project was able to achieve a number of joint statements and joint papers, agreed by the Soviet and American sides, is testimony to this close collaboration.

This Mutual Security Project began in informal discussions held among the directors of the two institutions during 1987. A Memorandum of Understanding, signed by both sides in July of that year, committed them to the undertaking. Some preliminary work was done later that year and in the early months of 1988.

The project was formally opened with a three-day conference, held in Moscow at the Institute for the USA and Canada in July 1988. A delegation of some twenty-five American specialists attended, including members of the national security advisory staffs to both candidates in the U.S. Presidential elections of that year. Some forty Soviet specialists attended, including representatives of the Ministry of Foreign Affairs, of the Central Committee of the CPSU, and of the armed forces.

Over the following sixteen months, research was conducted by six working groups. Each group was assigned its own area of responsibility, as follows:

Working Group on Principles and Criteria: Development of concepts about mutual security and its application, for use by the other working groups. Also development of theory and of historical and domestic context.

Working Group on Europe: Exploration of the applicability of the mutual security approach to the improvement of American and Soviet security in Central Europe, along with that of their allies. Chief emphasis on political rather than military matters, since European arms reductions are a topic for the Nuclear and Conventional Arms Reductions group.

Working Group on the Persian Gulf: Exploration of the applicability of the mutual security approach to the improvement of American and Soviet security in the Persian Gulf region.

Working Group on the North Pacific: Exploration of the applicability of the mutual security approach to the improvement of American and Soviet security, as well as that of their allies, in the North Pacific region. Chief emphasis on security problems on the Korean peninsula.

Working Group on Nuclear and Conventional Arms Reductions: Exploration of ways in which arms reductions and other arms control can contribute to mutual security, in selected areas involving strategic nuclear weapons and conventional weapons in Europe.

Working Group on Future Scenarios: Overall assessment of future prospects for the development of mutual security. Also an assessment of public opinion in both the U.S. and the USSR, regarding possible scenarios for the evolution of the foreign policy of each nation.

Certain areas of the world that might have been added, such as the Middle East, were excluded because other unofficial Soviet-American discussions were occurring on those topics, and the Mutual Security Project did not want to overlap that work.

As the reader will notice, the four groups that worked on specific problem areas did not begin from a dogmatic assumption that mutual security *is* the chief solution to either side's national security problems. Instead these groups defined their task as exploring whether, how much and how the mutual security approach could contribute to improving security.

Specialists from both sides working in this project felt free to suggest new methods and fresh ideas whenever these seemed appropriate, without limiting themselves to currently accepted lines of policy. In working together, their rule was to express any doubts about any idea openly, and to analyze ideas freely and as explicitly as possible. As readers will see from the papers in this book, no uniformity of views was imposed, or emerged. Mutual security is a roomy and very rich concept. The reader will find a significant diversity of views, all within the overall approach of mutual security.

The working groups met at times in Moscow, in Washington, D.C., or in Providence, Rhode Island where Brown University is located. A list of working group meetings, along with other sessions and discussions, may be found in the back of this book.

The Mutual Security Project closed with a six-day conference held in the United States in November 1989. The first portion was held at Brown University and the second portion in Washington. The Soviet delegation included some twenty Soviet specialists, headed by Academician Georgiy A. Arbatov and including representatives from the Foreign Ministry and the Central Committee, as well as scholars from the Institute for the USA and Canada and other Moscow institutes. Several sessions of the Washington conference were held at the U.S. Department of State, and the working groups met with diverse specialists from the U.S. government and from policy institutes in the Washington area. The purpose of the meetings in Washington was to brief the policy community on the results of the project. Meetings are planned in Moscow for the same purpose in the spring of 1990.

On the American side, the work of the Brown Center on the Mutual Security Project was supported by the W. Alton Jones Foundation, Inc.; the Joyce Mertz-Gilmore Foundation; an anonymous contribution from a member of the Rockefeller family; the Carnegie Corporation of New York; and Brown University. The Brown Center gratefully acknowledges this financial support. Editorial work by the American co-editor was done while he held a temporary appointment as a Visiting Senior Scholar at the Center for International Studies of the University of Southern California; and that Center's support is gratefully acknowledged. We wish to thank Lorraine Walsh for her extensive editorial work on the English-language edition, and Shirley Benson for her work in translating Russian material into English.

This Mutual Security Project has given birth to not one but a series of further projects. By the time of its closing conference, the directors of both the Brown Center and the Institute for the USA and Canada had decided that the mutual security approach was too useful for their joint work to be allowed to end. Joint research is continuing on issues involving the future of Europe and of the North Pacific region. A third continuing project is described in P. Terrence Hopmann's paper in this book. In addition, the Brown Center has decided to publish an annual report on developments in mutual security.

This book contains the most significant papers written during the original Mutual Security Project of 1988 and 1989. The book is organized into six major segments, one contributed by each of the project's six working groups. The reader will find brief biographies of authors at the back of the book, along with a list of all the members of each working group. A fuller description of the Brown Center and of the Institute for the USA and Canada will be found there as well. This book was completed in January 1990, so events since that date cannot be reflected in the chapters.

This book will be published at approximately the same time in English in the West and in Russian in the Soviet Union.

Richard Smoke (USA)
Andrei Kortunov (USSR)
January 1990

Part I

Working Group on Principles and Criteria

THE WORKING GROUP ON PRINCIPLES AND CRITERIA was responsible for developing concepts about mutual security and its applications. It also was responsible for developing useful theory and for the historical and domestic context of mutual security.

The Working Group has contributed five papers to this book. An introduction to mutual security, which appears first, is provided jointly by Viktor Kremenyuk, the chair of the group on the Soviet side, and by Richard Smoke, the convenor of the group on the American side. Mikhail Bezrukov and Andrei Kortunov contribute a chapter on interdependence. Alexander George provides a paper on the historical development of Soviet-American relations in recent years and the need for a "political framework" for further progress. Petr Gladkov contributes a paper on the domestic conditions required if mutual security is to be achieved. Finally, Richard Smoke provides a lengthy theoretical paper on the concept and implications of mutual security. Biographical sketches of these authors, and a list of the full membership of the Working Group on Principles and Criteria, are given at the back of the book.

— THE EDITORS

1

Joint Introduction to Mutual Security

VIKTOR KREMENYUK (USSR) and
RICHARD SMOKE (USA)

Mutual security is an approach to one of the most cherished values in human and social life, the value of security. Security has always been a focus of attention for individuals and for societies. It has always received priority because it incorporates such basic interests as physical survival, continuation of life, preservation of wealth and resources, and the survival of power and institutions. From this point of view, mutual security is only a modification or development of the traditional value of security, and of the ways people seek a durable and stable sense of security. An alternative point of view may also be found: that mutual security is a highly novel, even radical, idea. People who see it this way often feel that mutual security differs so much from the known and accepted approaches to security that they may doubt whether it genuinely seeks to achieve security at all.

What requires emphasis from the very beginning, then, is that mutual security in no way rejects security as an essential value for human society. Rather it aims, in fact, to achieve *greater* security for society than other approaches can achieve. It aims to accomplish this by understanding more deeply the meaning and implications of the latest developments in military technology, in the international situation, and in the real threats to our societies.

During 1989, the President of the United States, George Bush, spoke of the necessity to conceive the next phase in East-West relations — a new phase that, as he put it, moves "beyond containment" and reflects the great changes in the Soviet Union and in Eastern Europe. In his statement at the Malta Summit (December

1989), the President of the USSR, Mikhail Gorbachev, stated explicitly that the Cold War has come to an end. Both statements reflect what is now the dominant tendency in the official thinking of the United States and the Soviet Union concerning their relationship. Both statements are based, at least to a significant extent, on a reevaluation of the mutual threat; on a fresh assessment of the dangers that could arise in their relations if significant changes are not made; and on a desire to find new and innovative ways to enhance security at a time when the whole structure of the two sides' stances toward each other is becoming obsolete and politically disoriented. This similarity in thinking in the two governments suggests that strong effort should now be applied, on each side separately and also by both working together, to search for these innovative ways to enhance security.

It was within this framework that the Mutual Security Project discussed in this book was conceived, and the work presented here was done.

Background

Why is it that President Bush speaks of East-West relations entering an entirely new phase, and President Gorbachev speaks of the end of the Cold War? What is it about the present moment that causes great governments to think that new and innovative thinking is needed? Of course the answer is that for about forty years, from just after World War II until very recently, East and West were locked into a particular relationship. That relationship had definite characteristics and, in its fundamentals, persisted continuously.

The Cold War that arose just after World War II created a system of two great blocs. Those blocs were more than simple military alliances. They were profound political alignments based on mutual interests, shared values and a shared perception of threats. These two great blocs — NATO and the Warsaw Pact — were organized largely along ideological lines, dominated militarily, politically and economically by one unchallengeable leader, and geographically spread around the world but concentrated in Europe. Each bloc was created to try to achieve security for itself, and good "management" of the relations between them was supposed to prevent war and provide security for all. For decades these blocs were regarded (and are still regarded by some people) as the most reliable pillars for world security. They promoted both good relations within the alliances, and a somewhat controlled adversarial relationship between the two blocs, based on mutual deterrence. For about forty years this arrangement did provide a measure of security, and most of the time, peace of a kind.

But time has proven that this type of security arrangement cannot last indefinitely. First, it provoked and sustained a continuous arms race between the two sides. NATO developed into a strong alliance as a response to the first Soviet test of the atom bomb, which meant an end to the American monopoly of this weapon and demanded, in the opinion of U.S. strategists, a military alliance that could "deter" a possible Soviet conventional attack in Europe. The whole later history of the East-West relationship demonstrates that each side was inclined to counter a possible threat from the other with a new generation, or a larger deployment, of nuclear and/or conventional weapons. In time each side possessed such a huge quantity of weapons that the weapons themselves came to be seen as a threat. The tool for achieving security became a new source of danger. Both sides had to give attention to limiting the numbers of weapons, removing the most destabilizing weapons, and controlling the directions of military developments.

Second, the unchallengeable position of the leaders of both alliances was finally challenged. On the Eastern side, it took the shape of ideological debate, which led first to the Soviet-Chinese rift, and then to increasing anti-Soviet feeling in Eastern Europe, which in turn led to the so-called "Brezhnev Doctrine" to try to compel unity. On the Western side, the challenge was mainly economic in nature. The development of the West European economies (most powerfully in West Germany), the rapid growth of the Japanese economy, and then the rise of the "Four Tigers" (South Korea, Taiwan, Hong Kong and Singapore) did not directly challenge American military leadership. But these developments demanded changed decision-making procedures, and later produced something like economic warfare between the leader and at least some of its allies (notably Japan). Of course, these trends on both sides could not but have an impact on military security: both bloc leaders became unsure of the support they would have in some kinds of crises.

Third, the existence of the two great "collective security" blocs did not reduce military insecurity in other parts of the world. Third World conflicts became a serious source of international instability. They threatened to draw in the opposing superpower (and they did, in Vietnam and Afghanistan) or to escalate into a serious East-West confrontation (as occurred in the Middle East). They also raised the specter of new nuclear conflicts, as a result of nuclear proliferation. The two blocs found that they had to cooperate to try to forestall this danger, creating the Non-Proliferation Treaty of 1968, but that effort proved not to be entirely successful. Proliferation dangers continued, as did wars and insecurities in the Third World. Finally the two great blocs had to accept that those conflicts were less of a "playing field" for their own competition than they were a source of common dangers.

Fourth, wholly new kinds of threats appeared to both alliances, threats that were global in nature or that appeared nearly everywhere. New global threats included a threat of destruction of the ozone layer, pollution of the oceans and outer space, and the greenhouse effect, which may produce serious changes in climate. Other new threats appearing nearly everywhere included air and water pollution, new epidemics such as AIDS, risks from nuclear power plants and nuclear waste and other risks involved in high-technology operations, drug traffic and the growing social damage from drug use, and the growth of international terrorism (which in the future may include terrorism with nuclear bombs). It seemed that while the two military blocs were diverting their attention to their own competition, the very existence of their peoples was being jeopardized.

These four developments in the contemporary period are not mere temporary phenomena. They continue on and on. Hence they demonstrate fundamental weaknesses and flaws of the post-World War II security system made up of two hostile blocs. One is that real security for both sides was not achieved; threats back and forth continued. Another is that both found that, not only did they have to commit effort and resources to that competition, they also had to try to exert more efforts and find further resources to meet new kinds of insecurities. And another is that the mutual hostility constantly prevented or hindered the cooperation that so clearly was needed for coping with new dangers. The conclusion is inescapable: the post-World War II system cannot last indefinitely, because time and changing circumstances have proven it unable to provide sufficient, lasting security.

The growing realization of this truth in both East and West, combined with the great changes in Soviet society and Soviet policy in the second half of the 1980s, have led to the natural result. A demand has arisen for major revisions in traditional thinking about "national security," and for a search for new ideas about security. Mutual security is one of those new ideas. It is a concept that calls for a new way of conducting relations — and finding security — between East and West, a way that is distinctly different from the post-World War II system.

What is mutual security?

Mutual security is an approach to improving the security of two parties that are, or might be, in conflict with each other. The two can be nations, or two alliances, or in principle almost any two groups or individuals. Mutual security calls for each of them to seek to gain security by seeking more security for *both* of them. This approach stands in clear contrast to the approach of each side seeking security by trying to undermine or diminish the security of the other.

The mutual security approach could also be called a "cooperative security" approach. The alternative could also be called a "competitive" approach to security or a "unilateral" approach to security.

These two approaches to gaining security are just that: *approaches*. They are not automatic formulas or recipes. They do not immediately tell policymakers what to do in any particular situation. Every situation has to be analyzed itself. What they do tell policymakers (and everyone) is that there are two distinctly different ways of analyzing the situation. Which approach is taken is likely to lead to different conclusions for policy and for action. National leaders who hope to gain security for their country by undermining the other side are going to make different decisions from leaders who want to find ways for both sides to gain security.

At first glance, mutual security may seem the more appealing morally. Of course, as a general rule it is natural for human beings to hope to cooperate. But in fact, which approach is the more sensible is not always clear. Would anyone have wanted to cooperate with Hitler, to gain "mutual security" with the Nazis? Of course not. If the danger (or the evil) is sufficiently great, one can only hope to defeat it.

Even with a less virulent enemy the right path is not always clear. For instance, in the last few decades both the United States and the Soviet Union have felt that they needed to adopt a "deterrence" policy for their nuclear weapons. Each side has threatened to destroy the other if the other attacks first with nuclear weapons. Only *after* both sides had developed a very clear understanding of this threat back and forth (which required many years) were the two sides able to start talking about limiting and reducing their nuclear stockpiles.

As this example suggests, it is possible to mix together some elements of a unilateral approach and some elements of mutual security. Unilaterally the USSR deterred the U.S.; and unilaterally the U.S. deterred the USSR. Once this was well understood, they began to work together to keep the dangers under control. They could begin to work for some mutual security, for instance by agreeing to prohibit certain new, dangerous weapons that would make the situation more hazardous for everyone.

So "mutual security" and "unilateral security" are not absolutes. They don't exist in completely separate spheres. That is one of the reasons why a study like this one was needed and why this book was written. Nearly all the chapters show that today's problems are complicated, and a simple solution is not possible, at least not quickly.

But most of the chapters also show that the approach of mutual security needs much more emphasis in today's and tomorrow's world. When two great nations like the USSR and the United States, and their allies, have been competing for a long time, it becomes all too easy for people on both sides to think in a highly competitive way. As each fresh situation arises, it is very easy to think of the other side simply as "the enemy," and to think simply about ways to undermine or negate anything the other side does. Of course the other side is thinking the same way. This is a formula for a struggle without end.

The mutual security approach often provides a way to extricate ourselves from this struggle, without either side having to give up anything that is truly important.

Mutual security does not call upon either side to sacrifice its real security "for the sake of peace" or for some other reason. Mutual security calls upon both sides to *gain* more real security, by approaching the problems of security together and cooperatively.

Some time ago this might have seemed utopian. But as humanity approaches the end of the twentieth century, this approach is becoming increasingly possible, at least for many problems. The reform movement in the USSR, changes in Eastern Europe, and other developments around the world are creating a new situation. Increasingly the Soviet and American peoples, and their allies, are not thinking of each other as enemies. These developments make it possible for national leaders, and for specialists on policy matters, to rethink what can be done and should be done. Much more emphasis can now be put on gaining security mutually.

The possible steps are not necessarily confined to steps that these two alliances could take. There are many other nations in the world, and in principle, the mutual security approach can be applied more generally. Many nations can work together to gain what is now called "common security" for all, or "global" or "universal" security. But that process will take time. Meanwhile it makes sense for the two great alliances, who together control more than ninety-five percent of the nuclear weapons in the world, to work on improving their bilateral, mutual security.

For four decades, much of the competition between East and West has been conducted by means of threats. Often the threat has not been made in words (although sometimes it has); threats can be silently created and silently continued. Each side's vast nuclear arsenal is a standing threat to the other. Each side maintains a huge military machine in Europe that is a threat to the other. Each side has taken many kinds of actions around the world to improve its competitive position vis-a-vis the other, which is another kind of threat.

Now the two sides seek to greatly soften and even end their competition. Hence working toward mutual security will mean reducing and even ending these threats. In the project reported in this book, the Working Group on Principles and Criteria identified *mutual threat reduction* as a major principle for achieving mutual security. The powerful threats back and forth that have been created over decades need to be reduced, and as conditions permit, dismantled entirely. This principle of mutual threat reduction applies equally to the standing military forces, and to the pattern of taking competitive actions around the world.

It should be obvious that threat reduction must be mutual. It could be dangerous for one side to make great reductions in its threats, if the other side did not. (However, in some areas certain specific, limited steps can be taken by one side or the other by itself; and some already have been.) If East and West want to improve their mutual security, then, they need to carry out together a policy of mutual threat reduction.

It may be less obvious but it is equally true that most of what needs to be done to achieve mutual threat reduction is complicated, and much of it will take time. For example, the huge military machines each side maintains in Europe must be reduced carefully, or a moment could arrive when one side or the other suddenly finds itself vulnerable. This could even happen without the other side intending it or even expecting it. A similar observation applies to the huge nuclear arsenals. Moscow and Washington also cannot change their policies toward other nations around the world drastically and overnight. Doing so could disrupt a delicate balance in many regions, and perhaps even help lead to local wars. Most of the papers in this book discuss, in one way or another, the complications involved (and the time needed) for East and West to mutually reduce threats and move toward mutual security.

The exact criteria by which one decides how best to reduce the mutual threats differ greatly from one problem to another. Most of the papers published here represent only a beginning in understanding these problems. But the important step is for Washington and Moscow to discuss together, much more broadly and deeply than ever before, how to proceed. As the last chapter in this book suggests, new ways may need to be created for the two sides (and their allies) to talk together, and even to jointly study the problems involved.

Many questions about mutual security remain unanswered, and a great many points remain open to discussion. But what is clear is that, as we enter the last decade of this century, the two sides must move forward in developing their mutual security. No reasonable person can want a return to the intense competition of the Cold War. The Cold War yielded few gains for either side, but it did yield tremendous dangers and tremendous costs for both sides. May it now recede into history, and the nations that fought it now turn to the task of creating security together — mutual security.

2
Interdependence: A Perspective on Mutual Security

MIKHAIL BEZRUKOV AND ANDREI KORTUNOV

Wars are an evil that has existed from time immemorial. The history of human civilization is full of pages covered with blood. During thousands of years a *divided* humanity used brute force to settle disputes among its constituent parts.

Attempts to defend oneself from external threats are also of reputable age. And the first world here, beyond doubt, belonged not to a humanist but to people who were guided in their actions and decisions by pragmatic considerations. The moral dimension of the war and peace problem that is so important to us today surfaced later. The starting point was a struggle for survival.

The oldest way to ensure security is the accumulation of military power. "The strongest survives!" This slogan, so dear to social Darwinists, has been a cornerstone of foreign policies of many outstanding statesmen of the past. With the persistence of an ant, humanity created more and more powerful military arsenals. Huge material and intellectual resources were spent on the development of the capacity to destroy and to kill. By the middle of the twentieth century "progress" in the military sphere gave birth to armaments of such a devastating power that they threaten the very survival of the human civilization. Military muscles of men have become capable of ruining the world men live in.

But it turned out that growing piles of weapons were not a sufficient peace guarantee in a *divided* world. So long as division continued wars, and tensions were constantly reproduced; old enemies were only replaced by new challenges. The sword as such proved to be incapable of giving a final solution to the war and peace problem. More than that, its perfection was accompanied in the second half of the twentieth century by a gradual weakening of human control over decision making in the military sphere. Still facing the possibility of horrible wars, mankind started becoming a captive of the monsters created by human hands — modern means of destruction.

The search for security was not only tried through military power build-ups. History knows many attempts to avert armed clashes between states with the help of special agreements. Treaties regulating interstate relations were created to make the use of weapons an exceptional measure. Protective structures in international relations were steadily evolving in accordance with changing circumstances and (all the contradictions and problems connected with this process notwithstanding) were growing and becoming more far-reaching.

Among the agreements helping to preserve peace a special place belongs to those that regulated military activity. They existed even in ancient times. But it is only in the twentieth century that human civilization has discovered how important they are for its survival.

In the course of military negotiations that took place in the first half of this century, the issue of protection of a more and more vulnerable human civilization acquired a real significance for the first time in history. During those years not much was accomplished. The dialogue did not justify the hopes placed in it. Yet the experience has not gone to waste: it was used in the nuclear era.

Revolution in the military sphere brought about by the nuclear bomb initiated a qualitatively new turn in the use of agreements for ensuring security. The invention of nuclear weapons, the gradual evolution of the strategic situation created by them, the growth of the number of nuclear powers, the transition from traditional confrontation to what is called mutual deterrence (a situation where no nation can attack other nuclear powers with nuclear weapons without putting at risk its own survival) — all these things have turned agreements regulating military competition between the nuclear powers into an indispensable precondition for avoiding a nuclear catastrophe.

Simultaneously, the importance of other agreements stabilizing military rivalry between states also grew during the postwar years. The world was becoming increasingly too vulnerable to settling disputes by military means.

However the events of the second half of the twentieth century have not only brought to light a growing need for agreements regulating military activity of states; they also have demonstrated the imperfections of this instrument for ensuring security in a *divided* world. For example, large-scale agreements concerning the most destructive weapons were but an island in a sea of impasses relating both to nuclear and conventional armaments. It also became evident that the progress of negotiations could not keep pace with breakthroughs in military technology. This was especially visible in East-West relations, where acute confrontation and very distinct dividing lines were combined with intensive, constant military preparations.

More than twenty years of Soviet-American experience in the field is a long enough period to make a healthy and cynical judgment about its achievements and failures. The overall ratio between these failures and achievements does not give us much ground for unconditional optimism. Practical results stipulated by the SALT agreements were basically a by-product of a new version of Soviet-American geopolitical interaction, motivated and distorted by many things including acute domestic problems.

In the American case, one can trace in the origin of detente and SALT I the sobering impact of Vietnam. For the Nixon administration, arms control was a centerpiece of detente which — as Stanley Hoffman has elegantly put it — was essentially meant to be "containment by other means." In the Nixon-Kissinger strategy, arms control — sweetened for the Soviets by an unexpected "gift of parity" and by other potential American "goodies" — was supposed to stimulate a Soviet taste for status-quo behavior. This was seen as a crucial element for obtaining a quiet international environment, which was badly needed for limiting the damage from a planned American disengagement from competing world-wide.

In the Soviet case, the SALT agreements were regarded as a visible and cherished symbol of "equality" with the U.S. — however shaky and superficial that equality might have been — which the USSR probably did not hope to achieve in any other area or by itself. Thus SALT did help to ease an acute Soviet inferiority complex vis-a-vis a wealthy, powerful and envied adversary. Besides — as many Western analysts believed, and not without grounds — the SALT process, as the major and perhaps only manifestation of relaxation of tensions with the United States, was seen by the Soviet leadership as a useful key to getting access to Western credits and technology, which could help give another breath to the suffocating Soviet economy. There also were some hopes that a strategic modus vivendi with the United States could help to release some scarce resources for dealing with the problem of worrisome relations with China.

The Carter administration seemed to entrust arms control with an even more ambitious role. By significantly widening the scope of arms control, the Administration apparently intended to expand the frontiers of "containment by military detente" and to help shift the superpowers competition to non-military areas, where America was supposed to be better off.

For obvious reasons the Soviet side was seriously alarmed by these perverse ideas that promised to considerably narrow the only ground where the USSR could successfully compete with the United States. That alarmist outlook was aggravated by a frustrated overreaction to a "subversive" human rights offensive waged by the Carter team. The famous SALT II proposals brought to Moscow by Cyrus Vance in March 1977 — which were perceived as a volatile and unjustified departure from "sacred principles" agreed upon earlier in Vladivostok — gave a final touch to that dim Soviet picture. As a result, promising ideas that actually could have laid solid ground for a generally more functional and preferable SALT II outcome were blatantly rejected in Moscow without the serious and sober consideration they certainly deserved.

Unlike its predecessors, the first Reagan administration had no intention of toying with the idea of promoting a devaluation of military power in international politics through arms control or any other means. To the contrary, the Administration practically denounced arms control in its effort to demonstrate its will and resolve to openly challenge Soviets with a policy of vigorous, militant containment, and thus to expedite its desired transition "from weakness to strength." Later on the Administration decided to score psychologically and propagandistically by advancing a call for radical, equal and verifiable reductions of nuclear arms. This call was backed by arms control positions that were supposed to be simple, publicly attractive, yet absolutely unacceptable to the Soviet side. That was how the concept of START and the INF "zero" and "double zero" options were born.

For "customary reasons" the Soviet leadership decided to enter this uneven game. Struggling hard to keep a solid posture and not to lose face it fought back emotionally (and often abusively). The showdown came in late November 1983, when all bilateral lines of communication on issues of arms control were broken on the pretext that the U.S. deployment of INF weapons in Western Europe made any further dialogue redundant and senseless. The real driving force behind this hectic Soviet behavior was probably a deep and hopeless frustration stemming from a fear that the American side was going to play its European version of the Cuban missile crisis gambit, and win it the same way the U.S. had beaten the USSR twenty years earlier.

The same strange logic of subordinating the rationales of strategic arms control to mere tactical political considerations dominated the scene at the Reykjavik Summit. Both sides were eager to score by demonstrating their resolution to achieve a great breakthrough. That desire resulted in an agreed goal to cut strategic nuclear arsenals by fifty percent. This even figure, taken from nowhere, and the idea itself looked extremely appealing politically; but it had little or nothing to offer for dealing with the disturbing trends of growing counterforce capability and the shrinking margin of strategic stability. As former U.S. Secretary of Defense James Schlesinger bitterly noted in a famous *Foreign Affairs* article (referring to Reykjavik and to Reagan's idea of eliminating all ballistic nuclear missiles), this desire to score politically could have ended in a disaster for the American side. According to Schlesinger, in this peculiar and sole case, SDI indeed properly served American national security interests by blocking a deal that would have removed a vital pillar of the U.S. strategic deterrent.

One has to note that political instincts and motivations are not always bound to be harmful to the arms control process and strategic stability in particular. Unfortunately the U.S. arms control policy from the outset reflected an old American obsession with devising mostly technical fixes for mostly non-technical problems of security and stability. And the Soviet side — which was always eager to follow the American example, even a dubious one — willingly adopted the same simplistic approach. Of course, in some instances the custom played a useful and constructive role. For instance, it helped everyone to understand and further develop the strange laws and conceptual premises of the strategic nuclear field. But at the same time, a primarily technocratic approach led to the eventual isolation of this specific field from the overall political process. And with time the gap grew ever wider between rational political goals (which could have been anchored to a shared vision of a lasting international security structure) on one hand, and strategic arms control means on the other.

From this viewpoint, we can see that some of Reagan's unorthodox arms control gestures, motivated by his political instincts and promptly labeled by experts as "signs of arrogance and ignorance," may have been prompted ultimately by a natural and healthy desire to escape from hopeless conceptual and technical dead ends created by surrealistic strategic "wisdom."

*

The weak sides of the traditional approaches to the problem of security — the attempts to ensure it through power accumulation and/or stabilizing agreements — have promoted a deep pessimism about the possibility of abolishing wars from the life of the world. Many people have gotten the feeling — an understandable one — of participating in an endless and hopeless race. But in fact the situation proves to be not as hopeless as that.

What seems beyond reach in a *divided* world has already appeared as a *natural* outcome of a growing *unity* of humanity that develops first of all in the economic sphere. We refer to the interdependence of states that is constantly gaining strength in the twentieth century. Economic interdependence has started a radical transformation of the whole system of international relations.

Very often when people speak about the interdependence of states they mean dependence on each other as a result of economic exchanges, and also of the emergence of global threats to human survival, which require joint efforts by the international community (e.g., nuclear proliferation, pollution of the environment). The word "interdependence" is also widely used for new forms of international cooperation generated by the rapid development of science and technology (e.g., large-scale international research projects and global information exchange networks). All these applications of the term do reflect processes in our world. Much more rarely do researchers — to say nothing of the general public — pay attention to another important fact of modern life that should be taken into account when we study the question of the interdependence of states. At present we are witnessing the rapid formation of organic ties among different countries, i.e., an interpenetration of societies. The main driving force behind this process is the rise of economic complexes that overstep the limits of national frontiers. Inside these economic complexes the words "national" and "alien" lose their traditional meaning. This development in the economic domain is putting an imprint on other spheres of human activity as well, though there the process is slower and more contradictory.

The formation of transnational planes of organic interactions from national unities is a reproduction on a higher level of what has already happened inside states in modern history (for instance in Western Europe). Parallels are numerous. We can observe a number of common features. The lessons of the past provide us with valuable hints about the present and future. Let us single out some of them:

— Changes in the system of relations caused by emergence of a new plane of organic interactions bring with them qualitative changes in existing interests; new communities of interests appear; and these processes modify substantially the existing "rules of the game."

— This develops unevenly, gradually, but at an accelerating speed; and it influences different aspects of life.

— With growing complexity of ties inside a new plane of organic interactions the cruder and more devastating ways of solving "internal" conflicts gradually disappear.

If we look from this angle at relations between East and West, we must acknowledge that the economic "peace factor" is still in an embryonic state. For too long the socialist countries have been erecting barriers separating them from the rest of the world. For decades their leaders have been trying to keep East-West economic interactions under strict bureaucratic control, and this precluded establishment of organic ties in the economic sphere with other nations. As a result, mutual security in East-West relations has depended almost exclusively on military power and on political agreements.

Development of more mature relations between East and West will depend upon the success of economic reform in East European countries and the Soviet Union, and also upon the success of political reform, for these are two sides of the same coin. Of course more mature relations will also depend upon readiness of the West to react appropriately to positive changes in the East. Reforms in the Soviet Union and other East European countries provide a unique opportunity to put an end to the separation of East and West.

By any standard, the formation of organic links of this kind between East and West will be a monumental undertaking. It will mean creating a single East-West economic organism, one that is transnational but that leaves room for national identities and needs. Progress toward this goal should be facilitated by all available means.

Beyond doubt, we are on the threshold of the most challenging period yet in the history of East-West relations. It has two sets of characteristic features, one of which reminds us of the Cold War legacy while the other focuses our attention on what is still only surfacing. True, the reforms in Eastern Europe and the Soviet Union clearly indicate that traditional East-West ideological quarrels are passing into oblivion. We are facing a qualitatively new situation on the European continent. The spectacle of falling barriers gives reason for trumpeting the termination of decades-old hostilities, and even more than that, the disappearance of one of the principal dimensions in post-World War II international relations. The "historic dispute" is over, at least in its traditional form. On the other hand, the gap between East and West has so far been narrowed only slightly. There is still much work to do. Having rejected artificial East-West division (on moral grounds also) we now have to demonstrate our capacity to create together a better world.

As it has already been implied, with the emergence of transnational planes of organic interactions any resort to arms inside them becomes a luxury that all sides cannot afford. Military power loses its usefulness as an instrument of practical policy. In this sense, the reforms in Eastern Europe and the Soviet Union give hope for a more secure European future, free from specters of devastating wars that have been haunting the continent for so many centuries. But for the present this is only a hope waiting for a more solid footing.

The Soviet Union and the East European countries will experience many difficulties trying to reintroduce themselves into world economic interactions after decades of self-imposed isolation, and of state bureaucracies' domination of their national economies. It is well known how the overcentralized state socialism economies start to "cough" when even partially exposed to the fresh winds of outside competition. Breaking through political and military obstacles in relations between East and West is proving to be a much easier a task than overcoming their economic incompatibility. The road of the Soviet Union and Eastern Europe toward their integration into the world economy will be paved with painful crises and social collisions, as clearly witness examples in Poland and Hungary. Too many material and spiritual chains are to be broken. But there is no other choice unless the lands of the East wish to face stagnation, with the even greater tensions and social unrest that would follow.

The agenda for the West, in its turn, is shaped by conflicting considerations. On the one hand, it is widely recognized that external aid is of critical importance for reforms in the Soviet Union and Eastern Europe. The East needs huge investments for accelerated passage through the strains connected with economic restructuring. How to get this money is already a big question for the West. It is one thing to mobilize resources for defense, and quite another to ask society to share other peoples' burdens. "External threat," after all appeals more to a taxpayer than an invitation to pay now in the name of a future common prosperity.

On the other hand, Western business circles are having a number of second thoughts about investments. The availability of a large labor force in the East may be a big plus, as is the desire of leaders in the East to open doors for foreign capital. But the minuses are at least as impressive: weak infrastructure, financial problems, a shortage of local qualified managers, potential social instability and so on and so forth. In other words, the promise of the region is greater than what it can actually give right now. There is a big risk involved in its development and quite naturally private investors look for their governments' strong backing before making decisions. The picture is additionally complicated by a destabilizing influence of reforms in the Soviet Union and East European countries on their internal political developments and on relations between them. The temptation is great for the Western countries, especially the most powerful ones, to exploit the situation for obtaining one-sided concessions and short-term benefits. The West, as it seems, faces an important dilemma: to let ambitions and egoisms prevail, even partially; or firmly to subordinate its choices to the creation of healthier foundations for the world's future.

A transition from security relying predominantly on military power and political agreements to a more promising guarantee of peace in East-West relations demands exceptional wisdom on the part of political leaders. Abandonment of the balance of mutual fears can be successful only if both sides unite their efforts in creating a network of organic ties between them.

Of course it would be wrong to suggest that long-term interdependence processes will solve security problems automatically, just by the logic of their development. There is still plenty of room for "traditional" security promoting mechanism (negotiations, arms control agreements, confidence-building measures, etc.). But we have to keep in mind that durable mutual security is inseparable from societies' interpenetration.

This implies that our approach even to such negotiations should include a broader vision of the mutual security problem. Economic and humanitarian "unfreezing" has a profound impact on security issues.

In the context of Soviet-American relations, this also implies that the two sides should see to it that our "decoupling" in the military sphere goes hand in hand with multiplying and intensifying positive relations in other spheres. The existing negative interdependence between our two countries must be replaced with positive interdependence. Otherwise any changes for the better are likely to be ephemeral.

3

U.S.-Soviet Relations: Evolution and Prospects

ALEXANDER GEORGE

"The true use of history is not to make men more clever for the next time, but wiser forever." (Jacob Burckhardt)

This chapter focuses on efforts made by the two superpowers to move beyond the worst confrontational aspects of the Cold War towards a non-confrontational form of rivalry, one that gradually would be leavened by cooperation and collaboration on significant issues of mutual concern.[1] In both the Soviet Union and the United States this goal of a more "constructive, stable" relationship, as it has often been called, has been the source of important controversy. Even those who see the need to move towards a more moderate superpower relationship have disagreed and continue to disagree as to the type of relationship that would be desirable and feasible and on the ways of developing it.

It is probably correct to say that a serious search for a less confrontational, more constructive relationship began with the move towards detente that followed upon the Cuban Missile Crisis. I shall focus here, however, on the period beginning with the Nixon-Brezhnev detente of the early 1970s. This chapter addresses the following questions: What "lessons" have leaders on the two sides drawn from the abortive Nixon-Brezhnev detente? How are Soviet and American leaders assessing the implications for their relationship on new developments that have occurred in the international environment and in their domestic situations since the early seventies? What new conceptions have already emerged or are now possible regarding the development of a more constructive and stable relationship? What suggestions can be offered to stimulate joint U.S.-Soviet efforts to address this fundamental question?

These are questions that cannot be easily answered and on which judgments will differ. In addressing them here I shall assume the reader's familiarity with the history of the period and focus our effort on identifying specific lessons that many (though certainly not all) Soviet and American leaders have drawn from the abortive detente of the seventies and on significant changes in the operative beliefs and policy assumptions of important leaders on both sides regarding U.S.-Soviet relations. Given the limited space available to cover so much ground, the analysis will be presented in a condensed fashion without the refinement and nuances that would otherwise be desirable.

The erosion and collapse of the Nixon-Brezhnev detente of the early 1970s led to a revival of the Cold War in the late seventies and early eighties.[2] Not only were these years marked by rising tensions and lack of constructive engagement between Moscow and Washington; many observers feared the possibility of nuclear war should the two superpowers get into a new crisis comparable to earlier ones in Berlin, Cuba, and the Middle East. However, despite the harsh rhetoric of the second Cold War, various ugly incidents, and accentuated militarization of foreign policy, the superpowers managed — as they had in previous decades — to avoid a shooting war of any kind between their military forces. And, in fact, they worked their way out of the second Cold War without drifting into any dangerous war-threatening crisis.

Evidently, some useful learning had taken place in Moscow and Washington as to the modalities of crisis management and crisis avoidance and this served the superpowers well in managing the tensions of the second Cold War. Shared understandings and patterns of behavior that have helped U.S. and Soviet leaders to avoid crises and war have been discussed elsewhere.[3] Here I shall focus more broadly on "lessons" each superpower has derived from the abortive detente effort of the early seventies and on new developments since then that have a bearing on recent efforts to develop more positive relations.

It is often said that history seldom gives individuals and states who have failed a second chance. Since the mid-1980s U.S. and Soviet leaders have had just such a second chance to do better than Nixon and Brezhnev did in developing a less confrontational and more constructive relationship. Have leaders on the two sides avoided the temptation to reflect upon the past simply in order to be more "clever" the next time? Have they derived genuine "wisdom" from the disappointing experience of the earlier detente and the turmoil of the second Cold War?

Important elements of the leadership of both superpowers — and in the case of the Soviet Union particularly since Gorbachev assumed power in March 1985 —

should be credited with the good sense to re-think some of the fundamental assumptions, goals, and modalities that influenced their relations in the seventies and early eighties. As a result, the political and psychological climate in which the search for improved relations has proceeded since the mid-eighties differs significantly from that which characterized the earlier efforts of Nixon and Brezhnev. To depict these changes one needs not only to identify the "lessons" which each side has drawn from the abortive detente of the seventies but also to take note of some important structural differences between the two periods and new developments in the interim that favor their most recent effort to develop a more constructive relationship.

General "lessons" drawn by some U.S. leaders from the abortive detente of the 1970s

The erosion and collapse of detente left American opinion divided as to its "lessons." Those who had opposed Nixon's detente policy from the very beginning felt that the history of the seventies proved them to be right. For them, the correct lesson was to give full recognition finally to the fundamental threat posed by the Soviet Union and to build up strength to cope more effectively with it. At the extreme, their preference was for policies that would increase pressure against the Soviet Union and to "squeeze" it, hoping thereby to exacerbate its growing internal and external difficulties.

Others, however, while supporting an American military build-up and a tougher foreign policy posture towards Soviet expansionism, did not rule out the possibility of another effort in the future to "deal" with the Soviet Union under more propitious circumstances should Soviet leaders show evidence of greater restraint and willingness to address the agenda of issues put forward by Washington.

President Reagan's circle of advisers included both "squeezers" and "dealers," and rather sharp disagreements arose between them during Reagan's first term on issues of arms control and on policy towards the Soviet Union. Among those who did not exclude re-engaging with the Soviets a consensus of sorts developed regarding general lessons of the abortive detente of the seventies that should inform and constrain any new effort to improve U.S.-Soviet relations. For this group of American leaders, six general lessons appear to have been particularly important and influenced the cautious moves of the Reagan administration when, after Gorbachev succeeded Brezhnev in March 1985, the President began to explore the new Soviet leader's receptivity to the kind of improved relationship the United States favored. Briefly stated, these general lessons were as follows:

1. Avoid agreements with the Soviet Union, such as the Basic Principles-Agreement of 1972, comprised of high-sounding but ambiguous general

principles. Such agreements are likely once again to turn out to be pseudo-agreements that paper over important disagreements and, therefore, are likely to lead eventually to shattered expectations on both sides and mutual recriminations.

2. The United States must not allow Soviet leaders to believe that the American interest in improved relations stems from weakness or that it will allow the Soviet Union to build up its military forces and pursue gains in the Third World without responding.

3. Progress in arms control cannot be easily "de-coupled" from progress in other aspects of U.S.-Soviet relations. Moscow and Washington must engage each other seriously and simultaneously in the areas of regional conflicts, human rights and bilateral relations as well as in arms control.

4. The United States will need to formulate a clearer idea of the long-range goal of a "more constructive" U.S.-Soviet relationship than Nixon and Kissinger had when they stated this to be among the objectives of their policy vis-a-vis the Soviet Union.

5. Norms of competition and norms of cooperation and reciprocity will indeed be needed for the development of an improved U.S.-Soviet relationship. But such norms must not remain vague and undeveloped as tended to be the case in the seventies. Institutional and procedural mechanisms must be created — and existing ones put to better use — to enable the two sides to clarify, refine, and implement such norms.

6. U.S. leaders must not again "over-sell" detente to the American public as did Nixon and Kissinger. U.S. leaders must not allow the public to develop exaggerated, unrealistic expectations regarding the pace and benefits of improved relations with the Soviet Union. Also, the impact on the American public of inevitable ups and downs in U.S.-Soviet relations must be better managed.

Soviet "lessons" and changing foreign policy beliefs

In this section, the "lessons" some important Soviet leaders and policy influentials drew from the abortive detente of the seventies and the second Cold War will be combined with the much more significant changes in foreign policy beliefs that have emerged particularly from Gorbachev's efforts to adapt Soviet thinking and policies to new internal and external developments. These "lessons" and these changes of beliefs have been inferred from Soviet writings and conversations with Soviet academicians, and they have been checked with similar analyses of Gorbachev's "new thinking" prepared by many Western specialists on the Soviet Union. They are stated succinctly here, it should be noted, *without* attempting to assess (a) how deeply rooted such beliefs are in the contemporary Soviet leadership group; (b) how widely held they are among influential persons in the Soviet Union; (c) how stable they are likely to be, and (d) precisely what impact these beliefs are already having or will have on Soviet policy and behavior. These are all important questions which American policymakers and specialists on the Soviet Union must be concerned with and take into account in formulating U.S. policy towards the Soviet Union. Quite obviously, judgment will be needed as to how to balance the opportunities and risks entailed in responding to Gorbachev's "new thinking" or in putting forward initiatives from the United States and/or its allies.

Taken together, these lessons and beliefs which are attributed to Gorbachev and his supporters constitute an important part of the political and psychological framework within which contemporary Soviet leadership is attempting to develop a more constructive relationship with the West. Because these changes in Soviet beliefs are so much more basic and numerous than those of American leaders, they require more detail and space than was given in the preceding section on "lessons" drawn by U.S. leaders.[4]

Soviet conception of its superpower role:

1. However valuable the acquisition by the Soviet Union of strategic parity and "military equality" with the U.S., it did not yield the type of "political equality" Brezhnev desired and the benefits that such a status was expected to yield.

2. Soviet acquisition of a favorable "correlation of forces" in the late 1960s did not turn out to be as advantageous as expected; instead of enabling the Soviet Union to achieve hoped for gains it provoked the U.S. into strengthening its own military capabilities and pursuing a more assertive foreign policy.

3. Competition and rivalry with the U.S. led to misallocation of resources which exacerbated domestic Soviet problems; the Soviet Union must no longer allow its conception of superpower status and foreign policy to be shaped by the imperatives and modalities of the traditional game of geopolitical competition with the United States.

4. The main foreign policy interest of the Soviet Union should be the creation of favorable possibilities for dealing with its domestic problems.

5. The Soviet Union should "de-ideologize" its philosophy of, and approach to, international relations. The "interdependence" of states and peoples is the basis for redefining the Soviet Union's global role.

6. The Soviet Union should pursue the goal of transforming the entire system of international relations in the direction of "demilitarization" and should

emphasize the need for cooperative efforts for dealing with increasingly severe global problems of economics, food, energy, and ecology.

Soviet conception of security:

7. Strategic parity, it turns out, is not a reliable or sufficient guarantee of security for the Soviet Union.

8. The earlier conception of security as based on a great power's unilateral efforts must be replaced partially or entirely by a new concept of "mutual security."

9. The earlier conception of security against military threats must be replaced by the broader concept of "comprehensive security" against a variety of threats to human welfare and existence.

10. The Soviet Union should be more sensitive to the dynamics of what American specialists refer to as the "security dilemma." It should not attempt to enhance its own security by means that make the U.S. so insecure that it feels impelled to increase its own military capabilities that, in turn, exacerbate Soviet insecurity.

11. The Soviet Union is no longer threatened by a deliberate, unprovoked attack from the West; this development opens up important opportunities for reorientation of Soviet military policy and arms control, and for greater emphasis on domestic Soviet priorities.

12. The threat of premeditated nuclear aggression is decreasing, but the possibility of an accidental, unsanctioned outbreak of war and inadvertent war through uncontrollable escalation of a crisis continues and may be increasing.

13. Terrorism will continue to generate serious threats to security. The Soviet Union should cooperate with the U.S. and other states to combat certain types of terrorism.

U.S.-Soviet relations:

14. Soviet efforts such as were made in the past to persuade the U.S. to accept "de-linkage" of the central U.S.-Soviet relationship (and arms control) from competition in Third Areas — however rational such de-linkage is in principle — will not work. Whether or not U.S. leaders deliberately attempt to employ a strategy of linkage, the coupling of different issues in U.S-Soviet relations is inevitable in a populist democracy such as the U.S.

15. Soviet behavior in the past sometimes inadvertently strengthened the invidious image held in the West of the Soviet Union as a hostile, untrustworthy opponent. Soviet leaders should not only try to avoid such behavior in the future but should adopt new patterns of behavior that will develop a more

favorable image of the Soviet Union as a "partner" committed to cooperation in dealing with problems of mutual security and comprehensive security.

16. Soviet emphasis on secrecy in the interest of Soviet security, however necessary it may have been in the past, had serious negative consequences for relations with the West. Soviet secrecy contributed to insecurity in the West; it encouraged "worst case" interpretations of Soviet intentions; it gave ammunition to Western proponents of the arms race; and in consequence Soviet secrecy had the effect of indirectly increasing threats to Soviet security. Greater Soviet "openness" is needed to reverse this process and will operate indirectly to strengthen Soviet security.

Competition in the Third World:

17. The Soviet Union must give higher priority to improving the central U.S.-Soviet relationship than to pursuing marginal gains in the Third World. Such Soviet gains have proven in any case to be more expensive and less stable than had been expected.

18. The earlier Soviet concept of "crisis prevention" in the Third World, based on reliance on Soviet military power to deter the U.S. from provoking or exploiting regional conflicts and on efforts to get the United States to agree to a "code of conduct" limiting involvement in Third World conflicts, has proven to be inadequate. These earlier Soviet approaches to crisis prevention must be replaced by a variety of bilateral (U.S.-Soviet Union) and multi-lateral (regional organizations and U.N.) mechanisms to de-limit U.S.-Soviet competition in Third Areas. Crisis prevention, that is, has to be viewed more broadly as a political problem, not exclusively as a matter of credible commitments backed by military strength.

19. "Peaceful co-existence" in its old meaning as a tactic for continuing "class struggle" in the Third World is no longer a viable concept and has had an adverse impact on relations with the U.S. The essential meaning of "peaceful coexistence" should be reformulated to reflect the desirability of a permanent state of peaceful cohabitation with Western capitalist societies.

20. Not only the ideological dimension of U.S.-Soviet rivalry in Third Areas but also the *geopolitical* motivation and rationale for superpower competition should be moderated and replaced by greater restraint in pursuit of gains in Third Areas at each other's expense, and this should be coupled with sensitivity to each other's vital interests. In any case, the Soviet Union should reduce its involvement in existing regional conflicts and should encourage the United States to follow a similar path. However, this does not mean that

the Soviet Union should withdraw from all positions of influence it has acquired and retreat to isolationism.

22. The increasing turbulence in the Third World together with domestic economic problems experienced by both the Soviet Union and U.S. means that both superpowers must reconcile themselves and adjust to a gradual but substantial shrinkage of influence and control in the Third World. The Soviet Union should take the lead in redrafting its global role and encourage the U.S. to do the same.

Some important differences between the two eras

There are important differences between the earlier detente era and today. In the early 1970s the efforts of Nixon and Kissinger to improve relations with the Soviet Union stemmed in part from their recognition of the fact that they were operating in a new situation of relative decline in the position of the United States in the world. And, indeed, Brezhnev believed that it was rising Soviet strength — a shift in the "correlation of forces" — that forced detente upon the United States. In the late 1980s, on the other hand, it is Soviet leadership that seeks improvement of relations from a position of weakness.

Evident, too, is certain asymmetry between the superpowers as regards the desire for and receptivity to change in the international system. The Soviet Union under Gorbachev strives for substantial, indeed in some respects radical, change not only in its relations with the West but also in the structure and modalities of international relations. To be sure Gorbachev's general concepts for such changes are still evolving and many of them remain to be specified. The United States, much less dissatisfied with the existing situation, has been concerned lest the momentum for change get out of hand and undermine the gains the West has made in stabilizing the situation in Europe and in containing and, to some extent, eroding Soviet expansionism in the Third World. Moreover, the two superpowers have different as well as overlapping agendas for change that have to be sorted out and explored.

Related to this is another difference between the two eras. In the late seventies it was President Carter who tried at the outset of his administration to shift U.S. foreign policy away from a geopolitical preoccupation with the Soviet "threat" to a set of "World Order" goals that he favored; but at that time the Soviets seemed more interested in exploiting opportunities to increase their global influence. Now, however, it is Gorbachev who promotes his own vision of World Order towards which he seems to want to move boldly and quickly, whereas the United States wishes to move more slowly and cautiously. Dissatisfaction with the general state of international affairs is much greater in Moscow than it is in Washington. Convinced that changes in the structure of relations in Europe are necessary and desirable, the Soviet Union seems more ready to accept the risks of fluid, uncharted change than the U.S., which, although recognizing that the existing structure of peace and stability in Europe must and will change in ways that cannot be clearly foreseen, is more concerned with managing the risks of change and the transition to new forms than the Soviet Union appears to be. More generally, the fact that the two superpowers differ somewhat in their readiness to move away from traditional concepts of security and instrumentalities for achieving it results in a certain lack of synchronization in efforts to create a more constructive and stable relationship, and beyond that to restructuring the international system.

Still another important difference between the two eras concerns the People's Republic of China. In the early 1970s, both the U.S. and the Soviet Union attached considerable importance, though with sharply divergent goals, to China as a factor in superpower relations. Brezhnev wanted to use detente with the U.S. to serve as a kind of alliance for isolating and weakening the PRC. For his part Nixon not only rebuffed Brezhnev's overtures; instead he exploited the Sino-Soviet conflict using detente with China to exert leverage on the Soviet Union. These differences, some observers feel, contributed to the erosion of the Nixon-Brezhnev detente. In contrast to the 1970s, China in the 1980s plays a more neutral, balanced role vis-a-vis the two superpowers and it is not as important a complicating factor in the development of U.S.-Soviet relations.

New developments that enhance prospects for improved relations

In addition to drawing general lessons from the abortive detente of the 1970s, both superpowers have begun to adapt to important new developments in their internal and external environments. The ways in which they are responding enhance the possibility of a significant improvement in their relationship. These new developments and their implications are mostly well known and, hence, can be briefly dealt with here.

1. Both superpowers have experienced serious economic difficulties, the Soviet Union in a much more acute and immediate form than the United States. As a result, Soviet priorities have shifted from the pursuit of global aspirations in the early seventies to efforts to deal with serious domestic problems in the eighties. In the seventies Brezhnev attempted to expand the global position of his country, proclaiming that the Soviet Union was now the political as well as the military equal of the United States. Such claims are strikingly absent in Gorbachev's era; instead, Soviet leaders and writers acknowledge that their country cannot any longer afford an expensive foreign policy and that it must curtail military competition with the economically stronger Western powers.

2. Not only Soviet internal difficulties but also a series of foreign policy failures in the past decade or so have forced a basic reconsideration of the assumptions, aspirations, and modalities of Soviet foreign policy. The list of flawed policies and failures includes Afghanistan, the sterility of Soviet policy in the MBFR negotiations, the provocative deployment of SS-20s in Europe, the walk-out in 1983 from the Geneva arms control negotiations, and the optimistic expectations and over-investment in the Third World competition.

For its part, the United States encountered a number of difficulties and frustrations during the second Cold War that eventually created a willingness on the part of the Reagan administration to modify some of the policy objectives that it had proclaimed and pursued during the early eighties. The Administration's initiatives in the Middle East and in Central America failed to produce hoped-for results. The Vietnam syndrome continued to constrain the use of force and threats of force as an instrument of U.S. diplomacy. West European allies effectively resisted U.S. policies that they feared would undo the gains the first detente had achieved for Europe. The Administration's threat to undo or bypass major arms control agreements made by previous administrations, Reagan's ambitious SDI initiative, and his military spending plans eventually ran into stubborn resistance from Congress and public opinion. He was persuaded by public and allied opinion to resume serious high level contact with Soviet leaders in the interest of reducing tensions, alleviating the fear of nuclear war, and resuming efforts to develop a more constructive relationship with the Soviet Union. President Bush, although evincing a distinct preference for proceeding cautiously, has recognized that it is time to move "beyond containment" and to try to bring the Soviet Union into a better relationship with the rest of the international system.

3. Both Soviet and American leaders recognize a need to adjust to developments that are altering the nature of the NATO and Warsaw Pact alliances, their leadership role in their respective alliances, and relations between the East and West in Europe. Unlike the Soviet Union, which has exercised a dominating hegemonic position in the Warsaw Pact, the United States has had considerable experience — and difficulties — in trying to exercise a non-hegemonic leadership role in NATO. Under Gorbachev the Soviet Union is loosening its control over its East European allies, moving away from a hegemonic role to some kind of as yet undefined leadership role. The United States for its part, has entered a period in which some of its NATO allies are moving towards even greater autonomy within and outside the alliance. In particular, various developments are combining to encourage and

permit the Federal Republic of Germany to play a more influential role in Eastern Europe and even vis-a-vis the Soviet Union.

4. Both Soviet and American leaders recognize the need to adjust to the ever-increasing multipolarity and pluralism in the international system. Moscow and Washington are increasingly aware that the trend towards increased turbulence in the Third World and stubborn assertions of independence on the part of so many other countries, coupled with their own economic difficulties, means that they will have to adjust to declining control and influence in the rest of the world. In consequence, the shrinkage of their role as predominant global powers is underway, and Moscow and Washington face the challenging task of redefining what it means to be a superpower in the emerging international system.

5. In the 1980s, opinion leaders and some strategic analysts in both the Soviet Union and the United States became increasingly uneasy over the extent to which the superpowers rely on nuclear deterrence to keep the peace. Developments in military technology and deployments created deep concern that strategic deterrence, while stable and reliable in peacetime, could prove fragile during a tense crisis when, as is likely, strategic forces would be placed on high alert. Concern over vulnerability of their command systems to preemptive attack has led both sides to move towards a "launch-on-warning" and "launch-under-attack" policy, thus exacerbating concern over the possibility of accidental and inadvertent nuclear war. In this context of rising concern over the possibility of nuclear war, President Reagan and other Americans found attractive the idea that advanced technology — the SDI — might provide a perfect or near-perfect defense against incoming strategic missiles, an accomplishment that might even lead eventually to the virtual abolition of nuclear weapons. However, stubborn questions of SDI feasibility, cost and expected performance, and fear of triggering an arms race have eroded hopes that technology could abolish fear of nuclear devastation.

As a result, although both the United States and Soviet Union accept some form of strategic nuclear deterrence as necessary in the foreseeable future, there is an increasingly strong feeling in both countries that they should attempt to reduce reliance on nuclear deterrence as a basis for their security. Not only should Moscow and Washington work together — through the INF Treaty, a possible START agreement, and other bilateral as well as unilateral actions — to develop a more benign, less dangerous form of nuclear deterrence, they should above all now give much more emphasis to creating stronger *political* foundations for improvement of the overall U.S.-Soviet relationship in order to enhance their mutual security. (This is an important point to which I shall return in the next section of this paper.)

6. In both countries there has been growing awareness that their relations in the past have been adversely affected by the impact of the "security dilemma." Thus, what one side does to improve its security has generally been viewed by the other side as an increased threat to its security which requires an appropriate strengthening of its own capabilities; this reverberates back to the adversary and sets into motion a vicious cycle of interaction that feeds the arms race and increases mutual distrust. Greater sensitivity to the dynamics of the security dilemma has encouraged thoughtful persons on both sides to raise questions about the *offense-oriented* military postures and doctrines the two sides have developed. Such postures and doctrines exacerbate each other's insecurity and magnify distrust; they encourage "worst-case" fears of possible threats from the other side, feed the arms race, raise the specter of crisis instability and the possibility of accidental or inadvertent war. An important implication of this development is that it creates new opportunities for unilateral and cooperative steps for *mutual threat reduction*, about which more will be said in this and later chapters.

7. Similarly, in recent years leaders in both countries have come to appreciate that the ideological dimension of their foreign policies has exacerbated the workings of the security dilemma, creating additional distrust and hostility, and magnifying obstacles to the exploration of cooperative arrangements to enhance mutual security. Significantly, beginning in the mid-eighties both sides began to abandon the heavy ideological cast of rhetoric and policies towards each other. Consider the remarkable shift within a few years from Reagan's "evil empire" characterization of the Soviet Union to his expression of friendship for Gorbachev. Even more striking has been the openly stated Soviet policy of "de-ideologization" of its foreign policy and of its view of international relations. This has been accompanied by a concerted, well-orchestrated campaign to change the invidious, hostile image of the Soviet Union held in the West into that of a reliable partner ready to cooperate in dealing with all global problems. Under Gorbachev's rule, Soviet leaders and writers have also tried to alter the Soviet public's fear that the U.S. and NATO pose threats to Soviet security, going so far on occasion to admitting that unwise Soviet behavior in the past reinforced the negative Western image of the Soviet Union, and also that in the past Soviet leaders had deliberately exaggerated the image of a hostile West.

8. Gorbachev has taken important steps towards creating a more "open" Soviet political system. This shift manifests itself in many ways. Of considerable

importance is the quite remarkable willingness of the present Soviet leadership to open East European and Soviet territory to on-site inspection in furtherance of arms control and confidence building. In addition, Gorbachev has taken significant moves towards creating a more pluralistic and more open domestic political system — one in which policy issues are publicly debated, the distortions of orthodox Soviet history are subjected to sharp revisionist attacks, and past Soviet foreign policy errors are admitted and criticized.

If these changes associated with glasnost continue, they will eventually help bring about a significant amelioration of the distrust with which the Soviet Union has been viewed in the past and thereby contribute to improvement in the overall political relationship. In fact, such a development in the Western image of the Soviet Union is already well underway. It has proceeded further in Western Europe and among the American public than among American foreign policy specialists, but as of the end of 1989 it is developing among all groups.

9. Over the past twenty years American and Soviet leaders have come to the sober recognition that their countries are inescapably vulnerable to nuclear devastation. Strictly unilateral measures by either side to promote its security, as in the past, will no longer suffice; each is dependent on the restrained behavior and cooperation of the other side to assure its security and to lighten the burden of providing for it. Recognition of this condition of mutual vulnerability and mutual dependence has strengthened incentives to explore arms control, confidence-building measures, and other cooperative arrangements for enhancing their security. Each side has moved towards a recognition that the measures it takes to increase its sense of security must not have the effect, as so often in the past, of increasing insecurity for the other side. In this important sense, objective conditions have created the basis for the new concept of "mutual security" as a fundamental goal for developing a more constructive and stable relationship.

The importance of a basic political framework of U.S.-Soviet relations

Security for both sides — and indeed the security of much of the rest of the world — is affected by the quality of the overall U.S.-Soviet relationship, its *political* as well as its military dimension. The arms control process is indeed important but it cannot carry too great a burden for improvement in U.S.-Soviet relations; although arms control achievements contribute to better relations, arms control *per se* cannot overcome or compensate for fundamental problems in the relationship. *Political* stability in the U.S-Soviet relationship is just as important as strategic stability; the two are not unrelated, but achievement of strategic stability cannot assure political stability. Besides, the full potential of arms control cannot be realized in the absence of a viable framework and mutually agreed upon goals for the development of U.S.-Soviet relations. If such a framework is carefully constructed and clearly understood by both sides, it can provide an element of political stability that should help the two countries to weather occasional downturns and setbacks in their relations.

Agreement on a basic political framework helps to define the longer-range objectives the two sides believe to be worth pursuing, each through its own unilateral policies and together (and sometimes with other states) in agreed-upon joint activities. A basic framework can provide a benign "shadow of the future,"[5] thereby increasing Soviet and American incentives to work for cooperative, mutually acceptable solutions to at least some of their concerns and problems. Without a basic framework that offers a credible prospect of important mutual benefits in the long run, a superpower is more likely to yield to the temptation to exploit opportunities for unilateral short-term gains at the expense of the other superpower.

Given the opportunities the present historical situation provides for the development of a more constructive relationship between the two superpowers, it is highly relevant to consider the contribution to this goal that an agreed-upon basic political framework of relations can make. First, let me briefly indicate what is meant and encompassed by such a framework of relations. It is, quite simply, an agreed-upon statement that indicates how the two sides view each other, what kind of relationship they would like to work towards, what common or parallel interests they have in various issue-areas which they wish to promote, and what norms and procedures they wish to observe in dealing with conflicting interests.

But is it realistic to believe that a viable political framework of relations is at all possible for these two powerful nations, so different from one another in their political systems and ideology, which have a long history of mutual distrust and hostility? Certainly the difficulty of the task must be acknowledged and, indeed, a proper understanding of why it is a difficult task in Washington and Moscow is a necessary starting point for any serious effort to formulate such a political framework. Such an undertaking should be grounded in an understanding of why Nixon's and Brezhnev's effort to create a basic political framework of relations in the early 1970s proved to be abortive. With this in mind, let us briefly review the history of their effort to formulate such a framework.

We may recall that it was Soviet leaders at the outset of the detente process in the early seventies who, more so than their American counterparts, attributed considerable importance to securing a formal, written U.S.-Soviet document that would articulate the fundamental basis of the new relationship the two sides wished to develop. As Henry Kissinger's memoirs makes clear, he and Nixon attached much less importance to such a document, but aware of the predilection of Soviet leaders for formalizing the basis of their relations with other states by means of a joint declaration of principles, they agreed to go along. The result was the Basic Principles Agreement (BPA) signed by Brezhnev and Nixon at their first Moscow summit of May 1972.

In this document Nixon and Brezhnev identified the specific issue areas in which they would seek to promote their mutual interests. Thus they resolved to continue efforts to limit armaments and to develop long-term economic, scientific, and cultural ties between their two countries in order to strengthen the relationship. At least in this respect the BPA document was a business-like "agenda setting" agreement which had much to recommend it.

But elsewhere in the BPA document the two sides touched upon the more sensitive question of how they viewed the overall Soviet-American relationship and, in particular, made an effort to identify some general principles by means of which the relationship should be governed and their rivalry muted. In this respect, the BPA attempted to provide some very general norms of competition and cooperation. Thus, the two sides agreed that in the nuclear age "there is no alternative to conducting their relations on the basis of peaceful coexistence." Moreover, "differences in ideology and in the social systems of the U.S. and the USSR are not obstacles to the bilateral development of normal relations based on the principles of sovereignty, equality, noninterference in internal affairs and mutual advantage." Continuing, the BPA records that the two sides agreed that "the prerequisites for maintaining and strengthening peaceful relations between the U.S. and the USSR are the recognition of the security interests of the parties based on the principles of equality and the renunciation of the use or threat of force." U.S.-Soviet discussions and negotiations in the future were to be conducted "in a spirit of reciprocity, mutual accommodation and mutual benefit." The two sides pledged to "do their utmost to avoid military confrontations and to prevent the outbreak of nuclear war" and to "be prepared to negotiate and settle differences by peaceful means."

It should be noted that most all of these principles and general norms for regulating U.S.-Soviet rivalry and for moderating its adverse consequences were cast in political phraseology long favored and recommended by Soviet leaders and spokesmen. Seemingly of equal benefit for both sides, these principles nonetheless had special salience and significance at this juncture in the development of U.S.-Soviet relations for Soviet leaders. Nixon and Kissinger were aware of this but they were perhaps not sufficiently sensitive to the risks of subscribing to *general principles whose operational meaning and significance could be interpreted differently by the two sides.*

For example, Nixon and Kissinger were fully aware that Soviet leaders attached special meaning and significance to their ideological concept of "peaceful coexistence." (In fact Nixon had instructed Kissinger to make it clear in earlier pre-summit discussions with Soviet leaders that he understood and firmly rejected *their* version of "peaceful coexistence," and the "Brezhnev Doctrine.") Nonetheless, Nixon and Kissinger evidently decided to accept the inclusion of "peaceful coexistence" and other Soviet-favored concepts and principles into the BPA for several reasons: in part in a spirit of compromise, in part to "reward" the Soviet leaders for the military and diplomatic restraint they had observed recently in the face of U.S. air attacks against the Haiphong harbor in North Vietnam (during which Soviet vessels had been struck), and in part because U.S. negotiators introduced principles of their own into the BPA that ostensibly counterbalanced the connotations and implications of some of the Soviet-favored phraseology. Thus the document also stated that the two sides agreed to "exercise restraint in their mutual relations" and that "efforts to obtain unilateral advantages at the expense of the other, directly or indirectly, are inconsistent with these objectives."

Thus this part of the BPA was a compromise, containing phrases about which at least one side, perhaps both, actually had reservations. Hence it is not inappropriate to label this part of the BPA document — as some observers did within a few years — a pseudo-agreement, one that ignored or covered up basic, unresolved disagreements and gave a false impression of real progress towards regulating and moderating superpower competition and rivalry for influence throughout the globe. Indeed, in the next few years the behavior of the two sides in the Middle East and elsewhere exposed the ambiguities and divergent interpretations of key concepts imbedded in the BPA with respect to "equality," "restraint," "reciprocity," and "no unilateral advantage."

The persistence and clash of conflicting U.S.-Soviet foreign policy interests in the Third World made not only these general principles for moderating their rivalry but the entire framework of relations agreed to in the BPA highly vulnerable. It soon became painfully obvious that mutually inconsistent hopes and expectations had been attached to detente by Moscow and Washington, leading to deep disappointments and mutual recriminations. The result was a gradual erosion of the framework and the political stability that the BPA was supposed to provide for the detente process.

Although Carter and Brezhnev formally reaffirmed adherence to the BPA when they signed the SALT II agreement in 1979, the next president made it clear that he considered the BPA and detente as no longer operative.

The question of a basic political framework re-emerged in connection with the first summit meeting of Gorbachev and Reagan in November 1985. Statements by the two leaders and their joint communique did not allude to the Basic Principles Agreement of 1972. Neither side accepted the other's draft proposal for a joint declaration (the contents of the drafts have not been disclosed). During the summit there was even considerable doubt as to whether any joint statement would be issued at the conclusion of their meeting. Finally, as a result of a last-minute compromise, a joint communique was issued. Notably absent were any references to "peaceful coexistence," "equality," and other symbols associated with the BPA. However, the Gorbachev-Reagan statement did contain a few points of agreement that might be regarded as constituting a minimal basic agreement on interests and objectives. The paragraph on "security" contained three important declarations:

1. "[The two leaders] have agreed that a nuclear war cannot be won and must never be fought."

2. "Recognizing that any conflict between the USSR and the U.S. could have catastrophic consequences, they emphasized the importance of preventing any war between them, whether nuclear or conventional."

3. "They will not seek to achieve military superiority."

Despite the absence of a broader political framework of relations during the Reagan years, the superpowers held talks on a variety of subjects. In 1986 arms control discussions addressed a variety of issues: nuclear and space arms, confidence-building measures, mutual and balanced force reductions, chemical weapons, nuclear testing, nuclear risk reduction centers, and incidents at sea. Other subjects under discussion included nuclear energy, regional problems, cultural and scientific exchanges, trade, human rights, and people-to-people exchanges.

Finally, in 1987 intensified negotiations on intermediate-range nuclear forces (INF) and strategic arms reduction (START) resulted in agreement on an INF Treaty, ratified by the U.S. Senate just before the fourth Reagan-Gorbachev summit in Moscow in May 1988. In this improved atmosphere Gorbachev sought but failed to obtain Reagan's approval of a joint statement that echoed some of the language of the BPA of 1972. Gorbachev's draft statement would have had the United States and the Soviet Union agree that "peaceful coexistence is something that we resolve as a universal principal of international relations, and that the equality of all states, non-interference in domestic affairs, and freedom of socio-political choice should be recognized as inalienable and mandatory for all."[6] In a news conference immediately following the summit meeting Gorbachev complained that Reagan had initially conveyed a favorable view of the proposed statement but that by the end of the summit his advisers had persuaded him to reject it. Secretary of State

George Shultz and other advisers were said to have reacted negatively to Gorbachev's proposed joint declaration. One unnamed U.S. official called it "ambiguous, freighted with the baggage of the past," too similar to some of the language of the BPA; he specifically objected to the phrase "peaceful coexistence" as a propagandistic Soviet term, and rejected "noninterference in internal affairs" as possibly undercutting U.S. appeals for improvements in the Soviet human rights record.[7] Instead the joint statement finally agreed to by the two leaders, said to have been written by the American side, reiterated the minimal basic framework established at their first summit and stated that despite "the real differences of history, tradition and ideology," the "political dialogue" they had established "represents an increasingly effective means of resolving issues of mutual interest and concern."[8]

As this account of the Reagan-Gorbachev summits indicates, American leaders are wary of agreeing to statements of general principles that purport to define a framework of relations. Their wariness reflects not merely the sobering experience with the BPA and a determination not to repeat some of the errors of the first detente. In addition, an underlying difference between Soviet and American political culture comes into play. The Soviets attach considerable importance to an authoritative articulation of basic political concepts as a starting point for development of policies and choice of actions, both in the domestic and international arenas. In contrast, most American leaders come from a political tradition and a process of socialization in domestic politics that favor a more pragmatic approach, which leads them in many situations to attach less importance to prior agreement on concepts and principles. This difference, however, should not be exaggerated; it is a matter of degree and dependent on circumstances. American leaders have often themselves advanced general principles in articulating foreign policy goals and aspirations. But certainly differences in ideology as well as in political culture do contribute to making agreement on general principles more difficult.

It is entirely possible that progress will be made towards developing a basic political framework of relations between the Soviet Union and the United States that will be given authoritative statement in future summit meetings. But this is likely to be an *incremental*, ad hoc process whereby useful additions will be made from time to time to the core agreement already achieved at the first Reagan-Gorbachev summit, rather than take the form of a comprehensive agreement at one point in time.

There are various reasons why progress in this direction is likely to be gradual and incremental. The history of the earlier effort by Brezhnev and Nixon, as already noted, created considerable sobriety and caution in American leaders regarding the desirability of a second effort along these lines. There is a widely shared feeling among influential Americans that Nixon's adherence to the Basic Principles Agreement was a mistake of a kind that should not be repeated. Incidentally, the fact that Soviet leaders and academicians do not share this negative assessment of the BPA (although they have acknowledged on occasion that it was not followed up by appropriate mechanisms for implementation) and the fact that they have advocated a new agreement of this kind does little to encourage American leaders to view the idea more positively. There is no question but that American opinion, even on the part of those who favor a more energetic response to some of Gorbachev's initiatives, takes a skeptical view of further efforts to agree on "general principles," and is more impressed with the risks that such an agreement could once again backfire than with its potential long-range contribution to improved relations.

For these reasons one may well conclude that, if at all, only a cautious, incremental process of developing a basic political framework will be acceptable to American leaders. Moreover, it will have to be one that avoids commitment to general principles which, however well intentioned, are ambiguous and subject to different interpretation by the two sides as to the implications of the principles for their foreign policy behavior.

The formulation of acceptable general principles is more likely to follow, not precede, acceptable answers to the fundamental question: whether the two superpowers are reasonably close together in their conception of the kind of relationship they consider desirable and towards which they commit themselves to work. This will require both sides to share a realistic conception of the nature and dimensions of the competitive nature of their relationship and of ways to mute and control its dangerous potential. In addition, the two sides will have to have a clear and shared understanding of those aspects of their relationship in which cooperation of some kind would be mutually beneficial. To the extent that the two sides gradually develop a shared conception of an acceptable mixed competitive-collaborative relationship, then incremental development of an increasingly broader basic political framework will be possible and useful.

Such an incremental, evolving framework should offer reasonable assurance that Soviet and American leaders of this generation have not forgotten the important lesson of the disappointing detente of the 1970s — namely, that verbal agreement on a general framework of relations is at best only a start toward, and not a substitute for, the hard work of developing more specific norms of competition and cooperation.

The conception advanced here of an *evolving* basic framework of relations does not exclude agreement on unambiguous, carefully defined general principles. Indeed, I shall discuss one such general principle before concluding this chapter. But principles which can effectively define norms of competition and norms of cooperation must generally derive to some degree from and build upon existing behavioral patterns; only to a limited degree can they be expected to precede and legislate desired behavior. In other words, efforts to state explicit norms for advancing cooperation and limiting competition are more likely to be effective to the extent that they codify behavioral restraints already exhibited from time to time, which the two sides would like to regularize.

An additional question needs to be addressed: should norms and principles, once carefully considered and agreed-upon, be stated in formal agreements? In the past, even the recent past, Soviet leaders and foreign policy specialists have expressed a strong desire for stating all agreements of this kind in written form. American specialists, on the other hand, are more sensitive to the risks of written agreements on norms and principles and more inclined to see the merits of dealing with some issues via tacit norms.[9]

It may be useful to elaborate on the American viewpoint. In the first place, and contrary to expectations entertained when written agreements were drafted, it can become evident later that they suffer from a lack of clarity as to the nature of the commitment they ostensibly impose on the two sides. Inadequate attention to clarity in drafting an agreement is more likely if one side or the other does not attach particular significance to it. (Thus, for example and as already noted, Soviet leaders attached much more importance to the Basic Principles Agreement of 1972 than did Nixon and Kissinger, and Brezhnev and his colleagues interpreted it as bestowing advantages and benefits on the Soviet Union that U.S. leaders were not fully aware of and had not readily agreed to.) Moreover, since written agreements are more visible than tacit ones, real or imagined violations of them by the other side are more likely to arouse domestic public opinion. Even when U.S. (or Soviet) leaders in fact do *not* regard the other superpower's behavior as a clear violation of the formal agreement, important elements of the public may think so and demand reprisals and withdraw their support of the administration's policy of improving superpower relations. For example, important elements of the American public and influential political leaders — but not the Nixon administration — regarded Soviet support of Egypt's attack on Israel in October 1973 as grossly inconsistent with commitments implied by the Basic Principles Agreement and the Agreement on Prevention of Nuclear War (signed by Nixon and Brezhnev at their second summit in June 1973). While this type of misconception is more likely to assume importance in a democratic country, it can do so also in the Soviet Union. Thus, we may recall that Brezhnev felt obliged to give repeated assurances to influential people in the Soviet Union that the written agreements he had signed with Nixon did not mean that Moscow would curtail its support for "progressive forces" in the Third World.

In contrast, tacit understandings have several advantages. They are more flexible and adaptable than written norms. Real or apparent violations of formally stated explicit norms are more likely to require the offended government to charge its adversary with having reneged on its commitment, bad faith, etc., and this can lead to countercharges of some kind that heat up the political atmosphere and agitate public opinion. Tacit norms are more likely to survive occasional behavior that seems at odds with implicit standards; imperfect adherence will not destroy their utility. In either case, whether behavior seems in violation of written or tacit norms, the two sides should create procedural mechanisms (as they have done in the case of the Standing Consultative Commission and in the Incidents at Sea Agreement) or utilize existing diplomatic channels to discuss the matter and to try to clarify the norm in question.

At the same time, some issues in U.S.-Soviet relations might better be handled through formal, explicit agreements. A written agreement may lend more authority to agreed-upon norms and make it more difficult and costly to violate them. Commitments undertaken in a formal, written mode may also be less vulnerable to a deterioration of overall U.S.-Soviet relations. All this presumes, of course, that the written norms are free of ambiguity and that the two sides share a common understanding of their implications as to permissible and impermissible behavior. Indeed, efforts to formalize tacit norms and understandings in written form may be useful, even if not successful, insofar as they force the two sides to become aware of ambiguities and differences of interpretation of tacit understandings.

Notwithstanding the risks associated with written agreements, then, they can play a useful — at times indispensable — role if carefully crafted and clearly understood by both parties. Formal joint declarations by U.S. and Soviet leaders that create a political framework for the development of their relations are less likely to encounter difficulties of the kind encountered by the Basic Principles Agreement if they limit efforts to agree on too many general principles and focus instead on identifying *priority objectives* in *specific issue-areas* on which the two sides agree to engage in joint problem solving and if they *set an agenda* and *create procedural mechanisms* for such efforts.

Viewed from this perspective, should U.S. and Soviet leaders agree to explore more fully the goal of mutual security, the concept that constitutes the central focus of the joint Soviet-American study reported in this volume, there is considerable promise that it would facilitate further development and consolidation of the U.S.-Soviet relationship. As subsequent chapters will illustrate, the basic idea of mutual security is at once simple and applicable to many dimensions of the superpower relationship: each side can improve its security by taking steps, separately or jointly with the other, that will improve security for both. In other words, increased security for one side need not be at the expense of increased insecurity for the other. The modus operandi for enhancing security for both sides is via *mutual threat reduction.*

Mutual security, it may be noted, is not an entirely novel idea that has been neither tried nor tested. In fact, it has important *continuity* with past U.S.-Soviet experience in developing cooperation on security issues. The roots of what is now called mutual security go back almost twenty years to the SALT I Treaty, which was based on recognition of the fact that security from the threat of a devastating nuclear war cannot be achieved any longer at acceptable cost and risk by relying solely on one's unilateral efforts. Recognition that each side is dependent on the other's behavior to achieve the level of security it wants has steadily increased in the past twenty years. This has been manifested in a variety of cooperative arrangements — for example, the Incidents at Sea Agreement, the INF Treaty, and the Nuclear Risk Reduction Centers.

Adoption of the mutual security concept would provide a relatively *non-controversial, non-ideological* centerpiece for developing a new, more construc-tive and stable U.S.-Soviet relationship. Mutual security is entirely consistent with what Secretary of State Baker in his address of October 23, 1989 referred to as "our mission to press the search for mutual advantage." And mutual security dovetails nicely with President Bush's call in his November 22 speech for moving U.S.-Soviet relations "beyond containment to a new partnership."

Adding the goal of mutual security to the Administration's articulation of its policy towards the Soviet Union would enhance its appeal to the American public and to U.S. allies. Incorporating the goal and framework of mutual security into the general framework of policy planning in both countries would give useful focus and direction for efforts to deal with many dimensions of their relationship. As demonstrated in the following chapters, mutual security provides criteria and a flexible framework for achieving relatively modest improvements in the short term to possibly quite ambitious ones in the longer run.

Notes

1.   The writer is indebted to Richard Smoke and Steven Kull for valuable comments on an earlier draft of this chapter. This chapter draws upon many articles and books by scholars who have dealt with the development of U.S.-Soviet relations as well as from several of the author's earlier publications: Alexander L. George et al, *Managing U.S.-Soviet Rivalry: Problems of Crisis Prevention* (Boulder, CO: Westview Press, 1983); George, Philip J. Farley, and

Alexander Dallin, eds., *U.S.-Soviet Security Cooperation: Achievements, Failures, Lessons* (New York: Oxford University Press, 1988). The author expresses appreciation for support for the research leading to these works, provided by The Carnegie Corporation of New York, The MacArthur Foundation, The Ford Foundation, and The Rockefeller Foundation.

2. Here and elsewhere in this chapter I refer to the collapse of detente between the U.S. and the Soviet Union. A form of detente was partially preserved in Europe.

3. See, for example, George, "U.S.-Soviet Efforts to Cooperate in Crisis Management and Crisis Avoidance," in George, Farley, and Dallin, U.S.-Soviet Security Cooperation, pp. 581-600.

4. Some of these Soviet beliefs, including some of the quite important ones, have been operationalized in concrete changes in policy and behavior which, however, will not be documented in this survey. The reader will note that I have not attempted to distinguish explicitly between changes in very basic philosophical/ideological beliefs and what may be called policy concepts. Instead, I have thought it more useful for present purposes to list the new Soviet beliefs under four substantive headings.

5. The term "shadow of the future" was employed by Robert Axelrod in his important game-theoretic contribution to cooperation theory. See *The Evolution of Cooperation* (New York: Basic Books, 1984). Axelrod points out that the more the possibility of future gains is valued relative to the payoff from current interactions with another actor, the less the incentive to behave in an uncooperative manner in the present.

6. Gorbachev disclosed at least part of the text of his abortive proposal in a news conference held immediately after the Moscow summit. *The New York Times* (June 2, 1988).

7. *San Francisco Chronicle* (June 2, 1988).

8. *The New York Times* (June 2, 1988).

9. For a more detailed discussion of the analysis in the next three paragraphs see George, "The Search for Agreed Norms," in *Windows of Opportunity: From Cold War to Peaceful Competition in U.S.-Soviet Relations*, edited by Graham T. Allison and William Ury, with Bruce J. Allyn (Cambridge, MA: Ballinger, 1989).

4

Domestic Preconditions for the Transition to Mutual Security: A Soviet Perspective

Petr Gladkov

This chapter examines the relationship between domestic conditions of a nation and its capacity to develop mutual security with a potential adversary. In particular, I will address the current internal situation of the USSR and how the current rapid pace of internal evolution is influencing the Soviet approach to security. However some of my remarks also apply to the U.S. and indeed to any country interested in developing mutual security.[1]

Preliminary observation

Before turning to my main discussion, I want to remind the reader of one elementary fact about mutual security which is obvious to common sense. No country is going to create a relationship of mutual security if its people and leaders have deep feelings either of fear or of hostility toward the other country. This is the first and most basic of all "domestic preconditions" for the development of mutual security. The people and leaders must be ready to see a relationship of mutual security develop.

However elementary this point may seem, it must be mentioned, because most certainly this condition is not always met. Current and past history offers many examples of situations where the population and most political leaders of a country feel too much fear, or too much hostility, or both, toward the other country for anything like "mutual security" to be possible. In these situations, the people and leaders hold a harsh, extreme "image of the enemy." Correctly or incorrectly, they believe that the enemy places no limit on its ambitions and is ready to be aggressive, even militant, in achieving its ambitions. In peoples' minds the "enemy" has become evil, demonized. Believing an image of such an enemy, the people will, quite naturally, feel extremely threatened. And no population that feels extremely threatened can also be receptive at the same time to ideas about "mutual security." The people and leaders will not be receptive even if certain specialists may argue that some sort of mutual security might be desirable for complicated reasons.

In this sense, people's and leaders' image of the other side is decisive; and in this sense, the domestic situation within the country is decisive. Any number of books like this one would make little difference, if the population of the country and most leaders believe, for example, that the other side is an "evil empire" that is bent on endless aggression. The people and their leaders must believe *first* that the other side can be reasonable, can limit its ambitions, and can limit its threats. Then and only then is it possible for people to be willing even to think about mutual security.[2]

I have made this perhaps obvious point first for the simple reason that it applies universally. These generalizations apply to all nations. They are not limited to the feelings of the people and leaders of the USSR, or for that matter of the U.S. They do not apply to this time but not to some other time. They apply to any time and to any country.

Having made this preliminary observation, I turn now to my main remarks.

The interrelation of domestic and foreign policy in the USSR

The USSR has always sought to maintain an integration of its domestic and foreign policies. Following the principles of Marxism-Leninism, policymakers have approached policy as a dialectical unity, a unified whole. Marxism-Leninism holds that neither aspect can be divorced from the other, much less be opposed to the other. For example V.I. Lenin wrote that "there is no more mistaken or harmful idea than the severing of foreign from domestic policy."[3]

Despite this, the historical reality is that a few decades ago the connection between domestic and foreign policy was far more tenuous than it is now. Global problems and international relations (with the important exception of wars) hardly affected people's everyday lives, and this gave the political leaders of the country greater freedom of action in the field of foreign relations than in any other area. In the years following 1945, Soviet leaders deliberately sought to keep the USSR largely disengaged from many of the affairs of Europe and the world. In that period Soviet policy also sought economic autonomy for the USSR and its allies from the world economy. These policies also helped ensure that people's lives were mostly unaffected by external events. The government held nearly a monopoly on the country's foreign affairs; the foreign affairs of the country and the foreign policy of the government thus were more or less identical concepts.

Now this monopoly no longer exists. Today Soviet official foreign policy and the totality of Soviet foreign affairs are not identical concepts; and Soviet foreign affairs are made up of a complex combination of elements. They are made up of the government's foreign policy in the world arena, by the actions of private companies (where they exist), by the activities of public organizations, the mass media, and so on.

The internal conflicts and disagreements present within the Soviet Union (and within any nation) increasingly overstep the national boundary. In this respect, the USSR is coming more to resemble other countries, where it is considered normal for elements within the country to seek influence and take action beyond the national territory, at least in some ways. The very concept of "national interests," which is of key importance in determining national priorities, is becoming vague and sometimes contradictory, since the groups participating in the conduct of foreign affairs sometimes have conflicting interests.

These observations apply in full measure to the important processes of internal change now occurring in the Soviet Union, and to their influence on Soviet foreign policy and Soviet approaches to mutual security. We may suppose that these complications will apply just as much, if not more, to Soviet foreign affairs in the future.

These facts represent a new internal situation within the USSR. Until recently, debates on the interrelation of Soviet domestic and foreign policy were of a purely rhetorical nature, since domestic considerations played such an insignificant role in the formation and conduct of foreign policy by the ruling circles. This was true of direct and indirect influence both.

Direct influence

In a democratic system the people have an opportunity to exert a direct influence on the formation and conduct of foreign policy because their lawfully elected legislative bodies supervise the government's conduct of foreign policy. The goal of coordinating the interests of various political forces and developing a policy that takes account of the country's domestic situation is achieved through open discussion in the legislature of foreign and military policies, the financing of various programs, and so forth.

However, when genuine legislative bodies do not exist, and when their functions are performed by quasi-legislative institutions whose sole task is to legitimize the government's actions, internal limitations do not function and foreign policy becomes a "thing apart." Such a situation existed in the Soviet Union for a rather long period, and the government was free to carry out any foreign policy without regard for its "legislative" body, the Supreme Soviet, which had a purely formal existence.

Indirect influence

By this I refer to consideration given in policy making to public opinion, expressed both in direct polling and through the activities of public organizations. Here also the degree of influence was insignificant in earlier decades. This was so, first, because no one investigated public opinion, and secondly, because even if public opinion had been known nobody would have paid the slightest attention to it. In the framework of the existing political culture, public opinion and public organizations were allowed to exist and function only insofar and until they approved and supported the course already set, in total secrecy, by a narrow circle of the top leaders. Outside that "approval" their opinion was irrelevant, and since everyone knew it was irrelevant, it was of no interest.

However in the last few years, the policy of perestroika has been creating enormous changes in these areas. This is occurring in part because new political thinking has transformed the conceptual bases and practical conduct of the government's foreign policy. It is also occurring because perestroika, by democratizing Soviet society and expanding the range of political action by the people, is introducing a whole series of important internal factors which must be taken into consideration in the conduct of foreign policy. As President Gorbachev has observed, "We are transforming new approaches in domestic affairs into initiatives in foreign policy."[4]

The transformation of the Soviet political system

Mutual security is one of the core concepts of the new political thinking in the USSR pertaining to foreign affairs. Adoption of mutual security is part of the transformation of the conceptual bases of policy. However, this kind of change might be of limited significance if it were confined to a narrow elite made up, say, of intellectuals and some elements of the government. What makes this conceptual change something of far greater significance is the fact that it is embedded in, and is a part of, an immense structural change that is moving forward at nearly all levels of Soviet society.

At the center of the political reforms being carried out inside the USSR is the idea of democratizing the entire life of the country, i.e., "the full-fledged, full-blooded functioning of all public organizations, all production collectives and creative unions, new forms of activity of citizens, and renewal of those forms that have been forgotten."[5]

When applied to the basic question of any revolution — and the changes taking place in the USSR truly are revolutionary — the question of democratization denotes a radical change in power structure of the country. What are the basic elements in this change?

First, the rejection of all forms of centralized regulation of relationships. It means the transition from hierarchical, "pyramidal," vertical systems of administration and control to horizontal systems of self-administration, independent of the leadership.

Second, the creation of conditions favoring the formation and functioning of new elements on the political scene. These new elements will take the shape of various horizontal structures to express and protect the interests of different social groups and strata. These include the numerous national fronts, movements in defense of perestroika, ecological organizations, consumer protection unions, etc.

Third, the further intensification of glasnost as an instrument for democratization. Glasnost is sometimes viewed merely as the chance to speak out and discuss the facts of social reality, but it is more than that. A broader concept of glasnost means that various organizations, departments and administrative organs — not excluding governmental organs — have an *obligation* to involve as much of the population as possible, and all interested groups, in the decision-making process and in overseeing the implementation of decisions.

Fourth, the separation of legislative and executive powers on all levels, with obligatory control by the legislative over the executive. This is made necessary by the fact that executive organs, in contrast to legislative bodies, function continually and without interruption, and hence may often tend to hold the real power and a virtual monopoly over the making of actual political decisions. It is also made necessary by past history, in which the executive organs very often seized the legislative initiative and turned into organizations which interpreted laws — which in many cases meant, in practice, making laws.

Fifth, making a firm distinction between Party and state functions at all levels of the apparatus. Formerly the Party and state completely interpenetrated each other; now they are in the process of becoming separated. Furthermore a basic change is under way in the concept of the proper role and functions of the Party apparatus. We are moving toward a concept in which the Party's authority does not derive from it having earlier assumed the right to administer the state and the society. Rather its authority will derive from its ability, continually tested, to guide correctly the administration of the state, in the democratic interests of the people as a whole. This reconception of the role of the Party creates conditions that will allow for a polycentrality of power, and thus for a competitive struggle for power and for control over policy.

The core of the matter is that, at all levels of the governing system, victory in the competitive struggle for the control of policy should not be awarded by the organs who traditionally have held power, but by the representatives of those over whom that power should be exercised. That is, victory should be awarded by the representatives of the people. This means nothing less than the transference of ultimate power to the people, which is what democracy means.

In short, we aim for a system in which there will be a competitive struggle for the confidence of the people, among groups proposing their services as spokesmen for national interests and as executors of national power. Whether these groups are called "parties" or something else is of no fundamental importance.

Elements of a society in transformation

It may be useful to make a few observations about the changing roles of some elements of Soviet society, as perestroika and democratization continue, and particularly as these changes bear on Soviet thinking about security. Of course a great deal could be said about changing roles in contemporary Soviet society. But for the particular purposes of this book I shall be brief.[6]

The people and the Party rank-and-file

Here I distinguish between the "mass Party," which for our purposes may be considered part of the people, and the Party apparatus. A more complete analysis of Soviet public opinion regarding security is presented in a later chapter, so I shall limit myself to two observations.

On the mass level there is, generally speaking, a high degree of indifference toward problems of security and indeed of foreign policy generally. Such problems have always been regarded as the responsibility of the Party leadership, of the military, and of the state. Today especially, most people's attention is directed mainly on the country's internal problems. In the public mind neither the origin of these problems nor their solution is connected to the rest of the world.

For many decades, fear of a threat from the outside world — and primarily from the United States — was deliberately inculcated in the Soviet people. Decades of consistent effort were bound to affect the popular attitudes toward the outer world and toward security. A build-up of weapons was presented as the only way of ensuring Soviet security, and this policy successfully gained a high degree of public support under the slogan "anything to prevent war."

Recently these attitudes have begun to change. With the spread of glasnost and with a greater openness to the outer world, more and more people have been realizing that foreign countries, including the U.S., were not really preparing to attack the Soviet Union. Thus the "image of the enemy" that had been built-up has begun to erode. And the continuous build-up of weapons no longer seems so necessary for security. To some extent people are also realizing that the deflection to the military build-up of enormous amounts of money, the finest labor resources, and the best productive capacities has had an adverse effect on the economy as a whole.

My second observation is that the current Party structure does not provide an adequate framework for people to express their attitudes about foreign affairs. Most Party officials are not interested in the new attitudes. Consider in this context a statement made not by a rank-and-file Party member but by V. Malykhin, a member of the Party Central Committee and the foreman of electricians at the important Volga Automotive Plant. At a meeting with President Gorbachev, Malykhin remarked that "so far not much depends upon our position, since we really aren't able to have serious discussions with the disinterested Party officials in our local areas."[7]

Since rank-and-file Party members are not finding much response from the Party apparatus, they, like other people, are increasingly looking for other avenues by which they can express their opinions.

The Party apparatus

The functions of the Communist Party apparatus, once all-important in Soviet life, are being reduced and changed in many ways. Most of these changes are outside the scope of this paper, their effect is complicated, and they are still continuing at the time of writing. I shall confine myself to one observation especially significant for the question of security.

The Party's highest policy-making body, the Central Committee, has an International Section. This used to be dominated by an "old guard," the so-called Partocrats, most of whom possessed no professional qualifications and were noted for a highly traditional view of the world. But with the revamping of the role of the Party, new elements are being introduced into the International Section. These include younger, professionally qualified experts, some of whom come from departments of the government, some from research or academic institutes. This new generation is distinguished by ideological flexibility, professional competence, profound knowledge of the subject, and an absence of fear of the West.

These new specialists in the International Section are, with scarcely any exceptions, supporters of glasnost, perestroika, democratization, and new thinking in foreign affairs. Of course their policy views are not uniform. (One would hope that their views would not be uniform, since this group precisely rejects the idea of a single rigid policy line.) But broadly speaking this group advocates cooperation between the USSR and the U.S. in all fields, and certainly an end to the traditional hostility, which is seen as unnecessary and costly. This means that this group generally supports relatively far-reaching ideas of mutual security. However some disagreements might well be found among these specialists about what exactly mutual security should consist of and about just how far it should go.

The Supreme Soviet

As mentioned, the Supreme Soviet has changed from being a merely formal body that automatically approved the decisions of the Party and the government Executive organs, into being a true legislature. This change is so recent that indeed, at the time of writing it is not yet complete in all practical respects. For example the Supreme Soviet's Committee on Defense and State Security is quite new, and at this time has not completed the development of the staff it will need to function properly. For another example, the internal problems of the USSR are so urgent that the Supreme Soviet has had to concentrate upon them, and at the time of writing has not yet held many important discussions about foreign policy. Even so, one may confidently predict that during 1990 the Supreme Soviet will reduce the military budget, will urge the government to reduce its involvement in the Third World, and will raise questions about improving the Soviet economy by developing Soviet economic relations with the outside world.

A mistake sometimes made in the West is to assume that this new and genuine legislature is wholly or very largely progressive in its thinking, and is engaged in a struggle with conservative elements within the Executive branch. This is not so. A distinctive aspect of the present situation is that the watershed line runs vertically, not horizontally. Some important elements within the Supreme Soviet are conservative and favor a return to earlier ways. (And conversely, elements can be found within the Executive branch who genuinely favor perestroika.) The Supreme Soviet, being an elected body, mirrors the division of forces within the country and therefore contains all elements. This includes a fluctuating center, for whose support there is a constant struggle.

On questions of security, however, this center is likely to give support to advocates of mutual security and of cooperation with the West. I predict this because much of this center is made up, not of politicians and intellectuals with well-developed views and opinions, but of managers and workers drawn directly from the sphere of production. These practical people will understand that the USSR has much to gain from access to advanced Western technology and to Western experience in advanced methods of production. They will also understand that any renewed hostility will severely damage or nullify the chance for constructive economic relations with the West.

The state, the military and defense industry

As is well understood, many of the chief opponents of the revolutionary reform now under way in the Soviet Union are lodged within the structures of the state.

The organs of the Executive branch are enormous in their size and multiplicity; and needless to say in a socialist society, all industry and all means of production are themselves part of the state. Naturally this includes all industry related to military production. In a system where the state concentrates virtually all of society's material and financial resources in its own hands, the possibility for "bureaucratic interests" to determine policy is increased to a colossal degree.

It is predictable that people whose status, power and rewards come from the continuation and expansion of military production will oppose cutbacks in that production and oppose reductions in the military budget. In the area of national defense, the Supreme Soviet has not yet engaged these bureaucratic interests. We may expect that the Ministry of Defense and other ministries in the defense complex will make every effort to protect their affairs from any effective control by the Supreme Soviet. On the other hand we may also expect that, in line with Western experience, the legislature will, sooner or later, attempt to assert its rightful mastery in this sphere. This struggle has not yet really begun.

In the meantime, there are at least three major factors at work which will tend to limit the influence of the defense complex and will tend, in practical terms, to favor a mutual security policy. One, of course, is the supreme control that President Gorbachev and his Ministers maintain over the state, coupled with their determination to pursue a policy of mutual security.

The second factor is that the state is not, of course, a monolithic entity but is made up of a complex web of bureaucratic institutions, each of which has its own interests. Many important elements within the state will perceive that their interests are served by a transfer of resources away from military purposes and toward civilian purposes. Out of self-interest, those bureaucratic institutions will generally support a policy of mutual security and of economic cooperation with the West, even if sometimes they may dislike other aspects of perestroika.[8]

The third factor is one that has always been important in the USSR. Historically, the military and everything associated with it have always been under the firm control of the Party. The Party has taken strong and consistent measures to ensure that its control of the military remains unchallenged. The correctness of this Party control is also a part of the training of military officers. The supremacy of the Party over the military greatly limits the ability of the military to influence state policy in any direction contrary to the Party's line.[9]

Of course it is impossible to predict with high confidence the specific outcome, at any one time in the future, of the inevitable struggles over military policy. But the commitment of President Gorbachev and the Party to the policy of mutual security is firm and (we may confidently say) will remain firm. We may note that how far the President and Party are able to obtain not just the grudging acquiescence, but the genuine support, of the defense complex for a policy of mutual security with the West will depend very much upon the behavior of the West.

The mass media

If the main refuge of conservative, anti-perestroika forces are administrative structures (not only within the state, but also some formal public organizations), the main spearhead in society for perestroika is the mass media. Today the press, in complete accordance with the classic Leninist definition, is not a passive purveyor of information but a collective propagandist and agitator.

So far glasnost is the primary and most tangible manifestation of perestroika. However, glasnost has not yet become true freedom of the press, made secure by law. The zone of glasnost still has limits, and many important areas remain outside those limits. The limits sometimes open up under pressure from public opinion and sometimes contract at the bidding of unknown forces. The zones closed to public discussion are shrinking over time, but there are still vital subjects which the mass media have not addressed.

It is of great importance for the subject of this book to note that the foreign and military policy of the Soviet Union is still one of the subjects the press has not addressed, at least not in any major way. Very recently there have been animated discussions of some defense and military issues. But in the foreign policy sphere as a whole, silence still reigns.

The lack of real public debate over the main directions of foreign policy has not necessarily been unfavorable for mutual security. On the contrary, this silence has given the Party leadership what it also had prior to 1985 — great discretion simply to decide policy. Since the Party leadership has wanted a policy of mutual security, its freedom to decide without debate has in fact been favorable for mutual security.

Another mistake often made in the West is a belief that if the Soviet people were allowed to express themselves, they would always choose the path of cooperation. This is not necessarily the case. It is true that the people will always prefer *peace*. But they may not always believe that accommodating the West, and supporting mutual security, is the best path for obtaining peace. Under some circumstances they might believe that a better path is "peace through strength" (to employ a Western phrase) — that is, to build up Soviet military power. Again we must note that a major factor in peoples' view of the best path to peace is the behavior of the West itself.[10]

On the other hand, to the extent that the objective behavior of the West does support mutual security, then free discussion of foreign affairs within the USSR can and will observe this fact. As the media become increasingly able to discuss the various possible policies open to the USSR, they can report that the behavior of the West is in support of mutual security. Under those conditions, we may reasonably predict that public opinion will come to support mutual security also, especially as that remains the policy of the Party.

This review of the changing roles of certain elements of Soviet society does not permit us to make absolutely confident predictions about their roles in the future. Presently, the USSR is a political universe in rapid and fundamental transition. At this moment we cannot see what stable constellation will finally emerge. But assuming that the process of perestroika does continue in constructive directions, we can see strong indications that mutual security will continue to be a central principle of Soviet foreign policy. As even a review as brief as this one shows, there is a profound connection between the continuing development of perestroika and the successful creation of mutual security.

On the need for a concept of mutual democratic security

However it is not enough to realize that there is this profound connection. We must also come to realize that there is a profound connection between the successful creation of mutual security and democracy itself. Indeed it is not going too far to say that to be successful, mutual security will have to be mutual *democratic* security. This is an important theme not only for the USSR but also for the U.S.

It is perfectly possible that something called "mutual security" could arise that would not be healthy or desirable. One can imagine that either or both the USSR and the U.S. in the future might devise theoretical concepts and a practical system for a "mutual security" that would be far from desirable. This is perfectly possible given the traditions, the complications posed by treaty and legal obligations, and the current state of the social-economic and political development of each society. One or both societies might devise a form of mutual security that in fact was a form of condominium.

By way of illustration, take this example: to a degree it can be said that in 1939-1941 (up to June 22) there existed between the USSR and Germany a system precisely of mutual security. However this was an example of an authoritarian, undemocratic system directed *against* other countries. The national interests of those two countries (as understood by the leaders at that time) clearly, and one might even say crudely, prevailed over all-European interests or the interests of civilization as a whole.

Certainly something like this is not our ideal. Something that the USSR and the U.S. devise, directed against other countries, is not what we are seeking. This brings us to a fundamental question. A healthy form of mutual security necessarily must be acceptable to all mankind. Although mutual between the *two countries*, it must also have a form that has, in some way, a *universal character*, and thus deserves and receives the support of all (or at any rate, most) of the international community and of mankind. In other words, the form of mutual security we should seek should be a form that is not aimed against anyone else and does not threaten anyone else (even unintentionally). Indeed it might be helpful to others, if only by demonstrating to them how former adversaries can find security through cooperation.[11]

How can what seems an entirely bilateral conception attain a universal character? How can the rest of the world feel safe and comfortable as the USSR and U.S. create mutual security? Of course one answer is the progressive demilitarization of the bilateral relationship; this we recognize today. But there is much more to it than that. There are at least two further answers that are important. I shall take up one here and the other in the concluding section of this paper.

First, we must realize that *democratization* is a necessary ingredient for a healthy mutual security. Democratization is needed both internally, within the countries involved, and also in an important way, between them.

Internally, democratization is necessary to make sure that foreign policy conforms with the real wishes and needs of the people. We need to strengthen, and sometimes formulate anew, democratic traditions, institutions and ideas, encompassing not only the level of political leadership but also mass consciousness. Mutual security needs the underpinnings of broad democratic instrumentalities that have been elaborated by mankind over many centuries: "checks and balances," democratic elections, respect for the rights of the minority, recognition of pluralism of opinions and approaches, a tradition of freedom of choice, and so on. Without these, mutual security can dribble away — on the one hand into abstract musings of no practical value, or on the other, into some kind of crude Soviet-American condominium at the expense of other nations.

Democratization is also needed in the relations between the USSR and the U.S. The two societies need a much greater degree of openness toward each other. And each side needs, at all times, a vast amount of reliable information about the other and about what the other is doing. We may say that successful mutual security requires much mutual information.

Another part of democratization between the two countries is the development of norms and institutions for their behavior. Just as internal society becomes democratic when it follows established, accepted norms of behavior and works through regular institutions, so the behavior of the USSR and U.S. toward each other will become democratic when it follows established, accepted norms of behavior and works through regular institutions.

These norms and institutions can also help assure a rational, balanced reaction by each side to the unexpected, which is an important element for stability in the contemporary world of nuclear missiles and ecological fragility. Can we, by our joint efforts, lessen the dangers from the "attacks" of unpredictable events? Coping in a rational manner with the unexpected is one of the aims of democracy.

Often people speak of mutual security as if it were something primarily military in character. We do need to reduce the military dangers. However a healthy, developing mutual security will go on to embrace the whole of relations between the USSR and the U.S. And it will do it in a way that enhances democracy, both internally for each of them, and between them as well. In this sphere, there is much that still awaits development.

From mutual security to comprehensive security

An error sometimes still made in the West is to suppose that Soviet foreign policy is essentially disconnected from Soviet internal policies and the rapid internal changes within the USSR. It is sometimes thought in the West that our foreign policies of mutual security and other new thinking are not connected to, or not necessary for, our internal policies of perestroika, glasnost, and democratization. I have already suggested some of the ways in which this is an error. But let me emphasize here that perestroika *requires* mutual security and new thinking in foreign affairs; and what is more, that our new thinking embraces a concept that might rightly be called "perestroika at the world level." I shall briefly address each in turn.

It is widely understood that internal perestroika, in its purely economic sense, can benefit greatly from increased contact with the Western economies. Soviet policy to encourage the formation of "joint ventures" between Western companies and Soviet economic units is merely one example of many ways in which we seek to improve our economy through such contacts.

What is not so widely understood yet is that perestroika, even in its internal sense, is meant to lead to a *full normalization of economic relations* across the entire spectrum of economic affairs, between the Soviet Union and the rest of the world, including the West. We are looking forward hopefully and confidently to the day when there is nothing unusual or abnormal about Soviet economic relations with the rest of the world, and when the USSR is playing a normal role in the world economy in every respect. I need scarcely emphasize that this full normalization of economic relations is very much in the interest of the world economy, as well as of the Soviet economy. All will benefit.

It ought to be obvious that this normalization of affairs at the economic level requires a situation of mutual security at the political-military level. I emphasize "requires"; the connection is not accidental. It would be impossible for normal economic relations to develop while an atmosphere continues of mutual suspicion, mistrust, and insecurity. Development of normal economic relations among our respective nations can only occur as the nations feel increasingly secure with each other — in other words, as mutual security improves.[12]

This is one way in which perestroika, even in its internal sense, is connected necessarily and profoundly to mutual security. But there is something much larger coming into play as well. That is the "perestroika at the world level" that I mentioned.[13]

We in the USSR see an important analogy between the situation that our country has been in, and to some extent is still in, and the situation that the world as a whole is in. Perestroika within the USSR is our answer to the former. We also advocate a kind of perestroika for the whole world, as our contribution to the answer for the latter.

During the 1980s, many people in the USSR came to realize that our country had been stagnating. Many problems had been allowed to accumulate — economic problems, ecological problems, problems among different sectors and groups of society. Our perestroika is our attempt to come to grips with these problems and to solve them.

Presently, many people around the world are also coming to realize that, in a profound sense, the world itself is also stagnating. Many problems are being allowed to accumulate — economic problems, ecological problems, problems among different regions and countries. It seems to us in the Soviet Union that there is an important similarity between the stagnation we see in the world, and the stagnation that we are combating in our own country. Just as we have faced up to our problems and have launched our perestroika to solve them, we believe the world should face up to its problems and launch its own "perestroika" to solve those problems. Of course, no one is so foolish as to imagine that the problems of the world are identical with those of the USSR; and therefore no one imagines that the solutions are identical either. But the similarity between the Soviet and world problems is close enough to be noteworthy and significant. Certainly the similarity is close enough that people everywhere should be able to notice that some kind of major perestroika at the world level *is needed.*

For several years, President Gorbachev, Foreign Minister Shevardnadze and other Soviet leaders have been trying to draw the world's attention to the need for a major perestroika at the global level. They have raised this in major addresses at the United Nations and elsewhere. As first steps, they have advocated an immediate strengthening of the United Nations, and of international law generally. They have repeatedly invited world discussions, in almost any forum, about the problems facing humanity and their solution.[14]

Soviet leaders have emphasized that they do not believe the USSR holds a monopoly on wisdom and that the USSR does not seek to "dictate" or impose its own views on others, regarding any of these matters. They have emphasized that all issues are open for discussion and negotiation, and that they welcome proposals from the West and from anyone. However they have also reiterated that the world situation is worsening in some important ways, and that there is no time to waste in beginning a search for solutions.

One key element in the "global perestroika" would be the realization of comprehensive security for everyone. The correct path toward improving mutual security between East and West is one that would also help lead the whole world in the direction of comprehensive security.[15]

However, security in its traditional, military and political meaning can only be one part of security at the world level. The full fruition of global perestroika would be a Comprehensive System of International Security (CSIS), as has been proposed by Soviet leaders.[16] This comprehensive security would include general disarmament, the settlement of regional conflicts, the normal and successful management of the world economy for the benefit of all, and the general observance of human rights. A vital dimension of CSIS is the ecological dimension. Protection of the world environment and the rational use of natural resources are important to all of humanity.

Conclusion

The analogy that we perceive between the need for perestroika within the USSR and the need for perestroika at the world level is the broadest connection of all between domestic conditions and international security. In this paper I have addressed many connections between domestic affairs and world affairs, but none is larger in its implications than this one. In a sense, one might even speak of the USSR as being in an advantageous position compared to many other countries. The profound changes that we are now undertaking may make it easier for us, than it may be for others, to perceive the need for profound change at the global level also.

No country can be an island any more. Under the conditions of the late twentieth century it is impossible; and it will be even more impossible under the conditions of the twenty-first century. The security of one country has become interlinked with the security of others, and ultimately with the security of all. This is true not only of politico-military security but also of economic security, ecological security and other forms of security.

In recent years the USSR has been giving first priority to creating mutual security with the West. This has been the right choice. One cannot give first priority to everything at once, and relations with the West were and are the most urgent for our attention. Both East and West greatly need the huge economic resources that have been wasted in our fruitless competition; and after all, it is only the USSR and the U.S. that have the capacity to destroy the whole world, should the very worst situation arise. So East-West mutual security has rightly been the Soviet first goal.

But it is not our final goal. Our much larger goal is comprehensive security for the whole world. We must make sure that East-West mutual security contributes positively to movement toward comprehensive security for all. And we hope that the world soon will join us in perceiving the necessity that all of us move forward, together, toward that larger goal.

Notes

1. The author thanks Vladimir Savel'yev for his contributions to this chapter.
2. These observations apply to the "psychological state," as it were, of a country; I have not yet spoken here about the objective truth about the other side. In some cases the other side may have been misunderstood, partially or entirely. In other cases the other side may actually be an aggressive and dangerous enemy. Hitler's Germany in 1940 was, in fact, precisely an evil empire, bent on aggression.
3. V.I. Lenin, *Complete Works* 32 (Moscow: Politizdat, 1969), p. 335.
4. Quoted in *Pravda* (July 16, 1987).
5. M.S. Gorbachev, *Perestroika i novoye mysehleniye dlya nashy strany i dlya vsego mira"* (Moscow, 1988), p. 27.
6. To Soviet social scientists and to many other Soviet readers the following passage will seem highly oversimplified. But great simplification is necessary for two reasons. The subject of this book is not the changing Soviet system but mutual security, and the implications of changing Soviet internal affairs are only one aspect of the complicated subject of mutual security. Secondly, this book is being published simultaneously in the West, and many Western readers of a book about security cannot be expected to have either the knowledge or the interest to wish to read a lengthy, detailed analysis of Soviet internal affairs. All readers should regard this section of the paper as merely introductory. The discussion here is current as of January 1990.
7. Reported in *Pravda* (September 25, 1989).
8. Incidentally, something similar applies to the U.S. Within the American government there also are major bureaucratic institutions that stand to gain from a transfer of resources away from military and toward civilian purposes. There also are powerful social organizations and business corporations outside the government that will similarly gain. These elements may be expected to support an American policy of mutual security with the USSR.
9. Again there is an analogy to the American situation. In the U.S., the principle of "civilian control of the military" is considered a fundamental principle of the state system and of the constitution; and again, the correctness of this is included in the training of military officers.
10. Soviet public opinion is discussed in more detail in a later chapter.
11. It might also help set the stage for, and help create some elements for, a more global, comprehensive international security, along the lines that are already being advocated by the USSR, as I shall discuss further below.

12. Of course, what I have said here about economic relations applies equally to matters of ecology, another area in which the USSR seeks to cooperate fully and normally with the rest of the world, to the benefit of all.

13. Here I must say again, with sincere regret, that the new Soviet attitude has not yet been adequately understood or appreciated in the West, and perhaps in the world generally.

14. M.S. Gorbachev, "Speech at the U.N. Organization," Address at the 43d Session of the U.N. General Assembly, December 7, 1988 (Moscow: Novosti Publishing House, 1989); E.A. Shevardnadze, "For a New Thinking in World Politics," Address at the 41st Session of the U.N. General Assembly, September 23, 1986 (Moscow: Politizdat, 1986).

15. This is the second way in which we can and must make sure that bilateral, mutual security takes on a universal significance.

16. M.S. Gorbachev, Report at the 27th Congress of the CPSU, February 25, 1986 (Moscow: Politizdat, 1986), pp. 74-76; Gorbachev, "General Directions of Domestic and Foreign Policy of the USSR," Report at the People's Deputies' Congress, May 30, 1989 (Moscow: Politizdat, 1989).

5

A Theory of Mutual Security

RICHARD SMOKE

Introduction[1]

"Mutual security," also sometimes called "common security," is an idea that seems to be growing in visibility and significance. Although the idea itself has been implicit in some actual and proposed U.S. and Soviet policies for decades, the phrases "mutual security" and "common security" seem to have emerged only in the 1980s. In only a few years the phrases have become commonplace in literature and discussions about the national security affairs of the United States and Soviet Union, and a good case could be made that the concept is having a mounting impact on the national security thinking on both sides.

For many on both sides, the concept first came clearly into view with the publication in 1982 of the *Report of the Commission on Disarmament and Security Issues*, generally called "The Palme Report" after the Commission's chairman, Olaf Palme. That Report was published as a book with the title *Common Security*.[2]

Since 1982, it has been increasingly common in the West to find published and unpublished papers, reports and other documents that refer to common or mutual security as a basic idea that underlies various policies that the U.S. and/or USSR are or should be adopting to prevent war and to improve security.

After Mikhail Gorbachev became General Secretary in 1985, the idea of mutual security became an important element in the "new thinking" that Gorbachev and his supporters pledged to bring to Soviet foreign policy. By February 1986, mutual security was part of the declaratory policy of the USSR. Acknowledging that mutual security is a general principle whose full implications remain to be discovered and developed, Soviet spokesmen have repeatedly declared that the principle should be a fundamental one in East-West relations.[3]

It is natural that an idea that found its own name only a few years ago should be less than fully developed now. Nothing in what follows is meant to imply that there is a single way of conceiving these ideas that is theoretically or pragmatically "correct," and other ways incorrect. Rather the appropriate question is what formulation(s) of the ideas prove most useful in illuminating which issues. Decisions about the most useful conceptual formulations are inseparable from choices about which issues to focus upon and from our understanding of them. These are matters presently under very active discussion, and this paper is meant as a conceptual contribution to that discussion.

Prefatory remark about terminology

A preliminary clarification is needed about a purely verbal ("semantic") matter. From at least the publication of the Palme Report, *Common Security*, until the late 1980s, the terms "common security" and "mutual security" were used synonymously by nearly all Western writers. Both terms refer mainly or exclusively to security between East and West (that is, between the USSR/Warsaw Pact and the U.S. and its allies.) That was the nearly exclusive subject of the Palme Report.

By the late 1980s, Soviet and some Western writers began employing the term "common security" to refer to the security of *all* nations, reserving the term "mutual security" to refer to East-West security. This distinction in terms reflects a translation of two Russian terms, "vseobshchaya bezopasnost'" and "vzaimnaya bezopasnost'."[4] This more recent terminology may create some confusion for users of English, who already have a word of long standing for the security of all — *collective* security — and also have the term "global security." To sidestep any confusion, this paper will employ the term "mutual security" for the bilateral sense, which is my principal subject, and "collective security" or "global security" for the sense of all nations' security. I will not use "common security" here at all.

Sections I and II of this paper, which follow next, develop an abstract theory of mutual security. Readers who are more interested in practical theory for policy may wish to turn directly to Section III.

Section I: Outline of a Theory of Mutual Security

The root of the concept of mutual security

It seems clear that today's concept of mutual security has its origin in a form of interlinking between East and West that has developed in the nuclear age. Any sizable nuclear war between the two sides would destroy or profoundly damage them both. Thus for instance the Palme Report:

In the modern age, security cannot be obtained unilaterally...The security of one nation cannot be bought at the expense of others. The danger of nuclear war alone assures the validity of this proposition...We face common dangers and thus must also promote our security in common.[5]

Other actual interlinking between the security of East and West may exist and certainly other potential interlinking can be imagined, as discussed later. But the root of the mutual security idea is that one vital form of interlinking exists now and cannot presently be removed.

At least in the current period, the significance of the mutual security concept rests upon this interlinking being perceived as *intrinsic* in the situation now existing and being perceived as fundamental in importance. It is not a minor aspect of our condition, nor something that can be canceled by plausible efforts in any readily foreseeable future. Somewhat unwittingly, the two sides gradually created their profound mutual vulnerability over the first two decades or so of the nuclear age; and having created it, they cannot easily uncreate it. This relationship of mutual vulnerability might also be said to be a relationship of "mutual insecurity."

An important distinction should be observed at once. The existence of this "mutual insecurity" is a *fact*. But the conclusion that therefore we should strive to enhance the two side's mutual security is a policy *choice*. It is not the only possible choice in a situation of this kind. Two others are possible. One is simply to accept and live with a condition of mutual vulnerability and mutual danger, perhaps on an estimate that the real probability of a major East-West war is and has been extremely low. The other is for either side to strive for decisive superiority, perhaps in the form of a disarming first-strike capability, or the form of highly effective defenses against all means of delivering nuclear warheads, or in other ways. Some mixtures of these three broad choices are also possible.

Let me now advance several ideas intended to illuminate the concept of mutual security, and using them, suggest the outlines of a theory.[6]

A general definition of a mutual security policy

In its most general definition, a mutual security policy is simply a policy that aims to improve the security of both sides, under conditions of some mutual insecurity.[7] The two "sides" may be two nations; or two alliances of nations; or two militant organizations threatening each other; or in principle, any two "actors" who are able to threaten each other and are presently in a state of some mutual insecurity.

A game theory metaphor

Game theory provides a useful metaphor for thinking about this situation. Imagine that one side takes some action toward the other. In game theory terms, a "zero-sum game" is one in which one side gains and the other side loses by an equal amount. Often the gain and the loss "add up" to zero because one side has gained and the other has lost the same thing. A "negative-sum game" (in its simplest form) is one in which the result of the action is that both sides lose. A "positive-sum game" (in its simplest form) is one in which the result is that both sides win.[8]

Clearly, the concept of mutual security advances the idea that the two sides, presently in a state of some mutual insecurity, can take actions that create a positive-sum game — that is a game in which both "win" in the sense that both improve their security together. In today's East-West situation for instance, the idea of mutual security asserts that appropriate policies can make both sides more secure, together and in the same time period.

This idea of improving security has obviously not been the idea held by many people at many times. A great deal of the behavior of nations, and a great deal of thinking about security, has been based on a different assumption. Two nations in a state of insecurity toward each other have often acted on the assumption that their security relationship was, in essence, a zero-sum game. They have believed that, in general, the result of actions will be that whatever one side gains will equal, at least roughly, what the other side loses. A step by one side gains something for it, which improves its security by some degree; that "something" is lost by the other side. (Various illustrations will be given shortly.) In this way of thinking, policies by one side, aimed at improving its security, will necessarily operate at the expense of the other side's security. To continue the East-West example, leaders on each side during the Cold War decades often said that this or that advance by the other side in the competition represented a loss in security for "our" side. What the other side gained, "our" side lost in security.[9]

Let me advance this terminology: actions intended to develop *mutual security* are actions intended to create and further a positive-sum game in which both sides gain in security. I shall call actions by one side, intended to enhance its own security, actions for *unilateral security*. These actions for unilateral security typically involve the assumption (generally not stated) that the intended gain will result in an equivalent loss for the other side. I advance the terms "mutual security" and "unilateral security," in these senses, as being of general significance; their significance is not confined to today's East-West situation.

The concept of an interactive system

In this general sense, the idea of mutual security is a very old idea. Many examples could be found in European diplomatic history in recent centuries, and other history of nations and other political entities, of efforts intended to create mutual security. People simply did not use this name for it.

Today's thinking about mutual security contains another element which, though also not entirely new, is becoming more explicit and more widely noted than before. That element is the idea of an *interactive* relationship or system. An interactive system is one in which the actions of one side lead to reactions by the other side, which in turn lead to further reactions by the first side, followed by further reactions by the other, and so on. Today's mutual security theorists suggest, for instance, that the East-West security relationship has become an interactive system to an important degree. A belief also is taking shape that the global system as a whole is becoming an interactive system. Shortly I shall further explain what the idea of an "interactive" security relationship, such as the East-West one, may mean. Incidentally I am deliberately not using the term "interdependent," for reasons that will become clear later.

A well-known image that illustrates the idea of an interactive security relationship is the image of two men in one boat. One of them cannot make his end of the boat safer by trying to rock the other end of the boat. If the boat rocks, it rocks for both.

Central propositions of a theory of mutual security

There may be many ways to capture, in abstract theoretical terms, the essential concept of mutual security and why that concept may be extremely important in some situations. One simple way requires just two basic propositions:

1. *In a continuing interactive system, positive-sum games with positive outcomes for both parties will, in general, continue to lead to positive results for both sides.*

2. *In a continuing interactive system, zero-sum games played in the short run will generate a negative-sum game in the long run.*

The first of these is nearly axiomatic: games with positive outcomes for both parties are positive sum, and in an interactive relationship that continues over time such positive-sum games will continue to yield positive outcomes for both.[10]

The second of these propositions is certainly not axiomatic. Let me turn now to some reasons for believing that it is true.

Reasons why zero-sum games become negative-sum over time

The second proposition holds that, as time passes, the consequences of repeatedly playing zero-sum games will, on net, lead to greater costs than gains for each side over time. Thus over time the situation as a whole becomes a negative-sum game, in which both are losing on net (that is, compared to their situation if they were not playing.) In the most general terms, the reason for this is that the zero-sum games cannot be played without both sides incurring costs and risks in the act of play. How great and how significant these turn out to be will, of course, vary from one case to another. In this discussion, I will use the East-West example of recent decades to illustrate my points and to suggest that the negative sum can be highly significant. Five reasons at least can be suggested, employing that example, why a series of plays of zero-sum games in an interactive system will generate a negative-sum game over time.

One reason involves a form of what economists call "transaction costs." The transfer of an "asset" does not occur "free of charge" in terms of the actual mechanics of play.

For example, if one side in the East-West competition succeeds in removing a third party (e.g., a country) from the other side's camp and adding it to its own camp, then it has won a zero-sum game. It has gained, and the other side has lost, one and the same thing: the asset represented by that third country's alignment with "our" side. But while engaged in this play, both sides have incurred costs. The side that won expended effort to do so, and probably expended some political, diplomatic, economic or other assets in the effort. The side that lost presumably also made an effort to keep its ally and probably also expended various assets in the effort.

A second reason why a series of zero-sum games will generate net costs over time involves what might be called the "policy effects" of play. Seeing that zero-sum games are being played and may continue to be played, each side will adopt policies intended to position itself for future plays. Thus an effect of a series of plays is to create policies that anticipate the series continuing. Those policies are carried out on a continuing basis, whether the next play actually occurs immediately or not. And those policies are far from cost-free.

To continue the same example: once it became clear to both sides in the East-West competition that part of the competition consisted of zero-sum games aimed at shifting the balance of aligned and friendly countries around the world, both sides adopted policies to suit. Both sides created alliance systems. Both sides developed and maintained a panoply of mechanisms — diplomatic, political, economic, military and other — aimed both at preserving the alignment of the friends and allies it had, and of adding new ones. The alliances and these various mechanisms were then maintained on a continuing basis, and with worldwide scope, whether or not there was actually a "play" of a zero-sum game in any particular region in any one year. Some new play in the series of games could be anticipated at any time.

Alliances are not cost-free to maintain. The policy mechanisms aimed at preserving and adding friendly countries also are not cost-free to maintain, even in the sense of maintenance of diplomatic and other establishments. And the actual carrying out of various measures, merely to maintain the alignment of countries presently aligned, is far from cost-free. In short, the anticipation of continuing plays of zero-sum games has the "policy effect" of generating a variety of policies and mechanisms which are then carried out — and incur costs — on a continuing basis whether the next zero-sum game is played at once or not.[11]

These two reasons why repeated plays of zero-sum games in an interactive system will generate noteworthy costs over time might apply in many eras of international affairs. The remaining reasons apply mainly to the current era (and perhaps future eras) because they depend upon a context of rapid technological developments. Specifically, they depend on the fact that, in a competition like the East-West one, a major dimension of the competition will be a competition in developing and applying new technology to weapons. This is the arms race.

An arms race can be seen as a series of plays of zero-sum games in this sense: Each side is striving to achieve a competitive advantage in its weapons and forces, or to counterbalance and thus neutralize an advantage the opponent has gained. First consider achieving an advantage. The advantage the one side gains is equal to what the other side loses by falling behind. One side's gain equals the other's loss. Now imagine that the other side succeeds in catching up, thus counterbalancing and neutralizing the previous disparity. This second "play in the game" is also zero-sum. By catching up, the previously inferior side has gained, and that gain equals the other side's loss of its previous advantage. Unless one side can gain *and keep* a significant advantage, this series of "plays" back and forth is a series of zero-sum games.[12]

The third reason why repeatedly playing zero-sum games in an interactive system will generate a negative-sum game in the long run is simple. In this kind of arms race interaction, both sides are incurring major costs in the repeated play. In one play, one side incurs costs to obtain an advantage, in some weapons system or set of forces. In a later play in the series, the other side incurs costs to counterbalance and neutralize that advantage. At that point, neither side has the advantage in this aspect of the competition. Approximate equivalence has returned. But both sides have incurred costs, perhaps large ones, in the process.

A number of examples could be found in the U.S.-Soviet competition in nuclear and other advanced strategic weapons where approximately this has occurred. By the mid- to late-1960s the two sides were in rough equivalence in strategic nuclear power. Very large investments have been made in strategic weapons by both sides in the decades since. And today, the two sides are in rough equivalence in strategic nuclear power.

While one or the other gained certain advantages along the way, those advantages proved marginal at the time, and proved fleeting. The other side took steps to catch up. Indeed there is a potent reason *why* the two sides have usually been in rough equivalence: each side feels powerful incentives to make sure that it is not behind for long.

Arguably something analagous has occurred in the balance of European forces. In the mid-1960s the Warsaw Pact enjoyed some degree of advantage in that balance, with the West making up the difference by the threat of first nuclear use. Very large investments have been made in European forces by both sides in the decades since. And today, the Warsaw Pact enjoys some degree of advantage in the balance, with the West making up the difference by the threat of first nuclear use.[13]

A fourth reason why a series of zero-sum games yields a negative-sum game over time involves stability. For instance, the nuclear arms race has repeatedly threatened to create, and sometimes has actually created, a less stable relationship than existed previously between the two sides' strategic forces. Also, competition around the world for the alignment of other players has repeatedly threatened to create, and sometimes has actually created, East-West crises in various regions, with their attendant risk of crisis escalation. Thus a series of zero-sum games may produce risks to stability and has produced actual instabilities.

Both the arms race and the competition over alignments evidently have the disturbing feature that they seem *recurrently* to generate new risks to stability. The perception that this keeps recurring leads reasonably to the conclusion that these risks are an intrinsic feature in such interactive systems. Similar interactive systems involving similar international politics and arms race would presumably contain similar intrinsic risks.

At best, each new potential destabilization, in the arms race or in various regions, requires effort to analyze and understand and probably requires additional investments to forestall before it materializes. But we can hardly expect invariably to achieve the best case. Some destabilizations may not be forestalled and thus actually materialize. Destabilizations in the arms race may prove time-consuming, and difficult and costly to correct; and while they exist they may significantly and dangerously alter strategic perceptions, increasing the shared risk of war. Destabilizations in regions may also prove time-consuming, difficult and costly to correct, and while they exist they may erupt into dangerous crises, increasing the shared risk of war.

These four reasons would seem to apply to any interactive "mutual insecurity system" containing important international competitive politics and a significant arms race. An additional, fifth reason why a negative-sum game is generated over time in today's East-West system particularly is simply that, for many reasons, the risk of war is not zero. Each year, some probability exists of an actual nuclear war occurring that might destroy civilization. That probability means that, beyond the reasons already mentioned, "playing the game" is not a neutral activity. It is an activity that is constantly imposing some chance of catastrophe on both sides and in that sense is a negative-sum activity.[14]

To sum up this argument, there are at least five reasons why the repeated play of zero-sum games in an interactive system like the present East-West one will generate a negative-sum game over time. Zero-sum games in the international politics of the system have transaction costs. They have "policy effects" for each side, whereby each constantly carries out policies, which have costs, to position itself for future plays. Zero-sum games in the arms race part of the system lead one side to counterbalance the other's prior gain, or to gain itself, while both pay the costs of new weapons. Destabilizations in both the arms race and the international politics recur, generating costs and risks. In addition, in today's East-West case the continuing probability of a catastrophe for both sides is not zero.

Costs and risks in the interaction

One feature of this argument deserves attention before proceeding. This argument that a negative-sum game is created over time mixes together two kinds of "negatives" — security costs and security risks. The first, second and third arguments involve costs to both sides in the repeated efforts to achieve security by unilateral steps. The fifth argument involves a risk to both sides in such efforts. The fourth argument involves both costs and risks.

The distinction is important. A negative sum consisting of accumulating costs is not the same thing as a negative sum consisting of continuing or accumulating risks. From the policy viewpoint, the important difference is that a policy (perhaps labeled "mutual security") that is aimed at reducing the costs is not necessarily one that will also reduce the risks; or vice-versa. We *cannot* simply assume that any particular mutual security policy will generate both kinds of gains.

It is possible, for example, that the two sides could make various sorts of arms-control agreements and agreements to restrain their international competition, which did succeed in reducing their "costs of play" over time, but which also had the effect of *increasing* the security risks to one or both. For instance this might occur if the agreements included inadequate verification and one side or both exploited loopholes to cheat.

Conversely, it is also possible that the two sides could make various sorts of agreements which did succeed in decreasing the security risks to both, but at the price of actually increasing the net costs to one or both. This might occur, for instance, if certain arms-reductions agreements involved very high verification costs, but yielded only modest or zero savings in weapons costs.

The third possibility, of course, is the one where an agreement or collection of agreements did succeed in reducing both costs and risks to both sides. This possibility certainly cannot be excluded. But neither can it be simply assumed.

I conclude from this that arguments for mutual security policies should indicate which of these three outcomes will follow from any policies or agreements proposed. Expected gains of both kinds would be, of course, the most appealing outcome. Also very appealing might be major gains for security, even if equal or even greater costs were entailed. Sizable cost savings that actually generated increased security risks should not be appealing — and should not, as a matter of fact, be billed as proposals for mutual *security*.[15]

A necessary assumption

So far I have suggested reasons, involving both costs and risks, supporting my second proposition that in a continuing, interactive system, zero-sum games played in the short run will generate a negative-sum game in the long run. However the proposition does not follow from these arguments unless a basic assumption is also made. That assumption is that as time passes, neither side is cumulatively winning the series of zero-sum games. To be exact, the proposition assumes that neither side is cumulatively gaining, as a result of the series of zero-sum games, sufficiently to outweigh the costs involved.

This assumption would not have to be true. Imagine, for instance, two great alliances in competition, perhaps in the distant future or on some other planet. All of the reasons, discussed above, why the "interaction costs" in their competition add up over time to a negative sum might be true there too. Yet one side might be steadily winning, not in the arms race, but by advancing on the other geographically. It might be winning the series of zero-sum games played for the alignment of third parties, steadily adding to its overall position and shifting the world balance in its favor. In that case, the advancing side might decide that its overall gains were outweighing "the costs of play," and thus choose to continue to play and to continue to make gains at its adversary's expense.[16]

Observing this illuminates the character of the argument being made here. My argument focuses on what might be called "system interaction costs and risks" (or, in a positive-sum game, system interaction benefits). But naturally any one play of the zero-sum games yields direct benefits to one side (a victory) and direct costs to the other (a loss). My argument makes the assumption that, over time, neither side is winning so often that the accumulating direct benefits to it of repeated plays outweigh its long-term costs.[17]

Whenever this assumption does hold true, then the second the two propositions stated earlier follows: in a continuing interactive system, zero-sum games played in the short run will generate a negative-sum game in the long run. Both sides lose by continuing to play.

Indeed something more powerful can now be said. We may observe that *in the long run a positive-sum game or a negative-sum game are the only two kinds of games possible.* Over the long run, neither side can, in reality, play a zero-sum game in which it wins and the other loses. The common belief that this is always possible is now excluded. Only two long-term games are possible: a negative-sum game in which both sides accumulate costs and risks, or a positive-sum game in which both sides improve their security. There is no third basic alternative. (However, over time it is possible to play a complicated game that has both positive-sum and negative-sum aspects, a point to which I shall return later.)

We may draw an important conclusion for policy choices. In a continuing interactive system, the two sides have, in the long run, only two overall policy choices, not three. They can choose unilateral security policies and repeatedly play zero-sum games, which will generate a negative-sum game over time; or they can choose mutual security policies, which will generate a positive-sum game over time (or some mixture of these two). They cannot choose unilateral security policies and play a zero-sum game, on net and over time.

From theory to policy

So far this conclusion, and the two theoretical propositions by themselves, provide only a way of understanding certain situations. Two more steps must be taken before mutual security can be responsibly advocated as a policy for these situations.

One step is to show that a significant, shared improvement in security is actually *feasible* in any particular situation. It may not be. The foregoing argument has only suggested that a positive-sum security game is a major theoretical possibility. It is not self-evident that the situation will actually present significant opportunities for positive-sum interactions.

In fact it common for people to reach the pessimistic conclusion. They may accept the idea that the real choices are only between positive-sum and negative-sum games, and then conclude that a significant positive-sum game is not possible and thus that the only real possibility is a continuing negative-sum game. This view of an interactive relationship might be termed "tragic." The tragic viewpoint, as I would define it, is to agree that over time neither side can win or even play a zero-sum game, to believe also that a positive-sum game is not feasible (at least to any substantial degree), and thus to conclude that the two sides are locked into a negative-sum relationship. Both will lose and nothing can be done about it. Advocates of a mutual security policy must show that this tragic viewpoint is unnecessary and that a positive-sum game is indeed feasible.

The other step that must be taken, before mutual security can be responsibly advocated as a policy in a particular situation, is to show that it is *realistic* in one very important sense. It must be shown that security is, or can become, a chief political-military goal for both sides. This will usually mean convincing each side that security is or can become a chief political-military goal for the other side.

In many relationships involving intense competition between two sides, this will be far from self-evident. Many people on one side or both may reject this idea. In relationships involving intense competition, many on both sides may believe that the other side's chief political-military goal is not security but victory. These people commonly perceive such situations this way: the other side may say that its main goal is security. But this is a deception. In fact the other side's main goal is to win the competition — to defeat us. Security is in fact a secondary goal for the other side.[18]

Consider for instance the East-West competition of the Cold War era. Many in the West have believed that the principal Soviet goal, at least in the long run, is the domination of the world by the USSR; or at least by the Soviet way of organizing society, politics and economics (which as a practical matter would mean Soviet world domination). And they have believed that under some circumstances the USSR would employ force to reach this goal. Naturally Soviet leaders did not often proclaim this goal nakedly, but hid it behind the claim that Soviet political-military policy is aimed at protecting the USSR's security.

Similarly, many in the East have believed that the principal Western goal, at least in the long run, is the domination of the world by the West; or at least by the Western way of organizing society, politics and economics (which as a practical matter would mean Western world domination). And they have believed that under some circumstances the United States or the West would employ force to achieve this goal. Naturally Western leaders did not often proclaim this goal nakedly, but hid it behind the claim that Western political-military policy is aimed at protecting the West's security.

People who see the other side's dominant political-military goal as victory, not security, will regard the entire concept of mutual security as scarcely relevant to "our" side's policy. Preventing the other side's victory must, of course, be our own main policy. That is, we must protect our *unilateral security* against a dangerous adversary.

People holding this perception of the other side might even agree that "systems interactions" are generating a negative-sum game over time, perhaps a costly one. This tragic result is the inevitable consequence of the other side's intolerable goal. (It is inevitable unless, of course, our side wishes to surrender.) People holding this perception might also agree that a positive-sum game *would be* feasible, if only the other side would abandon its basic goal. That is, they might agree that in principle nothing in the nature of the situation prevents a positive-sum, mutual security game, except for the all-important fact that the other side does not want one.

In short, this perspective sees the conflict as a zero-sum conflict in the most fundamental sense. It is not merely that any given "play" or series of plays is zero-sum. The entire conflict is zero-sum at its most basic level. The other side's goal is intolerable and unlimited. Hence there is nothing left but for them to be defeated or for us to be defeated.

Only if *security* is a chief goal on both sides, is there a basis for attempting to develop *mutual security* as a policy. If security is one chief goal but others, potentially competing, are also centrally important, then a strong basis exists for mutual security, but the priority to be assigned to it and the form it takes will be dependent upon the competition with other goals. Parts of Section III below deal with this situation, and this theme is taken up again in the paper's concluding remarks.[19]

To sum up, a responsible advocacy of the mutual security approach to policy must be able to show that that approach is feasible, because actual opportunities for a positive-sum game exist or can be created; and show that it is realistic, because security is a chief goal for both sides. Unless both of these things are shown, there is no *policy* conclusion from the argument presented above. It might be true that a negative-sum game is being played over time, but no policy to change it follows from my argument. After it is shown that a positive-sum game is feasible and realistic, then the mutual security approach must be considered directly applicable to the development of policy.

Section II: Some Implications of this Conception

This way of conceiving mutual security generates various implications and consequences. This section addresses some of the significant ones.

The fundamental perspective: one system

The way of conceiving mutual security that I am advancing here is based ultimately on a fundamental perspective. In this conception, the bilateral relationships to which mutual security applies are being seen in a certain basic way: the two sides and their relationship are being seen as making up one system, not two. (This perspective applies at least to certain, critically important, aspects of the relationship, not necessarily to all aspects of their relations.

Let me explain briefly; and let me exaggerate for the sake of clarity.

People holding the contrary, traditional viewpoint are visualizing a situation consisting fundamentally of two separate things: there is "our" side and there is the adversary. As they visualize the situation, our side takes some action vis-a-vis the other, as part of our *external* affairs. People holding the mutual security viewpoint are visualizing a security situation consisting fundamentally of one thing: a single system made up of two halves. They are visualizing interactions between these two halves occurring *internally* inside the one system. These are interactions between two halves of one whole.

This distinction in perspectives may seem abstract, but its implications can be far-reaching. It may have implications both for how one thinks about specific problems, and for the solutions and policy recommendations one is likely to arrive at.

Once this difference in visualizing the situation is grasped, it may become clearer how the two viewpoints lead naturally to what I am calling the "unilateral security" and "mutual security" approaches. Again I will exaggerate for clarity. If one is visualizing two fundamentally separate things — our side and the adversary — then it follows naturally that the goal is to maximize our side's security (i.e., to employ the unilateral security approach.) If instead one is visualizing one thing — a single whole made up of two halves — then it follows naturally that the goal is the maximize the security of the one whole. Indeed in this way of visualizing the overall situation, this approach may be the only way security will be successfully achieved for either side.[20]

Put this way, these statements are an exaggeration, because I have isolated just one aspect of the way people think and have discussed it by itself. Of course skilled specialists have a complex and rich understanding of the situations they study. It would be an injustice to suggest that their understanding can be reduced to this, and I do not say that. Nonetheless, I believe this difference in the way of conceiving things runs like a thread through many debates.

Policy purpose and policy action

In conceiving mutual and unilateral security in the way I am suggesting, it is important to distinguish between the purposes or goals of policy and more specific policy actions. The policy purpose of improving mutual security does not necessarily require that actions always be mutually carried out. On the contrary, actions taken by one side may enhance both sides' security under some circumstances.

It is useful to distinguish three kinds of policy action, all of which might serve mutual security purposes under appropriate circumstances. Actions may be taken *unilaterally* by one side, *separately in parallel* by the two sides, or *jointly* by the two sides together. Comprehensive study of ways to increase mutual security would logically consider all three possibilities. Actions do not always have to be jointly undertaken. There may be many ways that one side or each side can improve mutual security merely by taking an action by itself, or the two can act simultaneously and in parallel.[21]

Verification

Even in situations where the two sides are developing their mutual security in an extensive and far-reaching fashion, there will be one class of actions that each side will want to continue to take unilaterally. Those are actions to verify that the other side is actually carrying out all steps agreed upon. It may seem to be a paradox that successfully achieving mutual security will require this one form of unilateral action. But the need for unilateral verification does not contradict the concept of mutual security in any way. It merely is a need that each side will have in situations where mutual security exists only partially.[22]

An alternative terminology

The reader will have noticed that in constructing my argument I have not yet used the phrase "national security," although that clearly is the subject. One reason is that that phrase can be used, in this context, in two alternative ways.

The perspective offered here is that mutual security is one approach *to* national security — one path by which national security may be improved. I have offered the term "unilateral security" to name the other approach.

There is an alternative terminology possible, and it can be found in some of today's discourse. In that terminology, the phrase "national security" is used as synonymous with what I call unilateral security. In that perspective, mutual security and national security are held to be alternatives to each other. *Either* one is interested in mutual security, *or* one is interested in national security.[23]

In my judgment, this way of naming things will generally confuse rather than clarify the issues. That terminology obscures something fundamental: the object of a mutual security policy between two nations is to increase *each nation's security*. The object of mutual security is not something other than the security of nations. The object of mutual security is precisely the improved security of nations. Thus mutual security is best seen as one approach to national security, not as something in competition with national security.

Goal and process

The question can readily arise whether mutual security is a goal toward which the two parties may strive, or is a process by which they gradually increase their security over time. The perspective being developed here suggests that it usually is best seen as both.[24]

Two parties, presently in a state of some degree of mutual insecurity, can certainly set some specified degree or form of improved mutual security as a goal. The goal may be modest and perhaps short term, or grander and perhaps longer term. The two may or may not succeed fully in reaching it. But in this sense mutual security, in that form or degree, is a "thing" that can be imagined, worked toward, and reached (or not).

In working toward it, the parties will find that they are engaged in a process which is also generating some mutual security along the way. This will occur in the tangible sense that successful steps toward an objective achieve some gains in their own right. It probably will also occur in the intangible, and sometimes more important, sense that the process will modify the perceptions that each holds of the other. To the extent that the two come to see each other less as zero-sum competitors and more as "working together" toward a shared goal, each side's calculus of risks changes. Putting it formally, their subjective estimates of the probability of acute conflict in the future are likely to be modified, by fresh perceptions.

The fact that mutual security may be improved by the process is largely a product, again, of the interactive quality of the system. Because the system is interactive, one side sees the other executing a parallel or joint step, which modifies its perceptions of the other, which encourages it to proceed with executing its own next step, which the other side perceives, which...etc. Sequences of actions are considered further in Section IV below.[25]

Regarding third-nation threats

Mutual security, in the sense being developed in this chapter, is a matter of bilateral relations between two sides. There is another possible meaning for the phrase, which needs to be kept clearly distinct from this meaning.

Obviously it is possible for both sides to be threatened by some third nation. (Or by third and fourth and...Nth nations.) If such a threat emerged, then the two sides might cooperate to meet it, and in so doing they would be jointly improving their "mutual security." This is a simpler, and quite different, meaning of the phrase than its major meaning in today's discourse.

An obvious example of the U.S. and USSR jointly acting to protect or improve the security of both against third-nation threats is the Nuclear Non-Proliferation Treaty. The two sides cooperatively championed that treaty during the period 1968-70 as it was being presented to nations around the world, and to a considerable extent have continued to support it cooperatively since.

Cooperative measures to forestall third-nation threats may be important to the security of East and West, and at other times to other adversarial pairs. But this form of cooperation should not be confused with improving "mutual security" in the sense of adjusting the interactions between the two sides themselves.

Incidentally, the fact that one side may be threatened by some other nation means that their bilateral relations to create mutual security may not meet the *complete* national security needs of that side. This is potentially a complicating element in their analysis and development of their bilateral mutual security.

Mutual security does not imply condominium

A related possible confusion involves the idea of condominium.[26] There is nothing in the concept of mutual security *per se* which implies the creation of a condominium, nor any domination of third parties. Of course it is obvious that certain steps may be *possible*, in a relationship between two parties, that would improve their mutual security by dominating others. But such steps are certainly not necessary to, nor intrinsically part of, a mutual security policy or the concept of mutual security, as I have developed it here.

Observe that it may be equally possible, in a strategy of *unilateral* security, to take steps to improve one's own security by dominating others. In fact this is common. During the Cold War, for example, both the USSR and the U.S. took steps (at least in the opinion of their critics) that meant the domination other nations. These steps were justified as necessary for achieving (unilateral) national security. There are many other examples in history where nations sought unilateral security, in the context of some perceived danger, by undertaking policies that meant the domination of others.

Thus the danger that "national security" may be used as a justification or pretext for dominating others is a danger that is not unique either to the mutual security approach or to the unilateral security approach. It is a dangerous possibility either way. It is also a possibility that may be avoided either way.

It will be obvious from these remarks that I regard any tactics, within some nation's so-called "mutual security" strategy, that involve the domination of others to be a perversion of the real meaning of mutual security. Besides the obvious moral reasons for my opinion, I would also point out a contradiction: for that nation to use tactics of dominating others means that the nation is not seeking mutual security with *those* countries.

May I draw the reader's attention to the method that I have employed in the last several paragraphs, namely to take a question that may be asked of the mutual security approach, and ask it of the unilateral security approach also. This method will apply across a broad range of possible questions. It would be a mistake to assume that unilateral security will be, in general, the preferable approach to national security, requiring no particular justification, and that mutual security requires special and elaborate justifications. In fact the same questions and challenges can and should be applied equally to both approaches. Which approach to national security is superior is not obvious *a priori* and will depend upon the particulars of each situation a nation faces.

The "security dilemma"

The concept of mutual security, as developed here, bears an important relationship to a concept called the "security dilemma," which has been of interest to theoreticians for a long time. Here I shall discuss the relationship between the two only briefly and in simplified terms.[27]

The idea of the "security dilemma" holds, in essence, that one nation will feel insecure if it makes no effort to protect its security, but that any effort to do so must threaten the security of one or more other nations. Feeling threatened, those others will take actions that, in turn, diminish the security of the first nation. Thus the first nation faces a dilemma: it will be insecure if it doesn't act and insecure if it does.

The concept of mutual security can shed much light upon this problem. Perhaps the most fundamental contribution that mutual security can offer is this: advocates of mutual security can say that, precisely because the security dilemma is a possible danger, the mutual security approach is all the more needed. It is not necessary or inevitable that nations take actions, trying *unilaterally* to make themselves more secure, that have the unintended result of making themselves and others less secure. The proper development of *mutual* security between these potentially insecure nations can forestall these problems before they arise.

In short, I and other advocates of mutual security can take this position: agreeing that the *potential* for mounting insecurity is present in the relationship, we proceed to conceive, and to advocate designing, the *actual* relationship so that that potential remains only potential, and hence the "dilemma" does not materialize.[28]

Mixed games

The conclusion drawn in Section I was that in interactive security systems, the two sides can play a negative-sum game over time (via unilateral security policies) or a positive-sum game over time (via mutual security policies), but no third general alternative is possible: there is no zero-sum game possible over time. However it was pointed out that the two sides can play a negative-sum game in some aspects of their relationship and a positive-sum game in other aspects, over the same time span. This combination could be called a "mixed game."

In one way this possibility is almost trivially true. It would be difficult to find an interactive security system which was so absolutely negative-sum that no positive-sum (mutual security) elements could be found in it at all. Even in the depths of the Cold War, for instance, East and West took certain positive-sum steps. In this sense every game is a mixed game. But a game that is heavily negative-sum is still extremely undesirable.

Where only two basic games are possible, and where it has also been shown that a mutual security approach is both feasible and realistic (in the senses described earlier), then the chief question of practical significance will be this: how and to what extent can a heavily negative-sum game be changed into a less negative one, and/or be changed into a positive-sum game? That is, how can the negative-sum elements of the system be reduced or removed, and how can positive-sum elements be created or enhanced?

This is an empirical question that depends entirely upon the particulars of any given situation. Observing this is the last general theoretical observation I will offer in this paper. There is no deductive solution to this question, that is no solution that can be derived merely by reasoning. Solutions require detailed analysis of the particulars. The solutions will differ from one pair of nations to another pair, and may also differ for the same pair at different times.[29]

Section III: Three Conceptions of Mutual Security and of Policy to Achieve It

Up to this point I have offered basic features of a theory of mutual security, without discussing variations that are possible within that overall framework. Extremely important variations are possible, and in this section I turn to those.

I believe that nearly all the important variations depend, at root, upon different assumptions or perceptions about the *degree* of interaction that exists between the two sides of the bilateral relationship. The "systems interactions" discussed earlier are not simply either present or absent. As we shall see, these differences in the perceived degree of interaction also involve differences in the kinds of interactions that exist and in the roles they play. People disagree about the extent and ways in which any particular bilateral security system is interactive. From that disagreement, I will argue, flow differing conceptions of what form and degree of mutual security can and should be developed. From those different conceptions flow, in turn, different views on what policy is appropriate. In what follows, I shall continue to use today's East-West relationship as the illustrative example.[30]

It seems useful to distinguish three broad conceptions of mutual security, each of which generates a viewpoint on what kind of policy can and should be undertaken to achieve its own form of mutual security. I shall give names to the three according to their viewpoints on appropriate policy. I term the three the *technical* conception of mutual security and policy, the *threat-reduction* conception of mutual security and policy, and the *supportive* conception of mutual security and policy.

These categories are not rigidly compartmentalized and some overlap in views can be found. But these categories represent identifiable main tendencies, and as we shall see each has its own distinctive logic. The categories are moderately roomy; each permits significant shadings and variations within it. Let us take up each in turn.

The "technical" conception of mutual security and of policy to achieve it

The "technical" conception of mutual security, as I term it, begins from an interpretation of the interaction that is the narrowest of the three. This viewpoint does not deny the existence of a security interaction. It agrees that unwise steps by either or both sides can increase the insecurity of both, and that wise steps can increase the security of both. But it interprets the interaction and the possible steps in terms that are considerably narrower than either of the other interpretations.

In the East-West relationship, a substantial amount of attention was given to this conception of mutual security in the early and mid-1980s, and some had been given earlier. Events since have been so dramatic that attention has largely shifted elsewhere. However if East-West relations should chill again, I would predict that this conception would again attract attention.

People holding the "technical" mutual security viewpoint on the East-West relationship, for instance, characteristically support the Hotline and the several improvements that have been made to it. They typically support the Nuclear Risk Reduction Centers that now exist. They usually support the existing regime of confidence- and security-building measures (CSBM's). They may support development of additional CSBM's, additional measures for "crisis control," and further quiet East-West discussions to help forestall new crises. (This viewpoint overlaps heavily with what some call the agenda of "owls.")[31]

However, supporters of this conception typically do not believe that the more far-reaching measures suggested by the other two conceptions are realistically feasible (or perhaps even desirable.) That is, the arms race and the overall political competition cannot be deliberately ended or altered in fundamental ways. These more basic interactions between the two sides are part of the underlying reality of their profound political differences. In this conception it does not seem impossible, especially now, that these political differences may be reduced as a result of deep political change occurring. The basic interactions may indeed change fundamentally, but *not* in a way that can be planned or designed by the two sides mutually.

The other two conceptions claim that indeed change in the basic interactions can be accomplished deliberately and mutually.

The technical conception focuses chiefly on what has come to be called the danger of "inadvertent" escalation — the danger that a developing crisis will escalate to levels that neither side wants. For example, many csbm's provide improved "transparency" between the two sides, helping each side to avoid misperceiving exercises or innocent military movements by the other as steps preparatory to an attack.

In this conception, in sum, the basic and continuing systems interactions between the two sides cannot be much changed by design, but it *is* possible to make, as it were, technical adjustments around the margins of those interactions, sometimes in ways that may be very useful. This advocacy of meaningful technical adjustments is the source of my label of the "technical" conception of mutual security. More will be said below about this conception, as contrasts are drawn between it and other conceptions.[32]

The "threat-reduction" conception of mutual security and of policy to achieve it

Supporters of the second conception agree that the dangers of "inadvertent" conflict must be forestalled to the greatest extent possible. But they go much further to advocate major reductions, and eventually the minimization, of the *deliberate* threats between the two sides.

In today's East-West case, these mutual security theorists argue that the time has come for the two sides to take deliberate, well-designed steps to reduce, in both degree and kind, the various threats between then. Those steps would proceed in stages and over time. Suitable steps will include joint, parallel, and unilateral measures, all three.[33]

In this conception, the U.S. and USSR and their major allies should, in other words, make substantial efforts to change the East-West relationship in the direction of reducing threats, especially the more dangerous threats. In this conception, a planned, sequential process of mutual threat-reduction is the principal strategy for developing mutual security.

I remarked earlier that each of these basic conceptions of mutual security may include significant variations. Those supporting this conception may differ considerably in the particular threats to which they give attention, in the degree of designed change they consider possible, and in their time horizon. Some, for instance, are focused primarily on the nuclear and/or conventional arms races and force structures. Others may be interested in regional issues, such as ways East and West could cooperate to "defuse" (and perhaps disengage from) potential crisis areas such as Europe, the Persian Gulf, and the Korean peninsula. In any of these topic areas, some may focus mainly on progress deemed feasible in the next several years; and others (especially in the weapons areas) may focus on possible arrangements for a time further away. Hence some discussions that fall under this second heading will concentrate on short-term, and others on longer-term, approaches.[34]

The point of agreement that unites these somewhat disparate thinkers is their premise that East and West should now be able to cooperate, at least to some considerable extent, in developing and carrying out mutually agreed measures that will substantially reduce mutual threats and thus substantially enhance the security of both sides. These thinkers implicitly agree that these measures can go beyond "technical" adjustments at the margins of the system to achieve important change in the system itself.[35] Thus the defining difference between the first conception on the one hand and the second (and third) on the other is that the latter say that deliberate changes are now possible in the basic systems interactions themselves, leading to an East-West relationship that is significantly different *by design*. Those holding the first viewpoint do not think so. The "by design" is conceptually essential, since of course everyone agrees that significant change in the relationship can occur in unplanned ways.

Another way to state the difference between the first and second conceptions of mutual security refers to their differing views of the *spectrum of relevant risks*. The second conception defines the spectrum of the risks relevant to mutual security much more broadly than the first, since the second includes deliberate threats in the spectrum. (Later we will see that the third conception embraces a still broader spectrum of relevant risks.)

Here, "relevant" primarily means relevant for policy, specifically policies for mutual security. Supporters of the technical conception do not, of course, deny that each side has been making important threats against the other. Rather they see those threats as not relevant to the question of *mutual* security or policies to increase it. In the technical conception, those threats are mainly relevant to each side's *unilateral* security, and policies to enhance unilateral security; and as such are very important to each side (separately).

Those holding the second, threat-reduction viewpoint regarding today's East-West relationship characteristically support not only a START agreement involving approximately fifty percent cuts in strategic nuclear forces, but also are strongly interested in further nuclear agreements thereafter, designed to decrease further the strategic threat each side feels from the other side's existing and potential forces. They may well be interested, in the long run, in finding a design for the two sides' forces that can remain constant and stable thereafter — that is, essentially a stable "end point" for the competition in deployed strategic weapons.[36]

Supporters of the threat-reduction conception of mutual security typically seek vigorous, successful negotiations on mutual reductions and redesign of European forces, down to much lower numerical levels than the existing levels, and to force configurations that each side finds less threatening than current configurations. Typically these theorists are strongly interested in ideas for creating defensively oriented postures on both sides in Europe that are much more capable of defense than of attack. Again they may be interested in the long run finding a design for the two sides' European forces, at low levels, that can remain stable thereafter, thus essentially designing an "end point" for the competition in deployed European forces. Alternatively they may be interested in a complete or nearly complete demilitarization of all of Europe over some time span.[37]

Finally, many advocates of this viewpoint are interested in ways of improving both sides' security by reducing the threat that each perceives from the other's past and present behavior in potential crisis areas in the Third World. A limited form of this mutual threat reduction can be created by explicit or tacit "rules of the game" for the superpower competition, globally or in a particular region. A more ambitious form might arguably be created by a scaling-back of the competition itself, perhaps leading over time to mutual superpower disengagement from parts or all of the Third World.[38]

The essential principle underlying all these ideas is *mutual threat reduction.* Whether the context is strategic weapons, European forces, or superpower interaction in the Third World, these theorists see many present and prospective mutual threats as being unnecessary, and in fact being counterproductive to both sides' real security. Well-calculated steps to reduce these threats can improve the security of both sides.

These mutual security theorists differentiate themselves sharply from, e.g., advocates of unilateral disarmament, by stressing that threat-reduction must be *mutual* threat reduction if it is to be stable and durable. Policies of mutual threat-reduction would suitably include measures that satisfy both sides' needs for independent verification.

Limited, calculated unilateral steps by one side to reduce its threat to the other may also be useful under some circumstances. Such steps may demonstrate sincerity and resolve. Under some conditions such steps might also succeed in initiating a series of reciprocal steps back and forth. But limited, calculated unilateral steps are generally conceived, in this second viewpoint, as one possible element (applicable only under some conditions) within the larger theme of mutual threat reduction.[39]

Section IV returns to other aspects of the threat-reduction conception of mutual security.

The "supportive" conception of mutual security and of policy to achieve it

The first two conceptions of mutual security focus upon military and political-military dangers or threats that both sides face: in the first, primarily inadvertent dangers; in the second, deliberate threats the two sides make against each other. Supporters of the third conception of mutual security strongly agree that all of these dangers and threats must be reduced to the greatest possible extent. But they go much further, to advocate a broader conception of mutual security, one that partially transcends political-military relations as these are traditionally conceived. As we shall see, this large conception embraces many possibilities and contains (at least at present) a number of important complications and ambiguities.

In this conception, the security of either side is diminished, perhaps endangered, by a wide range of potential dangers to the other side. Thus if the other side were to be threatened by, for instance, severe economic collapse, large-scale continuing terrorism, or societal breakdown, such dangers could not help but diminish the first side's security. To protect its own security, the first side has an interest in taking action to forestall such threats to the other side. This idea represents one version of mutual security because to the extent the first side helps forestall the emergence of such dangers the security of both is enhanced.

This idea goes well beyond the second, threat-reduction conception of mutual security. Under that conception it is necessary and sufficient for each side to reduce *its own* threats to the other. Nothing is said about other threats or dangers. Let us give the name "extraneous-origin dangers" to dangers that do not have their origin in the relationship between the two sides. In the third conception, each side reducing its threats to the other is necessary but not sufficient. In addition each side bears a responsibility to reduce and forestall extraneous-origin dangers to the other's security. Each bears this responsibility not — or not only — as a matter of good will or benevolence, but out of its own security self-interest.

Action to reduce and forestall extraneous-origin dangers to the other side's security can reasonably be called action that is supportive to the other. Hence my label for this third conception as the "supportive" conception of mutual security.[40]

An example of a significant extraneous-origin danger is the danger of domestic turmoil followed by reaction. Civil insurrection or substantial ongoing internal terrorism on one side might bring to power a "strong" new government prepared to use drastic measures to restore order. That new government might be of a kind that the other side would see as militaristic, fascistic, or tyrannical, or as one that might pave the way for such a regime. Almost certainly the other side would perceive an increased security threat to itself from a new government of this character. At the time of this writing, the possibility of severe domestic disorder in the USSR is the example of chief interest to most of those advocating supportive mutual security in the East-West relationship.[41]

How much one side can do to support the other, against threats such as this that do not have their origin within the bilateral relationship, is an open question. Advocates of the third conception may suggest that more can (and should) be done than others may believe. One avenue that may well be open and may help forestall such dangers to the other side is the economic avenue. In today's East-West case those holding this third conception characteristically advocate a rapid increase in East-West economic contacts: trade, joint ventures, and other forms of economic relations. Their motive is to aid perestroika and improve the Soviet economy for its citizens, with the intention of helping to head off any anti-Gorbachev counter-revolution. It would be consistent with this conception of mutual security, indeed, to advocate outright Western economic aid, perhaps even in large quantities, to Gorbachev's government.

In some future time, the same reasoning might apply with equal logic in the other direction. At a time of American or Western economic malaise and Soviet prosperity, the same reasoning would argue that Soviet economic power should be used to aid democractic governments in the West.[42]

Advocates of the third conception of mutual security also characteristically advocate much-increased exchanges between East and West of scientists, artists and many other groups. They typically favor joint U.S.-Soviet scientific research projects, including large ones, partly because scientific projects require close, continuing interaction. They often favor citizen exchanges on a large scale.[43]

Supporters of this conception also typically advocate East-West cooperation to cope with environmental and ecological dangers facing both sides, such as global warming, acid rain and the shrinking ozone layer. This observation brings us to an important feature of this conception.

Intersection with ideas about global security

The supportive conception of mutual security, unlike the other two, is heavily intertwined with another set of ideas. Many ideas in the supportive conception of mutual security are intertwined with ideas about global security — the security of all nations and peoples. And many of those advocating this conception of East-West mutual security are also advocates of some version of global security. This intertwining of ideas and this overlapping advocacy introduces an important element of complexity and ambiguity into current thinking about this kind of East-West mutual security. It is probably not too much to say that the supportive conception of mutual security, in today's thinking, cannot be fully understood without comprehending its links with notions of global security. At the same time, it would be perfectly possible to hold a coherent, detailed, powerful conception of supportive East-West mutual security while leaving all global questions aside. Many who advocate both seem to feel that the East-West relationship provides the best (or the paradigmatic) example of the larger ideas they are presently developing. In short: at this stage in the evolution of ideas, the relationship between the supportive conception of mutual security and thinking about global security is ambiguous. (This point and several further points about ambiguity that follow are meant merely as a theoretician's observations, not as criticisms.)

Today's thinking about global (or sometimes "common") security embraces a large number of ideas, which vary in scope and meaning among different thinkers and proponents. Often the ideas include the following: the development of international peace-keeping institutions and procedures to prevent and halt wars; a much greater reliance on international law; a shift in international focus away from potential conflicts and threats (with the frequent resort to military means) and toward ecological and economic dangers; hence a broadening of the idea of "security" to embrace, indeed emphasize, ecological and economic security for all; an emphasis on Third World development; and a long-term goal of full economic, environmental, political and legal security, both domestically and internationally, for all peoples, groups, individuals and nations. As of this writing, there does not yet appear to be any general accepted theory that coherently unites these elements, together with strategies for reaching these goals. But various statements exist, and in the United States a declaration is being circulated. Portions of this viewpoint have been advocated in speeches by Soviet leaders. A premise underlying much of this thinking appears to be that global affairs should be conceived as a single grand system, holistically united and made up of many subsystems (ecological, economic, political, etc.) which are intricately interwoven.[44]

Some who hold this view may see the East-West system as a microcosm of the global system, and hence believe that East-West mutual security is essentially an expression, or "translation down," of the principles of global security to the level of one bilateral relationship. Others may see the East-West problem as significantly different in kind, but one whose resolution requires some application of global principles and priorities. Most holding this view seem to believe that the U.S. and the USSR should take the lead in developing global security, both because that is the best way of achieving global security and because these two powers turning their attention and energies in this direction would be the best way of dissolving all remaining East-West problems.

The core of the supportive conception of bilateral mutual security

This glance at ideas of global security may provide helpful background for understanding current thinking about East-West mutual security, in its supportive conception. But as noted, it is not logically necessary to rely on global ideas to hold a strong supportive view of East-West mutual security. Also, some of the advocates of the supportive view might feel that at the present time, great emphasis on "global security" might make for unnecessary delays in developing a high level of East-West mutual security. With this background let me return then, to the analysis of the supportive conception of bilateral mutual security.

The supportive conception of mutual security is based on a broader and more multifaceted idea of East-West systems interactions than the other two conceptions are. Here the actual and potential interactions are both more numerous than in the other two conceptions, and take a greater diversity of forms. Of course, supporters of the third view would emphatically agree that the five systems interactions discussed in Section I of this paper exist and yield a negative-sum game, and they would assess those interactions as serious and the game as costly. But they would go on to emphasize that those five do not exhaust the important interactions in the East-West system; others are also important.

Similarly, this third conception advances a wider *spectrum of the relevant risks* than does the second, much as the second advances a wider spectrum than does the first. In the third, the relevant risks include extraneous-origin dangers, which are not part of the other two conceptions.

Thus, while strongly agreeing about the interactive effects of inadvertent risks and deliberate threats, supporters of the third conception also see interactive effects and relevant risks in other aspects of the situation. The heart of this viewpoint is that it sees some of those other effects and risks as suitable for preventive action by the two sides, conceived and implemented as policies for mutual security. Logically speaking, it is this feature of recommending broad action for security that is the most fundamental feature distinguishing this conception from the other two.

Supporters of the other two conceptions might well agree that a certain limited set of dangers may exist or arise, against which East and West should undertake policies in common — for instance certain ecological dangers like global warming. But these thinkers do not find it helpful, at least at present, to combine these dangers with the more traditional "security" issues and include them all within the concept of "security." Supporters of the other two conceptions might also agree that some problems that do involve security could arise which their conceptions do not address — such as reactionary governments emerging for internal reasons. But these thinkers do not believe that "mutual security" policies to meet such dangers are feasible and appropriate. Rather they see such policies as being ineffective in reducing these dangers, and/or counterproductive in their impact on other important goals and values.[45]

Thus the defining difference between the third conception and the others is that in the third, a broader range of actual and potential interactions and risks are seen as suitable for preventive action, to the goal of improving mutual security. In this third conception, suitable policies could be unilateral, separate and parallel, and/or joint; most often they will be joint.

Complexities and ambiguities in the supportive conception

In the supportive conception, the complete range of relevant interactions may not yet be fully known and the precise preventive policies may not yet be completely specifiable. Here is another element of complexity and ambiguity in the supportive conception of mutual security (in addition to its overlap with ideas about global security.) To my knowledge the claim has not been advanced, among those holding this viewpoint, that anyone presently has a comprehensive understanding of the interactions or of the appropriate supportive policies. To the contrary, the tendency among advocates of this third viewpoint is to suggest that all the significant interactions may not be evident yet; that is, that the full range of interactions in a system like today's East-West relationship (while certainly extensive) may not yet have been discovered.

I offer the observation that advocates of the third, rather than the first or second, conceptions of mutual security are most likely to employ the term "interdependence" for the East-West relationship. This word implies that the interactions between the two sides are not merely important: they are so important that they add up to mutual dependence on each other. Discussions of the "interdependence" of the two also typically say or imply that the interactions are numerous and of many kinds — not only military but also political, economic, ecological, psychological, cultural, etc.[46]

Another element of complexity and ambiguity in the supportive conception derives from the fact that its advocates evidently tend to see a high degree of interaction not merely as an objective feature of the situation, but also as something desirable. For them, high interaction is not only a *fact* but a value. In this conception, "systems interactions" between the two sides are not merely something that exists (to a degree that we may presently be underestimating) but also are something that we should want to increase further.[47]

Closely related is an ambiguity involving what is *inevitable* and what should be done as a matter of *policy*. For instance some people now say that it is inevitable that the Soviet economy, along with the economies of the East European countries, will becoming increasingly intertwined and "interdependent" with the West European economy. (Others do not think so, but that is not my point.) The ambiguity lies in the relationship between this supposed inevitability, and what it means for policy choices now, or at any given moment. It is not obvious that policies should be undertaken to hasten some process, even if one agrees that in time the process is inevitable and desirable. Wise policymakers know that trying to move too quickly can be counter-productive, even destructive. The idea that some long-term process is inevitable also may raise an ambiguity about the *time span* that is being considered, or that is relevant to policy.

Another complication is also closely related: mutual security is usually not the only end its advocates have in view. Those who hold a highly interactive, inter-dependent conception of the East-West relationship typically say their proposed policies will have a variety of benefits, of which mutual security is only one. *Multiple goals* will be served by the two sides aligning their policies with the great existing interdependence and by their increasing the interdependence further. Ever-increasing mutual security is certainly one goal to be served. A rapid increase in East-West economic relations will also have direct economic benefits for both sides. Similarly, scientific exchanges and joint projects will benefit science on both sides; and something similar applies to artistic and cultural exchanges. In a broader way, citizens' exchanges and a high volume of travel and communications back and forth will promote mutual understanding and good relations generally.

These various complexities and ambiguities in this third conception of mutual security also make the assessment of it complicated. For instance supporters of the first or second conceptions may well agree that the short-term economic, scientific, etc., goals are desirable for their own sake, and perhaps achievable, but may doubt that achieving them will really add much to mutual security in the short term. The immediate implications of long-term possibilities are not necessarily clear. For example, it would be possible for Westerners to agree that the Soviet and West European economies probably will become increasingly interdependent in the long run, without drawing any particular conclusion for Western policy in the 1990s. Instead, Western policymakers might feel that East-West economic ties will develop naturally over time, as business people on both sides find and create new business opportunities; and there may not be much that Western governments can or should try to do to hasten it.[48]

Supporters of the other two conceptions may also seek other policy goals and values which they perceive as being at least partly competitive with mutual security. Section I of this paper pointed out that in interactive systems, security may be a chief goal but not the only major goal. In such cases, the priority to be assigned to mutual security, and the form it takes, will depend upon the competition with other goals. An illustration of this arises in the assessment of the supportive conception made by those who do not entirely share it. These people may have other goals, to which the supportive conception would be at least partly counterproductive. In today's East-West situation, for example, people on one side may hope that the political system on the other side is going to evolve further, and believe that being too "supportive" to the *present* government and society might impede that evolution.[49]

Section IV below returns to further aspects of the supportive conception of mutual security.

Summary of the three conceptions of mutual security

This section of the paper has suggested that the existing, complex and somewhat amorphous ideas about mutual security, and appropriate policies to achieve it, can be usefully categorized into three broad kinds. Although the ideas have been discussed here in the context of East-West mutual security, these three categories would appear to apply to other bilateral situations where two parties find themselves in an interactive "mutual insecurity system." The three categories are not rigidly distinct; there is some gray area between them. But I suggest they represent identifiable main tendencies. Let me summarize them.

The *technical* conception holds that the risks relevant to policies for *mutual* security are chiefly the risks of inadvertent escalation and inadvertent conflict between the two sides. Supporters of this conception agree that deliberate threats back and forth and some dangers of extraneous origin affect each side's security, but they perceive such threats as either a problem for one side's or the others' *unilateral* security, or as hazards that cannot be forestalled by any feasible, non-counterproductive security policy. Which and how many such measures, beyond those already in place, would be useful are variables within this conception.

The *threat reduction* conception agrees that forestalling inadvertent dangers is important; but sees the two sides as having a major opportunity to reduce, by design, the threats to each other that each have been making. A well-analyzed, planned strategy for mutual threat reduction, in stages and over time, is the chief strategy for developing mutual security. Supporters of this conception would agree that dangers of extraneous origin can affect each side's security, but perceive these as hazards that cannot be forestalled by any feasible, non-counterproductive security policy. How far the mutual threats can be mutually reduced, over what time span, are variables within this conception.

The *supportive* conception agrees that reducing mutual threats and forestalling inadvertent conflicts are important; but holds that achieving real mutual security also requires each side to forestall dangers to the other that have their origins outside the relationship. These dangers too, by reducing one side's security, inevitably reduce the other side's security. And supporters of this conception hold that some, at least, of these dangers *are* amenable to policies by the other side aimed at forestalling them. How many of these dangers are suitable for preventive policies by the other side, and what policies should be applied to them, are variables within this conception.

Section IV: Some Implications for Policy Issues

This final section of this chapter tries to illuminate a few of the implications of this theory of mutual security for certain policy issues. Here I shall largely confine myself to questions involving East-West mutual security, although many of the ideas to be suggested may apply *mutatis mutandis* to other situations. Here "policy" refers to policy in a broad sense, not to immediate policy issues important at the particular time this book appears. Since the policy implications of mutual security are numerous, I shall touch on certain issues only. I necessarily must be brief.

The role of deterrence

Central questions in many discussions of mutual security involve the role to be played by deterrence, and especially of strategic nuclear deterrence. Advocates of mutual security disagree among themselves about the answers to these questions.

Supporters of what I call the technical conception believe that mutual security, as they conceive it, does not imply any great change in the goals of deterrence or in how it should be achieved. They may support some adjustments in current deterrent arrangements, at the strategic, European, or other levels.[50]

Many advocates of what I call the supportive conception often say that mutual security, fully achieved, would mean abolishing deterrence altogether at some time in the not-distant future. Certainly there should be no need for the terrible danger implicit in strategic nuclear deterrence. And if the two sides have become thoroughly interwoven, there would be no need for any military form of deterrence, just as there is no military deterrence today between the U.S. and Canada or within Western Europe.[51]

Supporters of what I call the threat-reduction conception have — and must have — more complicated ideas about the role of deterrence. On the one hand the essence of their position is that mutual threats are to be reduced, eventually minimized, and many of the mutual threats are deterrent in nature. Hence this school must (and does) advocate substantial reductions, and perhaps some abolitions, of these deterrent threats. That may mean great changes in today's deterrence policies.

On the other hand, many advocates of this conception are well aware that mutual deterrence between East and West has apparently created important forms of stability in the overall East-West relationship. At least this seems to be true in a basic way of the European and strategic nuclear deterrent relationships (in spite of their instabilities in other respects). It seems hard to deny that the dread of a catastrophic nuclear war has introduced great caution into the behavior, especially in crises, of East and West, and that this has contributed to the longest peace in modern European history. Any mutual security policy is supposed to *increase* mutual security, not decrease the existing level of mutual security and stability. Hence major changes in those deterrent relationships should be considered with care.[52]

Many advocates of the threat-reduction conception are also well aware of the great problems that seem to be raised by any effort to abolish nuclear weapons altogether. For instance it is almost inconceivable that the United States and Soviet Union would agree to abolish their nuclear weapons, unless all other declared and undeclared nuclear weapons states abolished theirs too, in some highly verifiable way. Achieving this might not be easy within any readily foreseeable time frame.[53]

For many supporters of the threat-reduction conception, the result of these contending considerations is a conclusion that strategic nuclear and European deterrence should be modified in stages and over time. Well-analyzed steps should be taken in sequence, which have the effect of steadily reducing the actual threats back and forth. The effects of early steps can be experienced and studied before further steps are implemented. How far this process can eventually go is a question that can be left open for now.

Many advocates of this approach believe that it should focus at least as much, perhaps more, upon the characteristics of military forces and weapons as on their numbers. This brings us to two ideas now widely discussed by those taking this approach to deterrence. Since both ideas are very rich and complicated in their own right and would demand lengthy treatment to be discussed in their substance, I shall mention them here mainly as illustrations of the theme that characteristics may matter more than numbers. (Both of these ideas are discussed further in the section of this book devoted to nuclear and conventional arms reductions.)

Defensive orientations in Europe

Much attention is now being given to the concept that arms reductions in Europe should focus upon the weapons and forces on each side that the other finds most threatening. This is a mutual threat-reduction approach *par excellence*. What each side finds threatening is chiefly the other side's offensive capabilities, especially high-speed offensive capabilities and offensive capabilities in which the other side is significantly superior. By reducing offensive threats, this approach leads toward a reconfiguring of each side's European forces. If each side comes to perceive that the other is relatively weak in attack capabilities and that "our" side is able to defend itself strongly, then both sides will be more secure (mutual security). The resulting situation still involves deterrence, but it becomes deterrence with a defensive emphasis.

Overall cuts in numbers of forces are desirable as well, for cost savings and other reasons, but only if the military situation afterwards is at least as mutually secure as it was before the cuts, and preferably more secure. It is possible for numerical cuts actually to increase the threat, one way or even both ways. Given this hazard, *threat reduction* must take precedence over numerical cuts per se, whenever this inconsistency may appear.[54]

Fundamental Deterrence in strategic weapons

As noted earlier, advocates of the threat-reduction conception of mutual security usually seek cuts in strategic nuclear weapons beyond the START regime currently under negotiation. But here the same principle comes into play: some numerical cuts could reduce stability and security rather than increase them. From the threat-reduction viewpoint what most needs to be "cut" are the threats that each side perceives in the other's strategic forces, beginning with the threats that each side finds most disturbing, and proceeding thereafter to less disturbing threats.[55]

Many specialists hold that the most disturbing strategic threats are (a) hazards of inadvertent or accidental launch of nuclear weapons; and perhaps even more, (b) contingencies in which one superpower or the other might have an incentive and opportunity to employ strategic nuclear weapons deliberately ("rationally").[56] Perhaps only by abolishing all nuclear weapons in the world can these risks be reduced to zero. However many specialists believe that an exceedingly low risk, in the East-West relationship, could be achieved if each side deployed only enough strategic nuclear weapons to deter the other side's nuclear weapons, and none for any other purpose. Such postures are usually called "Minimum Deterrence" postures.

In my opinion this name is an unfortunate one. To non-specialists, this name strongly implies either that the nation is doing the minimum to preserve deterrence, or that deterrence itself exists in some sort of minimal form. These ideas are (and ought to be) very distasteful. They also are the direct opposite of what advocates of such postures mean to suggest. Advocates believe that such postures, on both sides, would create an exceptionally strong and "robust" form of mutual deterrence, indeed perhaps the most robust form possible.[57]

I and others advocate a different name for the same posture: *Fundamental Deterrence*. This name captures the essential quality of this mutual posture. It is a posture in which each side's strategic nuclear arsenal is designed by the single criterion of achieving the fundamental goal — deterring the other side from any rational use of strategic nuclear weapons. No other goals are added, explicitly or implicitly, that might complicate or compete with the arsenal's capacity to accomplish its fundamental goal.[58]

A mutual posture of Fundamental Deterrence is arguably the posture that reduces the threat posed by nuclear weapons as far as it can be reduced, short of complete global abolition of them. Thus its promise is one of *threat reduction*. The task of defining it concretely is primarily one of subtracting out threats; it is a task of subtracting numbers of weapons only where subtracting numbers is a means to (and not counterproductive to) reducing threats.

Defensive deterrence in Europe and Fundamental Deterrence in strategic nuclear weapons are presently two major areas of interest for those holding a mutual threat-reduction conception of mutual security.

The role of trust

An objection sometimes voiced to the very concept of mutual security is that it depends on "trust." Mutual security cannot be an acceptable principle for policy, it may be said, unless each side "trusts" the other.

This objection may rest in part on an assumption that mutual security is something that either does exist or does not — something entirely present or entirely absent. The objection seems to overlook the possibility that mutual security can be something that exists in some degree and that that degree can be increased. Thus the objection overlooks the important policy possibility that a "mutual security policy" is something that seeks, as a matter of deliberate policy, to increase the degree over time (understanding that, indeed, one-hundred percent security will not be attained, at least not soon.)

On the other hand it is true that trust plays an important role in the supportive conception of mutual security. In that conception, developing trust is one of the goals of a mutual security policy, and mutual security remains seriously incomplete unless and until a high level of mutual trust has been built up.

But trust does not play so central a role in the other conceptions of mutual security. In the technical conception it plays only a small role. The inspections and verification in the existing regime of CSBM's and arms control substitute for it. Confidential discussions between the two sides to forestall misperceptions and unwanted escalation may depend to some extent on each side meaning what it says, but if one side does not, that usually will soon become obvious to the other. Something similar applies in the threat-reduction conception. If steps to reduce threats are taken in stages and over time, again each side can verify for itself that the other has actually carried out one step before undertaking the next.

The threat-reduction conception of mutual security is also able to provide another valuable possibility which makes trust less necessary. I will turn now to this. Incidentally all the ideas presented in the remainder of this section apply chiefly to the threat-reduction conception of mutual security, and to some extent to the supportive conception. The rest of this section does not much apply to the technical conception.

A demonstration and confirmation technique

A possible objection to the idea of "mutual security" is that it is a seductive idea that can be exploited for unilateral purposes. Skeptics on either side can charge that talk from the other side of "mutual security" is a deception that veils aggressive intentions. Thus skeptics in the West may say that Soviet talk of mutual security is a convenient new veil for the Soviet desire for a *peredyshka*, a breathing-space in the competition, before Moscow resumes it with renewed vigor.[59] Skeptics in the USSR may say that talk, in some quarters in the West, of mutual security distracts attention from new American weapons developments, intended for U.S. superiority.

Decades of experience have shown that arguments among people on one side about the true intentions of the other side are rarely resolved. The other side's behavior often provides ambiguous evidence that can sustain conflicting interpretations. However, the threat-reduction version of mutual security offers an opportunity to cope with this problem in another way. It does so not by attempting to refute the skeptics but by incorporating their arguments into the mutual security approach in a certain fashion.

Threats to one side, as identified by skeptics on that side, can be an important starting point for the threat-reduction approach. The same applies to threats to the other side, as identified by skeptics on that side. A mutual security analysis would then proceed to examine how those threats both ways can be reduced, on a mutual basis (and of course on a mutually verified basis.)

If mutual threat reduction is to be not rhetoric but a genuine operating method for enhancing national security, then it properly should work with the real threats that each side perceives from the other. In this process, the skeptics on each side have a legitimate role to play, by clearly identifying what those threats are. From the mutual security viewpoint that is a significant and useful role, and one without which the threat-reduction approach cannot succeed.

That identification being done, a sophisticated mutual security approach would then incorporate those threats, from each side, into a combined "threat assessment" that becomes a subject for *mutual* study, discussion and analysis by the two sides. That assessment can then become the analytic basis for developing well-calculated threat-reduction measures to be taken by both sides.[60]

Thus the best response to the skeptics on each side is neither to dismiss the threats that they fear as unworthy of attention, nor to allow their claims to become a criticism of the mutual security approach itself. The best response is to incorporate their feared threats *into* the mutual security approach, and then reduce those threats and fears.[61]

Appropriately carried out, this technique also provides an opportunity for each side to demonstrate its commitment to mutual security, by actually implementing its share of an agreed set of mutual threat reductions. That demonstration by each side, in turn, provides a confirmation for the other side that mutual security is indeed the first side's genuine policy, and is not a deception or mere rhetoric.

Such confirmations are needed. In a situation containing important doubts both ways and a history of sharp conflict, each side needs tangible confirmations that the other side is now willing to strive for mutual security. That need is not a sign of unhealthy suspicion, but of realistic prudence. A well-designed mutual security approach needs to respect, not deny, this need and to include specific means for meeting it.

By providing a means for each side to demonstrate, and thus confirm for the other, that mutual security is its real policy, this technique allows a step-by-step development of mutual security to proceed without either side relying on trust. In this fashion, neither side need fear that the other is employing the rhetoric of mutual security as a deception. This technique might be called a "demonstration and confirmation" technique.[62]

Joint study of mutual security policy options

I wish to emphasize the point that a process of mutual threat reduction, carried out in stages and over time, will require joint study, discussion and analysis by the two sides. The same will be true for many aspects of developing a much broader, "supportive" mutual security relationship.

The joint work required to carry out policies of these kinds goes far beyond what is normally meant by the word "negotiation." Indeed traditional ideas of "negotiation" are severely inadequate to achieve such goals. The traditional ideas revolve around an assumption that each side first prepares its own "position" by itself, and only after completing that process does it open talks with the other side. I believe that it would be impossible to achieve well-developed forms of mutual security with such a method. A much more sophisticated approach is needed, in which the two sides begin discussing and analyzing the problems together, informally, from a very early stage. Without making any commitments, they need to study the issues jointly, discuss their security needs jointly, examine known policy possibilities jointly, and develop new policy options jointly. This joint "research and development" of the possibilities and options must come *before* the two sides start "negotiating" what they will decide *actually* to do.

A theoretical paper of this kind is not the place to propose specific mechanisms by which this joint research and development of options could be conducted. Here I merely point out that the creation of research and development mechanisms that both can agree to is a necessary stage in the creation of any well-developed form of mutual security.[63]

On robust mutual security

A mutual security policy is intended to improve the real security of both sides in an interactive system. As this discussion has shown, such a policy may include components that are mutually analyzed and mutually planned; these and all components of policy are then implemented by joint, and/or separate parallel, and/or unilateral actions. A "policy success" follows, if the security of both sides actually enhanced by the actions taken.

A "policy success" in this sense may, however, be of one of two kinds, one of which is more desirable and more deeply successful than the other. The improved mutual security that has been achieved may or may not be "robust." I offer this concept with a specific definition and meaning.

The concept refers to the relative vulnerability of either side, once a mutual security posture has been achieved, to the other side later abandoning mutual security as a policy and making (perhaps even carrying out) new threats. In a "robust" mutual security posture, as I define it, one side is relatively secure against such a later policy reversal by the other. Here, the "posture" may refer to strategic nuclear postures, military postures in Europe (or elsewhere), other aspects of the security relationship, or some combination of these.

An essential feature of this definition is a careful use of the term "relatively." It refers to the comparison between the mutual security posture in question and any other *possible* security posture: any possible unilateral security posture or some other possible mutual security posture. The "relatively" does *not* refer to a comparison between the mutual security posture in question and "absolute security" or other postures that are not possible. No approach to security — neither mutual security or unilateral security — can offer absolute or perfect security.[64]

Clarity on this point is important because a lack of it can easily lead to serious confusions. For example, advocates of unilateral security may criticize some proposed mutual security posture on the grounds that the security it provides is imperfect. Such a simplistic criticism would overlook the fact that the security provided by unilateral security approaches is also imperfect. The correct standard of judgment, for assessing any proposed security policy — unilateral or mutual —

is the comparison with other possible alternatives, not with the impossible standard of absolute security.

A "robust" mutual security posture, then, provides each side with strong protection, relative to other possibilities, against the chance of the other side changing its policies later and making, perhaps even executing, new threats. Thus, in determining whether a robust mutual security posture is possible in any given case, the relevant questions involve the costs and risks to the other side in making such a decision and the response options and their costs and risks for the defending side.

There are several reasons why a well-constructed, robust mutual security posture may offer better protection against a later policy reversal than a unilateral security strategy can (or a poorly constructed mutual security posture can). To illuminate these reasons let us employ a simplified, illustrative example.

Let us imagine that NATO and the Warsaw Pact are considering creating, as of the year Y in the future, defensively oriented conventional postures in Europe. That is, in year Y both sides will have in place conventional forces much more able to defend than to attack. For simplicity let us contrast this possibility with a second: that in the year Y each side has offensively oriented postures, (based on an idea that national security means unilateral security.) The central evaluative question is whether the first, mutual security posture would offer each side more or less protection than the second, unilateral security posture, against a policy reversal and a fresh offensive threat later by the other side. In each of these two situations, how should each side evaluate the danger of later offensive threats from the other?[65]

One reason why this mutual security posture would offer superior protection involves the basic logic of the force structures. Let us say that in a later year the other side does decide to switch to a more aggressive policy. If it finds itself then with a defensively oriented force structure in place, it cannot just start making offensive threats. Such threats, to be credible, must be backed by forces with major offensive capabilities. Hence that side must wait, before making new threats, until it has restructured its forces to back the threats. In the second case, where that side finds itself with major offensive capabilities already in hand, it can proceed at once to making fresh offensive threats.

Another aspect of this comparison is that in the first case, the other side must take considerable time to make the necessary changes in force structure. This delay gives the defending side time to prepare its response. In the second case, the other side can make its new threats almost at once following its policy switch, after little or no adjustment of its already offensive force deployments. The defending side has little or no time to prepare.

A third consideration involves the costs of changing force structures. Creating and deploying powerful new offensive forces after year Y will require large new investments. Conversely, little or no costly investment is needed to be able to make new offensive threats, if offensively oriented forces are already in place in year Y.

A fourth consideration involves the warning that the defending side will receive. The costly and time-consuming fresh investments in strong new offensive forces will give the defending side warning of the policy switch, and of the likely fresh threats to come; and it would be warning of an especially unmistakable and unambiguous kind. In the second case, where strong offensive forces are already in place, the defending side may receive little or no warning of fresh threats.

All of these considerations should lead each side, in the year Y, to perceive itself more secure against a future policy switch by the other if mutual defensive deterrent postures are in place, than it would if strong offensive forces are then in place. This is the central evaluative question here. Hence, in this "robust" mutual security posture each side is *more, not less,* secure in the year Y against a later policy switch by the other than it would be with offensive, unilateral postures. This, in turn, speaks directly to the analysis today of potential alternative postures for the year Y, and to any concerns entertained today about later policy switches by the other side. While this illustration involving defensive deterrent forces in Europe is only one example, analogous reasoning would apply to other issues of force structure and military posture and to some other mutual security issues.

I have dwelt on this concept of "robust" mutual security because confusion in this area can affect practical policy decisions. An example involves, again, a misunderstanding about "trust." It is sometimes said on one side or the other that "we cannot adopt a mutual security policy because we cannot trust the other side to maintain its commitment to mutual security through the years to come." But this "trust" is simply not needed where robust mutual security postures can be created. Such postures offer more security against future policy switches than any available alternative. And whether such a robust posture is actually possible, in any given context, is a matter for detailed and objective analysis. This example suggests it may well be. At a minimum, one cannot proclaim ahead of time that it is not possible.[66]

Action sequences in interactive systems

The theory of mutual security developed in this paper is based on the idea of an interactive system. It was suggested earlier that when each side is striving for unilateral security at the expense of the other, various interactions between the two will generate a negative-sum game over time for both. Alternatively, mutual efforts to develop mutual security will generate a more positive-sum game over time for both. Hence *actions*, taken by the two sides as part of mutual security policies, will also prove to be interactive.

The interactive nature of action — and thus of policy — for mutual security may be best conceived in terms of sequences of action. As has been suggested, mutual security is not something that can be created all at once. Rather it develops (if it does) in steps, over time. It is a common and significant error during sequences of action for policymakers to think about policy only or mainly in terms of one step, usually the next step. However the true meaning and implications of any step include not only its immediate, direct consequences but also the consequences of that step for further interactions. Put this way, this idea may seem obvious, but in an interactive system it has an important meaning for policymakers that is not obvious. That meaning involves the range of possibilities.

Consider estimates made today about the feasibility of a policy option (for instance, some step for improved mutual security). Analysts on one side may say that "our" side cannot safely undertake that option because in the existing situation it would be too dangerous. That skeptical estimate may well be correct today. But a more complete and adequate assessment would go on to point out that the option would become feasible, if certain specified conditions change. Policy analysts have a responsibility to identify the changes in conditions that would change their policy conclusions.

A simple example involves defensively oriented postures in Europe. It is sometimes said in the West that NATO cannot safely adopt such posture because Soviet offensive capabilities against NATO are too great; there is too much danger the defenses would be pushed back or overwhelmed. That estimate may be correct with respect to today's Soviet capabilities. But the policy conclusion does not follow that therefore a NATO defensively oriented posture is not feasible within, say, a few years. It may well be possible to identify changes that would make such a posture feasible — namely some specifiable reductions in Soviet offensive capabilities. In a sequence of actions, those reductions would precede, and make possible, a shift in NATO policy.

A similar logic arises in a broad range of policy problems. Indeed this way of considering a problem is sufficiently important to policymakers and policy analysts that it might be useful to have a name for this identification of changes that would alter the policy recommendations. May I propose that this technique be called the identification of *enabling conditions*. In a context of potential sequences of action, an adequate policy analysis would identify the conditions that would enable "our side" to adopt a certain policy, even if under current conditions our side cannot. Naturally the same applies to either side.[67]

In the "research and development" of policies for improving mutual security between East and West, it might prove helpful, even necessary, to analyze steps within a sequence of actions in terms of specifying the enabling conditions that make them possible.

That actions may have to occur in a sequence, in an interactive system, is basic to grasping this kind of policy problem. For instance, it is entirely possible that the other side will not be able safely to meet our side's enabling conditions, until our side has first made some other change. That is, our side must first take some action to meet the other side's own enabling conditions, before that side can safely act. To continue the same example, certain reductions in Soviet offensive capabilities might prove to be not safe for the USSR to make, until after one or more changes were made in NATO's posture.

It might be tempting, but is misleading, for people on either side to say, in this kind of sequence, that our side is "helping the other side." The only "help" our side is giving is what helps the other side to make a policy shift that improves our side's national security. Improving our side's national security is the object of the mutual security approach (which accomplishes it in the act of improving the other side's national security also.)

The importance of sequences should not be overdrawn. In some situations, the two sides may be able to undertake a process of simultaneous actions, each side meeting the other's enabling conditions *as*, rather than after, the other meets its own. Of course each would need to verify carefully the other's performance.

Joint actions in sequence or parallel actions, by which each side meets the other's enabling conditions, are difficult and "advanced" policies to carry off. Achieving them will surely require the kind of joint analysis and discussion advocated earlier.

Interactive change over time

One final point needs to be made about the true range of possibilities in interactive systems. Over a *short* sequence of actions, it may be necessary and possible to analyze potential steps in terms of their enabling conditions. However, over an unfolding *long* sequence, it is not possible to do this. It is too difficult to visualize what later steps may make feasible still later.

This impossibility can lead to a significant practical error. There is a human tendency to assume that whatever we cannot presently visualize must be improbable. In a relatively static situation, this will generally be true. What we can visualize *will* resemble what is actually possible. But in a highly dynamic situation this may not be true. (The dramatic events of late 1989 in Europe provide an excellent example.)

An interactive sequence can be highly dynamic and can open wholly new possibilities later in the sequence. The practical error is to fail to recognize this, and assume wrongly that what we currently visualize includes all the realistic possibilities.

A dynamic, interactive sequence may be compared to driving around a bend in the road. It is simply not possible to see around the bend, until one is already much of the way around it.

The conclusion for policymakers is simple. In interactive systems undergoing change, it is unwise to believe that we or anyone can make estimates about the limits of future possibilities with any confidence. Hence it is unwise to make today's decisions on the basis of such limited estimates. The wiser approach is to recognize that the scope of the future possibilities is an unknown.

Concluding Remarks

This chapter has presented a theory of mutual security that rests upon perceiving a bilateral relationship as a single interactive system. The perspective is one that constantly focuses upon perceiving the two sides and their relationship as one whole, not as two independent entities who occasionally act on each other.

The argument has suggested that under some conditions, which are definable, each of the two sides may be able to best achieve its national security by seeking mutual security. That is, under these conditions each can achieve a higher degree of national security for itself if the two sides design and construct their situation mutually, than if each side strives to achieve national security unilaterally.

The chapter then attempts to develop ideas and theory to help understand situations of this character. Except to show how it is possible for two sides to find their security intertwined, the paper uses the East-West situation illustratively, to develop and illuminate concepts. The significance of the ideas does not appear to be limited to the East-West situation.

The mutual approach to national security differs from the unilateral approach in various ways. One critical one not yet mentioned is that the mutual approach requires the policy participation of both sides. It is impossible for one side to conduct a national security policy of mutual security (however sincerely it may wish to) if the other side is conducting a unilateral security policy. Thus each side can "compel" the other to follow a unilateral security policy by doing so itself.

A further theme, alluded to earlier, deserves emphasis by way of conclusion. The theory and practice of mutual security will always depend crucially upon each side adopting *national security* as a central goal in the bilateral relationship.

A nation may have other goals for its political-military policies besides national security. Nations build up their military forces and other forms of national power for various reasons, of which security is only one. For instance a nation may seek an image of strength and power in the world; seek particularly an image of being superior to its main opponent; seek influence in world or regional affairs based on military power; seek to intimidate its opponent; or seek a sense of national pride or feelings of internal cohesion based on symbols of power. (Or, of course, a nation may seek direct expansionist or exploitative goals vis-a-vis others via direct aggressive action.)

These goals involving power are not the same as the goal of national security. Of course, political leaders may often *present* their policies as being policies for "national security," when actually their policies are aimed, partially or largely, toward other goals such as these.[68]

The theory offered in this paper is dependent upon national security being clearly separated, at least conceptually, from other goals. And the more that national security is the chief goal of policy in fact, the more this theory becomes relevant to policy — within, of course, an interactive system. To the extent that national security is the goal in such a system, mutual security will be the indicated path to attaining national security (certain conditions, discussed earlier, being also met). To the extent that other goals involving power are also being sought, a mutual security approach will be constrained, and at the extreme nullified, since usually the other partner in the system will not share those other power goals.

In sum: national security, within an interactive relationship, may well be found most completely when it is found in the form of mutual security. And achieving adequate mutual security, in that relationship, requires that each side give its chief emphasis not to other goals for power but to national security.

Notes

1. This chapter is an abridged and simplified version of a longer publication with the same title. That longer version is being published by the Center for Foreign Policy Development at Brown University, as part of its series of research papers. This shorter version differs chiefly in that some of the abstract theoretical material in the longer version has been removed.

   In both versions, this paper has benefitted greatly from meetings of the Principles and Criteria Working Group of the Mutual Security Project, from other discussions at various seminars and group meetings, from many individual discussions, and from written comments on earlier drafts. The individuals involved are too many to thank all by name, but I would be remiss not to mention exceptionally valuable discussions with Mark Sommer and William Ury. An earlier draft of the paper also received especially useful commentaries from

Alexander George and Steven Kull. I am indebted to Jacqueline Berman and Gareth Cook for research assistance.

2. Independent Commission on Disarmament and Security Issues (the Palme Commission), *Common Security: A Blueprint for Survival* (New York: Simon and Schuster, 1982).

3. See Gorbachev's report at the 27th Congress of the CPSU, *Pravda* (February 26, 1986), translated in Foreign Broadcast Information Service, *Daily Report: Soviet Union* (February 26, 1986), especially p. O29: "The highest wisdom is not in only worrying about oneself or, even more, about damaging the other side; it is necessary for all to feel they are equally secure."

   See also his February 1986 interview with *L'Humanite*, a publication of the French Communist Party, in which he stated that there can be "no security for the USSR without security for the United States....Without their mutual security, there can be no universal security." Reprinted in *Pravda* (February 8, 1986), and quoted by Robert Legvold, "War, Weapons, and Soviet Foreign Policy," in Seweryn Bialer and Michael Mandelbaum, eds., *Gorbachev's Russia and American Foreign Policy* (London: Westview Press, 1988), p. 103.

   Since 1986, there have been numerous references to this principle. See, for example, "Gorbachev replies to journalist on U.S. ties," in *Pravda* (January 1, 1987), translated in Foreign Broadcast Information Service, *Daily Report: Soviet Union* (January 2, 1987), pp. A2 - A4, especially p. A3: "Our age...rules out the security of one to the detriment or at the expense of the security of the other."

   In 1989, the decree of the USSR Congress of People's Deputies, *On the Basic Directions of the Internal and Foreign Policy of the USSR*, states: "One cannot count upon strengthening one's own security while neglecting the interests of others."

4. The literal translation of the former phrase is "global security."

5. The Palme Commission, *Common Security*, p. 12.

6. In spite of its length this paper cannot, and does not claim to, exhaust all important aspects of mutual security theory. The concept of mutual security is a rich and fecund one.

   The theoretical viewpoint developed here is drawn loosely from General Systems Theory; and the core of this paper's perspective is the idea that some bilateral relationships, such as today's East-West relationship, can productively be viewed as one system, not two. Useful introductions to General Systems Theory can be found in C. West Churchman, *The Systems Approach* (New York: Dell Books, 1968); F. E. Emery, *Systems Thinking* (Harmondsworth, U. K.: Penguin Books, 1969); and Ervin Laszlo, *The Systems View of the World* (New York: George Braziller, 1972).

7. Technically the final phrase is unnecessary, as the *most* general meaning of mutual security could include efforts to further improve the security of two sides who already are rather highly secure vis-a-vis each other — the U.S. and Western Europe for instance. Security is a matter of degree. However, few people are likely to use the term in this meaning, primarily because measures that in fact do this are generally not thought of as "security" measures but as measures to further "improve relations," in a situation where relations are already good.

8. It is not necessary to assume that both sides lose in equal degree or that both sides win in equal degree. This statement of the concepts is substantially oversimplified from the viewpoint of game theory, but will suffice for the simple, metaphoric use intended here. For a more elaborate and more accurate use of game theory ideas, in a more rigorous argument, see the longer version of this paper. For a different conceptual approach to the question of repeated play of game-theoretic games, see Robert Axelrod, *The Evolution of Cooperation* (New York: Basic Books, 1984).

9. There is a third logical alternative, which is that action by one side neither improves nor diminishes the other side's security. For simplicity I will not take up this possibility here; it is discussed in the longer version of this paper.

10. If anything, a continuing and interactive relationship might be expected to magnify or amplify the positive result, because as time passes, leaders will recognize the positive outcomes of earlier games and have all the more reason to continue to seek further positive sums. I have included the phrase "in general" merely because it is not necessary to claim that this will occur every single time without exception.

    A scientifically satisfactory demonstration of the proof of this proposition would require extensive empirical research, which to my knowledge has not yet been done. The discussion that follows in the next section also does not advance a scientifically satisfactory demonstration of the second proposition. It merely advances some interesting preliminary evidence. The purpose of this paper is not to attempt scientifically adequate demonstrations. My purpose is merely to advance ideas and arguments for consideration.

11. To pick two examples of many, the U.S. provided foreign aid to Taiwan for many years in the 1950s, in substantial part to help ensure Taiwan's continuing pro-U.S. alignment; and the USSR has provided large amounts of aid to Castro's Cuba for many years, in substantial part to help ensure Cuba's continuing pro-Soviet alignment. While it might be argued that such aid was and is not actually necessary to preserve the small nations' respective alignments, it appears that policymakers in Washington, D.C. and Moscow did not wish to take the gamble, and were and are willing to pay substantial sums not to.

    Robert Axelrod has suggested the phrase "the shadow of the future" to name policymaker's anticipation that interactions will continue in the future; this anticipation has an effect on present interactions. Axelrod, *The Evolution of Cooperation*.

12. For some years now, the general assessment on both sides has been that ever since the mid- to late-1960s, neither the U.S. nor USSR has been able to keep, on net, any significant advantage for long. Of course each side has enjoyed fleeting advantages; for instance the U.S. possessed MIRVs and the USSR did not for several years in the early 1970s. And because the two force structures are constituted somewhat differently, each side has advantages in certain limited respects; these do not change the overall rough balance in capabilities against each other.

    Here I leave aside both the modest technical superiority of Western weapons overall, and the argument over the existence and extent of a meaningful Pact superiority in conventional forces in Europe. Neither changes the fact of rough overall equivalence in a global superpower war against each other. It is not changed either by the much greater U.S. capability for intervention at a distance against other enemies, for instance in the Third World.

13. This chapter is being written prior to any successful agreement in the Conventional Forces in Europe (CFE) negotiations. Such an agreement might modify the perception in the West of a Warsaw Pact advantage in the European balance. Whether a changed perception would result in NATO ending its policy of maintaining a nuclear first-use option is another question.

14. This fifth reason is not merely a by-product of the fourth because there are possible ways nuclear war could occur other than as a result of an arms race destabilization or a regional crisis — via certain kinds of technical or computer accidents, perhaps. Arguably we may not know all the ways a nuclear war could begin.

    This fifth reason might apply to other "mutual insecurity systems" in other times or places, where there was a possibility of catastrophic destruction to both sides resulting from a war between them.

15. This discussion is not a logical exercise. One of the most common criticisms leveled at mutual security proposals is that they might yield cost savings, but that they would generate hidden risks to security.

16. The possibility of one side gaining *and keeping* an important advantage in the technological game (arms race) cannot logically be excluded either, although this is improbable if the two sides are roughly evenly matched in their scientific and engineering *potential.*

    The second proposition also makes the assumption that one side cannot simply end the entire series of games, with victory. Neither side can find some move, however drastic, that enables it to win completely. This is really the extreme form of the same basic assumption that direct gains do not outweigh long-term costs.

17. To put it formally, the argument rests on the assumption that the system interaction costs and risks outweigh, for each party, the accumulating direct benefits of play minus the accumulating direct costs. Because each side wins some and loses some of the games, the direct benefits of play do not add up to a gain over time for either, large enough to outweigh the interaction costs and risks.

18. It may be felt that the other side is prepared to take risks to security, to achieve its goal of victory; or that it sees victory as the chief means of obtaining security; or some mixture of these. The former view sees security and victory as competitive goals and assigns victory the higher priority. The latter view sees them as non-competitive goals, where security is secondary in the sense that it is derivative from the direct goal, victory.

19. A small role might remain for policies to achieve a limited degree of mutual security, even if one or both sides' chief goal is victory, under certain conditions. If victory is thought to be well in the future, and meanwhile the two sides share certain common risks to the security of both, a limited kind of mutual security policy might be relevant for both. See, again, Section III.

20. It should be obvious that this latter viewpoint is not disloyal or unpatriotic. People holding this viewpoint (which, as I see it, leads to the mutual security viewpoint) do so because their understanding of the situation, *viewed in its entirety,* leads them to the conclusion that this approach is the best way (perhaps the only way) of achieving security for *their own* country under the existing circumstances.

    It should also be pointed out that people, even experienced specialists, may not be fully conscious of all the ways they are visualizing the situations they study.

21. Actions taken unilaterally by one side may be taken with, or conceivably without, the other side's awareness and approval. However the other side will presumably become aware of it at some point thereafter, and if mutual security has been enhanced, that side is unlikely to disapprove.

    It is analytically important to be clear that unilateral *action* by one side acting alone does not necessarily mean that that side is aiming only for *unilateral security.* There are examples even during the Cold War decades where East and West took all three kinds of actions. Example are mentioned in the longer version of this paper.

22. Notice that the need for elaborate policies for unilateral verification vanishes as two nations, such as the United States and Canada, develop very high levels of mutual security.

23. For example the January 1989 issue of the newsletter of Planetary Citizens (a public interest group) proclaims "the concept of global security...and the disappearance of 'national security'..." (Quotation marks in original.)

24. These remarks apply to parallel, separate measures and to joint measures, but not necessarily to isolated, unilateral steps.

25. This process of each side shifting perceptions and expectations strongly resembles the shifts in perceptions and expectations that occur during sequences of escalation (or de-escalation)

in warfare. The dynamics are both pragmatic and psychological. For instance, successful attainment of intermediate goals is also part of the process. I examine such dynamics in the context of escalation in my book *War: Controlling Escalation* (Cambridge, MA: Harvard University Press, 1977). See also Robert Jervis, *Perception and Misperception in International Politics* (Princeton: Princeton University Press, 1976).

In the context of mutual security there is a distinct possibility that these shifts in perception and expectation may be purely subjective and in fact delusory; and some mutual security efforts may provide opportunities for one side to deceive the other. A careful analysis of any particular effort for mutual security would not overlook this possibility.

26. A "condominium" refers to a situation where two or more parties cooperate to jointly dominate an entire region or the world.

27. A longer treatment of this relationship appears in the longer version of this paper, referred to earlier.

Pioneering statements of the security dilemma appear in John Herz's article, "Idealist Internationalism and the Security Dilemma" *World Politics* 2 (January 1950), pp. 157-180, and his book *Political Realism and Political Idealism* (Chicago: Chicago University Press, 1951). For another especially useful treatment see Robert Jervis "Cooperation Under the Security Dilemma," *World Politics* 30 (January 1978), pp. 167-214.

28. I do not regard this as merely an abstract or idealistic possibility. This is, for instance, precisely the relationship between the United States and Canada, neighboring nations who in fact do not face any security dilemma between them. In some situations, the development of mutual security may be able, over the short term, only to minimize, not completely forestall, any security dilemma.

29. This paragraph and the preceding one have slightly simplified an argument made in less simple form in the longer version of this paper.

30. As in the first Section, I do not assert that the ideas that follow are true of all instances because to do so would require the examination of all instances. There is a *prima facie* case that the significance of what follows is not confined to this one example of the East-West relationship, but I shall not attempt to demonstrate further applicability.

31. See Graham T. Allison, Albert Carnesdale, and Joseph S. Nye, Jr., eds., *Hawks, Doves, and Owls: An Agenda for Avoiding Nuclear War* (New York: W. W. Norton and Company, 1985).

32. The label is not meant to be prejudicial. Supporters of this viewpoint might call this one the "realistic" one and might prefer that label. But that label would be prejudicial, since of course advocates of each of the other two viewpoints also see theirs as the realistic one.

The technical conception receives a lengthier treatment in the longer version of this paper.

33. Sophisticated advocates of this conception of mutual security are well aware that drastic, too-sudden change in the international system might be destabilizing, even dangerous. See, for example, Richard Garwin, "A Blueprint for Radical Weapons Cuts," *Bulletin of the Atomic Scientists* (March 1988), pp. 10-13.

34. I do not mean to imply that these groups are in mutual conflict. Generally speaking those who choose one focus are also hopeful about others, although naturally individual analysts may disagree on some points about feasibility, scope, timing, etc.

The threat-reduction conception requires that each side accept that the other has genuine and legitimate fears about threats. In the past it sometimes has been difficult for some Westerners to accept that the USSR perceives real threats from the West; and sometimes difficult for some Soviets to accept that the West perceives real threats from the Soviet bloc.

35. I remarked above that the three conceptions being developed here are not rigidly exclusive categories. There is a "gray area" at each border. For instance, in addressing regional

problems there is a gray area between the first and second conceptions. As "technical" adjustments accumulate in a particular region, they could gradually add up to a more basic change in the East-West competition in that region.

Even so I believe there tends to be a distinction between those who believe that continuing East-West competition in and for the Third World is inevitable and can only be "managed," and those who believe that, over time, it can be significantly reduced (by intention and design, not as accidental by-products of something else).

36. This way of formulating the idea of an "end point" for the nuclear arms race ("deployed weapons") takes account of the likelihood that, at least for some time, laboratory research on potential new weapons would continue. I shall return in Section IV to the thorny questions around whether, over some significant time-span into the future, nuclear deterrence will continue to be needed at all, and whether complete abolition of nuclear weapons might then be safely feasible.

   For a discussion of the abolition of nuclear deterrence, and a stable endpoint, see E. Agayev, "Towards a new model of strategic stability," *International Affairs*, no. 3 (1989), p. 96.

37. A number of terms have been used to name postures that emphasize defense over offense, most commonly "non-offensive defense" or "non-provocative defense" in the West, and "defensive sufficiency" in the East. Another term is "defensive deterrence." The term "qualitative disarmament" has also been used to refer to the phased, negotiated, multilateral shift of national arsenals from offensive to defensive. These ideas came to prominence in the West in the so-called "alternative defense" literature.

   The alternative defense literature in the West (and in neutral nations of Europe) is quite extensive. See B. Moller, *Bibliography of Non-Offensive Defense* (Copenhagen: Centre for Peace and Conflict Research, undated). For the most current work, see B. Moller, ed., *Non-Offensive Defense Journal*, published at the same address; or *Defense and Disarmament Alternatives* (Brookline, MA: Institute for Defense and Disarmament Studies). See also Robert Neild, "Non-Offensive Defense: The Way to Achieve Common Security in Europe," Background Paper #25 (Ottawa: Canadian Institute for International Peace and Security, January 1989). Finally, see the September 1988 *Bulletin of the Atomic Scientists* for a special issue devoted to non-offensive defense.

38. A mutual scaling-back of the competition does not necessarily require explicit superpower agreements. It could be accomplished tacitly, by parallel separate action.

   A relatively modest set of "rules of the game" can well be part of the first, technical conception of mutual security. As noted above, this is a gray area between the two conceptions.

   In this context "mutual superpower disengagement" refers, of course, to their political-military behavior and specifically the portion of that behavior which is part of their present and past struggle for global advantage vis-a-vis each other. "Disengagement" here does not refer to either American or Soviet involvements around the world of other kinds, such as in trade, humanitarian aid, or environmental concerns.

   Those holding the threat-reduction viewpoint may also be interested in reducing, on a mutual basis, the threats embedded in both sides' naval deployments, weapons and strategies; and the threats embedded in both sides existing and prospective space weapons and space capabilities.

39. The idea of reciprocal steps to reduce threats is not, of course, new. One version of it is the well-known concept of "GRIT" — Graduated (Reciprocal) Reduction in Tensions, introduced by Charles Osgood in *An Alternative to War or Surrender* (Urbana, IL: University of Illinois Press, 1962). Writing at that time, Osgood emphasized a sequence of unilateral steps back and forth, rather than, say, mutually planned steps taken in parallel or jointly. As this

illustrates, there are a number of possible strategies within the larger approach of mutual threat reduction.

40. The word "supportive" is not as exact a term as I would like for the concept that one side may take action, out of its own *security* interests, to forestall dangers to the other side that originate outside the bilateral relationship. Unfortunately the English language does not seem to offer another word that names this more exactly. (The words "cooperative" and "interdependent" will not serve, because the other two conceptions of mutual security also involve forms of cooperation and interdependence.)

    Observe that this conception of mutual security is not the same as the idea, discussed in Section II, that the two sides may both face a "third party threat." Here, one side has a responsibility for the security of the other even if the first does not face the same threat itself at all.

41. The *perceptions* held on one side about the current trends on the other as precursors to future dangerous regimes are not always the perceptions that observers on the other side would expect or find reasonable. For instance, in the early 1980s many in the USSR perceived a possibility that the rise of the New Right in America and its election of Ronald Reagan as President represented a trend that, carried far enough, could eventuate in a quasi-fascistic government and society in America — something dangerous to the USSR. This perception may seem bizarre to most Americans, but that does not change the fact that the perception was widely held in the USSR. For numerous examples of how nations may misperceive each other, sometimes severely and sometimes in momentous ways, see, for instance, Robert Jervis, *Perception and Misperception.*

42. The Soviet motive would be to improve mutual security (and Soviet security) by helping to forestall the emergence of governments in the West that might prove threatening. In 1990 it is still worth noting that this is an un-Marxist idea. I believe the Marxist viewpoint would say that any Western economic malaise is the inevitable result of the internal contradictions of capitalism. Hence the USSR should, at the least, stand aside and let historical inevitability run its course. As this example shows, there may be a serious conflict between Marxism and the supportive conception of mutual security.

43. It is possible to advocate a moderate degree of citizen and scientific exchanges also on the basis of the second, threat-reduction, conception, if such actions are seen as symbolic or demonstrative of each side's intent to reduce its overall perceived threat to the other. This is another gray area at the borders between these conceptions.

    Supporters of the third conception being developed here should logically be expected to advocate extensive and uninhibited exchange of television, magazines, newspapers and other media, and uninhibited travel both ways for all, for the same reasons (to be discussed in a moment) as they advocate citizen and scientific exchanges.

44. The declaration, which I believe is representative of this viewpoint, is "A Call to Action: Common Security and our Common Future," (Cambridge, MA: Institute for Peace and International Security, 1989). Representative addresses by Soviet leaders are addresses by President Gorbachev at the 43d Session of the United Nations General Assembly on December 7, 1988 and by Foreign Minister Shevardnadze to the 41st Session of the United Nations General Assembly, September 23, 1986.

    Implementation of these ideas about global security would, of course, require the development of a somewhat different international system from the present one.

45. The English language does not offer a single word for the useful idea that even if policies succeed in reaching one goal, they may do so at the cost of being too counterproductive for other major goals. The best one can say is that policies should be non-counterproductive.

Supporters of the other two conceptions of mutual security might also agree in the abstract that "threats of extraneous origin" might arise, but assess them as less worrisome than supporters of the third conception do. For instance, supporters of the other two might argue that recent centuries have witnessed a number of "strong," even military-dominated or internally tyrannical, regimes that were not aggressively inclined in external affairs and posed little threat to their neighbors.

46. Some who say that the two sides have become "interdependent" may believe that the interactions are so numerous and of so many kinds that it has become pointless to try to dissect and identify them all. At that point the "interdependence" comes to be regarded as a primary, irreducible reality in its own right.

47. A Soviet analyst has suggested a useful three-way distinction among kinds of interdependence. There is the kind that has been unwittingly created by the two sides over forty years as a result of their decisions regarding weapons and their global competition. There is a kind, such as global warming and some other ecological matters, that result from advancing technology and industrialization. And there is or could be a kind that results from deliberate choices by the two sides to interweave themselves more closely. I am indebted to Alexander George (personal communication) for this report of a Soviet analyst's distinction.

48. A similar viewpoint might apply to Soviet or East European participation in global economic institutions such as the General Agreement on Tariffs and Trade (GATT): that participation should evolve naturally, as determined by economic factors.

49. A common Western viewpoint today, for instance, is this: The USSR and Eastern bloc are presently finding themselves forced, by economic failure, to evolve toward freedom and democracy. Too much economic support could unintentionally hinder their evolution, by "taking the internal pressures off" and thus reducing incentives that would otherwise lead toward further change. In this way it could be argued that implementing the "supportive" conception of mutual security, especially if carried very far, would be counterproductive for other central Western values.

This is one example of a competition among values where mutual security is a chief value but not the only central value. Other such competitions could arise under various circumstances. Notice that the existence of values competing with security is not a problem in the context of mutual security only; the same competition often arises in the context of unilateral security as well.

50. See, for instance, Allison, Carnesdale, and Nye, eds., *Hawks, Doves, and Owls.*

51. I must confine this statement to "military" deterrence since deterrence is so broad an idea that some forms of it can arise in even the friendliest relations.

Many advocates of the supportive conception might agree that parts, at least, of the threat-reduction approach are desirable as aspects of the path toward achieving full mutual security, and as we see that approach may include some deterrence at least for a while.

52. Thus there is an important paradox (but not a contradiction) within the threat-reduction conception. Certain threats may need to be deliberately *maintained*, at least at a minimum level and at least for a while, because the system as a whole would be less secure and less stable without them.

The most fundamental interaction between the two sides, as discussed at the outset of this paper, is the fact that they have interconnected their security: the two men in a boat cannot rock just one end of the boat. But from the threat-reduction viewpoint this truth depends upon the continuation of the basic nuclear threat between the two sides. Without that, the security of the two sides would not be so interconnected in the first place. Paradoxically, then, it is the existence of one or more basic mutual threats that "creates the system" (although those threats can be reduced to a certain minimum level.)

The supportive conception of mutual security dissolves this paradox, by proposing the development of many other interconnections and interdependencies. Once the two sides have become highly interdependent in other ways, they can afford to abolish the original interconnection of the basic mutual threat.

53. In addition, it is uncertain, to say the least, that the resulting world would be more stable and secure than today's world, unless other far-reaching steps were taken in accompaniment.

54. It is important to bear in mind that numerical cuts in armaments can actually leave each side feeling more threatened. If, for example, numerical cuts reduce both sides "defensive" weapons more than "offensive" weapons, then both sides will be better equipped to attack than to defend, leaving both sides feeling more threatened.

55. From the threat-reduction viewpoint this recommendation is all but axiomatic. It is not axiomatic that the process must proceed in stages over time, but I believe this is desirable because of the complexity of the problems, the very high stakes involved, and especially the possibility of unanticipated consequences.

56. I specify "strategic" weapons here and in what follows, only to avoid raising in this theoretical paper the complicated issues surrounding "no first use" in Europe and at sea. Similarly, for purposes of this paper it is not necessary to describe all the measures that must accompany the strategic posture I am about to mention, such as highly secure second-strike weapons and highly secure C^3I.

57. "Non-specialists" in this context may include such people as members of Congress and members of the Supreme Soviet. Such people are not usually trained in the arcana of nuclear terminology.

For two recent treatments of Minimum Deterrence, see Garwin, "A Blueprint for Radical Weapons Cuts," pp. 10-17, and Committee of the Soviet Scientists for Peace, Against the Nuclear Threat, *Strategic Stability Under Conditions of Radical Arms Reductions* (Moscow, 1987).

58. The task of defining, in concrete terms, a Fundamental Deterrence posture is a complicated and highly specialized task. For a more extensive discussion of Fundamental Deterrence, I refer the reader to the chapter in this book entitled "Fundamental Deterrence and Mutual Security Beyond START."

Other goals for a strategic nuclear arsenal might detract unintentionally from accomplishing the fundamental one, but detract nonetheless. For instance, it is difficult in an interactive system like the East-West one for either side to seek options for "prevailing" in a strategic nuclear conflict, without the other side feeling that its capacity is being threatened to deter rational use under *all* contingencies. Yet to deter rational use under all contingencies is just what each side must strive, above all, to maintain.

It must be noted that one of the most threatening aspects of the strategic arsenals, for each side, is the quantitative and qualitative additions and improvements to them that might be made in the future by the other side. Hence a comprehensive approach to mutual threat reduction, at the strategic level, must sooner or later seek to find a stable "endpoint" for the arms race.

The term "Fundamental Deterrence" was originally coined by Dr. Dan Caldwell, formerly an associate director of the Center for Foreign Policy Development.

59. For cautionary notes on mutual security from the Western viewpoint see, for instance, Bill Bradley, "Gorbachev's Stake in the West," in Bill Bradley et al, eds., *Implications of Soviet New Thinking* (New York: Institute for East-West Security Studies, 1987), or William Safire, "Break up the Russkies," *The New York Times* (March 27, 1989). For a still more concerned note, see, for example, Joseph Churba, *Soviet Breakout* (Washington, D.C.: Pergamon-Brassey's, 1988).

60. Examples may be found at many points in this book. This approach to a "combined threat assessment" and mutual agreement on calculated threat reduction measures requires each side to identify and present the threats it fears in a sober spirit. The method cannot employ exaggerated "threats" which take an extreme, alarmist view of the other side's behavior. However this is not a drawback for the mutual security approach, because the same is also true in analyses that take a unilateral security approach. A well-calculated strategy for unilateral security also must not employ exaggerated, alarmist threat perceptions, as good strategists have known for centuries.

61. If we say that "doves" are inclined to dismiss the fears of the skeptics as beneath serious attention, and that "hawks" are inclined to use those fears as a reason to criticize and dismiss the mutual security approach, then the mutual security approach (as conceived here) is itself neither dovish nor hawkish.

    The ideas about mutual security in this subsection and the remainder of this chapter have theoretical significance beyond their immediate relevance to today's East-West situation.

62. An interactive process of mutual demonstration/mutual confirmation is an idea appropriate to mutual security thinking. Conversely, a *failure* by one side to provide demonstrations of its commitment to mutual threat reduction would soon become important evidence that that side is not serious about mutual security. If one side's talk about mutual security were, in fact, merely rhetorical and for purposes of propaganda, this failure in action might be evidence of it. However caution should be observed in drawing this conclusion from just one or two instances, since domestic constraints on the other side may be an alternative explanation for a failure in action. One side's serious "misbehavior," as the other side sees it, in some area outside the bilateral relationship could also undermine confidence. There are many ways in which mutual confidence can be built up and many ways in which it can be undermined. The technique suggested here is only one way to increase it.

63. Advocacy of this kind of informal, joint research and development of policy possibilities is far from original with me. Academician Georgiy Arbatov has advocated essentially this, for example in *Pravda* (October 17, 1988). Harold Saunders, a well-known Western specialist on negotiation and a co-author of another paper in this book, has written along similar lines. See for instance his papers "We Need a Larger Theory of Negotiation," *Negotiation Journal* 1, no. 3 (1985), pp. 249-262, and "International Relationships — It's Time to Go Beyond 'We and They'" in *Negotiation Journal* 3, no. 2 (1987), pp. 245-274. The basic viewpoint that I suggest here goes back at least as far as Roger Fisher and William Ury's book, *Getting to Yes* (Boston: Houghton Mifflin Co., 1981).

    It is essential for the joint research and development I propose that specialists from the two sides be able to work together without appearing, in any way, to be taking or stating positions concerning what their governments may actually decide. But it is also essential that they not be so completely disconnected from their governments that their work is merely "academic" and can be too readily ignored by their governments. Real movement toward mutual security requires that the governments be committed to the joint process, without becoming committed, prior to negotiations, to any one policy choice.

64. Here and in the next nine paragraphs I contrast, for logical simplicity, mutual and unilateral security as if pure cases of each were the only two alternatives. Nearly all real problems permit a spectrum of possible policy approaches, most of which will be mixtures of more or less mutual security with less or more unilateral security. Nonetheless, many actual policy issues may come down to a debate between those who seek a policy employing more mutual security and those seeking more unilateral security, in the policy mix to be adopted for that problem.

65. Here I leave aside either's *political* estimate of the likelihood of such a later policy switch by the other. This example presumes that at least one side regards the danger as a real one.

    Significant assumptions are made in this paragraph which a thorough analysis would need to investigate. One is that NATO and the Warsaw Pact have successfully negotiated and implemented an agreement, in the time up to year Y, that yields defensively oriented, mutual security postures, and without creating dangerous instabilities or imbalances along the way.

66. At the time of this writing, this fear about "trust" is most often heard in the West, specifically regarding the fear that the Gorbachev regime in Moscow might be replaced at some point by a reactionary new regime that would reverse present Soviet policies, including mutual security. Some Westerners hold the additional concern that Western publics, having once lost their fear of the Soviets, would not then support the necessary restrengthening of Western power. But this concern makes unwarranted assumptions about the inability of the general public to distinguish, for instance, between offensive and defensive postures.

    Indeed, many mutual security arrangements have the important feature that any later policy reversal by the other side *would* be publicly "visible." By contrast, policy changes of modest size by the other side, within an overall, ongoing context of unilateral security approaches and offensive postures on both sides, are relatively *in*visible to the general public.

67. There is nothing new about this idea. Many competent diplomats, policymakers, policy analysts and others have been long familiar with this way of thinking about a problem. Many professional intelligence analysts, too, have long been aware of the need to identify the conditions under which their estimates of the opponent would need to be changed (sometimes called "preconditional analysis"). Even so, it is common to find evaluations of national security policy options which do not assess the ways that significant — but perfectly possible — changes in conditions would lead to a different conclusion.

    The concept of planning for development in an interactive system, as I discuss it here, is closely related to "design theory," as advanced by Herbert Simon in *The Sciences of the Artificial*, 2d ed. (Cambridge, MA: M.I.T. Press, 1981).

68. Under some conditions, some of these goals may be perceived or misperceived by leaders as contributing indirectly to security. Seeking other power goals on the grounds that they will lead indirectly to enhanced security may raise numerous analytical complications. These complications do not pose difficulties for analyses premised on mutual security alone; they also pose difficulties for analyses premised on a unilateral view of security.

Part II

Working Group on Europe

THE WORKING GROUP ON EUROPE was responsible for exploring the applicability of the mutual security approach to the improvement of American and Soviet security in Central Europe, along with that of their allies. Chief emphasis was placed on political rather than military matters, since European arms reductions were a topic for the Nuclear and Conventional Arms Reductions working group.

The Working Group on Europe has contributed six papers to this book. A Joint Statement, which appears first, is provided by the group as a whole. Williams Luers describes the key issues that emerged as the U.S.-Soviet dialogue on Eastern Europe evolved. Yuriy Davydov provides a perspective on the revolutionary changes in Eastern Europe and Soviet policies in the evolving situation. Mark Kramer discusses Western policies for dealing with Eastern Europe. Mikhail Bezrukov and Yuriy Davydov discuss the concept of the "common European home." Finally, Francis Meehan and Mikhail Kozhokin each offer a perspective on the future of Germany. Biographical sketches of these authors, and a list of the full membership of the Working Group on Europe, are given at the back of the book.

— THE EDITORS

6

Joint Statement

THE WORKING GROUP ON EUROPE

This working group has considered political steps that would help prevent an East-West confrontation over Central Europe. More specifically, as agreed in guidelines adopted at the Moscow conference in July 1988, the Working Group was responsible for "considering what means are available to assure that countries in the region can change in accordance with changing circumstances and their own peoples' desires without destabilizing crises and without outside intervention." Such steps were deemed, from the outset, to be a necessary complement to measures that the Working Group on Nuclear and Conventional Arms Reduction might recommend for Central Europe.

The efforts of both Working Groups derive from the general principle of mutual security, namely, that in the nuclear age the security of each side is closely connected to the security of the other. To apply this principle to concrete problems, the Working Group on Europe explored ways to support political change that will forestall internal crises which could have destabilizing international repercussions.

The case of Central Europe is especially important from the mutual security standpoint because it is the one region where several hundred thousand U.S. and Soviet forces have confronted one another since 1945, placing the security of both countries (and of many others) at risk. Moreover, even if the military stand-off had not been so intense, the whole question of Central Europe would be crucial to U.S. and Soviet security because it is the region where the Cold War started and where it has been fueled by recurrent crises. Historians in the United States have long debated whether the Cold War could have been avoided; a similar debate has recently begun in the Soviet Union as well (though it is still at an early stage). As these reassessments continue, we may eventually have a clearer understanding of what mistakes, on either side, were made and what actions, if any, could have reduced the scale of the confrontation.

In the meantime, and wherever the real "blame" may lie, policymakers on both sides have to grapple with the consequences: large and powerful armed forces, equipped with nuclear weapons, face each other; and the possibility of a destabilizing crisis in one or another country, stemming from national aspirations and economic conditions, hangs over the security of Europe. A future crisis that has serious international repercussions would also impede Soviet and U.S. efforts to resolve other security issues, and it would undermine any prospect for movement toward what Soviet participants refer to as a "common European home."

Thus, the Cold War has come full circle: if it is to be laid to rest, Europe must be its burial ground. The process of interment, however, will not be easy. The past four-and-a-half decades have witnessed the encrustation, in both East and West, of slogans that did not quickly lose their grip. For example, in the United States charges of "Yalta," stemming from a sense that the wartime agreement enabled Stalin to take advantage of the United States and to impose his control over the small countries of East-Central Europe, initially stood in the way of any discussion with the Soviet Union about those countries. Likewise, in the Soviet Union, the "defense of socialist gains" within the Warsaw Pact is a slogan sometimes used by those opposed to positive changes in the socialist countries.

Despite these inherent difficulties, events in the late 1980s have shown that Soviet and American leaders have increasingly recognized the importance of encouraging far-reaching political change in Central Europe to reduce the pressures that could give rise to violent internal crises. Remarkable progress has already been made, and at a much faster rate than anyone could have anticipated. Continued change of this sort, in a highly-charged international environment, will of course demand time and statesmanship. All parties should strive to ensure that subsequent steps will not increase the likelihood of destabilizing crises or endanger the security of either side. Such change, nonetheless, must come, for without it there will be a continued risk of future crises, with all the dangers they would entail.

Thus, during the next few decades at least, the mutual and overlapping security interests of the United States and Soviet Union will require active political and economic steps that will mitigate the risk of internal crises, by supporting the changes that any country in the region wants and needs to avert violence and dangerous unrest. Mutual security will also mean no sudden "reversal of alliances" nor active efforts to undermine each other's alliances. It is, in short, in the interests of both the United States and the Soviet Union to support a peaceful evolution in Europe: sweeping democratic reorganization where needed; broader, non-exclusionary economic and political connections among European countries —

and between those countries and the United States and USSR — as these become possible and mutually desired.

In each case, extensive consultations will be indispensable: consultations between the United States and the Soviet Union, consultations by each superpower with its own European allies and by each with the other's allies, and consultations among East and West Europeans themselves. Eventually, it may be useful to explore potential mechanisms, under the rubric of the CSCE or elsewhere, to help ensure that any crises that do arise will not provoke a military response from outside the country in question.

The cardinal principle guiding any such consultations is that all states in Europe, no matter how small, must have freedom of social, political, and economic choice, with genuine control over their own internal affairs, free of outside interference. A continued transition to a more stable political order in Europe must be allowed to proceed peacefully, without detriment to either side's security. As the process of political change unfolds, economic contacts and trade should burgeon, reinforcing the ongoing political evolution.

The future relationship between the two German states has emerged as a particularly important issue. It deeply touches the interests and emotions of the Germans themselves, and at the same time is seen by other peoples in and connected to Europe as affecting their own security — and not only in a narrow meaning of the word. The mutual security of all concerned requires on the one hand that other countries do not attempt to dictate to the Germans how they relate to each other, for to do so could sow the seeds of a future disaster. On the other hand, mutual security requires that any changes in the relationship between the two Germanies take place within a broad European process that takes full account of the security needs of all concerned.

By no means will it be easy for the Soviet Union and United States to encourage a continued peaceful transition in Central Europe, but no step will be of greater tangible benefit to the mutual security of the two sides and to the security of all of Europe.

7

A Soviet-American Dialogue on Eastern Europe

WILLIAM LUERS

The changes that took place in Eastern Europe in 1989 make possible a new era for Europe, but the full unfolding of that promise still lies ahead. For all parties involved to receive the greatest benefit, including the greatest mutual security, requires much thought and much care.

Foreshadowing these events was a series of discussions among U.S. and Soviet specialists about Eastern Europe that took place in 1988 and 1989, preceding and coinciding with the momentous changes in Poland, Hungary, the German Democratic Republic, Czechoslovakia and Bulgaria. Those discussions are worth reviewing because they record ways in which Soviet and American views changed in the heat of events. They also provided a vivid demonstration of the usefulness of addressing difficult issues within the framework of a mutual security approach.[1]

There was some initial uneasiness between Americans and Soviets in discussing these painful and historically burdened issues connected with the birth of the Cold War. But inhibitions soon gave way to frank and realistic exchanges. The shift was due in large part to a shared belief among most of the participants that the process of change in Eastern Europe is one of the most critical East-West issues in the current and coming period, and that candor in talking through the issues is best for all parties.

Common ground

The most important new dimension, as our discussions proceeded in 1988-89, was a growing awareness that the Soviet Union, the U.S. and the countries of Europe have important areas of common cause along the dividing line between the two parts of Europe. One fundamental common interest emerged, sharply illuminated by applying the test of mutual security to Eastern Europe: what is the threat, if any, to the security of the U.S., the USSR and the other countries of the region; and what can be done about it?

As discussions proceeded, participants gradually realized that the answer to the first question was that the threat comes mainly from the possibility that a domestic crisis in one or another country in Eastern Europe would quickly become a security threat to all concerned, if it became internationalized through outside interference. The threat could take the direct form of East-West confrontation, or — more likely — a freeze in East-West relations.

The answer to the second question — what can be done — came initially in the abstract: reforms are needed in Eastern Europe that meet national aspirations and remove the Soviet role as a bone of contention. Under the impact of events inside Eastern Europe and a rapid revision of Moscow's perceptions of its interests, theory quickly was put into practice.

Ambiguities and disagreements

In the course of the discussions, it became clear that disagreements among Soviets and among Americans were sometimes as sharp as those between Americans and Soviets. On some issues, attitudes also changed over time on both sides. For clarity, I shall review these ambiguities and disagreements, and some changes over time, topic by topic.

Eastern Europe as an appropriate topic for U.S.-Soviet discussion

In the summer of 1988, there were differences among Soviets on this matter. Some Soviet academic experts on Eastern Europe already believed it important to engage with Americans on the subject. A paper delivered at the Virginia conference[2] saw two "vitally important" reasons for such a dialogue: one is that the region is "pregnant with crises," which might even be stimulated by the needed reforms; the second is that the stakes are too high in East-West relations to neglect an open-minded review of policy behavior during crises in Eastern Europe.

On the other hand, at that time many Soviet academics who are expert on the United States were doubtful that it was useful or necessary to have a Soviet-American dialogue on Eastern Europe. Some participants in the Europe working group at the 1988 mutual security conference in Moscow argued that there is no danger of crisis in Eastern Europe, and in any case the Soviet Union would not directly interfere in such a crisis, even if one occurred. Nevertheless, when the issue was analyzed as a matter of mutual security, they came to acknowledge that the history of destabilizing crises gave reason for finding ways to assure that countries in Europe can change as their people desire, without outside intervention.[3]

By March 1989, attitudes had further evolved — not only among Soviet academics, but also among responsible Party and government figures, who discussed the subject freely with unofficial Americans and even expressed willingness to talk with American officials as well, under certain circumstances. This may have been partly the result of rapidly moving events in Eastern Europe itself. But it also developed partly because the mutual security framework of the discussions logically called for taking up every issue, however neuralgic, that had a bearing on both sides' security.

Meanwhile, on the American side differences on this issue had sharpened. Henry Kissinger floated his ideas about the need for a new U.S. dialogue over Eastern Europe, which were challenged by others, particularly State Department officials. They argued that official discussion along those lines would be taken as a U.S. affirmation of a Soviet sphere in Eastern Europe ("Yalta II"). Moreover, they believed trends in the region were in the United States' favor with no need for discussion with the Soviets. This dispute eventually subsided, however, and a quiet official dialogue ensued.

Interpreting the past

As noted in the joint introduction to the "Europe" section of this book, there are debates in both countries about the origins of the Cold War and what could have been done to avoid it. The arguments between American revisionist historians and their critics are well known. A new element at the end of the eighties was the critique by Soviet scholars of Soviet mistakes in Eastern Europe.

One analysis[4] pointed to the damage caused by "naive concepts" that there were not, and could not be, conflicts inside and among socialist states. A second major mistake was Soviet domination over the East European communist parties, which led to the crises in Hungary, Czechoslovakia and Poland. Individual Soviet observers came to see the Soviet interventions in 1956 and 1968 as mistakes even at a time when officially those actions were regarded as correct under the circumstances.

Americans generally believe that the root cause of the Cold War was Stalin's distortion of the Yalta accord by preventing free elections in Eastern Europe and imposing puppet regimes. That view leads to the conclusion that those regimes lacked legitimacy. In our discussions, that assertion normally elicited a sharply negative reaction from Soviet participants; when "legitimacy" was put on the agenda, the discussion tended to bog down.

In the Mutual Security Project, however, this impediment did not arise because the focus was on the operational question of how to deal with the common threat rather than abstractions such as "legitimacy." This moved the discussion naturally to the need for governments to meet the aspirations of their peoples. This could also be called "restoring legitimacy," but it was not necessary or useful to insist on Americans' nomenclature.

"Defending socialism"

The risk of unproductive, theological discussion also arose over the term "socialism." This could have been seen as an operational issue because the "international duty to defend the achievements of socialism," or the Brezhnev Doctrine as it is known in the West, raises the question: what is this socialism the USSR is bound to defend? Discussions with responsible Soviet officials, however, made clear that this was another area where actions are more important than abstractions. They steadfastly avoided talking about that particular international duty, preferring to talk about "universal human values" rather than class struggle. They declined to define socialism, saying that that is a matter for each country to decide. And, in the dramatic events of 1989, they stood by while power in East European countries devolved to non-communists.

Avoiding "extremism"

In the Soviet-American discussions, Soviet participants — particularly those with official responsibilities — sometimes pointed to "extremism" in Eastern Europe as a matter of concern, implying without saying so that some forms of "extremism" could lead to a reluctant Soviet decision to intervene. Presumably one thing they had in mind were the violent repressions of communists said to have taken place in Hungary in 1956. Some Soviets were inclined to interpret as "extremism" such things as calling for free elections or a multiparty system, but later events in Eastern Europe discredited such views.

Preserving the Warsaw Pact

Of all the potential causes of Soviet intervention, withdrawal from the Warsaw Pact seemed to evoke the greatest concern on the part of almost all Soviet participants in these discussions, however "liberal" they might be on other issues. Even this concern softened, however, at least in principle. For example Academician Oleg Bogomolov, on a visit to Hungary in 1989 told an interviewer that "even if Hungary was to become a neutral country like Sweden or Austria, that would not threaten the security interests of the Soviet Union."[5]

President Gorbachev himself, visiting Finland in October 1989, in an impromptu response to a question, agreed that neutral Finland was a good model for Soviet relations with East European countries.[6] But more formal Soviet statements made clear that the Soviet Union intended to try to maintain the Warsaw Pact intact for the present, gradually shifting its emphasis from military to political matters as circumstances change, until the need for military alliances in Europe disappears.

This is an issue where further East-West discussion would be appropriate and useful. As Lech Walesa has demonstrated, continued membership in the Warsaw Pact was not seen in 1989 in Eastern Europe as an unacceptable price for achieving democracy. And under the principles of mutual security, the West would not actively try to undermine Soviet security by encouraging East European defections from the Warsaw Pact. Furthermore, a dialogue is in order to assure that further evolution does not precipitately threaten anyone's security.

Constructive ambiguity?

One senior Soviet academic participant in our discussions said candidly that it is in the Soviet interest to remain ambiguous about the tolerable limits for East Europeans, and about the conditions that might provoke Soviet intervention. Later, however, the events of the autumn of 1989 vividly demonstrated in practice that the Politburo was prepared to accept, even welcome, very great internal changes in East European countries. Gorbachev had foreshadowed this attitude in his speech to the Council of Europe in Strasbourg on July 6, 1989, asserting that each people has the right not only to choose their social system but also to change it, and unequivocally rejecting any interference in internal affairs by "friends, allies or anyone else." As one Party official put it in private conversation, only the Politburo can decide in light of the circumstances of a specific crisis. And he confirmed his positive attitude at the joint press conference with President Bush at the Malta summit. Responding to a question about the changes in Eastern Europe that were by then well underway, he said, "The direction of these processes raises my spirits."7

U.S. and Soviet interests

As the participants in our discussions generally agreed, mutual security is a useful framework for Soviet-American discussions of potential crisis areas such as Eastern Europe only if each side believes the other willing to subordinate its other interests to the pursuit of mutual security.

In this connection, a senior Soviet participant in the March 1989 Moscow discussions put a series of questions to the Americans present about the United States' perceptions of its own interests:

— Does the U.S. aim to change the systems of the countries of Eastern Europe?

— Does that include dissolving the Warsaw Pact?

— Does it include downgrading close economic relations between those countries and the Soviet Union?

— Does the U.S. care about Soviet interests in Eastern Europe?

The Americans present answered yes, no, yes and yes to the four questions, with some disagreement on the third question about downgrading economic relations and also with the caveat that other Americans if asked would give different answers to several of the questions. There was agreement that these are indeed questions that Americans have to address if there is to be a meaningful dialogue.

The first question is a crucial one. The mutual security framework makes it possible to answer yes to that question in a way that Soviet listeners do not need to feel as threatening or disturbing. The effect is quite different from the effect when U.S. policy (whether it is called "building bridges" or "differentiation") is understood to be aimed at weaning Eastern Europe away from Moscow for the sake of weakening the USSR or the Warsaw Pact. In the mutual security context, change in Eastern Europe is seen as the best way to remove the threat to *both* Soviet and American security that would be posed by a crisis. If East Europeans are running their own affairs, as advocated by Gorbachev, there is less danger that a domestic crisis in one or another country would lead to anti-Soviet "extremism" that would, in turn, pose for Moscow the question of direct interference.

The question of Soviet interests in Eastern Europe is not easily answered. One *Soviet* academic participant reported, in fact, that he had asked that question in various quarters around Moscow and had gotten no concrete answers. The reason for the lack of clarity may be that Moscow's perception of Soviet interests in Eastern Europe is changing, under the impact of several factors:

— The rapid pace of glasnost, which has radicalized the political discourse about the Soviet role in the world.

— The pace of events in Eastern Europe, which have repeatedly reshaped and radicalized the options and challenges.

— And the relatively benign and constructive reaction of the West to changes in Eastern Europe, which encourages, in turn, a degree of Soviet detachment.

For decades, Western policy was predicated on the assumption that for reasons of military security, prestige and economic benefits, Eastern Europe was so vital to Moscow that control would be maintained at all cost. But under the impact of Gorbachev's reforms, questions began to be raised: What good were these states as a security buffer if the populations were anti-Soviet? Indeed, in the nuclear era, what use was such a buffer anyway? What kind of prestige flows from a region in decay and despair? Had Eastern Europe become an economic burden rather than a boon?

Soviet participants in this project who are closely involved in the Gorbachev reform effort said, not surprisingly, that their highest priority is the success of perestroika and that the Soviet objective in Eastern Europe therefore is to see that events there do not hinder, and better yet support, perestroika in the Soviet Union.

This is a helpful insight. Clearly a domestic crisis in Eastern Europe that raised a serious debate in Moscow about intervention would put Gorbachev in a lose-lose situation. If he agreed to forceful intervention, the East-West detente aspect of his policy would go out the window and so would domestic democratization. (Loud opposition in parliamentary bodies and the media would be both inevitable and intolerable.) If he failed to respond to drastic events in Eastern Europe such as a reversal of alliances, bloody reprisals against local communists, or humiliation of Soviet forces in Eastern Europe, he could face an overwhelming backlash within his own Party that would swamp him and his program.

Such an evaluation of Soviet interests suggests an interlocking of interests of many different players: the U.S., Western Europe, reform movements in East European countries, and the reformers in the Soviet Union. All have a mutual interest in far-reaching and effective domestic changes in every country where existing arrangements are not satisfactory to the people. But all also have an interest in avoiding actions that would end up damaging the interests of all.

Conclusion

The issues of Eastern Europe clearly are now on the U.S.-Soviet agenda. Academic discussions that encourage informal involvement by officials on both sides can continue to play a useful role, even as official discussions expand.

A useful direction for unofficial discussions would be to include broader representation from Europe, both East and West. There is a danger here: that both Soviet and American participants would be less candid and creative in the presence of others whose interests were more directly at stake. That risk can and should be dealt with in order to provide a forum that can explore all aspects of the problem, particularly those delicate ones that are not yet ripe for discussion at the official level.

Mutual security principles, broadened to an all-Europe context, can provide a basis for dispassionate discussion of delicate issues in multi-sided and multi-level forums. For example, unofficial Americans can explain the U.S. policy of helping East European countries that are helping themselves by reforming their economic and political mechanisms. If they employ the concept of mutual security, these Americans can succesfully communicate the message that the criterion for assistance is not anti-Sovietism but responsiveness to the people's desires.

Another set of issues that could usefully be discussed is the risks that go along with the advantages of Western programs in reforming countries. Programs now on the table for Eastern Europe range from a large-scale "Marshall Plan" to privately funded management and entrepreneurial training programs for the private sector. Governments, private foundations, educational institutions, emigre groups and religious organizations in the West have an interest in the development of civil societies, private enterprise, joint ventures, political parties and legal, media and political institutions in reforming countries. These "developmental" activities could be immensely influential in both positive and mischievous directions, and could also be disappointingly ineffectual. Thoroughgoing discussions can help reduce surprises and mistakes and help keep expectations within reasonable limits.

Finally, a broader and unofficial forum is an appropriate place for Americans, Soviets and Europeans to begin seriously probing the future. Should NATO and the Warsaw Pact be allowed to wither away as their military reason for being declines, transform themselves into political mechanisms for pursuing peaceful competition, or be the subjects of a grand renegotiation of Europe's future? How will "1992" affect the political-military divide between East and West? And the question at the core: what is the future of Germany?

This is without question an ambitious agenda. It is premised on continuation of the major shift in Soviet interests in Eastern Europe, which in turn is intimately linked to reforms in the Soviet Union itself and therefore could be transitory. It is also premised on a shift in perception by both Moscow and Washington of the U.S. role in the process of change in the region. It can force the U.S. to face up to the question of acknowledging Soviet security interests in Eastern Europe. It threatens a reincarnated political minefield of "Yalta II" or "Munich II." But the long-term vision of mutual security provides an effective lodestar.

Notes

1. The situation in Eastern Europe was discussed at the initial mutual security conference sponsored by the Center for Foreign Policy Development at Brown University and the Institute for the USA and Canada of the Soviet Academy of Sciences in July 1988 in Moscow; at working sessions in March 1989 in Moscow and in May 1989 in Providence; and at the final mutual security conferences in Providence and Washington, D.C. in November 1989. It was also discussed at conferences sponsored by the International Research and Exchanges Board and the Soviet Academy of Sciences in July 1988 in Virginia, and in October 1989 in Moscow, and the Council on Foreign Relations in June 1989.
2. "East-West Relations and Eastern Europe," *Problems of Communism* 37 (May-August 1988), p. 66.
3. This was acknowledged, among other ways, in the final document resulting from that conference, entitled "U.S.-Soviet Mutual Security Project: Guidelines to the Working Groups."
4. See "East-West Relations and Eastern Europe," pp. 61-62.
5. Academician Bogomolov is Director of the Institute of Economics of the World Socialist System of the Soviet Academy of Sciences. Foreign Broadcast Information Service, *Daily Report: Eastern Europe* (February 14, 1989), p. 24.

6. Moscow Television, translated in Foreign Broadcast Information Service, *Daily Report: Soviet Union* (October 26, 1989), p. 32.
7. Foreign Broadcast Information Service, *Daily Report: Soviet Union* (December 4, 1989), p. 12.

8

Eastern Europe and International Stability

Yuriy Davydov

Three world wars — two "hot" and one "cold" — began in Eastern Europe in our century, confirming the region's reputation as the "powder keg of Europe." An obvious question is whether instability is a characteristic feature of the region. To some extent it is. Eastern Europe has never been an organic whole either historically, economically, or from the perspective of culture and civilization. It was a conglomeration of weak, small and medium-sized states that did not share common interests. Diversity, heightened nationalism and discord, inflamed by ethnic and territorial problems, are all relics of the period when nation-states were being formed (defined by the term "Balkanization"). Their political leaders attempted to solve domestic and foreign problems by turning to various power centers in the modern world, which were willingly drawn into this game, rather than by regional cooperation. As a result, the region became a sphere where the interests of the great powers clashed. Even during the bitter postwar East-West confrontation, anti-socialist forces in these countries often tried to draw the United States into the resolution of internal conflicts in a particular country, and communists did the same with the Soviet Union. As a result, a region with a population of one hundred million attracted an inordinate amount of attention from both superpowers. Today their orientation toward mutual security cannot disregard this historical character of the region, without the risk of becoming hostage to local emotions, nationalistic strivings and insoluble ethnic quarrels.

Parting with the past

To say that socialism has brought Eastern Europe only problems and difficulties would be an exaggeration; every society produces them. In a number of countries it facilitated more rapid industrialization, greater social protection of the broad mass of the population, a higher level of education and access to the achievements of industrial society and world culture. State ownership of the means of production provided a sense of general equality. The ideology of socialist internationalism, being supranational, repressed local nationalisms.

However, having freed itself from some former sources of instability, Eastern Europe acquired new ones. It is quite obvious that it lost out in economic competition with Western Europe. The monopoly of the Party, or more accurately its top echelon, led to political paralysis of entire societies. The construction of socialism according to a blueprint imported from abroad not only traumatized society, but had other negative consequences as well: in the first place, an increasingly critical attitude toward this blueprint socialism; in the second place, a similar attitude toward the Soviet Union; and in the third place, antipathy toward socialism itself. This led not only to a crisis in society, but to a crisis in relations with the Soviet Union.

As the 1990s begin, the following are characteristic features of the situation in Eastern Europe:

— Eastern Europe is parting with its postwar past. Perestroika has taken hold in all countries of the region and is proceeding at unprecedented speed. What took years in the Soviet Union or Poland has occurred in months or weeks in several East European states. The former system collapsed with remarkable rapidity, proof that it had no mass support.

— The economic situation in almost all the East European countries continues to worsen. This is manifested by foreign debt, inflation, a lower standard of living for the population and a lag in the area of scientific-technical progress. It has not yet been possible to stop the deterioration of the economic conditions. A disjuncture in the level of political and economic modernization is typical for all East European countries.

— The Soviet policy of glasnost and perestroika has had a decisive influence on the tempos, essence and forms of change in Eastern Europe. An unusual circumstance is apparently responsible for this: although an anti-socialist mood at the level of mass consciousness has intensified in all countries of the region, sympathy for the Soviet Union not only has failed to diminish, but has generally increased. At the same time, thanks to the rapid pace of change, many countries in Eastern Europe have already passed the Soviet

Union both in the depth and fundamental nature of the economic and political reforms that have taken place. This disjuncture may introduce some complications in the general process of change, even though it is a result of the differences in scale of the problems to be solved: conservative forces in the Soviet Union can reproach Gorbachev for "losing" the allies; these same forces in Eastern Europe can interpret the Soviet Union's lag as evidence of its disapproval of the processes occurring in the region.

— The internal East European opposition to the communists, which is strong in the moral sense since it enjoys the support of the masses (it can easily bring hundreds of thousands of people onto the streets), is poorly organized, has no clearly defined program, and is not well prepared on a professional level to govern a country. On the other hand, the communist parties, though possessing organization, experience and members, some of whom are strongly in favor of reforms, are demoralized, have lost their authority, and, in most of the countries, are no longer in power.

— In the spiritual area, interest in the moral and political values of the Western world, whose roots go back to the common historical and cultural traditions of Eastern and Western Europe, has grown in Eastern Europe. Extensive contacts with the West, which have made it possible to compare the living standards and quality of life in East and West, have spread this interest to consumer-oriented sections of the population, which have traditionally stood outside politics. The "image of the enemy" is in the process of dissolution, and a growing number of citizens in East European countries no longer see the West as a threat to the political or national existence of their state.

— The East European public and official circles have a critical attitude toward the possibility of solving their countries' political and economic problems within the framework of the Council for Mutual Economic Assistance (CEMA)[1] and the Warsaw Pact. CEMA has not promoted either the existence of a common market or a rise to world standards in the scientific and technical potential of Eastern Europe. During past crises, the Warsaw Pact has not shown itself to be an organization capable of solving either East-West or internal problems. Different types of group cooperation without the USSR are now under discussion. At the same time there is considerable euphoria in the region at the prospect of cooperation with the West, a conviction that the West will assume the material burden of restructuring archaic economic structures, education, health care, ecology, etc.

— The differing levels of social-political and economic development in East European countries, the specific nature of their internal problems, their aspirations to outdo their partners and win a place in opening to the West, and an intensification of national consciousness, in some cases even nationalistic emotions, all lead to a situation wherein each country tries to act without cooperating with its partners. The sphere of cooperation with the USSR is also diminishing.

It is essential for both East and West to understand the scope and contradictory nature of the processes occurring in Eastern Europe. Otherwise their turn toward mutual security will become yet another scheme that crumbles when brought into contact with reality.

Transitional period

Eastern Europe is entering a period of transformation that may last ten to twenty years. A distinctive feature of this period is the interdependence of economic and political reforms.

The changes are obvious, their final result is less apparent, but it will hardly be identical in the various countries. Two trends are evident today in every East European society. One is represented by those who think that there must be a radical renewal of socialism, a reassessment of its basic features (property forms, commodity production, etc.), and greater orientation toward common human values. The other is by those who are disillusioned (permanently or temporarily) with the ability of socialism to achieve a high level of prosperity and democracy and think that it is not a matter of turning to the West, but of returning to the West. In the present emotional situation it is extremely difficult to determine the true strength of these two trends. It is also apparent that, while at the initial stage of East European revolutions representatives of both trends have been allies, as time passes they will grow further and further apart.

It may be said with certainty, in the first place, that Eastern Europe is moving toward a market economy, more diverse forms of property ownership, restrictions on state regulation of the economic life of the country, and encouragement of private enterprise, including capital investments from abroad. Does this signify a departure from socialism? That will depend on the orientation of society and of its basic political forces. It is possible to build either capitalism or socialism on the same economic base.

Eastern Europe has moved toward political pluralism, toward a multiparty system in which communist parties no longer automatically dominate. The basic question is not how other parties will be incorporated into the new political structure of society, but what place communist parties will occupy in it. Today they are trying to rid themselves of their past, of their monopoly on power, in a number of cases of their very name, and Marxism-Leninism, in favor of renewal, democratization of themselves, and constructive dialogue with other political movements. Many representatives of other movements realize that society cannot emerge from its social and political crisis without cooperation with communists; some are frightened by the burden of individual responsibility and by their lack of experience, members, and the necessary organization. It is likely, therefore, that coalition governments will be in power during this transitional period in many East European countries, though possibly not in all.

In principle the idea of a multiparty system does not contradict either Marxism or socialism. Socialist pluralism cannot be restricted to freedom of opinions, it inevitably leads to freedom of organizations, including political ones. At the same time, much depends on the specific historical aspects of societal development. In this context, it would be hard to see a real multiparty system emerge any time soon in the Soviet Union, although certain political counterweights to the Communist Party monopoly are already appearing (the Supreme Soviet, Popular Fronts, independent associations, etc.). Although the Soviet leadership quietly accepted the rise of a multiparty system in Eastern Europe, the absence of such in the Soviet Union will distance it from the processes occurring in the region, and will sometimes put it in opposition to them, which is naturally undesirable from the viewpoint of mutual security.

Finally, Eastern Europe is moving toward the establishment of more organic, more natural, more equal relations as partners with the Soviet Union, based less on ideological principles than on mutual benefit and a balance of interests.

Dissatisfaction with CEMA and with the nature of economic ties with the Soviet Union undoubtedly exists in Eastern Europe, but it is unlikely that any country in the region (including the USSR) can allow itself to renounce these ties today. In the first place, whole branches of production in the various states have become interdependent. In the second place, the existing level of East European economies is such that they are not yet able to switch from CEMA markets to Western ones without doing considerable damage to themselves.

The main thing that keeps Eastern Europe from developing greater economic cooperation with the West is its lack of a market economy and the nonconvertibility of its currencies. This brings it closer to the Soviet Union, although possibly that is not the best basis for rapprochement. Considering the common initial premises of perestroika in the USSR and Eastern Europe, it is likely that their economic ties will increase in the near future, for only by relying on a stable rear can Eastern Europe cooperate successfully with the West.

A skeptical attitude toward the Warsaw Pact also exists in Eastern Europe. In the first place, the events of 1956 and 1968 dominate the political thinking of many East Europeans. In the second place, as the European climate has warmed, the reduced external threat has diminished the Warsaw Pact's importance. In the third place, a military structure that includes states unequal in power leads objectively to the domination of the most powerful among them. In the fourth place, conservatives in Eastern Europe see the Warsaw Pact as a force opposed to change.

From the point of view of alliance relations, the Warsaw Pact is a moral and material burden to the USSR. (Not without reason does it propose dissolution of both blocs.) External circumstances are another matter. The military confrontation in Europe has been reduced but not eliminated. A unilateral dissolution of the Warsaw Pact could exert a destabilizing influence on East-West relations. Negotiations on disarmament, on a new structure for European security could drag on, and new suspicions and tensions could arise. A unilateral dissolution of the Warsaw Pact could create unprecedented tension in NATO and even among the former members of the Eastern bloc; it could open the way toward a "Balkanization" of Eastern Europe, increase uncertainty over the German Question, etc. Even the departure of one country from the Warsaw Pact would support a harder line both in the West ("This is a successful result of pressure") and in the East ("They've reverted to democracy"). If it is to be based on mutual security, the dissolution of the Warsaw Pact can occur only on a mutual basis with NATO, by means of a dialogue between them.

It is hard to predict the final result of the changes that have begun in Eastern Europe. One may hope that democratization of the political system and an orientation toward a market economy will, in the final result, create stable and durable societies that will be an integral part of the structure of mutual security. At the same time, it is obvious that this transitional period, like every revolution, is fraught with crises and uncertainties.

New threats to stability

It is clear that, with perestroika in the USSR, those figures in the region who were associated with the Soviet model of socialism and with Soviet domination of society will fall out of power. But people who attribute regional instability to these two sources alone will be disillusioned. The new situation in the region can engender new sources of instability, as well as reawaken certain illnesses traditional to it. What are they?

— The heterogeneity of Eastern Europe is acquiring a new dimension during this period of transformation. In some countries reforms will proceed faster, in others much more slowly; in some countries elements of socialism will predominate, while others will rapidly dismantle socialism; some will quickly join the world market, others will hold onto each other and to the Soviet Union; some will have quick results, while others may get stuck before getting under way. The correlation of conservative, reformist and extremist forces varies in each country, and so does the nationality problem. Heterogeneity does not necessarily lead to conflict, but it does usually lead to misunderstanding, which in turn usually leads to tension.

— A reduction of centripetal factors and of Soviet domination in the alliance awaken fear of the "Balkanization" of Eastern Europe. National ambitions revive, and are exploited by extremists; ethnic and territorial problems again rise to the surface; and historical injustices committed in the course of past settlements are debated.

— The prerequisites for destabilization are always present in society during a transitional period. The old structures are bad, but while working they are disintegrating, while the new ones arise slowly and do not yet yield results. As a result, people get the feeling that everything has grown worse than it was. Political changes occur faster than economic ones, a gap develops between hopes and their realization, which gives rise to popular dissatisfaction and social tension.

— Economic reforms require a regime of strict economy, belt tightening and "freezing" or lowering the living standard of the population. Difficulties arise which socialist societies are experiencing for the first time: inflation, budget deficits, increased taxes, unemployment, the egotism of independent producers, and a sharp rise in societal differentiation in a society ideologically oriented toward social equality. East European society, while prepared to accept the West's advantages, is not prepared to accept its problems. And when they appear (much earlier than do the advantages), people are dismayed, doubts begin to surface, and internal instability may develop into a crisis. We do not know what forces might take advantage of this situation to advance their own interests.

— There is a link between the processes occurring in Eastern Europe and in East-West relations. A deterioration in these relations would have a negative impact on Soviet security concerns, which could lead to a renewal of confrontation between the USSR and United States over Eastern Europe. During this transitional and unstable situation in a number of countries, all of these factors could lead to the growth of destructive factors in the region as a whole.

— A solution of the German Question which ignores postwar European realities could shatter Eastern Europe altogether.

Perhaps many of these fears will prove to be unjustified. Perhaps the preservation of CEMA and the Warsaw Pact will eliminate or neutralize some of these threats. But the imperatives of mutual security, oriented toward preserving stability during a period of change in Eastern Europe, require that both superpowers take these fears into account when considering their activities in the region.

The Soviet Union and Eastern Europe

The main questions here are: how does the Soviet Union view the changes in the region, and what reaction might it have to their expansion, and to the possibility that these changes may pass outside the framework of socialism and the alliance?

In carrying out perestroika, Soviet society and its present political leadership do not pretend to have a monopoly on the possession of truth, and they respect their alliance partners' search for a true path. Freedom of choice, socialist pluralism, mutual advantage — this is the only basis on which relations between the USSR and Eastern Europe can henceforth develop. Naturally, today there is a certain tension in these relations. The old structures of ties between the USSR and East European countries are ill-suited for new contents. Events in countries of the region are going substantially beyond the goals Soviet perestroika is setting itself at this stage. Two questions arise in this connection which trouble people in the USSR, Eastern Europe and the West.

First — Does the USSR continue to share the idea of collective responsibility for the fate of socialism in any particular East European country? This refers to the Brezhnev Doctrine. In the first place, under present conditions it is difficult to define what we mean by socialism. In its most general form, it is a structure oriented toward greater social justice. Not only is the model of Western democracy recognized, but so is the need to borrow some of its fundamental elements. Thus, many Western countries, such as Sweden, Denmark, etc., fall into the socialist category. In the second place, the critical reference point today for the Soviet Union is not some particular ideological diagram, but the will of the people, expressed by democratic means.

Second — Is the security of the USSR ensured only by the existence of a belt of socialist states along its borders, specifically in Eastern Europe? Practical experience has shown that there is no connection between the security of the USSR and the social orientation of its neighboring states. Capitalist Finland and Austria have been friendly countries, while Yugoslavia, China and Albania have been hostile. The present concept of Soviet security holds that security is ensured by friendly neighbors, not by their social structures. And the task of Soviet foreign policy is to ensure the friendliness of these neighbors, not the victory of socialism in any particular countries. These questions may be finally eliminated by the affirmation of mutual security principles in East-West relations, since these principles are based not on social or ideological criteria, but on the interests of the parties and of the system of values that today is accepted equally in Eastern and Western Europe.

However, it is apparent today that to eliminate the negative is not enough. The positive must be created, i.e., a structure of relations that takes account of the changes in the Soviet Union and Eastern Europe. The main features of this new structure are gradually becoming visible.

In the economic sphere it will be increasingly oriented toward market-type relations and mutual advantage. Participants in these relations will more often be independent enterprises, organizations and groups, not states. Elements of mutual assistance and an artificial division of labor will apparently be preserved for a time. The main difficulty is that neither the Soviet Union nor its allies yet have a market economy. Movement in this direction has begun, but is proceeding at different rates both in the Soviet Union and in Eastern Europe.

A reorientation from Party to purely governmental relations between the USSR and the countries of Eastern Europe is proceeding in the political sphere. Obviously a revision of bilateral Treaties on Friendship and Cooperation will be forthcoming, with the elimination of a number of provisions that do not correspond to the new situation. In general, relations between the USSR and East European countries will evolve toward political partnerships, which will make them more natural, and the situation in the region more stable.

In the sphere of military cooperation, changes will obviously move in the direction of greater politicization and de-ideologization of the Warsaw Pact Organization, if it is preserved. These changes presuppose a reduction, and in some cases elimination, of the Soviet military presence in the region. As an instrument for ensuring internal political stability it has definitely outlived its time. It has significance only as a means of ensuring security. Its level will depend on the general situation in East-West relations and on progress in disarmament and mutual security.

The most important indication of the perestroika that has begun in Soviet relations with Eastern Europe is that internal events in countries of the region are not leading to a crisis in their relations with the Soviet Union. As a result, the transition to reforms in a number of East European states has been accomplished without pressure, as a normal political process.

It is crucial today for the Soviet Union and Eastern Europe to find a new mutual understanding of each other and of their relations. The process of renewal, of democratization, and of glasnost going on both in the Soviet Union and Eastern Europe facilitates this task, while simultaneously laying the basis for a new European stability.

Conclusion

The European zone of socialism is today undergoing the most serious crisis in its history. It affects the content of socialism, the practice of its construction, and the relations of those countries drawn into the process. This crisis is a natural phenomenon in the development of societies, states, and alliances, when the principles on which they have been based come into conflict with reality. The crisis is also a process of renewal for society, socialism, and the system. That is the most important feature of the present crisis.

If this crisis has become a starting point for East-West rapprochement, rather than confrontation, the reason is obviously that both sides have increasingly based their decisions on mutual security principles.

Notes

1. Also abbreviated CMEA and Comecon.

9

Implications for Western Policy

MARK KRAMER

This chapter will consider how the United States can best apply a mutual security framework to U.S.-Soviet interactions in Eastern and Central Europe. Unlike the Working Group on Europe's joint statement, the chapter will reflect a distinctly American perspective and will concentrate on Western actions and policies. The main premise of the chapter, however, is the same as in the rest of the working group, namely, that in the nuclear age each of the superpowers can bolster its own security by taking account of the other's basic security interests and adjusting its own policies as necessary.

Two caveats about the chapter are in order:

First, for both geographical and historical reasons, mutual security in Eastern and Central Europe requires a greater degree of Soviet cooperation than in any other region. The remarkable political changes in Eastern Europe since early 1989 would have been impossible without a fundamental shift in Soviet policy. So long as previous Soviet leaders were determined to uphold orthodox communist rule in Eastern Europe, indigenous pressures for far-reaching reform were invariably thwarted. But now that Gorbachev has refrained from intervening to prevent the collapse of communist regimes, the whole political complexion of the region has been transformed. For the first time in the post-1945 era, the East European countries enjoy full leeway to pursue drastic changes in their political, social, and economic systems without interference from Moscow. This reorientation of Soviet policy has enabled both superpowers — whether consciously or not — to adopt a mutual security approach in the region, something that was inconceivable in the past. By the same token, a reversal or derailment of the reform processes in the

Soviet Union, combined with an attempt by Moscow to reimpose control over Eastern Europe, would undermine any hope of sustaining a mutual security framework. Thus, it should be made clear at the outset that a mutual security approach in Eastern and Central Europe will remain viable only so long as domestic reform and liberalization in the Soviet Union continue.

Second, Western influence in promoting continued reform in Eastern Europe will be limited, not least because of the uncertainty surrounding internal developments in Moscow. Responsibility for maintaining the pace of change rests predominantly with the local peoples. Nevertheless, if recent liberalizing trends in the Soviet Union are not wholly reversed, the United States and its allies will have a greater opportunity for a positive role over the next several years than at any time in the past. On such a crucial matter, even a modest difference would be worth the effort.

Mutual security objectives in Eastern and Central Europe

The one objective that the United States and the Soviet Union have shared in Europe throughout the postwar era is the avoidance of an East-West war. Virtually all observers agree that a deliberate attack by either NATO or the Warsaw Pact is implausible under current circumstances; the primary danger, instead, is that a large-scale war could arise inadvertently out of a severe internal crisis in Eastern Europe, a conflict involving two or more East European countries, or a peripheral conflict between an East European country and a NATO country (e.g., Bulgaria and Turkey).

Severe internal crises in Eastern Europe have occurred numerous times in the past: in East Germany in 1953, Hungary and Poland in 1956, Czechoslovakia in 1968, Poland in 1980-81, and Romania in 1989. To be sure, none of these earlier incidents precipitated a direct superpower confrontation, and the likelihood of Soviet military intervention in a future crisis has greatly diminished, at least for now. But the situation could change if reform in the Soviet Union goes disastrously awry, leading to a conservative backlash. Were that to happen, a future crisis in, say, Poland or East Germany might well provoke Soviet military intervention, especially if extensive bloodshed resulted. The hostilities, if prolonged, could then escalate and take a disastrous turn that might lead NATO and the Warsaw Pact — however unwillingly — into a wider conflict.[1] Moreover, even if the fighting did not result in a confrontation between the two alliances, a Soviet invasion of an East European country in the future would be a serious, and perhaps fatal, blow to reformist elements in Moscow and would create enormous tensions in East-West relations.[2]

As for armed conflicts between East European states — or between an East European country and a peripheral NATO member — these may, ironically, be more likely now than at any time in the last forty-five years.[3] In the days when the East European states were strictly subordinated to Soviet power, the Soviet Union could set the whole "political agenda" for the region. Territorial and other disputes that were so common before 1945 — such as those between Poland and Germany, Hungary and Romania, and Bulgaria and Romania, as well as the general phenomenon of "Balkanization" — ceased to be as important in an era of Soviet domination. But now that Soviet controls have been removed, long-submerged tensions and conflicts will surface more easily. If these tensions were to result in a military clash, the risk of escalation to a wider war between East and West — while small — could by no means be ruled out, especially if a NATO country were involved. It is worth remembering that virtually all the major wars in Europe over the last two centuries have originated from incidents in the eastern half of the continent.

Thus, from a mutual security standpoint, the fundamental goal in Eastern and Central Europe, for both the United States and the Soviet Union, should be to encourage continued political and economic reform that will bolster the internal stability of the local states, reduce the chance of violent unrest, and minimize the danger of armed hostilities between East European countries. The aim, in other words, is to *prevent* crises and conflicts, rather than trying to cope with them once they have arisen. To this end, the United States should seek to put in place measures that cannot be quickly reversed, even if domestic circumstances in the Soviet Union change drastically.

The prevention of internal crises and inter-state conflicts in Eastern Europe will be easier than before in some respects, but more difficult in others. For many years, the underlying source of internal crises was the existence of Soviet political and military hegemony, which all but guaranteed the recurrence of destabilizing nationalist unrest.[4] One of the prerequisites for ending this cycle of instability was the dissolution of Soviet control over the region. To a large extent that has now happened. Nevertheless, the potential for internal crises in Eastern Europe will remain high unless political liberalization and economic reform can take a stronger hold. It is here that the role of the United States and its Western allies will be especially important.

The risk of armed conflicts between two or more East European countries also will be likely to increase if economic conditions fail to improve. Nationalist grievances and animosities are most apt to emerge if living standards are stagnant or declining. The prosperity of Western Europe since World War II is one of the reasons that the European Community (EC) has proven so remarkably successful and that national differences and disputes in the western half of Europe no longer threaten to spill over into military clashes. Only when the East European countries begin to attain a comparable degree of economic buoyancy will the risk of armed hostilities truly fade.

The task confronting the two superpowers, therefore, is to facilitate — or at least not to inhibit — a continued peaceful transition to a more stable political and economic order in Eastern Europe. The guiding principle should be freedom of choice for every nation, without detriment to others' security. As is clear by now, this process will necessitate a fundamental restructuring of political and economic systems in the region, something that Gorbachev has been extraordinarily willing to accept thus far.[5] Continued Soviet adjustments to the rapidly changing situation in Eastern Europe will obviously be essential. The role of the West, meanwhile, will be threefold: to avoid any actions that would disrupt the process, to provide concrete support for the fulfillment of nationalist aspirations and market-oriented economic reforms, and to assure the Soviet Union (directly and tacitly) that Western countries will not exploit the ongoing changes to Soviet disadvantage. These and other aspects of Western policy will be examined in greater detail in the next section.

Policy options

Until recently, almost all discussions of Western options vis-a-vis Eastern Europe were limited to steps that would promote evolutionary change in a region still under Soviet control. The range of options available for even this circumscribed objective was much wider than often believed.[6] But now that the whole political configuration of Eastern Europe has been radically altered, it is necessary to think in more ambitious terms about steps that would expand on and lock in all the recent changes.

A "grand deal"?

One proposal to this effect, which was broached even before the events of late 1989 by some prominent American commentators, would amount to a "grand deal" between the superpowers.[7] In essence, the Soviet Union would formally relinquish all remaining control over Eastern Europe, including East Germany, in return for Western security guarantees. This exchange would be similar to the elaborate arrangements worked out under the Austrian State Treaty of 1955. The emergence of Austria as a liberal democracy, with its neutrality guaranteed by the two superpowers, does indeed provide a hopeful example of what might be feasible for most or all of the East European countries.

Under present conditions, however, a "grand deal" would be neither desirable nor necessary. No formal Western guarantees were required to bring about the momentous events of 1989; a low-key Western profile served perfectly well. Nor would formal arrangements be the best way to consolidate the emerging political order in Eastern Europe, especially in the near future, when any such arrangements would be likely to collapse if Soviet domestic political circumstances took a sharp turn for the worse.[8] In the years ahead, a posture of continued respect for the interests of East and West Europeans will be more appropriate than any sort of "guarantees." Over the longer term, as the political situation in the Soviet Union becomes less volatile and reforms in Eastern Europe take deeper root, new security arrangements in Europe may well evolve, including an appropriate U.S. role. But at no point should Western countries undertake commitments that could be construed as preventing the Baltic states (and perhaps other Soviet republics) from peacefully regaining independence, if they so choose.

The German Question

No issue will be more difficult, or more important, to resolve than the future of Germany.[9] From a mutual security perspective, any proposed "solution" to the German Question would be desirable only if it minimizes the danger of war. In that regard, several points are worth noting:

— Historically, Germany has been more frequently divided than united.[10] Following the break-up of the Holy Roman Empire at the start of the nineteenth century, Germans were scattered among hundreds of city-states, principalities, and fiefdoms, which were consolidated into thirty-nine separate states after the Congress of Vienna in 1815. Not until 1871 did Bismarck manage to unite these entities into a single German state, which lasted for just over seven decades (within varying boundaries). This period of seventy-four years, from 1871 to 1945, is the only time that Germans have ever been united in their own cohesive state. That brief experience stands in marked contrast to the centuries of unity that the French, English, Russian, and other European nations have known.

— Despite the historical record, the drive toward German reunification has gathered overwhelming momentum on both sides of the inner-German border. The question is no longer whether, but when, a single German state will be formed. Every major political party in the two Germanies supports reunification, and numerous public opinion surveys since November 1989 have revealed that the vast majority of East and West Germans want a united country.[11] Moreover, de facto economic unity between the two Germanies, including a common currency, has been proceeding at an ever faster rate. Thus, if the United States and Soviet Union delay at all in trying to manage the German Question, events will overtake anything they attempt to do.

— The Germans are by far the most numerous of the European peoples and, historically, have tended to be the most economically dynamic. When united before 1945, they also repeatedly sought an international role commensurate with their numbers and economic strength. Since the end of World War II, however, the division of the German nation and the emergence of the United States and Soviet Union as global superpowers have precluded a more salient political and military role for Germany on the world scene.

— Nationalism has long been a potent and unpredictable force in Germany. Adolf Hitler enjoyed greater popular support among Germans during his reign than any leader has either before or since. Although no one would seriously argue that West Germany today is comparable to the Weimar Republic, which gave way to the Nazi regime, the extreme-right Republikaner party has garnered nearly ten percent of the vote in recent local elections. No doubt, this support would grow (though by how much is anyone's guess) if the West German economy experienced a severe recession or if some other unforeseeable development provided an opening for nationalist demagogues to make a bid for power. East Germany, for its part, was never de-nazified, so there is little way of knowing the depth and passion of potentially dangerous nationalist sentiments in that country. Certainly the cries of "Deutschland, erwache!" (the Nazi slogan "Germany, awake!"), "Wir sind ein Volk!" ("We are one people!"), and "Deutschland, Deutschland über alles!" ("Germany, Germany over all!") that have been ringing on East German streets do little to inspire confidence.

— The movement toward German reunification has generated widespread unease in several East European countries, especially Poland. Several high-level Polish officials have been expressing concern for some time that "the establishment of a united [German] state, the very thought of which gives all of Europe goosebumps, would almost automatically reopen the question of Poland's territorial shape."[12] The fact that even a mainstream leader like Helmut Kohl has avoided a direct endorsement of the Oder-Neisse (Odra-Nysa Luzycka) line as Germany's eastern border has raised increasing doubts about future German intentions, whether legitimately or not.

— A few hard-lined communists and other extreme leftists in East Germany are so strongly opposed to the idea of a reunified Germany that they may resort to guerrilla warfare, if necessary, to try to prevent it. The effectiveness of such a campaign would probably be extremely limited, however.

In short, the German Question does not lend itself to any straightforward solution. Although mutual security in Europe must be based on "freedom of choice," this principle will have to be applied cautiously in the case of Germany. On the one hand, a failure to permit self-determination for the Germans could lead to festering resentment and an ugly nationalist backlash that would increase the risk of war.[13] On the other hand, a precipitate reunification of Germany without proper safeguards could result in a more aggressive and assertive German state that would seek to press its irredentist claims against Poland and Czechoslovakia.

To resolve this dilemma, the United States and its allies must pursue three objectives:

First, they should obtain a clear reaffirmation of Germany's adherence to the Nuclear Non-Proliferation Treaty, which has been signed by both the FRG and the GDR. Any attempt by a united Germany to renounce its NPT commitments would warrant immediate U.S. (and Soviet) action.

Second, Western governments must obtain unambiguous assurances of Germany's willingness to accept its post-1945 borders. That will be the only way to alleviate the concerns of Polish, Czechoslovak, French, and other European officials.

Third, the United States and its allies must ensure that the FRG remains firmly rooted in the Western democratic community, regardless of its eventual status vis-a-vis the GDR. Proposals for a neutral Germany, such as the plan advanced by Hans Modrow in February 1990, are dangerous because they would create a power vacuum in Central Europe and attenuate Germany's connections with Western democratic influences. Instead, Western governments should make clear their desire for West Germany to remain within NATO, including the integrated military command, even if some modification in the alliance (e.g., selective troop withdrawals) is required. Likewise, West European countries should strive for continued economic and political integration of the European Community, enabling West Germany — and, over time, a single Germany — to be united ever more closely with its democratic neighbors. The United States should lend strong political support to the full integration of Germany into the EC.

Future of NATO

The pivotal role of NATO in dealing with the German Question is one of the many reasons that the alliance will remain crucial in the years ahead. In the past, NATO's primary mission was to deter and, if necessary, defend against an invasion by the Warsaw Pact. Now that this threat has substantially receded, the chief tasks for NATO will increasingly be political. Just as Gorbachev and other Soviet authorities have spoken of transforming the Warsaw Pact "from a predominantly military and political alliance to a political and military one," so too NATO will be an indispensable political mechanism for the West in this time of profound change.[14] The proposals that some Soviet officials have advanced for the prompt dissolution of both NATO and the Warsaw Pact could not be more inappropriate.[15] The next several years would be precisely the wrong time to dismantle the most effective means either side has of preventing volatile change from spinning out of control.

This, of course, is in no way to suggest that the future of NATO need be strictly parallel with the future of the Warsaw Pact. NATO has always been a voluntary alliance of democratic states, whereas the Warsaw Pact, at least until very recently, has simply been an outgrowth of Soviet hegemony over Eastern Europe. Soviet leaders are now seeking to convert the Warsaw Pact into a genuine alliance and adapt it to the radically new circumstances in Eastern Europe, but it remains to be seen how successful they will be. Pressures for withdrawal from the Warsaw Pact are already growing in at least a few of the East European countries, and the alliance could eventually collapse of its own weight. Whatever the fate of the Warsaw Pact may be, NATO should be retained on its own merits as an organ of political stabilization. The dissimilar origins and nature of the two alliances explain why NATO can continue to serve a useful function long after the Warsaw Pact has become obsolete.

Indeed, even most Soviet leaders seem to recognize, if only implicitly, that NATO's continued existence will be essential to forestall a power vacuum in Central Europe and to reduce uncertainty about the long-term future of Germany. In contrast to Soviet posturing in the late 1940s and early 1950s, when Stalin constantly sought to play the "trump card" of German neutrality, Gorbachev has been loath to force the issue. No doubt, this change of course stems from Soviet officials' awareness of the risks of disrupting NATO and the EC and leaving Germany as a powerful state on its own. The views expressed by the Polish foreign minister about Germany in early 1990 — that a failure to keep a united Germany in NATO would endanger European security — seem to have gained increasing currency in Moscow as well.[16]

To bolster the new Soviet approach, Western countries should be careful to exercise discretion vis-a-vis the Warsaw Pact and avoid actions that would appear provocative. This means, for example, that so long as current trends in Soviet policy continue, NATO should refrain from actively enticing states like Hungary and Czechoslovakia to withdraw from the Warsaw Pact. It will probably soon be feasible for some or all of these states to pull out, and NATO should welcome that when it happens. But any explicit Western encouragement of such a step in the near term would almost certainly be futile and counterproductive. Restraint and patience on the part of the West are the best policy now that events are moving in such an auspicious direction.

Economic options

One of the primary obstacles over the long run to a process of stable liberalization in Eastern Europe is the continued stagnation or deterioration of many of the local economies. Economic grievances have consistently been one of the major catalysts of violent unrest in Eastern Europe during the post-Stalin era, whether in Czechoslovakia and East Germany in 1953, Poland and Hungary in 1956, Poland in 1970, 1976, and 1980, or Romania in 1977 and 1987.[17] This pattern, of course, may change now that the communist regimes in those countries have been replaced by governments that enjoy greater legitimacy.[18] But what seems more likely is that even if political liberalization continues, stability in Eastern Europe will remain fragile until sustained economic improvements are achieved.

The weaknesses of the East European economies are so pervasive and deeply entrenched that even vast infusions of Western assistance will be of no avail in the long run unless the local states carry out sweeping, market-oriented reforms. As the dismal experience of the 1970s shows, the success that the East European countries have in implementing such reforms will be what ultimately determines their economic fate.[19] Hence, Western economic support will be beneficial only if it it contributes directly to — and is contingent on — systemic reforms of the kind that the International Monetary Fund (IMF) normally requires. These include the decentralization of economic decision making, the lifting of price controls, the convertibility of currency, the imposition of wage restraints, the development of a rational incentives structure, and, above all, an expansion of the private and cooperatives sector.[20] Most Western assistance should be targeted specifically to the private sector, with loans and grants to East European governments reserved exclusively for improvements in transportation, communications networks, and environmental controls.

Direct investment by private Western firms and banks will be the most important source of economic aid for Eastern Europe, but Western governments can play a key role in encouraging and underwriting private investors and in helping to channel funds to the East European states that have adopted the most far-reaching political and economic reforms. The IMF and the new Bank for Reconstruction and Development in Eastern Europe will be of critical importance in providing technical assistance and economic advice, as well as in extending loans and loan guarantees with strict conditions attached.

To maximize the efficacy of the new loans and grants, Western governments (i.e., the seventeen members of the Paris Club) should soon begin offering debt relief for countries like Poland and Hungary on a much larger scale than has been contemplated up to now. The existing hard-currency debts are one of the pernicious legacies of the previous regimes in Eastern Europe; it would be unwise to compel the fledgling reformist governments to shoulder the burden of their predecessors' mistakes. Beyond providing debt relief, the United States and its allies can gradually ease and lift restrictions on civilian high-technology transfers to Eastern Europe. Of particular importance in this regard will be the sale of equipment to bolster the local states' telecommunications systems and pollution-control devices.

Finally, Western countries — particularly the members of the European Community — must be willing to liberalize their trade policies vis-a-vis Eastern Europe as reforms begin to take hold. The aim should be to integrate the East European states into a broader European economy, providing markets for East European manufacturing and agricultural exports. Over time, formal membership in the EC would be desirable for East European countries that have made the transition to a market-oriented economy.

All of these measures should be of direct benefit to the Soviet Union as well as to Eastern Europe. Soviet officials have already indicated that they would like to restructure the Council for Mutual Economic Assistance (CMEA) along more flexible lines, with transactions exclusively in hard currency.[21] Although the Soviet proposals do not yet go far enough to satisfy all reformers in Eastern Europe (and Moscow), they are certainly a step in the right direction.[22] However, without progress on *internal* market-oriented reforms, the East European states (and the Soviet Union, for that matter) will be unable to participate effectively in a more market-oriented CMEA. Thus, the domestic policies that will allow the East European countries to assume a greater role in the world economy will also provide for more "organic" trade links with the Soviet Union. In addition, the reforms that the East European governments undertake should pave the way for the adoption of similar measures in the Soviet economy, revealing both the pitfalls and the benefits.

Military/arms control measures

Selected military and arms control measures will be valuable in consolidating the new political order in Eastern and Central Europe. On the military side, the United States can best ensure continued East-West stability in Europe by maintaining a strong nuclear deterrent. Throughout the postwar era the existence of nuclear weapons has had an enormously inhibiting effect on superpower behavior in Europe and elsewhere. Indeed, one of the main reasons that the likelihood of an East-West war in Europe has been so small is that nuclear arsenals on both sides have been so large. As U.S. and Soviet strategic nuclear forces have expanded over the years, leaders in both Moscow and Washington, D.C. have been increasingly unwilling even to contemplate the sorts of military ventures that were so common in the pre-nuclear era. Drastic nuclear reductions would disrupt the whole strategic relationship that has evolved over the past few decades, and should therefore be eschewed.

By contrast, efforts to reduce *conventional* weaponry will undoubtedly bolster European security. The cutbacks envisaged under the Conventional Forces in Europe (CFE) negotiations will require the Soviet Union to reduce its troop presence in Eastern Europe by roughly two-thirds and its tanks, armored personnel carriers, and artillery by even greater proportions.[23] Moreover, a CFE agreement will facilitate the complete withdrawal of Soviet troops from three of the four East European countries in which they are now stationed: Czechoslovakia, Hungary, and Poland. Once all Soviet forces are out of those countries and effective verification measures are in place, it would be extremely difficult and costly for Moscow to reintroduce large numbers of troops, not least because a CFE agreement will require the dismantling and destruction, rather than just the redeployment, of withdrawn units.

In the absence of a CFE agreement, Gorbachev might still end up pulling most Soviet troops out of Eastern Europe, but he would be under no obligation to disband them. Instead, he could simply move the Northern, Southern, and Central Groups of Soviet Forces across the border into Belorussia and the western Ukraine.[24] That would be enough to meet Czechoslovak, Hungarian, and Polish demands for the withdrawal of Soviet forces, but it would also enable Soviet officials to redeploy troops swiftly into Eastern Europe during a crisis. A CFE agreement, by contrast, will effectively rule out that option. Thus, CFE will provide a concrete assurance of the Soviet Union's intentions not to interfere in the domestic affairs of East European countries, reinforcing the stance that Gorbachev adopted during the crises of 1989. Even if domestic circumstances in the Soviet Union change, the constraints that CFE will impose on Soviet interventionary capabilities should be of lasting value.

The same applies to the other salutary effects that CFE will have in Europe. For the Western alliance, reductions within a CFE framework will provide a far more orderly and coherent means of paring conventional forces than would be possible if the individual NATO countries are simply left to make their own unilateral cutbacks. In addition, as East-West force levels become more equitable over time, CFE will permit the burden for conventional defense in NATO to be shifted increasingly to the West Europeans, at lower cost for all.[25] Finally, CFE can contribute to a resolution of the German problem by facilitating large reductions in the military forces of the two Germanies, especially East Germany. Such steps will mitigate the threat that neighboring countries perceive as the German states draw closer together politically. A follow-on CFE agreement might even provide for the full-scale demilitarization of East Germany, with NATO troops to be located only on the current territory of West Germany, regardless of whether a united German state emerges.

Further impetus for positive change in Central and Eastern Europe can come from confidence- and security-building measures (CSBMs), such as those agreed to under the Stockholm round of the Conference on Security and Cooperation in Europe (CSCE) in September 1986. Certain "stabilizing measures" will be included in the CFE accords, and additional CSBMs are to be arranged under parallel negotiations in Vienna. To the extent that these measures will allow for greater predictability about troop movements and complicate any Soviet preparations for armed interference, they will alleviate tensions that may arise within Eastern Europe (and vis-a-vis NATO) as the pace of reform accelerates. The CSBMs will also provide solid evidence of Western intentions not to exploit future crises in Eastern Europe to Soviet disadvantage. In the longer term, the whole CSCE framework could prove useful if both East and West seek to fashion a new security regime for Europe. Although the CSCE should not become a substitute for NATO, it does offer a number of existing organizations and functions that can be adopted for a united Europe in the future.

Conclusion

The revolutionary changes that have swept over Eastern Europe have opened up new opportunities for mutual security. The manner in which Soviet and American officials handled the events of 1989 was invaluable in demonstrating the benefits to be gained by accommodating each side's interests and thereby providing greater security for both. The chances of continued reform in Eastern and Central Europe are now incomparably better than anyone could have imagined even a few years ago.

This does not mean that the process will be easy. Western influence in Eastern Europe is still relatively limited, and the future of the region will ultimately depend on complex internal developments in both the Soviet Union and the East European countries. Violent instability and disruption could still occur, with all the adverse consequences that would ensue. Even if both superpowers are wholeheartedly committed to adopting a mutual security approach in Eastern Europe, the actions of indigenous forces may undo the best efforts of the two sides.

Nevertheless, by consistently supporting increased political liberalization and free-market economic reforms, the United States and its allies can help expedite the transition to a new and more stable European order. Ideally, U.S. officials should seek to devise as many measures as they can that will endure even if Soviet political conditions change. Should they be successful, the positive trends in Eastern Europe and in Soviet-East European relations over the past few years could prove to be a lasting phenomenon. No result would be of greater tangible benefit to the security interests of both East and West.

Notes

1. It is worth noting, in this regard, that during the 1968 invasion of Czechoslovakia the Soviet Union placed its nuclear missile forces on full combat alert. See R. Jeffrey Smith and Patrick E. Tyler, "To the Brink of War in the Prague Spring," *The Washington Post*, National Weekly Edition (December 11-17, 1989), p. 15.

2. The unique case of Romania in December 1989 is an interesting exception to this statement. If the Soviet Union had dispatched troops in support of the anti-Ceausescu forces, East-West relations would not have suffered. On the contrary, French, British, and American officials publicly expressed support for a possible Soviet military intervention, though Gorbachev did not take up their suggestion. Since this special set of circumstances is not likely to be repeated, it is safe to posit that Soviet military intervention in Eastern Europe in the future would have highly adverse domestic and international repercussions. The effects of past interventions were frankly discussed by Yuriy Levada in "Reaktivnaya otdacha," *Moskovskie novosti*, no. 34 (August 20, 1989), p. 7.

3. This statement excludes the use of force by Poland, East Germany, Bulgaria, and Hungary against Czechoslovakia in 1968, which was obviously done at Soviet behest (albeit with the eager approval of the East German, Polish, and Bulgarian authorities at the time).

4. This has been acknowledged by a leading Soviet Academy of Sciences' research institute, the Institute of Economics of the World Socialist System (IEMSS), in "East-West Relations and Eastern Europe: The Soviet Perspective," *Problems of Communism* 37, no. 3 (May-August 1988), especially pp. 60-62.

5. The first clear indication of Gorbachev's willingness to tolerate such changes came during his speech before the European Parliament in July 1989: "The social and political orders of certain countries changed in the past, and may change again in the future. However, this is exclusively a matter for the peoples themselves to decide; it is their choice. Any interference in internal affairs, or any attempts to limit the sovereignty of states — including friends and allies, or anyone else — are impermissible" ("Rech' M. S. Gorbacheva," *Izvestiya*, July 7, 1989, p. 2). Since then, statements by Gorbachev and his colleagues have been even more strongly supportive of the East European states' "freedom of sociopolitical and economic choice." Most notably, Soviet foreign minister Eduard Shevardnadze has stressed that the Warsaw Pact "need not be associated with ideology" and can accommodate "whatever political system and structure [each East European] people wants to establish" ("Devyat' chasov v Bukhareste," *Izvestiya*, January 8, 1990, p. 4).

6. See, for example, Mark Palmer, "U.S. and Western Policy — New Opportunities for Action," in William E. Griffith, ed., *Central and Eastern Europe: The Opening Curtain?* (Boulder, CO.: Westview Press, 1989), pp. 388-400, and Lincoln Gordon, ed., *Eroding Empire: Western Relations with Eastern Europe* (Washington, D.C.: The Brookings Institution, 1987).

7. See Henry Kissinger, "Reversing Yalta," *The Washington Post* (April 27, 1989), p. A30, and Irving Kristol, "Forget Arms Control...," *The New York Times* (September 12, 1989), p. A19. For a more elaborate article on a similar theme in the pre-Gorbachev era, see Zbigniew Brzezinski, "The Future of Yalta," *Foreign Affairs* 63, no. 5 (Winter 1984/85), pp. 279-302. Brzezinski's more recent views on the matter, which depart somewhat from his earlier article, are in "Ending the Cold War," *The Washington Quarterly* 12, no. 4 (Autumn 1989), pp. 29-34. The most recent proponent of a "grand deal" is Stanley Hoffmann, in "How a Reunified Germany Can Benefit All Europe," *The Boston Sunday Globe* (February 11, 1990), p. A23.

8. To be sure, the Austrian State Treaty has been impervious to fluctuations in Soviet domestic and foreign policies; but it applies only to Austria. A more ambitious scheme for the whole of Eastern and Central Europe, including states contiguous with the Soviet Union, would be far more susceptible to derailment. Western countries would therefore be entering into formal arrangements without any assurance that those arrangements would last. What is more, they would undoubtedly have to make substantial concessions as part of a "grand deal" (including the withdrawal of American troops from Europe), which could prove highly detrimental later on if Soviet policy changed.

9. For other perspectives on the German Question, see the chapters in this book by Francis Meehan and Mikhail Kozhokin.

10. For a useful overview, see Diether Raff, *Deutsche Geschichte vom alten Reich zur Zweiten Republik* (Hamburg: Max Hueber Verlag, 1985).

11. John P. Gillis, "How Different Is Germany?" *The Wilson Quarterly* 14, no. 1 (Winter 1990), p. 87; "Steps to German Unity: One, Two, Three...Crash," *The Economist* (January 27, 1990), pp. 50-52; "Poll: E. Germans Back Reunification," *The Boston Sunday Globe* (January 14, 1990), p. 9; and "Deutschland, Deutschland über alles," *The Economist* (January 13 1990), pp. 43-44.

12. R.D., "Zamiast rozwagi . . .," *Trybuna Ludu* (Warsaw), (September 19, 1989), p. 4. See also the similar comments about Germany in "Przemowienie Mieczyslawa F. Rakowskiego na zakonczenie XV Plenum KC PZPR," *Trybuna Ludu* (Warsaw), (September 20, 1989), p. 3.

13. It is on these grounds of "realpolitik," rather than on grounds of morality, that I would concede the importance of self-determination for the Germans. If morality were the only criterion, the claims of, say, the Kurds to self-determination should be accorded much greater precedence than the claims of the Germans. The reason that the Mutual Security Project has focused on the claims of the Germans rather than the claims of the Kurds is simply that a failure to deal with the German Question could substantially increase the risk of an East-West war. No comparable risk would attend a failure to satisfy the Kurdish claims, no matter how morally deserving the Kurds may be.

14. See, for example, "Interv'yu M. S. Gorbacheva Sovetskomu televideniyu," *Pravda* (July 10, 1989), p. 1; and "E. Shevardnadze: 'Nuzhno vesti dialog so vsemi,'" *Argumenty i fakty*, no. 2, (January 13-19, 1990), p. 2.

15. Many Soviet commentators, in fact, have acknowledged this; see, for example, the recent comments of TASS's main commentator on military affairs, Vladimir Chernyshev: "The creation of a common European home and the destruction of the Warsaw Pact and NATO at one stroke, having skipped over all the problems and difficulties that now exist in many spheres of international life in Europe, is hardly possible. It is hardly possible to consider such an approach as anything other than illusory, for it has nothing in common with practice....At the present stage of historical development, the necessity of preserving the conceivable prospects for the North Atlantic alliance and the Warsaw Pact Organization should be heeded, since these may make a contribution toward strengthening European security and...preserving stability on the continent." From Moscow Radio, transcribed in U.S. Foreign Broadcast Information Service, *Daily Report: Soviet Union*, (January 8, 1990), p. 1.

16. Polish Press Agency report of news conference with Krzysztof Skubiszewski, 14 February 1990. Hungarian and Czechoslovak officials have made similar statements.

17. For a review of such incidents as of 1980, see J. M. Montias, "Economic Conditions and Political Instability in Communist Countries: Observations on Strikes, Riots, and Other Disturbances," *Studies in Comparative Communism* 13, no. 4 (Winter 1980), pp. 283-299.

18. Long before the events of 1989 it was clear that the foreign imposition of the communist regimes in Eastern Europe, and the subordination of those regimes to Soviet preferences and

policies, denied them any legitimacy beyond the economic "outputs" they could generate for their populations. A few Western scholars, however, used to insist that the East European communist regimes had indeed managed to establish a more diffuse form of legitimacy; see, for example, Stephen White, "Economic Performance and Communist Legitimacy," *World Politics* 38, no. 3 (April 1986), pp. 462-482. White's arguments have not fared well, to say the least, in the face of recent developments.

19. For a concise overview of the lessons from the 1970s, see Wlodzimierz Brus, "Economic Reforms as an Issue in Soviet-East European Relations," in Karen Dawisha and Philip Hanson, eds., *Soviet-East European Dilemmas: Coercion, Competition and Consent* (London: Heinemann, 1981), pp. 84-89.

20. For a cogent discussion of such measures, see Jeffrey Sachs, "Eastern Europe's Economies: What Is To Be Done?" *The Economist* (January 13, 1990), pp. 21-26.

21. See "SEV: na poroge bol'shikh peremen," *Izvestiya* (January 10, 1990), pp. 1, 4.

22. The reservations that some East Europeans have about the proposed changes in CMEA stem from concerns of an opposite nature as well. In particular, East European officials recognize that the adoption of world prices for intra-CMEA trade will lead, in the short term, to a considerable windfall for the Soviet Union. The prices for Soviet exports of energy supplies and raw materials will rise, whereas the prices for East European exports of machinery and consumer goods (which generally are well below world quality standards) will go down. See Yu. Popov, "SEV: Vtoroe dykhanie," *Pravitel'stvennyi vestnik*, no. 3 (January 1990), p. 2. To the extent that this short-term dislocation stimulates more rapid reform in Eastern Europe, however, it may actually prove beneficial in the longer term.

23. For data pertaining to the proposed CFE agreement, see Michael R. Gordon, "A Troop-Cut Assent," *The New York Times* (February 10, 1990), p. 6; U.S. Congress, Congressional Budget Office, *Budgetary and Military Effects of a Treaty Limiting Conventional Forces in Europe* (January 1990); and Michael D. Scanlan, *Conventional Forces in Europe (CFE) Negotiations: Facts and Figures*, Report No. 89-497F (Washington, D.C.: U.S. Congressional Research Service, 14 October 1989). Also see Andrew Slade, "CFE Special Report: Dismantling the Cold War," *Jane's Defence Weekly* 13, no. 2 (January 13, 1990), pp. 72-75; Jonathan Dean, "Negotiated Force Cuts in Europe: Overtaken by Events?" *Arms Control Today* 19, no. 10 (December 1989/January 1990), pp. 12-16; and Rüdiger Hartmann, "The CFE Negotiations: A Promising Start," *NATO Review* 37, no. 3 (June 1989), pp. 8-12.

24. This, in fact, is roughly what has happened with many of the unilateral "reductions" of Soviet weapons in Eastern Europe that Gorbachev announced in December 1988; see Douglas L. Clarke, "The Unilateral Arms Cuts in the Warsaw Pact," in Radio Free Europe, *Report on Eastern Europe* 1, no. 5 (February 2, 1990), pp. 43-47, esp. 44-45.

25. On this point, see CBO, *Budgetary and Military Effects of a Treaty Limiting Conventional Forces in Europe*, pp. 25-27.

10

The Common European Home and Mutual Security

Mikhail Bezrukov and Yuriy Davydov

The problem of mutual security in Europe should not be reduced to that of stability inside different European regions or countries. It is in fact much wider. The future of the European continent depends to a great extent on the general evolution of East-West relations.

Stability in Europe, divided into two blocs opposing each other, was assured in the past several decades by three interrelated factors:

— The existence of external threats for each bloc (whether they were real or imagined is another question);

— Military mutual deterrence based on a growing capacity of the sides to destroy each other;

— The predominance of the superpowers — the Soviet Union and the United States — in their respective blocs.

This kind of stability proved to be strongly built though it had three important shortcomings: a) it was very expensive; b) it distorted perception of real problems and needs of the region; and c) it was potentially dangerous, for its collapse could have brought about a nuclear catastrophe. In other words, the situation was stable but not sufficiently secure. In the past that was perhaps the only possible kind of stability given the realities of the international situation, and it survived the crises of the Cold War era.

The end of the 1980s will, beyond doubt, enter the history of international relations as a period of rapid erosion of the walls that have been separating East and West.

The break through the dividing lines is due primarily to the reform movement that is gathering strength in the East. Mounting reforms of economies and political structures in some of these countries here are accompanied by a radical revision of their foreign policy concepts. Rejected or substantially weakened are many "idols" of the past; many basic ideas about the outside world are reconsidered. Parallel steps are visible in the West: The "image of the enemy" has faded; the division of the world into "us" and "them" is being replaced by a more promising idea of unity of humanity. The consensus achieved in the Vienna follow-up meeting of the CSCE reflects this new reality.

There are other signs indicating that we are in a process of fundamental changes in East-West relations on European soil. Following the INF Treaty, we witness sincere efforts of the East and the West to lower the balance of conventional forces in Europe. Both in the West and in the East the superpowers are losing their dominant Cold War style positions. It is quite understandable why Mikhail Gorbachev's appeals for "new political thinking" are echoed by President George Bush's calls to move "beyond containment."

It is now more and more widely recognized both in the East and in the West that relations between the European states could surpass the limits set up by the Cold War confrontation. Mutual fears and enmity can and should be replaced by a growing East-West cooperation and dialogue. Already several generations of politicians on both sides have tried to lead their countries to victory in our "historical dispute." In doing so they were convinced of the validity of a black-and-white formula "we or they." Now it is clear more than ever that this approach has been *erroneous*. "We *and* they, together" is the principle that should guide our efforts in East-West relations.

The evolution of the situation in Europe gives rise to discussions about its future and about a new European political order. At the core of these discussions is a striving for a European identity. Among many ideas that have emerged is Mikhail Gorbachev's idea of a "common European home." In Prague on April 10, 1987 he said: "We now turn ourselves resolutely against the division of the continent. . . we have introduced the idea of a 'common European home.'" In this connection at least four questions arise: Are there any preconditions for building this "common European home"? What can every side gain from it? What serves as a basis for the edifice? What difficulties may the process of constructing it face?

The idea of a unified, peaceful Europe is an old one. In the past many of the best minds of the continent embraced it in one form or another — Kant, Voltaire, Rousseau, Saint-Simon, Mazzini, Garibaldi and even Metternich, among many others. The main reason for the present surge of interest in the idea is simply that now the time is ripe for it. A set of preconditions now exists, making it possible to move beyond the postwar European system of relations.

The most general of these preconditions are: the historical memory of the European people with its deep understanding of inadmissibility of a new war; a high level of mutual understanding among the nations of the continent (higher than in any other region); a uniquely diversified system of bilateral and multilateral interactions, especially the Helsinki process; and a common cultural and historical heritage. These are good starting ground for building a system of relations in Europe based on the principle of mutual security.

The present situation gives us some additional reasons to believe that Europe is ready for a gradual dismantling of the system it has inherited from the past.

First, it is evident that Europe has already been living for many years under circumstances where the Cold War has exhausted itself. The states of the East and the West have reached most of the goals they had been aiming at when participating in it. At the same time some goals, which proved to be unattainable, were dropped. By now many of the social and political differences that once had been the main reason for confrontation have eroded or even disappeared totally. Some of the differences are, of course, still present, but they are much less acute than they were forty years ago. Today, the high level of military preparations do not correspond to the level of social and political differences existing between the countries of Europe.

Second, representatives of a new generation are entering active political life in European countries and in the United States. They are free from the stereotypes of the 1940s and 1950s; they fear less; and they believe more in the peaceful development of East-West relations. They do not share some of the allegiances of the generation of their fathers and above all they refuse to accept the system of political-military division of Europe.

Third, the perception of a threat to survival is changing. Traditionally both sides were obsessed with the specter of nuclear and conventional wars. But as it turned out there are other important sources of danger as well. And they are common both to the East and to the West: deterioration of environment, international terrorism, drugs, and so forth. Global problems can not be solved by one state, one alliance or even one social system. This means that besides national and regional interests there are also those of the European and global communities.

Fourth, both in the East and in the West we observe more tolerance towards other belief systems and more readiness to listen with patience to the arguments of the other side. The age of uncompromising "theological disputes" between advocates of capitalism and adherents to the socialist idea is clearly becoming a thing of the past.

Fifth, democratic institutions are gaining strength in both parts of the European continent. And as we know from our historical experience, democratic societies have convincingly demonstrated their preference for non-military solutions of any disputes that arise between them.

One can draw the conclusion that the process of change in Europe has reached a critical point. The area of shared interests in East-West relations has considerably grown while their confrontation has drastically diminished. This process gave a powerful impulse to the idea of mutual security. Let us hope that both the East and the West will take advantage of the current situation.

Possible positive outcomes

Overcoming of the division of Europe and construction of the "common European home" based on mutual security principles can be successful only if both the East and the West perceive the advantages of a new system of relations in comparison with the old ones. What are these advantages?

— The emergence of a system of mutual security, eliminating fears and suspicions, would allow both sides to use huge resources that are now spent on the arms race for solution of other problems;

— The enlargement of a European network of economic ties; a big European economic market could provide dynamic economic development for the whole region;

— Strengthening of political stability on the European continent, by the creation of all-European institutions, could help to solve political, economic and other problems;

— Organic ties between East and West European states can be created;

— An all-European consciousness can emerge, as opposed to national and group egoisms.

Principles and stages

It is possible to overcome the division of Europe only on the basis of common approaches to such fundamental issues as mutual security; trust between peoples and states; non-interference into internal affairs of the other nations; human rights; democracy; legal foundation of the functioning of the international, state and public life; role of the market forces in the economy, etc.

The desire expressed by the Soviet Union to join some of the international agreements worked out by the Council of Europe reflects a readiness of the Soviet side to reach common understanding with the West on these issues. The final document signed in the Vienna follow-up CSCE conference demonstrates that the values of the East and the West are closer to each other than many skeptics might have expected. This document is a very important step towards the "common European home."

The construction of the "common European home" could be divided into several stages.

In the initial stage, dramatic changes in the existing European structures are undesirable. NATO, the Warsaw Treaty Organization, the European Community and the Council for Mutual Economic Assistance could play a role in a positive transformation of relations among the European countries, especially if their functioning undergoes appropriate reforms. At the same time the emergence of new forms of regional cooperation should not be excluded, first of all in the East.

The Warsaw Treaty Organization and NATO should in any case stop performing their traditional functions, determined by the East-West confrontation of the Cold War years.

Reform of the Warsaw Treaty Organization, if it is to be implemented, should develop along the following three interrelated lines. First, there should be a resolute shift from military to political cooperation among its members. Especially important in this connection is the question of the Soviet military presence on the territories of other WTO countries. Second, the WTO should be transformed from a Soviet dominated organization to a flexible union based on a real equality of the rights of its participants. Without that, the "superpower legacy" in the organization cannot be overcome. Third, the political institutions of the WTO should be developed. The existence of a Political Consultative Committee and a Committee of Ministers of Foreign Affairs only obscures the fact that the WTO political structures are in an embryonic state, compared to the military ones. The problem could be at least partially solved by the creation of new permanent and/or ad hoc political bodies inside the WTO system. These could help to coordinate the efforts of the member states in seeking common interests and also facilitate the process of reaching compromises acceptable to all sides.

The spheres of political cooperation among the WTO members are potentially large. To name but some of them: political support of their multilevel existing and developing economic ties; preservation of stability in the region; development of all-European structures; and coordination of efforts aimed at creation of a new security system in Europe, based on cooperation with the West.

The reformed Warsaw Treaty Organization could become an important instrument for solving problems inherited from World War II, especially those connected with the German Question.

During this initial stage, both the East and the West, having in mind mutual security principles, should concentrate their efforts on the following three goals:

— Levels of military confrontation on the European continent should be lowered.

— National laws and foreign policies of the European states should be brought in line with international agreements, especially those worked out through the Helsinki process.

— Both sides should encourage development of transnational economic ties between independent producers and agencies (that is, those whose activity is not directly guided by government bodies and is based on market principles).

The last goal will not be easy to reach, given the current economic difficulties being experienced by East European countries and the Soviet Union, and also the incompatibility of the Western market economies and the highly centralized ones that are still largely in place in the East European countries and the Soviet Union. But it should be kept in mind that without such ties it is hardly possible to move toward the creation of what could be termed organic ties between the countries of the East and the West, and therefore towards the "common European home."

Thus the mutual security idea has also an economic dimension.

In later stages, emerging common or comparable features in the national structures and foreign policies of European states would create the necessary preconditions for intensive cooperation between them. Formation of transnational economic complexes would make them more interdependent economically and would facilitate economic integration. Similarities in political structures and legal regulations would make it much easier to establish all-European institutions.

In these later stages, all-European institutions would be increasingly relied on in regulating relations in different spheres: security problems, economic exchanges, foreign policy, culture and education, etc. They would be moving forces behind European integration. The precise forms of their activity will be determined by the process of construction of the "common European home."

The "common European home" would include, first, all the territory from the Atlantic to the Urals. But this in no way means the exclusion of the United States and Canada, for they are linked to Europe by extensive historical, political, economic and cultural ties. Any attempts to erect artificial barriers between North America and Europe will inevitably fail. They contradict the very goal of forming a new system of relations in Europe based on mutual security principles. It will never be possible to create the "common European home" at the expense of the United States and Canada, who have played an important role in the Helsinki process.

Politically and economically, North America is even more a part of Europe than even some European nations presently are. Modern technology has drastically shrunk the Atlantic, and the United States and Canada (especially in security terms) are as close to Europe as Great Britain was at the beginning of the present century, or even closer.

The United States and Canada should in some form be involved in the European mutual security system. Their dependence on and their involvement in it will increase the stake of both countries in European stability. One also has to take into consideration the possibility that if the United States withdraws politically from Europe, that could create fears and feelings of insecurity in some of the West European nations, which could be highly destabilizing in the long run. It should also be kept in mind, as history shows us, that there is a certain positive and healthy European influence on the behavior of the United States in the political-military sphere, an influence one would like to keep.

It is often said that the Soviet Union is too big and has too many problems to be part of a stable European system. This argument in favor of exclusion of the Soviet Union from all-European cooperation may look a weighty one. But other considerations should be also taken into account. First, historically and culturally, the Soviet Union belongs to Europe. For many centuries we have influenced European developments and have felt in turn their impact. European countries are our traditional and natural partners and though the Soviet Union (Russia) differed in the past and still differs from our European neighbors, our mutual attraction should not be overlooked. Second, the Soviet Union and other European countries are interdependent in many respects. Soviet problems would inevitably knock at the doors of other European nations. Third, the USSR may not be so big after all. The United Europe that would surface after 1992 would be large and powerful by any standards. Fourth, any attempt to exclude the Soviet Union from the "common European home" would renew Cold War fears and suspicions and would destabilize the situation in the whole region. In other words, it will be impossible to create a viable system of relations in Europe based on the mutual security principle without the Soviet Union.

Transitional period

Transitional periods are usually difficult ones, and the present course of events in Europe is not an exception. Any transitional period is marked by the coexistence — and the conflict of — the old system of relations that has outlived its time, and the gradually emerging new approaches and structures. This very conflict by itself may be a significant destabilizing factor. For the moment the legacy of the Cold War is still with us and a new era of East-West cooperation free from military threats is making but its first steps.

Cold War symptoms are still numerous, unfortunately. Large armies face each other. Many institutions brought to life by the East-West confrontation continue to function. The temptation to gain one-sided concessions has not disappeared, nor has the habit to rejoice at misfortunes of the other side. We still hear "fatherly" advice in speeches as to what is to be done in this or that part of Europe.

Sprouts of a new type of relations on the European continent have to grow through stones of enmity and estrangement inherited from the past decades. But they do grow. Both in the East and the West, understanding is growing that Europe now has an unprecedented opportunity to draw a final line between its future, and its past marked by confrontations and wars. The "new political thinking" calls precisely to remove all political obstacles that bar the road towards unity of Europe and to open a new page in the history of this continent.

The main problem facing Europe today is to ensure the stable (and peaceful!) evolution of Europe toward a new political order. Where could possible threats to this evolution come from? There are several potential sources of instability:

— There could be attempts both from the East and the West to exploit contradictions and problems inherent to the processes of change in both parts of Europe to obtain one-sided advantages.

— There could be failure or unsatisfactory results of negotiations on conventional and nuclear weapons or confidence-building measures, or violations of the already existing agreements.

— Technological innovations could arise in the military sphere that could complicate negotiations between East and West and upset the military balance in Europe.

— There could be active efforts to undermine the Warsaw Treaty Organization or NATO.

— Reforms in the Soviet Union and East European countries could fail or "skid"; there could be a failure to create a common (market) base for economic interactions between East and West.

— Hazards could arise from the difference in the levels and characters of economic and political integration in the East and in the West; and the gap could deepen between integrating Western Europe and transforming the East.

— Attempts could be made to exclude the Soviet Union or the United States – or both of them – from the new political order in Europe.

— The process of military integration in Western Europe could pose a hazard if it led to a rapid growth of West European military capabilities.

— There could be risks in any attempt to force reunification of the two German states without reaching consensus among other interested sides in Europe and North America.

Most of these sources of instability could undermine the foundations of the mutual security system in Europe.

Both East and West have an interest in a peaceful transition to a more stable political order in Europe. They should do everything in their power to reduce these and any other threats to the present positive developments on the continent. The "common European home" and European political stability are not identical ideas. But they are interrelated ones. It is hardly possible to build a "common European home" in an unstable international environment. On the other hand, only gradually overcoming the division of Europe can ultimately assure a more stable European political order.

11

The German Question: A Mutual Security Approach

FRANCIS MEEHAN

Central Europe was the breeding ground of two world wars in the first half of the twentieth century. After the defeat of Nazi Germany in 1945, Europe became divided into two opposing systems and alliances. The two German states became the focus of a maximum concentration of East-West confrontation of forces and arms.

Current developments are rapidly changing the political face of Central Europe as we have known it over more than four decades. Due largely to indigenous movements for political and economic reform in the various countries of the region, but also to the positive view of the reform processes on the part of the USSR, an entirely new situation has been created. If it continues, it could open the way for radically more constructive approaches to East-West relations in general, and in particular to relations between the countries of Eastern and Western Europe.

A growing sense of the possibilities for positive change is expressed in President Bush's call for the creation of a Europe "whole and free," and by President Gorbachev's concept of building a "common European home." The European Community is increasingly preoccupied by the implications of current developments in Central Europe for its own further evolution.

While the impression that the political ice age in Europe may be drawing to a close inspires hope for a more rational European order, history and realism teach that self-determination and democratic institutions do not in themselves constitute an irrevocable guarantee of national or international security. The loosening of the domestic and international constraints that have bound Central Europe for almost half a century could, if misdirected, revive the national animosities, divisions and power struggles that brought Europe, and the world, to disaster in the past.

It is all the more necessary, therefore, for the international community to approach the construction of a new, undivided Europe in all prudence, with due regard for the interests of all the parties concerned, and with the paramount goal of assuring mutual security for East and West and for all parties.

These precepts are relevant generally, but they have specific application in considering German issues, not only because of past history but also by reason of the continuing centrality and weight of these issues in any rearrangement of the European political landscape.

It has to be recognized that for many, in both East and West, the division of Germany into two states with membership in the opposed alliance systems, has been seen as in itself the surest guarantee of security in Europe. German reunification has been a dead, or at most a theoretical, issue for well over a generation. Now, largely — but not solely — because of current developments in the GDR, and the reaction to these events in the FRG, reunification is suddenly alive. It seems likely to remain so, in the two German states themselves and in the international community at large.

Two broad approaches to German issues (including reunification) are possible, negative and positive. The former would proceed basically from fear, rooted in the past, the latter from the conviction that the division of Europe cannot be ended without addressing the German Question positively. Indeed, it would be argued in the positive mode that a solution of the German Question is the essential prerequisite for a genuine international effort to build a new Europe. The rebuilding of Germany would be seen not as an unacceptable risk, but rather as a historical opportunity, not to forget the past but to put it behind and move ahead into a truly new European era.

Current East-West efforts to reach agreement on reductions in levels of the opposing forces and weapons systems in Europe, the bulk of which are deployed in the FRG and GDR, open up new perspectives for a reappraisal of German issues based on mutual security principles. It is hardly conceivable that significant reductions in levels of forces and arms in central Europe would not be accompanied by considerable readjustment of relations between the two German states.

The fundamental guiding principle of any reordering of the German situation must be that the new arrangements, whatever they might be, should enhance mutual security in Europe as a whole by removing potential sources of instability and tension.

One such major source lies in the two German states themselves. Current developments in the GDR, and their possible implications for relations between the FRG and the GDR, support the view that the German situation is inherently dynamic. This dynamism, if it is not channeled constructively through new approaches based firmly on the principle of assured mutual security, could jeopardize East-West efforts to reduce international tensions.

The most effective means of managing the dynamic potential of German developments is through unequivocal application of the principle of political self-determination. The Germans, in the two states, cannot be made an exception *ad infinitum* to that principle, solely because of past history. Efforts to maintain them as an exception will sooner or later produce resentment and lead to difficulty and ultimately insecurity. The Germans in the two states should be seen, and should see themselves, not as objects of international political processes but rather as those primarily concerned with deciding upon their domestic political institutions and their international status, including the form of association between the two states, or their fusion into a single state. Decisions on issues of such magnitude cannot be imposed from without.

At the same time, because of the central importance of the German Question for East-West mutual security in Europe, the conclusion of the process by which the Germans in the two states decide upon their international status should be subject to ratification by interested parties, and principally by the member states of the two alliance systems.

It is clear that consideration of issues of the scope indicated, in the German states themselves and in the international community, is a complex process that will take time. The process should not be compressed, neither should it be extended deliberately and indefinitely. It should ensure an orderly, prudent and progressive review of German issues by the Germans and other interested parties.

In a real sense, the process has already begun, both in the FRG and the GDR, and internationally. Its shape will presumably become clearer in the two German states in the time ahead. In particular, the domestic political developments now in train in the GDR should afford better insight into the views of East German citizens on the key political issues now before them. The outcome must be awaited by the others concerned, as the point of departure for further deliberation.

While those primarily concerned in the process are the Germans themselves, the Four Powers with responsibility for issues concerning Germany as a whole, and for Berlin, have a special role.[1] Not only is it special, it is peculiarly delicate. Their responsibilities date from the unconditional surrender of 1945 and the installation of military government in the respective zones of occupation.

The Four Powers will not wish to act, or be seen as acting, as occupying powers enforcing their views on the two German states at this juncture. On the contrary, in accordance with the self-determination principle, they will wish to receive and respect German views.

At the same time, because of the scope and pace of events, and in light of their special status in regard to Germany as a whole and in Berlin, it would seem prudent for the Four Powers to take the initiative at some point soon to inaugurate broad-based international consultations at an appropriately high level on German issues. Tackling the German Question is a massively complicated task which calls for the closest East-West consultation and coordination. The Four Powers have a special role to play in determining how the task is addressed.

It is not feasible to try to prescribe precisely how the international process of deliberation upon German issues should proceed. Nevertheless, a sequence can be indicated. The Four Powers should draw in the two German states at an early date, and arrangements should be established for thorough consultation with member states in the two alliance systems thereafter.

It will be important to eschew using the German Question for one-sided advantage. Failure to do so would have divisive effects, and would sow mutual suspicion and mistrust. The essence of an approach based on mutual security is that it should create confidence — as among the Four Powers, the Germans themselves, the two alliances, and in the international community at large.

Depending on the actual course of events, there could be an extended interim period during which the international process of addressing German issues continues, but before final conclusions are reached and ratified. The status of the two German states — that is their mutual relations, and their international status — will be a question of first importance during this period.

It would seem prudent, and in the general interest of creating confidence and assuring mutual security, for the two states to continue to function as separate state entities during the interim period. By the same token, they should continue to participate as member states of the respective alliances for the duration of the same period.

The international process of reviewing German issues should have as an essential accompaniment the broadest normalization of relations between the two German states. The form and content of normalization are essentially matters for the two states to decide upon themselves, but freedom of movement and contact between them is a prerequisite.

It can be assumed that the two states will be exploring various aspects of political, economic, cultural and other cooperation in the time ahead. Their efforts in this direction should be encouraged by the Four Powers and the international community at large.

While conclusion of a German peace treaty, finally bringing the Second World War to an international juridical close, still lies in the future and will depend, among other things, on the future status of the German states, or state, the Four Powers should take the issue under active consideration. There may have been no concrete grounds for addressing the issue in the past, but in the radically changing situation which is developing a positive approach to the peace treaty issue would in itself be a major contribution to the creation of the new Europe which now beckons.

Notes

1. The Four Powers are, of course, the four chief victors in Europe in the Second World War: the United States, the USSR, Great Britain, and France. These powers occupied Germany in 1945. The occupation zone of the three Western powers later became the Federal Republic of Germany; the occupation zone of the USSR later became the German Democratic Republic.

12

The German Question and its International Dimensions

MIKHAIL KOZHOKIN

The system of international relations in Europe has entered a period of transition. 1989 became the year when the Cold War was finished, the year that marked the end of the postwar era in the development of international relations in Europe. In the international sphere the confrontation between the countries of state-socialism and the highly industrialized Western nations is coming to an end. Eastern Europe is returning to the natural stream of European policy and this metamorphosis has already marked the first outlines of the future "common Europe," based on mutual security.

This new era not only creates new problems, but also urges resolving those whose existence politicians failed to notice or tried to ignore in the past decades. The most important among these for Europe is undoubtedly the German Question. Only a year ago it was widely believed that the question was not of reunification, but one of the character of the relationship between the two German states and its impact on European security. Today one has to acknowledge the evident truth known already in the nineteenth century, namely that a nation cannot live artificially divided. Emergence of a United Germany is an objective reality, determined by the requirements of the internal development of the German nation.

In theory it is possible to oppose this process, but only from outside and with the help of military force. In the contemporary world there are no states that would risk using such extreme measures, taking into account their inevitable consequences.

But it is also obvious that the Germans' progress toward a united state should take place without cataclysms, without upsetting the European and world balance of power, and without creating threats to the neighbor states.

The very beginning of practical rapprochement of the two German states is evoking concern in the West and East alike.

The first alarming signal for Eastern Europeans came on the day when the Berlin wall went down. On learning about the decision of the government of East Germany to open the border with West Germany, West German Chancellor Helmut Kohl interrupted his official visit to Poland for one day and returned to Bonn. In this way he openly indicated that relations with Poland are of secondary importance to the FRG compared to the events in the GDR. Thus many Poles, irrespective of their political inclinations, were given reasons to think about whether West German businessmen would be eager to invest capital in their country's economy, if equally good or better opportunities opened up in East Germany. It is also time to think about the fact that in historical perspective the principle of inviolability of frontiers is not always tantamount to the principle of their immutability.

So far it is not quite clear in what specific ways Poland, as well as Czechoslovakia, will react to the emergence of a United Germany: whether it will push them in the direction of more balanced assessment of the utility of the Warsaw Treaty Organization and political links with the Soviet Union; or whether it will become an additional stimulus for creation of a new regional community (such as, for instance, a Warsaw-Prague-Budapest axis).

The German Question is generating frictions even inside the European Community (EC). One can hardly speak of fear of the "German Threat" in the form that existed some decades ago, when the scars of World War II were still festering. (NATO, incidentally, was regarded by its architects as a means to prevent the rebirth of German military power in the future.) Even if this fear does exist, it exists at a purely emotional level and can be disregarded. Today West Germany's partners are worried by entirely different problems. First, a United Germany may be too large an entity for the EC's framework. Even today West Germany dominates the European Community, widely exploiting this dominance to secure its interests. Many EC member countries would be only too pleased if the final solution to the German Question could be postponed until after 1992 when, they hope, deep integration would leave little room for national ambitions and egoism.

The West German government speaks of German reunification in the context of constructing a united Europe. But will these declarations really be followed with concrete actions? Or will West Germany be less willing to support the common aims of the community? Will it become less compliant? Will it prove more reluctant to heed the interests of other EC members?

The second "big question" for West Germany's partners is whether East Germany becoming an "internal factor" within the EC framework could naturally slow down the rate of Common Market integration. The community still remembers the difficulties it had when "digesting" Greece and Portugal. EC representatives have repeatedly stressed that the community is uninterested in expanding its membership, since the adaptation of new members to the level of development achieved by the community and to the regulations within it will be complicated and will inevitably constitute a drag on the whole of the community. A tendency can be discerned in EC activities to protect the interests of the "privileged few." Even Austria has been listed as "undesirable." Even now there are projects that stipulate the division of outsiders into several classes or subgroups (for example, theory of concentric circles).

Integration of the Germanies could lead to changes in the alignment of forces within the EC, in the character of its further development, and in its relationship with the outer world, all of which cause concern among European countries not belonging to the Community. Their involvement in integration processes in the EC might meet with additional obstacles that, in turn, would inevitably make them pay more attention to alternative ways for resolving their problems. Of these alternative ways the most seriously debated are: the reinvigoration of the European Free Trade Association, other mechanisms of regional interaction such as exist in Northern Europe, and finally, establishment of new "alliances" with participation of those East European countries that have embarked on the road of restructuring their economies along the lines of a free market.

These processes have, in turn, given birth to counterprojects for overcoming the emerging contradictions. Thus, President Mitterand tried to gain the initiative by putting forward a plan of a European confederation. Soon after that the Chairman of the Council of the EC, J. Delore, proposed a piecemeal program for building a United Europe, including both parts of the continent. Delore considers the creation of a genuine federation of twelve West European countries by the year 2000 the most important and necessary precondition for the implementation of the "Mitterand Plan."

The American position on the question of German reunification can hardly be described in clearcut terms. Washington has been advocating German reunification for decades. This issue, generated in the years of the Cold War was used by Washington as a means of Western consolidation and exerting leverage on the USSR and its allies, rather than a question of practical German policy. Now that the prospects of reunification are real, the U.S. attitude is being formed under the influence of a more complex cluster of considerations.

Officially, the U.S. declares itself favorable to German reunification, stressing the continuity of the U.S. position over decades. On the one hand, Washington takes into account the views of the West German government (its leading political ally in Western Europe) and on the other hand, it admits the objective nature of the emergence of a United Germany.

At the same time, the U.S. administration is aware of the fact that the merger of the two Germanies may create serious problems. Rapid changes in the status of East Germany could complicate the conclusion of the treaty on radical reductions of armed forces in Europe. Moreover, these changes will inevitably affect the entire East-West dialogue.

The reunification of the two German states belonging to two opposing political-military blocs — in whatever form it might occur — could result in the prompt disintegration of the existing structures of European security. If this happens, a political vacuum could appear and it would take some time to fill it. This course of development is difficult to predict and it could potentially destabilize the situation in Europe.

If the situation around the German Question starts developing into a zero-sum game where Soviet losses are the West's gains, and the strategic situation evolves in a direction dangerous to the USSR, the Soviet leadership might be tempted to assume a tough and uncompromising stance.

Despite West Germany's priority position on the list of U.S. allies, Washington cannot afford to ignore the views of other West European countries when the United States' role as the political leader of the West is at stake.

The reemergence of a United Germany also revives many problems that appeared in Europe after World War II, as, for example, economic and territorial ones. So far nothing definite can be said about a mechanism that could help resolve them on the basis of a reasonable compromise. Disruption of the postwar status quo in Europe will also raise the question of how unshakable the results of World War II are in the world at large.

The objective interests of the United States favor gradual and controlled progress towards the solution of the German Question; and Washington has declared this interest repeatedly. Today we can define the following parameters of the U.S. stance:

— Reunification of Germany must be linked with the EC integration processes; thus the German Question is transferred from the national context to a broader, international one.

— The American side's official declarations recognize in principle the necessity of preserving the postwar borders in Europe fixed in international accords.

— The American side is displaying interest in variants of a pan-European solution to the German Question, as well as to the problems of Eastern Europe at large.

The Soviet Union's stand with respect to the German Question is based on the need to provide safe political, juridical and material guarantees to prevent the German unity from creating in perspective any threat to the security of other states and to peace in Europe. The main approaches of Soviet diplomacy toward the unity of Germany have already been identified:

— Measures to bring together the two German states must be synchronized with the all-European process, realized stage by stage and within its basic framework.

— Solution of problems originating from World War II and postwar development must be found either through the conclusion of a peace treaty with United Germany or through arrangements within the Helsinki process.

— There must be recognition and strict observance of existing borders in Europe.

— The Four Powers must reach an agreement on the scope of their rights and responsibilities in resolving the German Question.

— The most complicated problem is the problem of the United Germany's membership in the existing political-military structures, or alternatively, its demilitarization and military neutrality. Evidently, the solution of this problem will be very difficult, as well as protracted in time, and may require certain interim stages. (In particular, the issues of the Four Powers' military presence and rights; and also of nuclear weapons present on German soil are still open.)

In sum, the current political situation in the world demonstrates that for the first time in history objective prerequisites exist for peaceful solution of the German Question — the creation of a United Germany — on the basis of the mutual security principle, and serving the interests of all European states.

Part III

====

Working Group on the Persian Gulf

THE WORKING GROUP ON THE PERSIAN GULF was responsible for exploring the applicability of the mutual security approach to the improvement of American and Soviet security in the Persian Gulf region.

This Working Group decided to concentrate its efforts upon the development of a single joint paper in which both the American and Soviet sides could concur. In one part of this chapter there are specific short passages that explicitly are American statements and questions or Soviet statements and questions. Otherwise the chapter represents the shared views of the participants from both sides. Biographical sketches of the authors, and a list of the full membership of the Working Group on the Persian Gulf, are given at the back of the book.

— THE EDITORS

13

Toward Mutual Threat Reduction in the Persian Gulf

JO-ANNE HART (USA), HAROLD SAUNDERS (USA)
AND ANDREI SHUMIKHIN (USSR)

Introduction

Analyzing the dynamics of conflict, peacemaking, and development in a region such as the Persian Gulf is important in its own right, but that has not been the primary focus of the dialogue which generated this chapter. Our Working Group has discussed Soviet-American interaction in the Persian Gulf region.[1] Our purposes have been threefold: (1) to understand as deeply and to define as accurately as possible the real interests that guide our policymakers in this region; (2) to understand how this interaction affects the overall Soviet-American relationship; and (3) to explore how the mutual security framework suggests solutions to practical problems.

Our ultimate focus has been the overall superpower relationship because it is the totality of the interaction between the whole American and Soviet bodies politic that will determine the ability of these two nations to cooperate on problems in which they have a common interest, ranging from arms control to environmental protection. The two sides' ability to persevere through policies based on the concept of mutual security will depend on their capacity to sustain a sound overall relationship.

The joint nature of our discussions has allowed us to think about situations using the other side's assumptions, and allowed us to experience whether and how this changes our own thinking. Our hope has been to experience, to some degree, what changes when we see a situation not only as an American or Soviet analyst but as partners in the Soviet-American relationship. That relationship may have needs and interests in its own right. The ability to see problems through common lenses while preserving respect for our individual identities is essential for developing mutual security.

We conducted this experiment in applying the concept of mutual security to a particular situation because we believe that the conceptual lenses that a policymaker relies upon to understand a situation will partially determine how he or she will act in that situation. Public servants in the U.S., for instance, felt the difference between the approach of Richard Nixon, who saw the world through strategic lenses, and that of Jimmy Carter, who focused on human rights. Public servants in the Soviet Union felt the change between working for Leonid Brezhnev, who saw the world largely from an ideological perspective, and Mikhail Gorbachev with his imaginative "new political thinking."

At the same time, we recognize that policymakers will only accept that concepts make a difference if they are persuaded that using one set of assumptions rather than another would actually improve their behavior in particular situations. We hope that the experience of this working group will demonstrate the possibilities for such improvement.

There is an asymmetry of American and Soviet interests in the Gulf. We believe that recognizing this asymmetry, through a give-and-take in discussion, can lead to fuller understanding of our deeper concerns and our way of identifying our own interests. The very process of taking into account each other's deeper concerns helps to enlarge understanding of what each side identifies as its real interests. The more deeply we probed, the more clearly we were able to see the unique roots of certain interests and to understand that, in many cases, those interests were *not* in competition or in conflict. As the process of dialogue deepened, it became more and more possible to move away from a zero-sum notion of our respective interests.

A fundamental assumption of the mutual security approach is that superpower rivalry is not intractable and that a relationship based on reducing the threats perceived by both sides would increase their own and international security. Major domestic and foreign policy reforms within the Soviet Union and adjustments in American foreign policy thinking have made possible a restructuring of superpower relations. This restructuring has consisted, so far, in progress in the broad strategic relationship and in arms control.

Both superpowers are also aware of the importance of regional issues in solidifying improved relations. U.S. Secretary of State James Baker called for greater attention to regional problems in talks with the Soviet Union where, in his words, "it is important to move from competition to cooperation." Likewise, Soviet officials are on record recognizing the importance of regional policies to the overall superpower relationship. Officials on both sides have also stated that recent gains in Soviet-American relations may be jeopardized by regional conflicts. Their concern is justified: recent history demonstrates that rivalry in the Middle East can derail improving U.S.-Soviet relations. Despite this concern, the competitive nature of superpower behavior in the peripheral areas seems to have changed little by January 1990. Both powers are still at odds in Kampuchea, Afghanistan, and Central America and are not yet working together in the Persian Gulf or in the Arab-Israeli conflict.

This potential "end of the Cold War" challenges the Soviet Union and the United States each to reorient its Middle East policy. The alternative security context suggested by the concept of mutual security allows superpower relations in the Gulf to escape the limitations of zero-sum rivalry. The two countries have the opportunity to work together to build a more constructive relationship in the Persian Gulf.

The Persian Gulf at this moment is a particularly good time and place in which to consider such superpower interaction. There are salient interests on each side, and the superpowers are not distracted there by regional crises. There is time to think through what regional changes are possible in the near future and to consider how the superpowers might affect that future, as well as their own relationship, by operating within the mutual security framework. Furthermore, because events in that part of the world are not easily controlled by the superpowers, a firmer understanding of each other's perception of interests, threats, limitations and potential reactions would enhance their capacity for crisis prevention and management.

The dialogue

In order to provide a solid foundation for understanding the Soviet-American relationship, those participating in the dialogue of this working group took two steps together:

First, we attempted over several meetings to discuss as fully and candidly as possible the real interests of both nations in the Persian Gulf region. In doing so, we did not rely on the brief traditional statements of interests, but rather attempted to probe for operative concerns in concrete situations beneath the stated concerns — that is, what our two nations *really* fear and want to achieve or avoid in this region.

Second, against the background of that understanding, we discussed two likely conflict situations which might develop in the area. We attempted to identify steps that each partner might take to allay the other's fears to avoid appearing to threaten the interests of the other side. Working from a recognition of these fears, we then grappled with the conceptual and practical issues of what each side *can ask of the other* to assuage its fears, and significantly, what each side *would be willing to forego* in pursuit of threat reduction. This paper addresses mainly these last questions. We explore here a set of circumstances through which we can propose how actions taken within a mutual security framework may differ from unilateral, zero-sum behavior. This discussion leads to the formulation of specific proposals to promote mutual security between the superpowers in the Gulf. (The consideration of these proposals by policymakers on each side would also further clarify reservations and the analysis of obstacles to such agreements.)

The way people and governments of each nation perceive the intentions behind the other nation's action will affect the quality of the overall relationship. Understanding what the other side would regard as unexpected and threatening, our working group recognized the need for communication and actions that would avoid the worst interpretation of actions in a critical situation. This last point describes our ultimate ambition in the dialogue — to identify the kinds of threatening situations that may develop and to suggest behavior on each side that the other would find reassuring.

*

In laying the foundation for an improved Soviet-American relationship in the Persian Gulf region, we quickly recognized the importance of two factors in the present situation:

First, we agreed that the complexity of people, interests, and trends at work in this region sharply constrained the ability of either superpower to achieve everything it wants. Factors included the pressures of nationalism and fundamentalism, different political systems ranging from the most traditional to the more modern, widely different levels of economic development, and a wide spectrum of military capabilities.

Second, we recognized that any Soviet-American cooperation in this area risks the danger of appearing as an effort to develop a superpower condominium. While we write here about the process of developing shared perceptions of problems and the possibilities of cooperating to improve the interaction of the Soviet Union and the United States, we also recognize that any steps these two powers take together will have to be designed to reduce any concern in the area about the two "ganging up" on the smaller countries of the region.

Superpower interests in the Persian Gulf

We agreed at the outset of our discussions that it is necessary in today's world to understand interests on two levels. It remains important to begin from an analytical or objective definition of a nation's interests. But while such a definition is a necessary starting point, experience in both governments increasingly suggests that an objective definition is not by itself an adequate guide for a policymaker dealing with a particular situation. In addition to that analytical statement, policymakers also see interests as reflecting judgments of a body politic about what is important at that moment in relation to other interests with a claim on the nation's attention and resources. In understanding how that political definition of interests comes about, it is essential to understand (acknowledging that significantly different political systems are involved) exactly how the interests of different groups and individuals express their view of society's interests in a particular situation.

We establish this point to underscore that it is not only important for one side to hear the other state *what* its interests are; it also is an important part of credibility to understand the thought processes and the internal political interactions that define those interests. In other words, a central purpose in a good discussion is to understand *how* the other side will go about defining its interest: what factors will be important; what individuals or groups — for example, foreign ministries, defense ministries, ethnic or religious groups, ideological groups — will feel strongly about a particular situation and *why*; and what other priorities will be competing for resources, including the energies and political capital of leaders?

With this broadened concept of interests in mind, the Working Group exchanged statements on the interests of each superpower in the Persian Gulf area over a span of more than a year. As the dialogue deepened, the way we talked about interests evolved. The discussion began in 1988 with a review of the respective interests of the two nations as they emerged from the experience of Soviet-U.S. interaction in that area since World War II. Our purpose was not to review the recriminations of the past but rather to understand the feelings that had grown up around certain interests over those four decades. Each side explained its past fundamental considerations and concerns in the following way:

Soviet statement
The criterion of geographic proximity has played a strong role in Soviet conception of its interests in the area and the need felt for security guarantees against threats at its borders. Most Soviets considered their actions legitimate, or at least understandable, from this perspective. But American moves in the area have been regarded with suspicion and alarm, especially since these moves are made thousands of miles away from American shores but close to Soviet borders. To underscore the argument, Soviets compare their preoccupation with the Middle East and the Gulf to U.S. concerns in Central America.

The Soviets have explained the U.S. desire for power and influence in the region primarily by pointing to perceived American global ambitions, and a desire to encircle the USSR with bases, military alliances and regimes inimical to Soviet interests. A long list of evidence to that effect is usually presented including: the

Tripartite Declaration, the Truman and Eisenhower doctrines, restoring the Shah to the throne in 1953, and so on, up to the creation of CENTCOM and the American naval build-up in the Gulf in the mid-1980s.[2]

Also, in the Soviet view, the U.S. often "added insult to injury" by trying to ascribe to the USSR some of its own ambitions in the region. Allegations about Soviet "craving for Gulf oil" or Soviet "thrust towards warm-water ports" were regarded as pretexts for enlarging America's own presence and discrediting Soviet policy.

It was also perceived that the U.S. initiated and helped disseminate offensive ideas about the "incompatibility" between communism and religion (be it Islam or Judaism), and between Soviet social experience and local traditions.

A notion also emerged that, despite pronouncements in support of human rights and democracy, the U.S. would support reactionary elements and ideologies in the region if they had an anti-Soviet orientation.

At the same time, American and Western economic interests in the region, however enormous, were often regarded as only secondary to military ones. Also, certain traditional, cultural, and emotional links that attracted the U.S. to the region and some of its states in particular, were either over- or underestimated by Soviet analysts, which obscured understanding of true American interests and intentions.

Many of these perceptions and concepts began to change with the emergence of "new thinking," as it developed in the Soviet Union from 1985 on, and with the newly emerging Soviet-American rapprochement. Increased mutual trust in super-power relations, generated primarily in Europe and around arms control matters, could not fail to affect Soviet and American policies in Third World regions. As the result there are presently fewer Soviet suspicions of American competitive intentions in the Persian Gulf area (i.e., suspicions that the U.S. seeks to actively isolate the Soviet Union from regional affairs, or to increase/promote a hostile American military presence at Soviet borders).

However, it may not be assumed that the change in perceptions is final and irreversible. Former negative experiences are still vivid and may be brought back as the result of various U.S. actions such as in Panama. Possible conclusions are that improved relations in Europe either do not include other regions or are being deliberately used to undermine the Soviet position in these regions and Soviet relations with third parties.

U.S. Statement

The U.S. continues to have a near vital interest in the free flow of oil and access to the oil reserves of the Gulf. The degree of direct U.S. dependence fluctuates. But Gulf oil is essential to the economic health of Western Europe and Japan, and much of the developing world, and thus to maintaining the world economic environment in which the U.S. operates. Even if the U.S. may understand Soviet concern about hostile forces in neighboring territories and seas, it does not see Soviet interests as symmetrical to Western interests.

Rightly or wrongly, many Americans in 1990 are still too close to the Cold War and the 1973-74 oil embargo and are still too uncertain of how the Soviet Union intends to pursue its competition with the U.S. in the Third World to let go of their fear that the Soviet Union in some way at some future time might try to affect the flow of oil to the disadvantage of the West.

The longer-term U.S. military interest has been to position itself to deter a Soviet military thrust which could permit Soviet forces to attempt to gain control over any oil producing facilities or shipping routes, or would permit Soviet forces to play the kind of political role they played in Afghanistan. Since the collapse of the Persian Gulf security system in 1978 and in the context of the threat from post-1978 Iran, a more recent U.S. military interest has been preventing Iranian attacks on the Arab nations of the Gulf.

Some Americans understand that, before 1978, Soviets saw the U.S. military and intelligence presence in Iran, the maintenance of CENTO, and the U.S. naval presence in the Gulf and nearby Indian Ocean as threatening. The creation of the U.S. Central Command, the completion of U.S. facilities arrangements in the area, and the substantial increase in naval forces in 1987 were also causes for Soviet concern, although Americans believe Soviets assign relatively low probability that these actions alone signal a U.S. intent to attack the Soviet Union.

A central U.S. interest is to preserve the freedom of the nations in this area to govern themselves, to set their own internal and foreign policies, and to shape their relations with other nations without unusual external influence or intimidation. A more specific corollary of this is the U.S. interest in preventing the Soviet Union from repeating post-World War II attempts to establish positions in Iran and Turkey or from repeating the invasion of Afghanistan in a future breakdown of central authority in Iran. Difficult to define precisely, this U.S. interest would be affected if the Soviet Union attempted to establish the kind of influence it had in South Yemen in any other country in the Arabian Peninsula or Gulf areas.

Soviet understanding of this U.S. concern is critical for continuing to develop the overall Soviet-American relationship. Rightly or wrongly, Americans see Soviet attempts to extend controlling influence into this and other areas as signs of Soviet expansionism. The invasion of Afghanistan is seen as evidence too massive and too recent to ignore. Americans are watching the withdrawal of Soviet troops from Afghanistan to see whether the Soviet government will seek to preserve its influence through intelligence and security involvement and in that country, by trying (with military support) to keep in power the Najibullah government which was established while Soviet troops controlled the country.

The point here is not Afghanistan, although that experience makes this a critical subject for discussion. Both the Soviet Union and the U.S. will need to understand clearly how their actions and positions will be read by the other side when future regime changes take place in the region.

Joint summary of the two sides' interests

Against this background of the evolution of American and Soviet views of our interests in this area, and in light of past concerns and emerging circumstances, we eventually came to a summary statement of the interests of the two nations.

The Working Group agreed that interests are defined and rank ordered most significantly within specific contexts and with real political considerations and assessments supporting them. During the dialogue we discussed current interests by talking about specific regional circumstances that might develop. The following is not intended as an exhaustive list, but rather a guide to the primary interests on each side. (Lower priority interests are not listed.)

The Soviets have described their interests along the following lines:

— preventing any threat to the territorial and political integrity of the Soviet Union from a hostile presence and/or activities directly aimed at or construed as dangerous to the Soviet Union;

— interacting with the U.S. in the region in ways which would not undermine the superpowers' ability to cooperate and avoid conflict on other issues;

— strengthening existing cooperative relations with regional states;

— maintaining certain power projection capabilities in this theater.

Americans have described their interests in the Gulf as centering around:

— preserving Western access to affordable oil from the Gulf;

— limiting perceived Soviet influence in the area which may diminish America's role or threaten American regional interests;

— supporting American friends and promoting orderly rather than disruptive change in order to preserve an atmosphere not hostile to American economic, cultural, social, political, and security relationships;

— insuring unimpeded lines of communication for transit in the area and maintaining a military presence to preserve these American economic and political interests.

Three essential facts about these interests stand out. First, these interests are critically important to each side. Second, these interests are asymmetrical. The primary American interests are economic. The Soviets' profound geo-strategic interest, based on proximity, is completely unmatched by the U.S. Third, the superpowers have divergent interests in the price of oil. The U.S. prefers lower oil prices, whereas the Soviets, as oil exporters, benefit economically from higher prices. (It could also be noted that in terms of a military interest neither superpower has sizable military resources devoted to the region, though the American presence is larger than its Soviet counterpart.)

From this point on, the purpose of the Working Group's dialogue was to gain insight into how to move from a zero-sum competition to a scenario of interaction that takes account of the continuous interplay of interests and improves mutual security. It became productive to think through these questions in the context of specific situations that might evolve in the future.

The superpowers and the Gulf

The U.S. is primarily anxious to protect the West's vast economic interests in Gulf oil. Under some circumstances, protecting these economic interests and commitments might, in Washington's judgment, necessitate an American unilateral move in the Gulf. Such a move could be in response to regime instability, a series of terrorist activities in the Gulf, a period of sustained uncertainty and threat to U.S. allies there, or a combination of the above. On the Arab side of the Gulf in the foreseeable future, the U.S. may want to act on its own. It might not be able to forego responding to a crisis threatening its interests.

The question is, what would the U.S. like to *ask of the Soviets* in this type of circumstance?

The U.S. would probably like to assert its asymmetrical economic interests, having gained some kind of Soviet understanding that these interests can warrant unilateral action which need not threaten the Soviets and thus not trigger superpower involvement. This raises the question of what the U.S. would be willing to offer the Soviets in return for their tolerance in the Gulf.

A particularly interesting aspect of such a discussion is that it does not identify mutual or precisely common superpower goals in the same location. This bears elaboration. *Balanced* sets of interests may not always exist, but they are not mandatory for the mutual security approach to be useful. The Soviet view is that asymmetrical interests should not necessarily correspond to asymmetrical influence.

Due to geographical proximity, the Soviet Union would be greatly concerned by any American military build-up or intervention in the Gulf. The Soviets would attempt to minimize their fears by limiting U.S. options in the region. Of course, this runs counter to American desires to act with a relatively free hand in Gulf contingencies. The Soviets caution that the U.S. should consider possible negative Soviet reactions to such action.

The entire issue depends to a considerable extent on how each side evaluates and interprets the use of force in international relations. Though the goal of non-use of force remains the ideal it may obviously not be reached for some time. We should ask what facilitates the attainment of this goal. Developing mutual security arrangements is one of the ways to the desired ideal. Increasing trust in international affairs is another.

However, in the meantime, hard questions remain. What should be done with local conflicts, situations of large-scale violence against civilian populations, terrorism that affects the physical and moral well-being of thousands, etc.? There are situations when force can be countered only by superior force. We cannot beg the question of means: how force should be used and to what ends?

The United Nations Charter specifies concrete situations when the U.N. may and should act to reduce threats to international peace and security. It also suggests practical mechanisms and procedures to follow in such circumstances. One path to the legitimate use of force as a remedy for internationally unacceptable conflict may be to follow the Charter's recommendations and rules. But they themselves need further elaboration and improvement in view of the changes in international affairs over the course of postwar decades. Under the U.N. Charter, the USSR and the U.S. bear special responsibility for the maintenance of the international peace and security, and they should be at the forefront of attempts to preserve and develop international legal norms. Until effective norms are widely accepted, the USSR and the U.S. will need to work, via intensive dialogue, toward norms and understandings to govern their own uses of force.

The Working Group discussed, for example, the American operation, during the Iran-Iraq War, of reflagging and protecting shipping. The Group thought it possible that future situations might arise in the Gulf, not entirely dissimilar, in which Soviet-American talks in the spirit of mutual security could yield useful cooperation.

American members of the Group also raised the hypothetical contingency of some future U.S. unilateral military action in the Gulf. The response from Soviet members was to warn that such action would be bound to raise Soviet premonitions. The Soviets suggested that American policymakers should consider whether or not force may be undertaken through the auspices of the U.N., or by way of other appropriate international arrangements, which would involve the Soviet Union. The very power of a superpower agreement to act together, properly advertised, could be sufficient to prevent or terminate a conflict. Otherwise the conflict may be inflamed through separate, unilateral activities, especially if these are in opposition to each other.

On the other hand, it must be kept in mind that Soviet-American cooperation in circumstances requiring the use of force may produce a serious backlash among third parties both involved and uninvolved in particular conflict situations. As the functions and shape of such cooperation in the Persian Gulf are studied in the future, the discussion must address the threat of Soviet-American "condominium" as perceived by regional powers and other members of the international community. It must be noted that other nations may perceive a "condominium" even where Washington and Moscow do not intend one.

Iran as a special case

Iran presents a particularly good case for revealing each side's interests and fears as well as a current application of the principles of mutual security in the region. The Working Group discussed Iran in detail only as a particularly important case, not as the only possible topic. Both the Soviets and the Americans have an interest in the reintegration of Iran into international politics. Neither superpower wants to see the political division in Iran result in further exportation of revolution and regional instability. The Soviet Union currently has better relations with Iran than does the U.S. The U.S. hopes that the Soviet Union will use its influence to promote interests beneficial to both superpowers and to regional stability. Each side's relations with Iran are worth elaborating upon.

Relations between the U.S. and Iran

Following the bitter American experience with the hostage crisis, there was essentially no important interaction between the U.S. and Iran until the covert American arms sales to Iran in 1985 and 1986. The U.S. made overtures to Iran in part explicitly to gain longer-term influence with the nation that is the "strategic prize" of the Gulf region. The American intention was not lost on the Soviets, who fear an American attempt to regain their privileged pre-revolutionary position in Iran.

The Iran-Contra affair was followed by another cycle of overt hostility between the U.S. and the Islamic Republic. After maintaining some distance from the Iran-Iraq war, the U.S. became directly involved when it undertook reflagging and military escort operations in the Gulf from 1987-88. As a result of the reflagging operation, Iran and the U.S. directly confronted one another on several occasions. From the military viewpoint the most intense of these came in April 1988 when the U.S. damaged much of Iranian naval capacity in retaliation for damage sustained by the U.S. warship *Roberts*, presumably caused by renewed Iranian mining of the Gulf. The most destructive encounter occurred when the U.S. shot down an Iranian civilian airliner in July 1988, killing nearly three hundred passengers. Sustained military action by the U.S. was one of the proximate causes of the Iranian acceptance of a cease fire in the war with Iraq.

In the fall of 1989, the Bush administration agreed to release part of the remaining Iranian assets which had been frozen in American banks during the 1979-81 hostage crisis. Currently, the U.S. hopes to encourage a possible trend toward moderation in Iranian international behavior, with an eye on the fate of Western hostages held in Lebanon. It is widely recognized that the U.S. has significant long-term interests in having workable relations with Iran. It is the largest non-Arab Middle Eastern country, has significant oil reserves, and is strategically located at the crossroads of Gulf commerce and on the border of the Soviet Union.

Recent relations between the USSR and Iran

The Soviet Union has a substantial interest in restoring relations at all levels with Iran. Despite the close pre-revolution U.S.-Iranian relationship, the Soviets maintained fairly good relations with the Shah. After the Islamic Revolution the Soviets were not able to replace the U.S. in Iran, and gradually became embittered about the "unfulfilled" goals of the revolution and about Iranian intransigence in the Gulf. Furthermore the war in Afghanistan created animosity between the Soviets and the Islamic Republic. As a result of changes within the Soviet Union, the end of the Iran-Iraq War, and the shift in the Soviet policy toward Afghanistan, the Soviets have recently been able to pursue more active relations with Iran.

After little contact from 1983-1987, there were numerous meetings between Iranian and Soviet diplomats during 1989. These included meetings between Gorbachev and Rafsanjani, then Iranian Speaker of the Parliament and subsequently President. A series of accords signed in June and the Joint Soviet-Iranian Communique of August 1989 constituted a qualitative improvement in relations. The two countries signed specific and large-scale economic agreements heralding a "new era of cooperation." The agreements include long-term trade and scientific-technical exchanges.

The joint declaration included a pledge of non-interference in each other's internal affairs. This formally prohibits Iran from "exporting revolution" to Soviet Transcaucasia or Central Asian republics. Significantly, the new agreements explicitly include Soviet arms sales to Iran. While the Soviets sold a limited number of arms to Iran during the Iran-Iraq War, the new agreements (which include surface-to-air and anti-tank missiles) are expected to surpass former levels.

Soviet policy toward Iran is also affected by the situation in Afghanistan, where the USSR sees Soviet and Iranian interest to be sharply at odds. Since the Soviet

Union currently needs to press Iran to refrain from various actions in Afghanistan that would be inimical to Soviet interests, the USSR's freedom of maneuver in its policy toward Iran is somewhat limited. This may apply particularly to Soviet policies that the U.S. might prefer.

American concerns

What are some of the reasons that the U.S. could perceive the Soviet-Iranian relationship to be threatening?

An underlying and basic American fear about Soviet influence in Iran is that the Soviets could strengthen Iran, while allowing it to act against vital American interests in the Gulf. For example, if an Iran armed by the Soviet Union threatened other Gulf states, the U.S. could easily see the Soviet Union as seeking to expand it own influence at the expense of U.S. interests.

An important worst case scenario is that Iran might ultimately achieve a degree of political and military dominance in the Gulf that would enable it to force a major price rise by Arab oil-exporting countries in the Gulf, and then continue to manipulate oil prices. For the protection of its interests the U.S. depends on the preservation of sufficient power on the Arab side of the Gulf to block Iranian aggression. A mini-cartel dominated by Iran and enforcing discipline among the Saudis, the United Arab Emirates, Kuwait and Iraq could effectively control world oil prices. In the context of Iranian coercion or intimidation to set oil prices, the appearance of Soviet support or encouragement for Iran in a situation of Iranian aggression against the Arab side of the Gulf in some form — from militarily supported efforts to undermine present governments to overt attack — would negatively affect the Soviet-American relationship.

The U.S. is increasingly sensitive to the issues of oil availability and price as its dependence on oil imports continues to rise. In July 1989, U.S. oil imports surpassed the fifty percent level and dependence on Gulf oil will increase over time. It is therefore a major American concern that the Soviets, in their policy toward Iran, may not take sufficient account of the dire American national economic and security interests surrounding oil.

What would the U.S. want from the USSR with respect to Iran?

For the United States, the fundamental issue in its relations with the USSR, involving the Persian Gulf region, is that the USSR not develop its relationship with Iran in a way that would undermine the U.S. and Western need for affordable oil. Specifically, the U.S. would want the USSR not to support, encourage, or exacerbate Iranian assertion in the Gulf. If the U.S. believed that the Soviet Union recognized this interest, the U.S. would probably feel less threatened. This is a substantial request because the Soviets benefit from higher oil prices. Furthermore, this type of request may entail asking the Soviets to forego increasing their influence in Iran if pro-Soviet radicals, such as the Mussavi faction, come to power in Iran.

Soviet concerns

A resurgent American politico-military position in Iran, especially if it acquires anti-Soviet dimensions, may be perceived as particularly harmful to Soviet interests in the Gulf. Consider for example an Islamic ideological campaign by Iran encouraging Soviet Muslims to rebel; or some type of Iranian material support for nationalist-secular struggles within the Soviet Union, such as the Azerbaijani movement in the Nagorno-Karabakh dispute in the Transcaucasus. These scenarios would be greatly exacerbated if they are perceived as enjoying American support. Furthermore, the Soviets consider the possibility that improved American relations with Iran may lead to oil price reductions which are detrimental to Soviet economic interests.

What would the Soviets want from the U.S. with respect to Iran?

The Soviet Union would fear these scenarios less if it was reassured that the U.S. would not seek to reproduce pre-revolutionary relations with Iran (which allowed intelligence stations near the Soviet border and U.S. military advisors stationed in Iran). Naturally the USSR does not want the U.S. to engage in any drastic, unprecedented acts such as installing long-range missiles in Iran. Soviets would likewise want the U.S. to resist supporting, encouraging, or exacerbating conflict in Iran which could work against Soviet interests; and they would want to be able to respond to perceived Islamic or other threats on their southern border or to their own republics without risking confrontation with the U.S. or the deterioration of overall relations.

Depending on the level and nature of support, Moscow might need to stop Iranian intervention across the Soviet border. It is important for the U.S. to keep in mind that Iran borders the Soviet Union. The Working Group considered the extent of American sensitivity to conflict "in its backyard" and concluded that reciprocal allowance should be made for Soviet perception of threat. The principal question which this immediately raises is whether the U.S. could recognize these Soviet fears as legitimate and accept a Soviet unilateral move to prevent or stop an Iranian challenge. The question also arises whether some sort of multilateral action could substitute.

Summary of this discussion

To a large extent, the Soviets and the Americans share the goal of encouraging Iran to re-enter the mainstream of international and regional politics and to focus on its own social, economic and political internal development. Both sides may be able to agree that their security would be enhanced if Iran was not aggressive in the Gulf region. In this sense, superpower relations with Iran need not be treated as a zero-sum situation. In fact, increased Soviet influence in Iran can promote American interests.

The Soviets seek improved relations with Iran that allow them regular contact and involvement with a country that is as close to it as Mexico is to the United States. Such improved relations include economic, commercial, cultural, defense, and diplomatic ties between the two states. The Soviets can demonstrate their interest in seeing Iranian politics stabilize and use their influence to discourage Iran from provocative or disruptive regional policies, such as exporting revolution, hostage taking, and military training for insurgents. This is particularly important because, for complicated reasons, U.S.-Iranian ties will probably not improve substantially in the short run. Hence the U.S. has a particular interest in seeing another major actor working to influence Iran in a direction which the U.S. also desires. The U.S. is unaccustomed to, and thus uncomfortable with, this role being played by the Soviet Union. Under what conditions need the U.S. *not* be threatened by Soviet influence in Iran and vice-versa?

Applications of the mutual security approach

The mutual security approach cannot change the fact that superpower interests in the Persian Gulf are highly asymmetrical. But it does suggest constructive ways of coping with this fact, to the benefit of both sides. To begin with, the approach vividly draws attention (as this discussion shows) to critical questions that lie at the heart of Soviet-American relations involving the Gulf region. What is each side's perception of the other side's role — both its role at the moment, and its underlying role over time? How can each side constructively change the other side's perception of its role? How can each successfully reassure the other about its intentions? For example, what might the U.S. exchange for Soviet behavior that concretely demonstrated Soviet awareness of vital American interests in the Gulf? For a second example, what might the USSR exchange for American behavior that concretely demonstrated American awareness of vital Soviet interests on and near its border? For another example, what ways could be found to allay Soviet fears about possible American military action in the Gulf? And how might the two sides think together and work together ahead of time to prevent situations emerging where the U.S. felt so threatened that it felt it had no choice but to take military action?

The Working Group advances the following concrete suggestions as useful ways of taking the mutual security approach to superpower relations in the Gulf region:

First, it is important for representatives of the military forces of the USSR and the U.S. to conduct discussions that would permit military-to-military cooperation in situations that posed a threat to both, or to act in at least implicit concert where common purposes seemed to be involved. It was not a function of this working group to go into detail on these issues, but the experience of 1987-88 when the military forces of both nations were actively involved in the Gulf, suggests that a military dialogue include considerations of problems peculiar to the region.

These may lead to arrangements for *prior notification and other confidence-building measures*; exchanges of military data, briefing on policy initiatives or significant contacts with, and/or developments inside, i.e., Iran, or on hostage crises. There also is a need for policy coordination on terrorism.

Second, a significant way to affect each side's fear of the other's intentions toward Iran is to come to an agreement which vastly reduces the impulse to compete through re-arming Iran. The Americans in the Working Group propose accomplishing this through an *understanding between the U.S. and Soviet Union whereby neither will supply sophisticated weaponry to Iran,* for some period of time.

This type of superpower understanding would recognize the mutual interest both sides have in maintaining Iran as an arena of non-competition. Both sides would abandon the desire for significant unilateral advantage over the other. This policy could strengthen the superpower relationship in a regional context. The U.S. and the Soviet Union would agree not to go beyond a certain point in selling arms to Iran (i.e., prohibiting the sale of fighter aircraft, long-range missiles and possibly tanks). Other ties between the superpowers and Iran would continue but the instrument of sophisticated arms sales would be excluded.

It is essential to note that this kind of arrangement would, on its own, not prevent Iran from re-arming: there are many other arms suppliers on the market.[3] The suspension of sophisticated superpower weapons into Iran may in fact have marginal impact on Iranian military capabilities. The more salient consequence would be the mutual demonstration of a superpower ability to agree on restraint which specifically promotes threat reduction.

The proposal for mutual restraint toward Iran would affect current improved Soviet relations with Iran more than the minimal American ties to Iran. Thus it entails more of an immediate cost to the Soviets. Hence it should be considered together with further proposals examined below or in exchange for some quid pro quo.

Third, a related question is the prevention of the further proliferation of more esoteric weaponry to the area — chemical, biological, nuclear. This question has two aspects. One is working out programs with other potential suppliers for limiting the supply of technology and weapons. The other is the more complicated question about what actions the Soviet Union and the U.S. might take jointly, or in complementary ways, if intelligence indicated that a state in the area was on the verge of achieving a significant capacity in one of these areas. Merely talking through the question of whether or not the two powers would be willing to take joint action or how to place such action in a larger multilateral context would be valuable. It would provide an important context for working through in advance — even if not definitively — what interests would be at stake and what actions would be feasible.

Fourth, *there may be circumstances where one side or the other may feel justified in acting unilaterally if it consults with the other side, and informs the other of its intent and operational plans. The other side would then be expected to observe certain limits in its reactions.*

For Soviet forbearance in the Gulf, would the U.S. be able to grant the Soviets the same asymmetrical right to intervene on behalf of their interests in Iran? In further recognition of the reciprocity of mutual interests and threat reduction, the U.S. might consider offering to give no support or assistance to secessionist movements in the Central Asian republics. As this suggests, the salient trade-offs may not involve just one territory, but could involve an analogous legitimate interest granted to each side. This requires adjustment for both superpowers. Even a tacit agreement to tolerate unilateral military action in the region would be most useful if it included mechanisms which promote transparency for the other's sake. This issue is posed for further discussion because it raises extremely sensitive issues for both sides.

Fifth, the Working Group has discussed the possibility of a resumption of hostilities in the Iran-Iraq War. The Group believes that the superpowers continue to have a shared interest in a final resolution of the conflict between Iran and Iraq. This is a good place to think through how the Soviets and the Americans can work for the same goal. Here we highlight *strengthening the peace process* between Iran and Iraq. This has obvious consequences for wider issues of regional conflict resolution.

Sixth, we propose *regular meetings* between permanent American and Soviet consultative or study groups, hopefully mandated at the Secretary of State/Foreign Minister level. These meetings would consist of three or four people on each side who would sit down together every two to three months and discuss the overall interaction in the region in terms of U.S.-Soviet relations. They would assess developments and discuss the perceptions about and the impact of behavior. These people should grow to speak frankly with one another and should have a fundamental understanding of real interests and fears on each side.

Seventh, *agreed immediate consultation during instability*. The superpowers could agree further to talk to each other *first* before recognizing a new regime or supporting sides in a struggle for power in the Gulf region. For example, the U.S.

and Soviet Union could agree to withhold reaction for a set period of time, for instance, forty-eight hours, and meet to discuss the situation. This would create a firebreak in a time of great instability and uncertainty, and would be a mechanism to reduce tension and threat perception between the superpowers.

If either side decides to act unilaterally in the Gulf region (though the possibility should be made as remote as possible), that side should clearly communicate intentions and plans to the other side.

Conclusion

The exploration of mutual security in the Persian Gulf offers a good case for probing real interests, by asking difficult questions about what each side wants to prevent and what each might be willing to forego. This exercise of delineating fears, and real operative interests, helps to uncover ways in which each side can demonstrate its true intentions and reduce the other's fears.

In the present, early, stage of our testing the application of the mutual security approach, our Working Group has identified three categories of interests:

— objectively *divergent* interests on oil prices where there may not be much more to do beyond achieving workable and common understandings of the issues and feelings on each side;

— *common* interests involving the same territory, which raises opportunities to remove, through mutual restraint, competitive superpower impulses and perpetuation of threats in and around Iran;

— and *asymmetrical* interests, which may necessitate unilateral responses under certain circumstances, requiring forbearance by the other side.

Finally, the Group would draw attention to one additional point. Taking steps ahead of time to reduce the other side's perceived threat (even while pursuing one's interests) significantly decreases the most dangerous possibility of all — the chance that Soviet and American forces could come into direct contact or confrontation.

In its deliberations to this stage, the Working Group on the Persian Gulf feels confident of its overall conclusion about the best approach to the superpowers' problems in the region. The careful, frank investigation of what stimulates real fears, and of what each side is willing to ask of the other and to offer the other, is a good starting point for working toward increasing security for both.

Notes

1. We have defined the Persian Gulf area as primarily including the countries bordering the Gulf, but we have also recognized that relationships between those countries and their neighbors beyond the region, such as Afghanistan, must sometimes be brought into the discussion.
2. CENTCOM (Central Command) is the American command structure and group of forces with responsibility for the Persian Gulf area.
3. At a later stage in the relationship, and under certain conditions, the superpowers may be able to prevail upon other arms suppliers to join the restraint on sales to Iran.

Part IV

Working Group on the North Pacific

THE WORKING GROUP ON THE NORTH PACIFIC was responsible for exploring the applicability of the mutual security approach to the improvement of American and Soviet security, as well as that of their allies, in the North Pacific region. Chief emphasis was placed on the security problems on the Korean peninsula.

The Working Group has contributed five papers to this book. A joint statement appears first, formulated and endorsed by members of the Group. Next appear two papers about the region as a whole, a Soviet paper by Aleksis Bogaturov, Vladimir Lukin, and Mikhail Nossov and an American paper by Donald Zagoria. Two papers then follow about security on the Korean peninsula, a Soviet paper by Aleksis Bogaturov, Mikhail Nossov, and Konstantine Pleshakov, and an American paper by Alan Romberg. Biographical sketches of these authors, and a list of the full membership of the Working Group on the North Pacific, are given at the back of the book.

— THE EDITORS

14
Joint Statement

THE WORKING GROUP ON THE NORTH PACIFIC

This Working Group has explored ways of applying the idea of mutual security to U.S.-Soviet interactions in Northeast Asia. As in the rest of the project, the concept of mutual security here implies that the United States and the Soviet Union might each improve their own security by taking account of the other's security needs and by cooperating insofar as possible to improve both sides' security. The Working Group has found that although each side must always work in the first instance to promote its own security, there may be substantial room for the two countries to pursue a mutual security approach in the North Pacific region. Such an approach, of course, will require the cooperation not only of the two superpowers but also the cooperation of both Korean states, Japan and China.

The discussions in the Working Group have touched on a wide variety of questions, including the Korean peninsula, regional military competition in the North Pacific, the war in Cambodia and Soviet economic ties with East Asian states. The first two of these issues — the Korean peninsula and regional military activities — have been particularly useful in illustrating how a mutual security approach might bring tangible benefits.

The Korean peninsula

The Working Group has agreed that the political and military confrontation on the Korean peninsula, if left unchecked, could endanger the whole region. The possibility of renewed hostilities between North and South Korea is always present; the risk of escalation if hostilities broke out would be great; and the possibility of a full-scale U.S.-Soviet confrontation could not be ruled out. For these reasons, the

United States and the Soviet Union would both stand to gain (mutual security) from a diminution of tensions between North and South Korea.

To reduce the danger of a new war on the Korean peninsula, the United States and the Soviet Union should encourage a detente between Seoul and Pyongyang, starting with a genuine dialogue between the two Koreas. Such a dialogue, all members of the Working Group agree, could succeed only if it came at the initiative of the two Korean governments; similarly, most constructive changes on the peninsula would require the cooperation of both Japan and China as well as of the two superpowers. Presently there would be formidable barriers to any such process. Nevertheless, if the United States and the Soviet Union are determined to apply a mutual security framework to Northeast Asia, they should each seize whatever opportunities may arise over the next several years to promote even limited improvements in relations between the two Koreas. All countries concerned should continue to place high importance on this question and to take appropriate opportunities to discuss it among themselves.

Because the establishment of a meaningful dialogue between North and South Korea is the most important first step, the Working Group has considered a number of joint and unilateral actions that might promote such a dialogue. In this respect, the recent initiation of an informal dialogue between the United States and North Korea, and of unofficial contacts and trade between the Soviet Union and South Korea, is a healthy trend, as is the tentative expansion of contacts between the two Koreas. Soviet participants in the Group felt the United States should step up its contacts with North Korea to parallel, at least in some measure, rapidly evolving Soviet ties with South Korea. American participants in the Group agreed that the U.S. steps taken so far — amendment of trade regulations, permission for North Korean scholars to travel to the United States, and even the increasingly institutionalized dialogue between U.S. and North Korean diplomats in Beijing — were limited, and could be increased somewhat even now. But the Americans believed that, without a more positive North Korean response to those initiatives already taken by the United States since October 1988, and without meaningful progress in North-South dialogue, there would be minimal prospects for the success of any further steps. Without these things, further U.S. steps now would only create concern in South Korea and likely complicate the South's own efforts to reduce tensions on the peninsula.

Although encouragement of an inter-Korean dialogue is the most important near-term step toward reducing tensions on the peninsula, the Working Group agreed that the superpowers should also consider ways of seeking to reduce tension and constrain the military competition between North and South. In this regard, the United States and the Soviet Union should both exercise restraint in their military policies with respect to the peninsula. U.S. participants in the Group emphasized this point in discussions of recent Soviet shipments of MiG-29s, Su-25s, SA-5s and other sophisticated weaponry to Pyongyang; and Soviet participants emphasized it in discussions of U.S. shipments of F-16s to South Korea. Although mutually agreed restraints on arms transfers may prove difficult to arrange, other steps may prove more feasible and, at the least, merit further exploration; these include a scaling back of military exercises in both the North and the South, and mandatory notification of large maneuvers. The initiative in each of these areas will have to come from the two Koreas, but the role of the Soviet Union and the United States, as well as of China and Japan, will be crucial.

Participants in the Working Group's discussions agreed that it would be desirable to achieve a final settlement of the Korean problem but that under present circumstances, such an achievement would be difficult. Nevertheless, the majority consider that it is both possible and desirable to move step-by-step toward a gradual de-escalation of tensions and reduce intensity of the military stand-off on the peninsula at a balanced level.

U.S. and Soviet participants disagreed about the role of American forces in South Korea, though all recognized that those forces would remain there for the time being. The American participants believed that, under present circumstances, a United States withdrawal of its troops could lead to greatly increased anxiety in Seoul of an attack from the North. This in turn could easily lead to a South Korean military build-up far out of proportion to the forces removed by the United States, and lead to escalation of the military competition between Pyongyang and Seoul, suspension of any North-South dialogue, and, therefore, greater danger for all. While some U.S. reductions could be considered as South Korea's own capabilities grow, it would be undesirable for the United States to withdraw most or all of its troops from the South until there is genuine political stability on the peninsula.

A proposal by some on the American side to withdraw any nuclear weapons stored or deployed in South Korea (while preserving both the nuclear umbrella and the right of transit) was welcomed by Soviet participants, who said it would evoke a Soviet response in terms of restraints on arms supplies to North Korea. All participants stressed the importance that both Koreas adhere to the terms of the Non-Proliferation Treaty, accept full-scale IAEA safeguards and controls, and refrain from acquiring sensitive nuclear equipment and technology.

Regional military issues

The Working Group has explored various ways to apply a mutual security framework to the overall U.S.-Soviet military competition in the North Pacific. Although many disagreements surfaced on specific issues, general agreement emerged on the desirability of at least having the two sides consider confidence-building measures and criteria for arms limitations.

One confidence-building measure that could be achieved relatively quickly would be an expansion of the Prevention of Incidents at Sea Agreement. Among possible amendments to the agreement are provisions for mandatory notification of all U.S. and Soviet naval exercises including joint exercises with allies in the Northeast Asian area, the option of inviting delegates from the other side to observe large-scale exercises (akin to the observers required in Central Europe under the CSCE accords), and the establishment of fixed distances to be maintained during encounters of naval vessels and aircraft. Other provisions might be included to bring China and Japan, and perhaps other countries, under the terms of this agreement.

Another useful step would be to build upon the 1985 Accord on Civilian Air Traffic Safety in the Pacific. The scope of the accord could be extended to include some military flights as well as civilian air operations. Although the coverage of military aircraft would have to be limited, provisions might be added to require notification of large-scale exercises of land-based aircraft, especially those operating in conjunction with naval forces. Further provisions might be added for improved communications among flight control centers regarding military air operations in times of tension.

The Working Group agreed that mutual "transparency" of forces in Northeast Asia would be a useful contribution to stability. One step in this direction would be an official exchange of accurate data on the two sides' military deployments in the region. Another avenue to pursue would be bilateral discussions of U.S. and Soviet military doctrines. The aim in both cases would be to remove unnecessary fears, to clarify ambiguities, and to prevent tensions from arising out of misunderstandings.

On the questions of U.S. and Soviet force limitations, no consensus was reached on specific steps, but the Working Group did establish some broad principles that could govern future talks. First, regional arms reductions will not work, and indeed might be dangerous, unless they are achieved in the context of global constraints. Forces in the East Asian theater can be transferred to other theaters, and vice versa in time of war. Second, arms limitations must take due account of the different geographical circumstances and political relationships of the two sides. The Soviet Union has tended to give more emphasis to land forces, while the United States has always depended heavily on naval power. Third, the aim of arms control negotiations in the North Pacific region, as with any other arms control negotiations, is not to achieve reductions per se, but to achieve reductions that mitigate the intensity and limit the dangers of military competition between the two sides. Any discussions will have to proceed cautiously to ensure that force reductions, if deemed feasible, will lead to greater stability and predictability, not less.

Notes

1. This statement has been formulated and endorsed by members of the Working Group on the North Pacific. A list of Working Group members appears in the back of this book.

15

International Security in the Asia-Pacific Region: Confrontation or Balance of Interests?

ALEKSIS BOGATUROV, VLADIMIR LUKIN, AND
MIKHAIL NOSSOV

Introduction

The Soviet Union's vigorous involvement in the dynamic processes under way in the Asia-Pacific region (APR) is an integral part of its new political thinking in action. It is thinking that seeks to overcome previous Soviet attitudes of estrangement, confrontation, unconstructiveness and inflexibility in approaching some crucial international problems.

What are the basic reasons for the Soviet Union to pay much closer attention to developments in Asia and the Pacific?

First, Soviets are fully aware of the region's economic vigor, fast-growing productive forces, technological capability and the growing role it plays in the world economy and international relations. As a major Pacific power the USSR is naturally interested in seeing the process evolve successfully, on the one hand, and in making its own contribution to its overall progress, on the other. It stands to reason that the Soviet Union's economic situation in Asia and the Pacific should be a matter of special concern to us.

Second, the Soviet Far East has a special role to play in the perestroika that has encompassed all aspects of public life in the Soviet Union, for that area is exceptionally rich in natural resources and poor in population. That area is located far away from the Soviet Union's major industrial centers and, at the same time, lags far behind industrially and socially. It comes as no surprise that it was miners in the eastern regions of our country that initiated stormy social unrest in the summer of 1989.

The USSR seeks effective foreign economic contacts between the Soviet Far East and Siberia on the one hand, and the countries of Asia and the Pacific on the other, in the service of social and industrial development in those parts of the Soviet Union. This is a long-term and a strategic goal, not a tactical one.

Third, the USSR realizes that without reduced tensions in Asia and the Pacific it is impossible to succeed in creating a comprehensive international security system any place, including Europe. Also, in Asia and the Pacific there are various areas where the alleviation of confrontation and the settlement of conflicts are urgent.

At the root of the new Soviet approach to the problems of preserving international security lies a belief in the unity and indivisibility of the world. The political embodiment of this idea is the concept of an all-embracing system of international security, proposed by the Soviet Union. This concept is based on the notion of the interdependency of security of states and regions, which hypothesizes that it is impossible to achieve global security while there exists insecurity in any one state or region.

The aims of Soviet policy in the Asia-Pacific region are formulated in the context of this concept, and in the context of practical steps in building a system of international security encompassing all areas of the world, especially relations with the United States. In the official declarations of the Soviet government, the connection between the proposals for maintaining security in the APR and world-wide policy aims have frequently been emphasized. Soviet initiatives always include the presumption of mutual consideration and agreement of interests as the basis for regulating problems of security with the U.S.

However, it must be admitted that in spite of considerable progress of Soviet-American dialogue on global and European problems, the APR is still subordinate. This is in part due to conceptual differences in the approaches the USSR and U.S. have toward the question of maintaining security in this part of the world.

The United States evidently believes that before attempting a general settlement of all security questions in Asia and the Pacific, the present regional conflicts and disputes should be resolved. Washington feels secure enough in its position to maintain this viewpoint. The Soviet Union is concerned that the U.S. seeks to preserve American domination while minimizing Soviet influence in the region.

Both positions are logical in their own way. At the same time, it is hard to overlook the essential similarity of the approach of many Pacific countries to that of the United States. The situation in the Asia-Pacific region being what it really is — with the U.S. commanding powerful political, military and economic means of pressure, whereas the USSR has no such means — it would obviously be reasonable to use what is objectively valuable in the U.S. position. This does not mean that the USSR should renounce the idea of advancing toward its ultimate goals, which are to strengthen security in the region at both the upper, global and the lower, regional levels.

There are significant pre-requisites for this approach. Of course, the spectrum of Soviet-American relations encompasses many global issues that need to be resolved. Issues of this sort that are highly relevant to the APR include central strategic nuclear weapons and tactical nuclear weapons in the region; the regulation of naval activities in the oceans of the region; the steady provision of energy and raw materials to the regional economy; and environmental protection of the region.

Along with these, there are many (and interconnected) problems of the Asia-Pacific region itself, which can hardly be solved in a satisfactory manner without constructive Soviet-American dialogue or a substantial narrowing of the gap between these two powers' points of view. Their primary tasks in this context are preventing any uncontrolled escalation in Korea and Kampuchea; normalizing relations with Japan; drawing the USSR into economic cooperation in the Pacific; and guaranteeing the security of sea and air traffic.

Arms issues: a Soviet view

Official declarations of the Soviet Union have frequently stated that without U.S. participation it will be impossible to solve the problem of increasing security and cooperation in the Pacific region. However, Washington continues to ignore Soviet initiatives in the APR, and the region remains one of the greatest sources of Soviet-American strife. Soviet and American evaluations of the political-military situation in the region do not coincide.

The Soviet Union is deeply concerned with the escalation of the arms race in the region, as it has been indicated not only by repeated and varied proposals for arms reductions in the region but also by practical steps to this end. The USSR is eliminating its medium and shorter-range missiles in the country's Asian regions as part of Soviet-American agreements.

Asian and Pacific countries also responded with interest to a series of proposals we addressed to the United States for a direct dialogue between the USSR and the U.S. on confidence-building measures in the military field, and on lowering military confrontation levels in the region. The Soviet government's unilateral decision not to increase land- and air-based nuclear systems in the region, which has been implemented since 1984, has also found positive response.

In addition, in 1989-1990 Soviet troops deployed in the region will be reduced by 200,000, including 120,000 in the Far East. The decision was taken to reduce land-based troops there by twelve divisions and to disband eleven air force regiments, as well as to decommission sixteen warships from the Pacific fleet.

In recent years the level of military confrontation along the Soviet-Chinese border has decreased noticeably. Structural changes in our troops were introduced there, corresponding to the principle of reasonable sufficiency. During last year's visit by President Gorbachev to the People's Republic of China, an agreement in principle was reached with the Chinese to work towards reducing the strength of the armed forces confronting each other to a minimum, and establishing to this end a special negotiating mechanism.

In May 1989 the Soviet Union started another stage, reducing troops in Mongolia: in 1989-1990 three full divisions, including two tank divisions, as well as the entire air force group, which make up about seventy-five percent of all Soviet troops in that country, will be withdrawn. The complete withdrawal of Soviet troops from Mongolia is a realistic prospect.

In the spirit of glasnost and the new thinking, the USSR is also revealing fresh information, hitherto secret, about the numbers and types of its military forces in the eastern portion of the country.[1]

The Soviet military believes that the armed forces of the United States and Japan, taken together, have a considerable superiority over Soviet troops in the Asia-Pacific region: more than a two-fold superiority in personnel strength; nearly four-fold in the number of large surface ships armed with cruise missiles having the range of over 600 km (the Soviet Navy has no such weapons although it has shorter-range cruise missiles) and a more than two-fold superiority in the number of strike tactical and naval aircraft. The Soviet Union in this region has, as a land power, a two-fold superiority in tanks and about a 1.5 superiority in armored infantry fighting vehicles, armored personnel carriers and artillery systems. These forces may be regarded as defensive forces compared to air and naval forces of a naval power.

In the summer of 1989, the USSR invited military experts of Asian and Pacific countries to witness the maneuvers of the Soviet Pacific Fleet. Unfortunately, not all of those invited took up the opportunity: our main opponents — the United States and Japan — preferred to observe the maneuvers using their own national means.

In the USSR there is a hypothesis that the U.S. is not interested in negotiating with the Soviet Union on security problems in the APR, even though it is becoming increasingly difficult and expensive for the U.S. to maintain its position of leadership in the region.

Forty years of the American policy of "containment of communism" has created a situation in which the U.S. spends fifty billion dollars annually to maintain its military alliances in the Asia-Pacific region. Meanwhile the U.S. has a trade deficit of $140 million, seventy percent of which is deficits to trading partners in this region. The U.S. is carrying much of the cost for the defense of the very countries which are the main contributors to the U.S. trade deficit.

Recent Soviet policy has lessened the tension and confrontation that existed in the region. In May 1989 Soviet-Chinese relations were normalized. By February 1989 Soviet troops had left Afghanistan and in September 1989 Vietnamese troops also left Kampuchea. These steps opened the way to a resolution of both conflicts. Soviet steps towards the improvement of relations with the countries of the APR, including Japan and Australia, have eased tension in the region. Thus Soviet activity has made it difficult for Washington to justify U.S. military presence in the APR, and the U.S. feels that the countries of the APR want to lessen American military guardsmanship over them. Washington is now facing an anti-American public mood in South Korea, a movement against the presence of American military bases in the Philippines after 1991, and anti-nuclear sentiment in the majority of the countries of the region.

While the concentration of military forces in the Asia-Pacific region is not (except Korea) as great as in Europe, in our judgment the military situation there is much more volatile than in Europe. This is due to the immeasurably greater instability of both the domestic situation in many states of the region and to political relations between them, which in many instances are constantly on the brink of war or in the state of quasi-war. Everything is much more fluid and less fixed in the region as compared with Europe, and the uncertainty in the Asia-Pacific region is aggravated by the multilateral character of the military confrontations there and the absence of negotiating machinery on disarmament issues.

All this makes for a greater complexity and a more contradictory nature for the military situation in the Asia-Pacific region, and for considerable difficulties in finding ways to reduce the levels of military confrontation. Unfortunately, the positive aspects of the European experience are not applicable to the Asia-Pacific region. What is required there is a search for fundamentally new and innovative ways for reducing the military threat and enhancing universal security.

Mutual security in the Asia-Pacific region

The Soviet Union has probably not used all its opportunities to bring the U.S. to a serious dialogue on the problems of regional security and to curb the arms race in the Asia-Pacific region. In Europe during the Helsinki summit there was no serious dialogue on this topic until the Soviet Union made proposals. The Soviet proposals, which were meant to be beneficial to all, are regarded by the U.S. as being beneficial only for the Soviet Union. So the only way to solve the problem in Asia is to offer the American side terms that will express not only Soviet interests but American interests and priorities as well.

It might be good to start with an analysis of the military doctrines and the national interests of both countries in the region. Doctrines should be adequate and compatible in terms of regional policy as well as in terms of Soviet-American relations in general. The Soviet Union should be more precise in formulating and discussing its military doctrines in the APR. The analysis of these doctrines, in turn, by American specialists could help reveal their drawbacks and help the USSR to alter them for mutual benefit. American ideas for controlling the arms race in the APR are also important to us. Any proposals and initiatives concerning this region should try to find a balance of interests, and at the same time be concrete and realistic, and consider not only the interests of USSR and the U.S. but also the interests of their allies and partners.

Settlement of regional conflicts is of acute importance for Asia and the entire Pacific basin. Although the problem is as yet far from being solved completely, nevertheless certain favorable signs have already appeared.

The signing of the Geneva Accords on Afghanistan and the withdrawal strictly on schedule of all Soviet troops from that country was a real breakthrough in resolving one of the sharpest crisis situations in Asia. Developments since the last Soviet soldier left Afghanistan graphically demonstrate, first, that their introduction was a grave mistake both politically and morally, and secondly, that the Soviet factor is not even the main one, still less the only one, in this complex conflict. In any case the daring decision to eliminate an element of the Afghan crisis that was born out of the psychology and stereotypes in the USSR during the Cold War, has already played a positive role in the intensified search for settling crises in the world at large and in Asia and the Pacific in particular.

Both the USSR and the U.S. want to prevent the outbreak of instability in the region of the Korean peninsula. The present tentative dialogue between North and South is a positive feature. However, serious disagreements and polemics between Seoul and Pyongyang may aggravate conflicts inside Korea. It is important to note that people in the USSR and the U.S. are beginning to understand that both parts of the country, South as well as North, are responsible for the remaining tension. This has been pointed out by specialists on public opinion in the Soviet Union and the U.S. At the same time it seems that the officials in both countries do not want to admit this. It would be very useful to take public opinion into consideration and to discuss the Korean problem in an informal setting. This could help in creating an understanding of the respective responsibilities of each power in maintaining stability on the peninsula. The Soviet Union should stop selling arms to North Korea while the U.S. should stop its military activities in South Korea.

However, these steps alone are not enough to increase stability on the peninsula. There should also be a nonaggression pact between South and North Korea as well as a withdrawal of American military forces from South Korea. There need to be effective international guarantees against any forced changes in the social, economic and political systems of either part of the country.

Clearly there can be no normalization of relations in Korea without the development of economic and cultural ties to the rest of the world. An increase in Soviet-Korean relations in this area is as important as the increasing contacts among Korea, the U.S. and other industrially developed countries. As with any other regional conflict, the Korean conflict should be regulated taking into account the interests of all the countries involved.

The situation in Kampuchea should be approached in the same way. The Soviet Union should try to come to an agreement not only with China, but with the U.S. as well. In particular, the visit of the U.S. Vice-President to Southeast Asia and the region of the Thailand-Kampuchean border in May 1989 revealed the interest of the Bush Administration in Kampuchea. The Soviet Union and China are ready to contribute to the normalization of the Kampuchean situation, as it was stated during President Gorbachev's visit to Beijing in May 1989. The key aspect of a settlement today is the issue of outside support for Kampuchean participants fighting in the conflict. Whereas the withdrawal of Vietnamese troops means at least a considerable reduction in the outside military backing for the Heng-Samrin leadership, the United States still refuses to stop aiding the Son Sann and Sihanouk leadership.

The USSR should assist the Socialist Republic of Vietnam to establish normal relations with all countries of the region, including China, and to establish better relations with the United States.[2] A positive Soviet contribution to this process could reduce the mistrust of the developing countries towards the Soviet policy. This could also clear the way for the Soviet peace initiatives in the region and create a better political and psychological climate for Soviet participation in the economic development of the region.

It now becomes important for the countries of the Pacific to alter their hostile and distrustful attitude towards Soviet policy in East Asia and for them to break their stereotype of a Soviet and communist threat. The new Soviet policy is nonconfrontational. The Soviet Union is not going to use its military power to increase its influence in the region; instead it wishes to participate economically.

Unfortunately, the Soviet Union has been traditionally associated in the minds of the countries of the region with military affairs rather than as an economic partner.

In developing mutual security in the Asia-Pacific region, it is important that Soviet policy take the American side into consideration. This is especially important in Soviet-Chinese relations. There is no doubt that the U.S. and Japan, as well as the Socialist Republic of Vietnam and other developing countries of the region, are worried about the fact that the Soviet Union and China are growing closer, which might lead to the reconstruction of a powerful Soviet-Chinese political and ideological union.

It is already high time for the USSR's new, nonconfrontational, policy to be transferred from the speeches of politicians into practical Soviet policy. The USSR should now orient its policy towards semiofficial and official consultations on the questions of political settlement in the region. This type of diplomacy and the principles of mutual security should become the main basis of Soviet policy in the near future. The old policy of "breaking-through" at different frontiers of international relations (Chinese, Japanese, South Korean) can only damage the regional balance and generate distrust.

Soviet-Japanese relations

Much will depend on Soviet relations with Japan, which is the U.S.'s main ally in Asia. It is going to be very hard for the USSR to develop good relations with Japan. First, so far Japan is not much interested in economic relations with the Soviet Union and second, it maintains territorial claims against the Soviet Union. In addition to this, any presumption of inalienability of all parts of the territory controlled by the Soviet Union along the Soviet-Japanese border is not going to contribute positively to Soviet-Japanese relations. In our judgment it is more sensible for the USSR to start thinking about economic cooperation with South Korea rather than Japan.

At the same time it appears that relations between Moscow and Tokyo are gradually moving from confrontation to dialogue, from ultimatums to flexibility and recognition of the other side's interests. In this context, Foreign Minister Shevardnadze's talks in Tokyo in December 1988 were constructive and substantive. On both sides there was a desire to narrow the areas of disagreement and to expand the areas of agreement. This was reflected, among other things, in the agreement to begin discussions, within the framework of a special working group, on the entire complex of issues that could constitute the subject of a peace treaty between the two sides.

Japanese attempts to encourage territorial claims against the Soviet Union and to present them, in effect, in the form of ultimatums are counter-productive, for they delay, rather than bring closer, the resolution of issues in Soviet-Japanese relations. The proponents of "an immediate handover" of the islands often invoke Japanese public opinion and attempt to contrast the "Kremlin's intransigence" with the "will" of the Japanese people. In so doing, they are taking advantage of the fact that before perestroika and glasnost in the USSR, Japan's territorial claims were not even discussed openly and publicly. Today, when that taboo has been lifted, we discover that the South Kuril Islands are seen by public opinion in the Soviet Union, and particularly in the eastern parts of the country, as *originally* Russian, Soviet territory. Thus, the problem is not with the "Kremlin's intransigence," but rather with issues that historically are difficult and deep-rooted, and touch a very sensitive national chord in both countries. That is where the heart of the matter is, and not in the Kremlin's flexibility or inflexibility.

From a technical perspective, the situation seems difficult. The Bush administration openly supports Japan's territorial claims. But despite the complicated nature of the problem, Soviet-American talks on the Japanese situation are not out of the question. We should prepare for such talks irrespective of the eventual participation of Japan, because it is obvious that Tokyo is very worried by the possibility of superpower talks. Japan may even try to prevent them.

We should discuss with the United States the strength of land forces, air forces and other types of arms along the Soviet-Japanese border in the areas of Hokanda, the Kuril Islands and the Sakhalin Islands. In discussions with the U.S., it would be wise to try to develop a mutual understanding of the preconditions and potential for arms reduction in the area, and to try to halt the modernization of old military bases on both sides. It would be good if we could establish direct contact between Soviet military headquarters in the Far East and the U.S. military headquarters in Japan, including a direct hotline between the two headquarters. Each side should also observe military maneuvers in the region.

U.S. participation in Soviet-Japanese dialogues would also help in solving the problem of regional security (and it will cause the U.S. to consider more carefully its conception of the Soviet military "threat" to Japan). This may at last put some limits on the economic concessions that the U.S. makes to Japan, because the U.S. exaggerates the importance of its strategic partnership with Japan.

Soviet economic goals in the Asia-Pacific region

American economic plans in the Pacific region have been made without considering the possibility of Soviet participation, while the Soviets feel that the USSR could contribute positively to such plans for the betterment of all the countries in the region. The Soviet Union is very much interested in the most progressive forms of cooperation with countries of the Pacific region, which can be a positive factor for the further development of the whole region. We should make it clear that when we speak about

Soviet economic participation we speak not only of the eastern portion of the Soviet Union but of the entire Soviet Union. Progress along these lines should create additional opportunities for the development of the Pacific market and the overall intensification of international cooperation. In this respect it must be admitted that the present Soviet program for the economic development of the Soviet Far East is inadequate. Simply increasing local exports is not enough. Future plans must include the creation of the infrastructure necessary for full Soviet participation in the regional economy.

At the same time it is important not to underestimate the importance of specific short-term goals. For example, joint business ventures are a new and effective way to develop the processing of raw materials in the Far East. Special economic zones in the USSR, especially in the coastal regions, will help to develop the territory. Joint ventures are also important as a tool for developing small manufacturing enterprises, which can use even waste products. The decades of "gigantomania" of the Soviet economy have resulted in huge losses. Real profits were lost to a few huge and impractical projects which consumed all of the available resources.

At the same time, it is important that we make our plans from the perspective of a transition to totally new forms of economic cooperation in the Pacific region. The U.S. could play a special role in this endeavor. In the early 1970s the U.S. and the USSR reached a series of scientific and technical agreements on research in the Pacific Ocean, and actually began work which proved beneficial to both sides. We might mention two such Soviet-American agreements: an agreement on cooperation in environmental protection (May 23, 1972); and an agreement on research in world oceans (June 19, 1973). Normalization of Soviet-American relations could make it possible to continue this work. We could also set lofty goals for developing economic relations between the Soviet Far East and the West Coast states of the U.S.

The large scale of the processes that should take place on the Pacific Coast of the Soviet Union will require great concentrations of financial, technological and organizational power from the potential participants. Differences in interests, financial opportunities, technological development, and markets, among other things, are a natural basis for the organization of multinational business undertakings. So far, the only such agreement that we have is one on economic and cultural cooperation between the Magadan region of the USSR and the U.S. state of Alaska.

One of the most attractive types of cooperation is in construction. The qualifications and capabilities of American construction firms are well known. It would be good if we could also use Japanese equipment and technology, and the labor forces of other countries, to foster rapid construction, the opening of industrial zones, and also tourism in the Soviet Far East.

Such developments could positively contribute to the military and political situation in the Asia-Pacific region and in the Soviet Union itself. The integration of the eastern Soviet regions into the Pacific economy would enormously reduce tensions in this part of the world. This alone would provide the USSR with more security at less cost.

Conclusion

Genuine Soviet-American cooperation is much more realizable in the short run, in cases where Soviet and American positions are comparable, as in Korea and Indochina. Much will depend on the flexibility of Soviet policy, which can now be influenced by public opinion and the legislature. The USSR can also give concrete proofs that its "new thinking" represents actual policy, for instance the observation of human rights and proofs of fidelity to previously made agreements.

Meanwhile, it is obvious that constant efforts are needed to continue discussion of possible approaches to the improvement of the situation in the whole region. The USSR has several times already offered its views on ways to reduce tension. However, our opponents have their own version of the situation, and indeed all the countries of the Pacific have their own opinions on ways for achieving stability. Adequate discussion by all the affected countries could make possible a confluence of their positions, which are now quite contradictory. And although it might be difficult to have a dialogue, it is just the lack of such a dialogue which is the source of the remaining mistrust. On the verge of the 1990s the USSR has at last summoned the courage to admit that the U.S. and the Soviet Union have not only diverging interests, but parallel and converging ones as well. Admitting this fact is not enough, however; we must also do something about it. In this respect, Soviet-American discussions of Asia-Pacific problems become very significant, and currently their absence limits the flexibility of Soviet policy in the Asia-Pacific region.

Recently views have been expressed in Washington, too, that raise hope that the new U.S. administration will engage more vigorously in dialogue on problems of peace and development, with the participation of other Asian and Pacific countries.

Admittedly, a stronger peace and greater security in Asia and the Pacific are still a long way away. Today the challenge is to extend to Asia and the Pacific the positive trends that have emerged in the international arena in general and in Europe in particular. It is necessary to use the potential of new thinking more actively, and to tap the potential of realism and common sense to resolve the problems of the region. The fewer the ideological demons we have hovering over our work in the Pacific, the better it is for us, for the world and for the prosperity of future generations.

In advancing its new concepts for security and cooperation in Asia and the Pacific, the Soviet Union emphasizes that it is necessary to develop a collective and mutual approach to Pacific problems. In putting forward its proposals, the Soviet Union is not guided by the expediency of the moment, and lays no claim to any unilateral advantages, privileges or special rights. Rather the USSR wants to play a constructive role in the regional community and has no intention of gate-crashing or violating the existing rules. On the contrary, we are prepared to pay a fair entrance fee.

Notes

1. The data appears in *Pravda* (May 28, 1989) and results from an interview with the Minister of Defense, D.T. Yazov.
2. In addition, the USSR should assist Hanoi in normalizing its relations because any rapid withdrawal of the USSR from Southeast Asian affairs, or any rapid Soviet-Chinese rapprochement, might otherwise cause misunderstandings and insecurity in Hanoi.

16
Creating a More Stable Security Structure in the Asia-Pacific Region

DONALD ZAGORIA

Some forty years after the beginning of the Cold War, the world is now on the verge of a new era, one that promises more stable, peaceful and even cooperative relations between the two superpowers that have dominated the postwar period. Within reach is a world in which: the Soviet Union and the United States cut their nuclear strategic forces in half while removing substantial numbers of troops from Europe; help end the division of Europe in a peaceful manner that does not threaten stability; cooperate in ending regional conflicts; and come to realize that they share a number of overlapping interests in an increasingly multipolar world. Also within reach is a world in which the former East European satellites of Moscow move towards political pluralism and market economies while improving relations with the European Community, all with Soviet acquiescence; East Asia becomes increasingly prosperous, stable and peaceful as the major powers in the region move towards detente and as the forces for regional economic cooperation grow; and greater attention is paid to collective global concerns such as the environment, pollution, terrorism, poverty, drugs, etc.

Of course, such a momentous change in global international relations is by no means assured. Its outcome depends on many factors, not the least of which is the continuation of glasnost and perestroika and the success of President Gorbachev's historically ambitious task of profoundly redefining Soviet foreign policy and improving Moscow's relations with its neighbors.

But such a change in international relations also depends on the two superpowers coming to redefine their views of national security in terms of the concept of mutual security which informs this volume. Both Washington and Moscow must learn that in the new post-Cold War era now unfolding, they can become secure only by becoming more secure together. Washington and Moscow must learn to understand and to respect each others' legitimate security interests. While recognizing that their interests do not always converge, they must come to see that, in the increasingly multipolar world, they will have a number of overlapping interests in various regions of the world, including the Pacific.

In order for a stable post-Cold War world to be brought into being, it will be necessary to reduce East-West confrontation in the Pacific as well as in Europe. But the situation in Asia is quite different from the situation in Europe, and the patterns of accommodation in Europe cannot be mechanically transplanted to the Pacific. Whereas in Europe there are two multilateral alliance systems, NATO and the Warsaw Pact, in the Pacific there are no such multilateral security arrangements. Whereas in Europe regional integration is far advanced via the European Community and other organizations, in Asia the forces of regional integration are still rather weak. Whereas in Europe it is possible to make arms control trade-offs because of the symmetries in NATO and Warsaw Pact force structures, both of which are largely ground forces, in Asia the asymmetries in the force structures of the United States and the Soviet Union make arms control much more difficult.

To reduce East-West tensions in the Pacific, a formula quite different from the one applied in Europe will need to be employed. Several conditions will need to be met. First, the United States and the Soviet Union will need a realistic sense of strategic direction that takes into account the peculiar political, cultural and geopolitical circumstances of the region. Second, there needs to be continuing improvement in the bilateral relations between the major powers whose interests intersect in the region — the United States, the Soviet Union, China and Japan. Third, there must be a radical breakthrough towards a political resolution of the outstanding regional conflicts in Korea and Cambodia. Fourth, there needs to be continuing progress towards regional cooperation. Fifth, there must be continued movement towards political and social pluralism throughout the region. Finally, there should be efforts to reduce the military confrontation in the region.

So far as the superpowers' strategic direction is concerned, it is my own view, and the view of several "new thinkers" in the Soviet Union, that the traditional Soviet approach to Asian security, which envisages the creation of a broad, comprehensive security dialogue, modelled on the Helsinki Conference in Europe, is premature. Few countries in Asia have been attracted to Moscow's pan-Asian security proposals either in their Brezhnevian or Gorbachevian forms. Economic, political and cultural differences in the region are simply too great to allow for the creation of a broad, collective security system at this time.

A second important reality that must be taken into account is that the U.S. system of bilateral alliances in the Pacific, and the U.S. system of forward deployment which supports these alliances, have helped preserve the peace and to stabilize the military, political and economic environment. This is not only the American judgment, but the opinion of many of the countries in the region. Without the stability brought about by the American presence, it is doubtful that the region would have achieved such extraordinary economic and political success in recent decades. Moreover, all of non-communist Asia, and China as well, continue to look to American naval power as a necessary counterweight to the land-based military potential of the Soviet Union and to the military power of other potential regional great powers. None of American's allies and friends in Asia are calling for a reduction of the American military presence in the Pacific.

Yet a third crucial reality is that the existing military and political status quo in the region strongly favors the United States and is therefore more acceptable to Washington than to Moscow. Unlike the situation in Europe, the United States is under no great pressure from allies in Asia to respond to Gorbachev's various initiatives.

The Soviet Union's unsatisfactory position in Asia is largely attributable to its economic weakness, which inhibits economic interaction with the dynamic economies of the region, and to unwise policies of the past. To the extent that Gorbachev succeeds in changing these policies — and he has already gone some way in this direction — the Soviet Union will be able to normalize its relationship with most countries of the region.

The single most important way to begin laying the foundations for a more stable system of international relations in the Pacific is not through premature calls for pan-Asian security schemes but rather by improving bilateral relations among the major powers. There are already many encouraging signs of progress in this direction.

For the first time in postwar history, there is no "odd man out" among the major powers in the Asia-Pacific region. The United States and the Soviet Union are making progress on a new START agreement and on conventional and chemical weapons agreements, and they are discussing a variety of other ways to improve their bilateral relations. Soviet relations with China have been normalized after Gorbachev's visit to Beijing in May 1989, the first such meeting between top Soviet and Chinese leaders in thirty years. Soviet-Japanese relations are also improving. Gorbachev will visit Tokyo in 1991, the first such visit to Japan by a Soviet leader in the entire postwar era. Even Chinese-Indian relations are improving. Rajiv

Gandhi, the former Indian Prime Minister, visited China in 1988. He was the first Indian leader to visit China since Nehru went to Beijing in 1954.

This improvement in major power relations is accompanied by a variety of measures to increase transparency and mutual confidence. Soviet and American military leaders are beginning to exchange data and to visit each others' military installations. The Soviet Union has announced its intention to remove some twelve divisions from the Chinese border and to withdraw the majority of its forces in Mongolia, while China has already demobilized a million men from its armed forces. A joint Sino-Soviet political-military commission is now considering how to implement mutual force reductions along the border. During Rajiv Gandhi's visit to China, there was also an agreement to institute confidence-building measures along the disputed border.

An important factor that has led to the improvement of major power relations in East Asia is the revolution in Soviet foreign policy under Gorbachev. Moscow withdrew its troops from Afghanistan; announced a unilateral cut of some 200,000 troops from its forces in Asia; agreed to dismantle its SS-20 intermediate range missiles in Siberia in accordance with the INF Treaty; put pressure on Vietnam to withdraw from Cambodia; indicated a desire to join Asia-Pacific economic organizations; passed new joint venture laws; displayed new flexibility towards old adversaries such as China, Japan, South Korea and the ASEAN countries; and made a number of arms control proposals.

There are several important factors that are driving this revolution in Soviet foreign policy. The first is tactical but the other two are more fundamental. The tactical explanation is that Gorbachev inherited a policy in Asia from Brezhnev that was extremely counterproductive. Brezhnev's rigid, U.S.-centered, and over-militarized foreign policy was leading in the early 1980s to a united front of all the major powers against the Soviet Union. Any post-Brezhnev Soviet leader would have reevaluated Soviet policy in Asia.

Second and more fundamental, so long as Gorbachev's highest priority is to reform and to modernize the stagnant Soviet economy, he will need a peaceful international environment, stable relations with all the Western powers, especially the United States, and arms control agreements that will enable him to justify the drastic reductions in the Soviet military budget that he needs to revitalize the civilian economy.

The third reason behind the revolution in Soviet foreign policy is the most fundamental of all. Gorbachev has come to understand the limits of military power in the modern world and the fact that the very nature of power is changing. In the world of the information revolution, the progress of science and technology, not the expansion of arms and territorial aggrandizement, is the key to power and influence.

In sum, there are some very encouraging trends in the relations among the major powers in East Asia. A strategy designed to develop a more stable and secure structure of international relations in the region should build on these trends.

*

Two sets of bilateral relations among the major powers need to be improved. The first is U.S.-Chinese relations; the second is Soviet-Japanese relations.

U.S.-Chinese relations suffered a sharp deterioration after the brutal crushing of the pro-democracy movement in Tiananmen Square in June 1989. As a result of the Tiananmen massacres, the Bush administration imposed a number of sanctions on China, and the U.S. Congress wants to go even further. By sending National Security Advisor Brent Scowcroft to China in December 1989, the Bush administration signalled its interest in preventing any further deterioration in the relationship, and the Chinese leadership has made some modest response. Neither side wants to see a further downturn in a relationship that has been built up so painstakingly over the past twenty years and that is based on a variety of common interests. But the harsh crackdown on the students, the executions and arrests that followed, and the continuing imposition of martial law, as well as efforts by the new hardline leadership in Beijing to restore central control over the economy and to reimpose a more orthodox ideological line, have contributed to a negative image of China in the United States. Already President Bush is under fire from Congress and the media for allegedly "kowtowing" to China by sending the Scowcroft mission.

China, for its part, is blaming the West in general and the United States in particular for fostering the democracy movement in China. Beijing accuses the United States of trying to subvert socialism in China and of intervening in China's internal affairs.

Complicating the issue is the fact that China is probably entering a period of political instability. Deng Xiaoping and many of the other leaders in China are in their eighties and a new generation of leaders is not yet in place. It is questionable whether Deng's newly anointed heir, Jiang Zemin, will be able to get the support of the military and the Party after Deng's demise. More likely is a protracted struggle over power and policy at the top. Under these circumstances, it is difficult to be sanguine about the immediate future of U.S.-Chinese relations.

Over the longer run, however, the underlying forces for reform in China remain strong. And the common interests that bind the United States and China together are powerful. It is likely, therefore, that these two great powers will seek at some point to restore their relationship.

Soviet-Japanese relations have been hampered in the past by a history of conflict going back through most of the late nineteenth and twentieth centuries, by mutual distrust, by a belated Soviet recognition of Japan's importance, and by a territorial dispute over the four islands north of Hokkaido. Gorbachev has gone some way already to develop a more flexible policy towards Japan and some progress has been made in improving relations. There has been a resumption of scientific and technological cooperation that had been suspended after the imposition of martial law in Poland, a new five year trade and payments agreement, a new coastal trade treaty, a treaty for the avoidance of double taxation, and a cultural exchange agreement. But the Soviet leader will have to find some way to resolve the territorial dispute if there is to be any genuine breakthrough in Soviet-Japanese relations.

*

In addition to improving relations among the major powers, a second condition for a more stable Pacific is the need to achieve a breakthrough in resolving the outstanding regional conflicts in Korea and Cambodia. The stark facts of life in the Korean peninsula are that more than a million armed men face each other across the thirty-eighth parallel and there has been very little genuine progress in moving towards a North-South Korean detente. The principal obstacle to peace in Korea is the unreconstructed, Stalinist regime in Pyongyang which refuses to accept the legitimacy of the government in the South and which continues to try to reunify Korea on its own terms. North Korea remains one of the most highly militarized, secretive, and isolated countries in the world.

There are, however, some reasons for cautious optimism. Both Moscow and Beijing, Pyongyang's two allies, have begun to establish trade relations with Seoul, and the Soviets (undoubtedly to North Korea's chagrin), are even establishing quasi-diplomatic relations with South Korea through the opening of so-called trade offices which will be manned by high ranking foreign service officers on both sides. Also, several East European countries have formally extended diplomatic recognition to Seoul.

Moreover, the reform wave sweeping the communist world would seem to indicate that the days of the Stalinist dictatorship in Pyongyang are numbered.

But until and unless North Korea moves towards glasnost and perestroika, it seems unlikely that there will be any substantial diminution in tension on the peninsula. Recent developments in Eastern Europe, where communist party monopolies on power have been overthrown, may even be strengthening the North Korean dictator's resolve to take a harder line.

Still, the great powers must do what they can to encourage North Korea to come to an accommodation with Seoul. The immediate objective should be a new dialogue between the two Koreas which leads to a substantial drawdown of forces along the thirty-eighth parallel, family reunification, the beginning of trade, and a variety of contacts between Seoul and Pyongyang. A later goal is a peace treaty between the Koreas and the entry of them both into the United Nations. The critical first step is for both Seoul and Pyongyang to enter into arms control negotiations that will result in substantial numbers of forces and equipment being moved away from the demilitarized zone, so that neither side has the capacity to launch a surprise attack. In Korea, as in Central Europe, mutual security can be improved by the opposing sides restructuring their armed forces into a mode of "defensive defense." (This would be an appropriate form of "mutual threat reduction" for the Korean peninsula.)

In Cambodia, the great powers should increase their efforts to arrange a political settlement and to stop the fighting. There are some encouraging developments in recent months. The five permanent members of the United Nations Security Council, meeting in Paris, have agreed on a plan to bring Cambodia peace and free elections. The plan calls for Hun Sen's Vietnam-backed government to surrender the top administrative positions in Phnom Penh to U.N. officials. This is to be followed by a ceasefire between the Hun Sen regime and the three-party opposition coalition, headed by Prince Norodom Sihanouk but militarily dominated by the Khmers Rouges. The ceasefire would be supervised by the U.N. as would a subsequent election. The U.N. would then withdraw and leave the elected government to rebuild Cambodia.

For this plan to succeed, it will require a fair amount of money. But Japan has already promised to underwrite much of the cost. A more serious obstacle may be the Khmers Rouges. Will they stop fighting and agree to participate in the electoral process? If they do not, the big powers and the U.N. will be forced to organize a much more potent peacekeeping force, not just an election-watching operation.

Still, recent developments suggest that a settlement in Cambodia may be at hand. The Vietnamese have evidently become so alarmed at the deterioration of Hun Sen's battlefield position (and so desperate for Western credits and technology) that they are willing to sacrifice Hun Sen to the whims of the ballot box. And China seems now to understand that the West will not tolerate the idea of the Khmers Rouges shooting their way to power.

*

A third condition for moving towards a more stable Pacific is to foster the development of regional political and economic organizations such as ASEAN, the

Asian Development Bank, the Pacific Economic Cooperation Council (PECC), and the newly created regional economic organization which brings together most of the market economies in the region.

Once there is a political settlement in Cambodia, Vietnam may be invited to sign the Bali Treaty, which led to the creation of ASEAN. Following this, there could be an increase of political and economic relations between Vietnam and the non-communist countries of Southeast Asia. The Prime Minister of Thailand has already outlined a plan for turning all of Indochina into a market place and there is a considerable potential for the development of economic relations between Vietnam and the ASEAN countries and between Vietnam and the other market economies of the Pacific rim.

For some time to come, the Pacific economic organizations will be largely confined to the market economies. But the Soviet Union has already become an observer at PECC meetings and at meetings of the Asian Development Bank. Over time, as the Soviet Union and other socialist countries in the Pacific move towards market reforms, these ties to regional economic organizations can be expanded.

Any stable security structure in the Pacific will also require continuing progress in the region towards political and social pluralism. The attempts by the new hardline leadership in China to turn back on reform, and the continuation in Pyongyang of an anachronistic Stalinist regime are incompatible with any genuine progress towards regional security and stability. By the same token, much will depend on the continuation of political and economic reform in the Soviet Union.

Finally, there need to be some efforts to reduce the military confrontation in the region.[1] There is, however, no need for formal arms control negotiations of the type that are taking place in Europe. The severe asymmetries in the military forces of the two sides rule out the approaches of common ceilings or equal percentage reductions that arms control politics almost inevitably demand. The Soviet Union is a land power while the U.S. depends upon maritime power; and the military forces of other countries in the region also play an important role.

There are some possibilities for a selective development of confidence-building measures, but (as the principles of mutual security suggest) these measures should be chosen with care so that they do not benefit one side more than the other. Many of the confidence-building measures proposed so far by the Soviet Union are likely to be counter-productive, because they are considered by many Western analysts to be self-serving and designed to hamper the access of the United States Navy to the Pacific. As a maritime nation, dependent on the seas for its economic health, and with critical alliances across both oceans, the United States will always be reluctant to enter into any agreements that interfere with the freedom of movement of its navy.

This does not mean, however, that nothing can be done to reduce the level of military confrontation in the Pacific. Some reduction of Soviet and U.S. military forces in the Pacific are almost certainly going to be brought about by defense budget constraints on both sides. Some of the existing forums, such as the incidents-at-sea talks between the Soviet Union and the United States (which have been among the most successful of the various Soviet-American dialogues), could be expanded to include China and Japan. All four of the major powers could begin to exchange data on the respective defense budgets and defense plans. High ranking naval officials from all four countries could enter into regular exchanges to discuss their respective naval doctrines and their future force projections. Military exercises could be reduced and made less provocative.

In addition, since it is in the common interest of all of the major powers in the Pacific to discourage nuclear proliferation and the spread of ballistic missile and other advanced military technologies in the region, talks might begin on this subject.

It will also be necessary for the United States to reassess its military strategy and its military deployments in the Pacific. If there is a CFE treaty that substantially reduces Soviet forces in Europe, and if the East European countries continue to move in the direction of political pluralism, the danger of a Soviet attack on Western Europe will be greatly diminished. As a result, the current U.S. strategy of deterring a Soviet attack in Europe by posing a threat of horizontal escalation in the Pacific will lose much of its credibility.[2]

The United States needs to develop a strategy in the Pacific that focuses less on the threat from the Soviet Union and more on the multiple threats from other sources that can be expected to continue in the 1990s — threats to secure oil supplies from the Persian Gulf, threats of maritime interdiction, and, above all, threats from several flashpoints which could involve the U.S. in conflict at lower levels. Any U.S. strategic reassessment in the Pacific should, however, bear in mind that for some time to come there will be a need for a substantial U.S. presence in the Pacific not just to shore up or protect threatened allies but to underpin U.S. political/economic policy.

In this paper I have suggested that mutual security for the United States and USSR, and for all the nations of the Asia-Pacific region, can be considerably enhanced if these nations make progress along six paths. The superpowers in particular need to take realistic account of the particular political, cultural, and geopolitical circumstances of the region. Further improvement is needed in all the bilateral relations involved, and especially in U.S.-Chinese and Soviet-Japanese relations. Resolutions must be found to the serious confrontations in Korea and Cambodia. Progress toward economic and other cooperation within the region needs to continue. So must progress toward political and social pluralism. And finally, efforts are needed to reduce the military confrontations in the region, especially the U.S.-Soviet confrontation. Progress in all these directions is certainly possible in the years to come. If that progress is made, there are real grounds for hope that all the nations in the region will be able to enjoy greater security.

Notes

1. The military confrontations in Korea and Cambodia have been discussed above. Other military confrontations, such as the ones between China and the USSR, China and Vietnam, and others, are outside the scope of this paper. The Working Group on the North Pacific took as its main focus of attention the U.S.-Soviet relationship in the region.
2. The term "horizontal escalation" refers to enlarging a war by opening a new theater of operations. The *threat* to engage in horizontal escalation can be one means of strengthening a policy of deterrence in another theater, and it is part of U.S. policy now for deterring attack in Europe.

17

The Korean Problem and Possible Forms of Soviet-American Interaction

ALEKSIS BOGATUROV, MIKHAIL NOSSOV, AND
KONSTANTINE PLESHAKOV

The confrontation in Korea

One of the more significant threats in the North Pacific region remains the political-military tension on the Korean peninsula. Along with the Democratic People's Republic of Korea (DPRK) and the Republic of Korea (ROK), also involved are the United States, which is in a political-military alliance with the ROK, and the Soviet Union and China, which are allied with the government of the DPRK. Indirectly, Japan is involved in the confrontation as an ally of the U.S. Despite the fact that the USSR and the U.S. are on the "opposite sides of the barricade" in the conflict, they have in common (as do China and Japan) an interest regarding the possible escalation of the conflict on the peninsula into a military confrontation. Mutually understanding this hazard, and under conditions of increased economic and humanitarian contacts between the USSR, the U.S., Japan, and China on the one side, and both parts of Korea on the other, a search is possible for mutually acceptable efforts to resolve the conflict.

The Korean conflict occupies a special place in international relations, significantly different from other "hot spots"; therefore it demands a specific approach. The following qualities can be delineated which define its uniqueness:

— Extremely prolonged character. Existing for forty years, the Korean conflict has lasted longer than others (with the exception of some in the Middle East), reflecting a kind of chronic illness of international relations in East Asia.

— Stagnating character of the conflict. After a sharp intensification — the Korean War — the situation on the Korean peninsula has been in a state of stagnation for thirty-five years. On the one hand, this gives rise to a known (although a rather dangerous) stability, but on the other hand, it also leads to a psychological fatigue, a sensation of a deadlock of the situation.

— Unusually clear polarization. Perhaps no other conflict on Earth has such a clear delimitation of forces. Large, medium-size and small powers around the world, with few exceptions, express with determination their attitude toward the conflict, sharply emphasizing which side is "correct" and which is "to be blamed." This polarization does not facilitate a resolution of the conflict.

— There is a heavy involvement of great powers, especially the USSR and the U.S., up to a level of direct military presence or political-military responsibility for the fate of its ally (corresponding to the ROK and the DPRK).

— The internationalization of the conflict. Although originally the conflict erupted between the North and the South, and is still based on the national tragedy of the Korean people, a situation has emerged in which the DPRK and the ROK cannot by themselves resolve the conflict. Only the international community can find paths out of the deadlock.

— An irrational character of the conflict, to a certain degree, as neither side can realistically claim victory in the situation; meanwhile, the conflict continues and heated feelings remain.

— A large number of false perceptions of the two sides by each other's allies. This, on the one hand, hinders the search for constructive ways of resolving the conflict, and on the other hand, intensifies the tension on the peninsula.

— The emotional character of the evaluations. Practically all the countries involved in the conflict first turn to emotions, and not to sound judgment. On the one hand, for instance, there is the theme of "North Korean terrorism," and on the other hand, a definition of the South Korean government as a "puppet clique."

— Potentially colossal explosive power. The Korean peninsula can be viewed as a possible detonator for nuclear war: the domestic instability on the peninsula, the high degree of military involvement of the superpowers, the absence of mechanisms for stabilization of crises, or even consultations, and the saturation of the region with nuclear weapons attest to this possibility.

— The particular economic environment of the conflict. If the majority of regional conflicts develop in underdeveloped countries, then South Korea is one of the flagships of the Third World, one of the economic centers of the Asia-Pacific region (APR). All the countries of the region are interested in developing cooperation with South Korea.

— The territorial proximity of the conflict to the borders of the USSR, China, and Japan. This, on the one hand, involves the dangers of the Korean problem with the security of these countries. On the other hand, this proximity helps provide grounds for close economic cooperation with both the South and the North.

It is especially necessary to discredit the many false notions that prevail about the situation in Korea. Of course they differ somewhat from one country to another. Nevertheless, some typical characteristics can be outlined here:

— There is a widespread tendency to assign to the image of the enemy (North or South) an absolutely negative aspect, that is, to be convinced of the other Korea's ability to carry out to the highest degree treacherous and unpredictable acts, and to believe that it is striving, by military means, to impose its conditions on the opponent.

— In parallel, there is widespread belief in the other Korea's willingness to resolve the conflict or to negotiate; thus there is a dialogue of the deaf.

— These misperceptions in turn generate others:

  — the exaggeration of the dependence of both Korean countries on their respective superpowers;

  — a lack of understanding of the real facts of Korea, including the forces of nationalist feelings of the Korean people (hence the false parallel to the resolution of the German Question);

  — an underestimation of the aspiration of both sides (North and South) toward the unification of the country.

The development of regional conflicts

Regional conflicts go through common stages of development; the characteristics of these stages demand study. However, the stages are these:

— The origin, connected with a socio-economic crisis in the country. This crisis is accompanied by alignment of opposing forces to the superpowers (as a rule the U.S. and the USSR, the leaders of the two main socio-economic systems in the world).

— The split of the nation, at times even to the creation of two governments and two state establishments.

— An attempt to find a way out of the deadlock by military actions, with the support (direct or indirect) of the corresponding superpowers. The military conflict leads to a sharp aggravation of the international situation; therefore it is followed by:

  — An armistice, an acknowledgement of a stalemate situation, where neither side is capable of achieving a decisive victory.

  — Stagnation, under which the opposing sides develop in isolation, psychologically preparing for the renewal of open conflict, but actually not planning for it.

  — The search for compromise. A clearer example of this today is demonstrated by the Kampuchean conflict.

The superpowers and the Korean confrontation

In evaluating the possibilities for Soviet-American cooperation, with the goal of reducing tensions on the Korean peninsula, it is necessary to proceed from a calculation of objective circumstances. These determine the particular approach of each side. One issue is the understanding on the part of the Soviet Union and the United States of the potential for maintaining close relations simultaneously with the DPRK and the ROK. The USSR will not be able to interact with the U.S. to such an extent that it could threaten to break the Soviet alliance with Pyongyang. It is unlikely that doing so would make the policy of the DPRK any more predictable or the situation on the peninsula any less explosive. It is also necessary to keep in mind that the Soviet Union has at its disposal, as compared to the U.S., fewer possibilities for direct influence on its Korean ally concerning concrete questions of the political-military situation in the region. The USSR, as distinguished from the U.S., does not have at its disposal its own contingent of troops, military arsenals, or strategic infrastructure on the territory of the peninsula.

The United States has at its disposal a wide spectrum of possibilities for positive influence on the situation by means of less radical steps. Examples are a refusal to further expand its military presence in the South; lowering the level of activity in conducting joint military maneuvers (Team Spirit), which increase the suspicion of Pyongyang; and the application of measures of trust which are acceptable to the American side.

The Soviet Union supports such proposals of the DPRK as transforming the Korean peninsula into a non-nuclear zone, limiting in the years 1988-1992 the armies of the North and the South to one hundred thousand, with the corresponding gradual evacuation from South Korea of American troops and their nuclear arsenals, conducting negotiations between the DPRK, and the U.S. and the ROK about political-military negotiations with a high level of Korean representation. The U.S. has categorically refused these proposals.

Nevertheless, the USSR and the U.S. remain objectively interested in stabilizing the situation in Korea, ensuring there a stable peace. This goal should be the top priority compared to all other problems arising from political, economic, and ideological aspirations of the countries in the region (which are far from coinciding).

In spite of these tactical divergences, the similarity of Soviet and American long-term goals in relation to stabilizing the situation creates objective grounds toward searching for forms of bilateral interaction. Advancement to such interaction is possible in three directions.

First each can avoid direct opposition of the other's unilateral actions regarding the DPRK and the ROK, and also regarding the region as a whole.

This requires an open and clear account of Moscow's and Washington's opinion about the necessity to subordinate particular interest groups in Pyongyang and in Seoul to the interests of humanity as a whole and to the establishment of peace in Korea. An understanding that there are joint goals for the USSR and the U.S. should not only belong to a narrow group of specialists. In the end, not only Pyongyang and Seoul, the USSR and the U.S., but many other countries in East Asia are interested in the stability of the situation — above all, China and the countries in ASEAN. Furthermore, open discussion of the mutual aspiration of the Soviet Union and the United States to stabilize the situation will strengthen the feeling of responsibility on the part of the governments of the DPRK and the ROK for their political actions and will be a source of pressure on them.

From the point of view of political psychology, the rejection of the habitual stereotype of perceiving any Soviet action toward Korea as anti-American, and any American initiative as anti-Soviet, will permit the avoidance of unnecessary polemics. This will also facilitate the formation of favorable circumstances for the creation of an informal coalition of various forces which are not always in agreement, but can be united by their interest to normalize the conditions in the region.

Second, Soviet-American interaction could be realized in the form of parallel actions. It would be useful to create standing working groups, which would consist of experts and representatives of the corresponding departments of the USSR and DPRK, as well as the U.S. and the ROK. The formal goal of such groups could be the discussion of the situation on the Korean peninsula and in the area surrounding it; but the actual goal would be the search for possibilities for conducting direct dialogue between the North and the South in one way or another. Perhaps in their planning, the Soviet and American foreign policy departments, independently of each other, could work toward the formation of such groups and also toward regular working consultations with China. In the broad view, it is just not worth it to reject the creation of such Soviet-American working groups.

Third, and most effective, but also more complicated and requiring more cooperation between the USSR and the U.S., could be the direct coordination of policy in relation to Korea. In the sphere of potential understandings it is pertinent to include the questions of decreasing the supply of Soviet arms to the DPRK and simultaneously decreasing the American presence in the South. As it can be imagined, such steps should be undertaken in the broad context of taking measures to improve confidence, including the regulation of conditions for conducting Team Spirit and the military maneuvers of the DPRK.

Incidentally, there would be less of a negative reaction of the DPRK toward the establishment of economic relations between the Soviet Union and the ROK if it could be accomplished with the simultaneous establishment of such contacts between the U.S. and the DPRK.

Finally, the adoption during the next Soviet-American high level meeting of a separate joint declaration on Korea would have important political significance. Such a declaration could include the expression of the readiness of the USSR and the U.S. for open dialogue with all of the governments of the Asia-Pacific region on the basis of acknowledgement of existing political realities, and only if such dialogue responds to the interests of securing peace and stability. The point of such a voluntary expression consists of the high-level recognition of both superpowers of the priority of interests of the world as a whole, compared to ideological dogmas and the persistent stereotypes of confrontational politics. It might be thought that the development of the Korean question has brought the interested countries to a search for a compromise. Indeed, evidence can be found in the July 21, 1988 proposal of the DPRK and also the various specific steps on the part of the ROK. But it is necessary to emphasize that if the search for compromise does not lead to anything — because the two Koreas are unready, or because of any inadequacy of the superpowers — then the conflict could escalate to a second round of the usual development, up to the level of military confrontation.

Policy possibilities

Four variants of solving the Korean question are known to be presently under discussion.

First — Continuation of confrontation on the Korean peninsula, with the North and the South expecting each other to become weaker as a result of the political crisis arising from mass demonstrations or a change of top leadership. Such a political crisis would enable the opposing side to solve the Korean question on its own terms. This variant is not realistic. Gambling on a political crisis may result in violence breaking out on the peninsula, perhaps going as far as to directly involving superpowers in the crisis.

Second — Cross recognition (USSR and PRC recognize South Korea, and the U.S. and Japan recognize North Korea). Advocates of this model usually cite the experience of solving the German Question, when the GDR and FRG not only won cross recognition but also became members of international organizations. They make the case that cross recognition will legalize the existing political reality once and for all, will ease the tension of confrontation, will bring Korea into the norms of international law, and will enable the Korean people to quietly determine their future fairly soon. These arguments would probably be good ones if the Korean question were equivalent to the German Question. The differences, however, are striking. Germany was historically familiar with being broken up (actually it had been undivided for only seventy years — from Bismark to Hitler). For years after World War II the Germanies were occupied countries repenting of the sin of fascism. Later West Germany wanted to revive democratic institutions and restore its economy destroyed by the war; the idea of community of nation became an issue of secondary importance.

In Korea, the picture is quite different. Even during the many years of Japanese occupation the Korean people had a sense of a community of nation. Nowadays there is a growing interest in traditional culture in Korea, both in the North and the South. It is significant that the activists of the youth movement in South Korea decry the erosion of national traditions under the pressure of American culture and believe that in the North traditional values of Korean culture remain inviolable. Besides, it should be taken into account that the division of Germany into two states took place in the time of the most intense confrontation between the West and East, and it would be anachronistic to resort to the methods of Cold War problem-solving in a time when everybody realizes the world's interdependence. Of course we should get rid of any superstitious fear of certain terms and conceptions; cross recognition is to be discussed as one of the chief possible variants. However, we should also be aware of some characteristic features of national self-identity in Asia. For example, were it not for Taiwan being part of the Confucian area of culture (which includes Korea too), it would be expected to be anxious to declare its independence and enter the community of nations as a sovereign nation. However, Taiwanese leaders regarded this as unthinkable, as they claim themselves to be the only "true China." Many political figures in South Korea are in favor of cross recognition, and this approach seems to be acceptable for many countries. However, a series of discussions of this approach should be held, with South

Korea's opposition taking part, in addition to representatives of official quarters, for both have something to say about Korean identity. The presence of North Korea's representatives seems unlikely at this point.

Third — Peaceful reunification of Korea. By peaceful reunification of Korea we mean that neither South Korea nor North Korea would try to suppress its opponent, or impose its own social-economic structure or ideological values. In this connection the most serious attention should be paid to the conception born in the PRC: "One country — two systems." Needless to say, it would be much more difficult to realize this principle in Korea. Taiwan and Hong Kong are not nearly as large as the PRC is. On the Korean peninsula, we are talking about uniting two state formations of equal status and worth under the slogan of "one country — two systems." (South Korea is of course much better developed in military terms).

Obviously the most vulnerable points in any plan of creating one Korean Federation are the military question and the question of foreign ties. Not only in terms of today's confrontation but also in terms of future hypothetical detente on the Korean peninsula, these two questions are certainly going to block any agreements. And only in some distant future, provided the political and psychological climate on the Korean peninsula changes radically for the better, may it become possible to seriously discuss this possibility. However, it would be irrational to refuse to have anything to do with it now. Today the ruling principle in many formal discussions is "an eye for an eye"; that is, if the Soviet side refuses to discuss cross recognition, many American specialists refuse to talk about the reunification of Korea, sensing a propagandistic campaign in the very presentation of the idea.

The happy medium, a compromise for some near future, may be reached through the *fourth* variant of solving the Korean question: recognition of the two Korean states by all the members of the world community — not de jure, but de facto — and with North Korea and South Korea opening a dialogue. This variant by-passes the useless argument about which of the states on the Korean peninsula is "true," the national tragedy of the Korean people is not perpetuated, there still remains a chance of reuniting the country in the future, and no-one's interests are hurt. In this alternative the status quo is preserved, but it takes civilized shape, and tension is drastically eased. The de facto recognition does not make it impossible to negotiate peaceful reunification of Korea later. If we are to be realistic we have to admit that these negotiations will take supreme effort and long years, impossible in today's conditions.

The presence in both Pyongyang and Seoul of diplomatic missions of the states willing to participate in this process (by all means including the U.S., USSR, the PRC and Japan), and the unlimited promotion of economic, scientific, technical and cultural cooperation of these states with both the North and the South, will benefit the interests of the whole Korean nation, and not just the interests of some political factions. The importance of economic cooperation between North Korea and South Korea is self-evident.

Today, this alternative (merely as it is) for solving the Korean question has to be accepted as the best, because this is the only possible compromise. Of course, there is a great gap between the "only possible" policy and the generally acceptable one. However, here we can probably ask a question; what guidance should be chosen in trying to find a reasonable way out of this deadlock? Should we be guided by the interests of groups or by the interest of the whole Korean nation, which turned out to be a victim of Cold War?

It is only natural to say, too, that there should be Soviet-American cooperation in ultimately solving the Korean question, i.e., in establishing the Korean Federation. We must not ignore the fact that the USSR and the U.S. are second, only after North Korea and South Korea themselves, in bearing the responsibility for normalizing the situation on the peninsula.

Proposals

Despite many serious proposals and interesting initiatives, the process of easing the tension of the Korean peninsula is actually making very little progress. In our view many things depend on "outsiders" taking part in the process. We believe it is high time now to convene an international conference on Korea, in which all the parties concerned could take part, including the two Korean states. Considering the tense relations between North Korea and South Korea, as well as both countries' fears of possible aggression, the conference could discuss the set-up of a step-by-step lifting of the militarization of the peninsula, and ways of guaranteeing security for both sides during the practical realization of the above plan. Within the framework of such discussion it would be appropriate to raise the question of international guarantees of preventing a military conflict on the peninsula if such may arise.

At the initial stage the USSR, U.S., the PRC and perhaps some other countries, acting under the auspices of the United Nations, could act as guarantors of a nonviolence treaty between North Korea and South Korea. The next stage could deal with the issue of limitation and then cessation of military assistance rendered to the Korean states, and the issue of establishment of an international commission, with the two Korean states' representatives taking part. This commission would act to prevent any chance of a surprise attack and to elaborate a system of measures strengthening military confidence. The third stage could include the setting up of buffer zones on both sides of the demilitarized area. These buffer zones would be free from any kind of offensive arms and nuclear weapons; any military maneuvers would be banned in these zones. As a next step, the parties could agree to reduce the scale and frequency of military exercises. The fourth stage could provide for parity in the reduction of troops in North Korean and South Korea and for a progressive withdrawal of American military units from the peninsula. Simultaneously with the realization of this plan, and in accordance with it, the governments of both Korean states could proceed with the discussion of the inter-Korean relationship, and ways of achieving national reconciliation and reunification of the country.

The dialogue could be improved through the promotion of inter-Korean economic cooperation. Various possible forms of this cooperation, in particular the forms of guarantor countries' participation in it, could become a subject of discussion at the international conference. Such cooperation would have the prospect of widening perspectives, the more so as interest in it is displayed on both sides of the thirty-eighth parallel. In accordance with a Seoul economist's calculations, an "integrated" Korea could generate a GNP of the North and the South together of $360 billion by the year 2000, while under the existing situation the volume of GNP of the two parts of Korea added together will amount to only $260 billion. Big joint projects in such fields as the use of natural resources, fishery, agriculture and the possible participation of the USSR, U.S., the PRC and Japan in these projects would contribute to not only economic but military and political stability on the peninsula.

Obviously the most important thing in promoting economic cooperation is to contribute to making Korea one single economy. Without economic interdependence, any political declarations and obligations will inevitably remain under a constant risk of failure.

It is an objective fact that the economic standards in North Korea are inferior to those of South Korea. Therefore the North can be regarded as a good object for using the economic and technical potential of South Korea coupled with the labor market of North Korea. It also appears the U.S. and the USSR could largely cooperate today in facilitating the economic interaction between the North and the South. The American side has a big potential for such cooperation as many American companies are closely connected with South Korea. The Soviet Union could assist North Korea in the economic validation of joint projects, and the potential of the Soviet Far East could be drawn into this cooperation.

Considering recent changes in domestic policy in South Korea, it now is especially appropriate and timely to expand contacts. A dialogue between the USSR and South Korea will strengthen the democratic forces in the country and would create preconditions for extending a dialogue between the North and the South. South Korea could become an important trade and economic partner for the Soviet Union. South Korea would be a partner keenly competing with Japan, who so far has in fact monopolized our economic ties in the Far East. Also, an important factor for the USSR is a chance to obtain the latest technical know-how from South Korea. Those possibilities are the more interesting as the Seoul leadership makes no secret of its great interest in promoting trade and economic ties with the USSR.

Conclusion

The Korean conflict could be put to an end if active contacts were established among Moscow, Seoul, Pyongyang and Washington. It is hard to define now the forms of these contacts and their follow-ups, but the necessity of such contacts is obvious. Cross-contacts will not only create pre-conditions for a more extended dialogue among all the participants of the Korean process (the PRC would be a de facto participant and Japan might become one) but also will make the conditions for inter-Korean negotiations more favorable.

Any progress in Soviet-American interaction in the Korean question could pave the way to a discussion of the problem of making the Korean peninsula a nuclear-free zone. It could also create pre-conditions for adapting the "European" and Soviet-American treaties on arms control to the Asia-Pacific region. Now that Soviet-American relations are improving, it becomes both possible and extremely important to reach an agreement on issues of security on the Korean peninsula. Here especially, if the process of easing military tension and limiting arms supplies can be made, at a minimum, an explicit, acknowledged bilateral concern, then Soviet proposals for securing measures of trust in the Asia-Pacific region could be defined concretely.

As the natural guarantors of security on the Korean peninsula are the U.S., the USSR, the PRC and Japan, it would be advisable to hold a series of meetings of policy specialists and representatives of business circles of these countries. Such meetings to some extent would prepare the ground for governmental contacts.

An intensive dialogue on the problems of Korea is now vitally important. If the various sides refuse to conduct this dialogue and fail to accept de facto one of the existing states on the Korean peninsula (either for political or moral considerations), it can only result in deepening the existing crisis in Korea. Stagnation may turn into an outbreak of violence. The consequences of this not only for East Asia but for the whole world would be serious.

18

The United States, the Soviet Union and Korea: Beyond Confrontation

ALAN ROMBERG

Introduction[1]

For over thirty-five years, since the end of the Korean War, massive formations of troops have faced each other in hostility across the Demilitarized Zone; it has been one of the most dangerous confrontations in Asia. The two Korean states are armed to the teeth and are backed by powerful allies. While there has been no renewal of outright war, there have been numerous incidents, including commando raids by North Korea against the South some years ago and the construction of enormous tunnels under the DMZ. In the past five or six years, there have also been a number of terrorist incidents directed from Pyongyang, the capital of North Korea. Meanwhile, the South has built up a formidable modern arsenal and, in conjunction with its American ally, has developed into an imposing middle power. Relations between the two halves of Korea have been dominated by total mistrust.

In certain key respects, the situation is now changing. Not only has South Korea significantly altered its previous policy of confrontation toward the communist world, but the People's Republic of China (PRC) and the Soviet Union, North Korea's principal allies, have also moved in important ways to reach out to the South despite Pyongyang's obvious displeasure. This essay examines these changes as well as possible policy initiatives to reduce the level of tension between the North and South and, with it, the potential for superpower conflict.

The analysis and policy prescriptions offered here are obviously developed from an American perspective, but an effort has been made to account for the interests of the other parties as well. In this respect, and in the broadest sense, this paper accepts the concept of "mutual security": at least in the long run, the security of each party will — indeed, only can — be enhanced by assuring the security of all. In the short run, however, when the will for political accommodation is lacking on the part of one of the key parties — North Korea — this may not be the case.

U.S. interests

Forty years ago, the United States fought a war in Korea, suffering over 54,000 dead and more than 103,000 wounded in helping the Republic of Korea (ROK) defend itself against invasion from the North. In the period since, the United States has committed itself to the safety and prosperity of the ROK through a mutual security treaty, the stationing of tens of thousands of American combat forces in the country, and massive aid programs (terminated a number of years ago).

From an American viewpoint, this policy, which was initially marked by considerable confusion and much frustration, has finally met with outstanding success. South Korea's economic development is a model, with both less developed countries and socialist nations today seeking to emulate it. Politically, after years of authoritarian rule with a heavy military overtone, the South is now launched on the road toward a more liberal and stable society. And in security terms, the combined strength of the U.S. forces and treaty commitment, and the South's own increasingly powerful and professionalized military forces, constitutes a credible deterrent against future aggression.

All of the problems are, of course, not resolved, especially on the political front. Though South Korean party leaders are learning the importance of accommodation, their deeply ingrained instinct against compromise has not been rooted out, and some difficult issues have already begun to test the viability of the current structure.

Nonetheless, against the background of solid successes to date, and imbued with a new spirit of democratization, the Roh Tae Woo administration has moved since mid-1988 in a number of ways to smooth roiled domestic waters and to reach out to the North in an effort to reduce tensions across the DMZ. The new openness in Korean society has given vent to anti-Americanism among idealistic and nationalistic elements, especially radical students. Overall, however, the changes are compatible with American interests. They will not only contribute to greater security on the peninsula, they also conform with the aspirations of most Koreans. Accordingly, the United States has strongly supported Roh's initiatives.

Consistent with this approach, Americans will judge any proposals for U.S.-Soviet cooperation over Korea against the criterion of their contribution to the well-being of the Korean people in political, economic and security terms. Efforts to deal over the heads of the Koreans will not be acceptable.

With those caveats in mind, let us consider the problems on the Peninsula and possible moves to reduce or eliminate them.

The nature of the problem

From the very beginning of the postwar period, when the nation was divided at the thirty-eighth parallel, the two halves of Korea have confronted each other as mortal rivals. Only two years after both the Republic of Korea and the Democratic People's Republic of Korea (DPRK) were proclaimed in 1948, the North seized on a misperceived lack of American commitment to try to unify the country by force under communist rule.

Not long after the devastation of the ensuing war, South Korea embarked on a program of reconstruction and development which has led, today, to a country whose economic success is the envy of most of the world, whose political evolution has now brought it out of the stage of authoritarian, military-dominated rule to a course of increasing democratic pluralism, and whose military strength will soon be adequate to deter the larger North Korean forces essentially on its own.

Americans recognize that, with the aid of China and the Soviet Union, North Korea also rebuilt its economy rapidly and achieved substantial growth for a period of time. In addition, it was led by a regime acknowledged even in South Korea as a defender of Korean nationalism. Nevertheless, the net American impression today is of a rigid, regimented and doctrinaire political system, a stagnant economy, and a huge military establishment poised for offensive action.

Some years ago, Americans and others worried that militant leaders of South Korea might seek an excuse to attack north of the thirty-eighth parallel, assuming they could drag the United States into supporting what would surely have proven a costly and highly dangerous war. That fear disappeared with the development of South Korea in the 1960s and the accompanying desire — indeed need — for coexistence with the North. The one-fourth to one-third of the population and the modern sector of the economy located around the capital city of Seoul, a scant twenty-five miles from the DMZ, would be vulnerable to massive destruction in the event of hostilities.

While anxiety about a "northward thrust" has thus abated, concern with DPRK intentions remain, especially in this era of modern weapons. The North has continued to engage in various acts of terrorism and to plan and direct military and political provocations against the South.

Both sides have built up their military forces so that now over 1.5 million heavily armed troops face each other across a 150 mile-long demarcation line. For the

North, this build-up is estimated to cost nearly twenty-five percent of gross national product (GNP). For the South, with its far more rapid economic growth, the burden has now dropped below five percent of GNP, not nearly so onerous but still substantial.

In the context of this armed confrontation, for the past forty years South Korea has tried to prevent or suppress any domestic attraction to the North or political diversity within the ROK that might give Pyongyang an opening to exploit; diplomatically, Seoul has sought to isolate the DPRK. Despite talk of "reunification," it was obvious that until recently any affiliation with the North was not high on the South Korean agenda.

The record is replete with "proposals" from both sides for dialogue and even reunification. The North has focused on grandiose schemes such as confederation, the removal of American forces and reduction of Korean forces as the first tasks to be accomplished, with day-to-day relations in trade and travel to follow. The South, on the other hand, has advocated creation of mutual confidence through economic and other links, building to a stage where more overarching political ties and reduction of forces could be contemplated.

The United States has consistently supported the South's approach as the more realistic. Even so, it has generally been realized that the proposals from both sides always included some element that made them predictably unacceptable to the other.

Now, however, though suspicions of the North's intentions remain high, President Roh Tae Woo has responded to the increasingly outspoken South Korean sentiment for contacts with the North by proposing a different course. Roh's policy, supported by the opposition parties, rests on a fundamentally new premise: it would be in South Korea's interest to welcome North Korea into the world rather than seeking to shut it out. Thus, his declaration of July 7, 1988, and his speech to the U.N. General Assembly of October 18, 1988, suggested a number of steps that would not confront the North with a challenge but, rather, attract it with an invitation.

Specifically, Roh proposed the facilitation of visits across the DMZ between private citizens including members of divided families, the opening of trade between North and South, the welcoming of nonmilitary trade and other relations between the ROK's friends and North Korea, and an end to competitive and confrontational policies. As Roh put it in his U.N. speech: "[W]e are determined to pursue a relationship of partnership with North Korea....It is our sincere hope that North Korea participate fully in the international community."

An important part of the rationale for moving ahead in this fashion is obviously to deal with domestic sentiment in the ROK and to rob the radical students of their (currently) central issue. However, it also reflects the sense of confidence that the

South's enormous economic, security and, now, political modernization has created within the ROK government and society. Such responsiveness to the will of the people and the ability to see ROK interests in larger perspective represent significant departures from the past.

This confidence in South Korea's security, stability and prosperity has also been a critical factor underlying Seoul's encouragement to its friends in the United States, Japan and elsewhere to approach the North with trade and other initiatives. The steps announced by Washington on October 31, 1988, were designed in significant measure to support the ROK's new policies. These included restoration of permission for American diplomats to talk with North Korean counterparts in "neutral" settings, encouragement of private academic exchanges, and permission for some trade in humanitarian items.

The new U.S. approach is also consistent with the exhortations from China, and more recently from the Soviet Union, that the West reach out to North Korea in order to reduce Pyongyang's sense of isolation and vulnerability, strengthening the DPRK's confidence that it could safely abandon its reckless policies. Since 1988, the lack of North Korean responsiveness to American overtures has sharply limited the extent of bilateral contacts, in contrast to the rapidly burgeoning economic and even political relations between South Korea and the Soviet Union. Nevertheless, the new U.S. approach at least partly mirrors recent steps by both Beijing and Moscow to establish practical ties with the South.

Many, including Soviet and Chines experts, question whether any real progress is possible while Kim Il Sung is still the leader of North Korea. But whether a change can come under Kim or must await a successor — be it his son Kim Chong Il or someone else — many have argued that gestures now would eventually pay off.

Recent policy developments

In years past, especially at the height of Sino-Soviet tensions, Moscow and Beijing used to vie for favor in Pyongyang or, at the least, sought to avoid being outflanked. Each would try to take advantage of any cooling in the other leg of the triangle to strengthen its own position. In turn, the North was able to play its two large neighbors off against one another to its own — often considerable — advantage.

More recently, however, that situation has changed significantly. In the early 1980s, China determined that its interests required it to reach out quietly and cautiously to the South Korean economic miracle and engage it to the PRC's benefit. As it developed trade and other economic contacts, relations with the North cooled. At that time, Moscow, while firmly opposed to North Korean adventurism, played the traditional triangular game and moved to strengthen its links with

Pyongyang, supplying Kim Il Sung with a number of new, advanced military weapons systems in return, inter alia, for overflight rights of North Korea.

As the Soviet Union, itself, has come to emphasize non-military dimensions of national power, however, and to realize that economic reform and modernization are essential to its own future, it too has decided to risk some good will in Pyongyang in order to take advantage of South Korea's economic prowess. Though its trade with the ROK is only about one-sixth of the current annual level of roughly three billion dollars exchanged between China and South Korea, the USSR moved decisively to strengthen its ties with South Korea in 1989.

Having seized on the 1988 Seoul Olympics as a way, among other things, to educate its people about the true nature of South Korean successes, Moscow has now exchanged "unofficial" trade offices with Seoul and in other ways, including through consular arrangements and political dialogue between academic institutes, deepened and broadened its contact with the ROK.

The ambiguity of Soviet policy toward Korea is still manifest in its military deliveries to the North, however. Some Soviets explain this as fulfillment of commitments made years ago. Others contend that it is necessary to offset ROK purchases of F-16s (and prospectively, F-18s) and other modern weaponry from the United States. Still others point to many "interest groups" in the Soviet Union, including the military, who want to maintain good relations with their North Korean counterparts and who value the overflight rights and other privileges received in return.

Americans recognize that, though there is no credible war scenario that rests on ROK aggression, and though ROK systems are defensive in nature and have never been used to attack the North, the very significant growth and modernization of South Korean forces has doubtless given pause to the DPRK. So while the North outstrips the South quantitatively not only in military manpower but also in most categories of artillery and heavy weapons, it was to be expected that there would be some qualitative improvement in the North's inventory, especially of air defense systems. Thus, the Soviet supply of MiG-23 fighter aircraft and SA-3 surface-to-air missiles in the mid-1980s was not viewed with great alarm. Yet, even though the combined strength of the United States and the Republic of Korea still is sufficient to deter or, if need be, fend off any North Korean aggression, Moscow's more recent provision of MiG-29s, SA-5s and "Tin Shield" warning-and-control radar system to the North seemed to go beyond the requirements of a normal upgrade. Equally worrisome was the provision of Su-25 ground attack aircraft, which are well suited for an offensive thrust.

While one could argue that Pyongyang would never launch an attack because war would inevitably devastate the North as well as the South, the facts must weigh heavily. The pattern of North Korean behavior, and the disposition of its forces, leave one with considerable concern about the kinds of calculations that may be made in Pyongyang. The newly received aircraft and missiles, and the way they have been deployed (with the SA-5s close to the DMZ), raise the level of this concern.

The danger goes beyond even the extraordinary cost of any war to the Korean people — throughout the peninsula — to the possibility of direct involvement of the major power allies of the contending Korean governments. The fact that both Chinese and Soviet authorities state they would not support North Korean aggression (but only come to Pyongyang's aid in the event of an attack from the South) does not eliminate the problem, because of the potential for being drawn into a war arising out of incidents of ambiguous origin.

So what are the solutions, or at least policies that could be adopted by the United States and the Soviet Union to help alleviate tensions and support movement toward reconciliation between North and South Korea?

Policy considerations

We start from the premise that neither superpower wants war on the Korean peninsula and that both desire to see a reduction of tensions between Seoul and Pyongyang in order to minimize the likelihood of any such eventuality. We also assume that, whatever difficulties each may have with its Korean ally, neither is willing to sacrifice the fundamental interests of that ally in pursuit of better relations with the "other" Korea.

In the case of the United States, South Korea is already a significant political, economic, and military partner, and is growing in importance daily. Washington would see no advantage in ignoring its ally's interests in favor of relations with the North.

In the case of the Soviet Union, North Korea will remain an important ally but largely in terms of narrowly conceived military benefits as well as for "negative" strategic reasons (to prevent disaster in a sensitive area) rather than because the relationship helps the Soviets to achieve their new priority goal of modernization. The North's sluggish economy offers much less to the USSR than does the South.

The policy issues for both Moscow and Washington include how they can encourage North-South dialogue and a reduction of tensions as well as how they can protect their own interests. This includes questions of military supply to the two Korean entities, the two superpowers' own deployments, and the policies each adopts toward its erstwhile Korean adversary.

Military supply

It is inarguable that any meaningful progress in North-South relations and in reducing tensions on the peninsula will come not from one party overwhelming the other but from a sense on both sides of the DMZ that each is secure to pursue its own interests in peace and that neither will be able to impose its solution on the problem.

Viewed from the South, this means maintaining and strengthening the confidence that the North cannot credibly threaten either a cross-border attack or disrupt the South through other, less blatant means. Not only the economic strength of the South, but also its relatively new-found political liberalization will contribute importantly to establishing such a base. Democracy is not without its problems — including the enhanced opportunities for manipulation by the North — nor is the overall state of the world economy, on which the ROK depends so heavily. But the new, flexible attitude of the South toward the North seems well-grounded, and those conservative elements in the ROK who are concerned about the dangers entailed in opening to the North — and have contributed to some slowdown in the North-South dialogue and some slippage in domestic political liberalization — will increasingly find reason to feel reassured.

A key component of this setting, however, is the military security of the South. Regardless of whether there is a sizable U.S. military force stationed in the country, if the ROK felt vulnerable to either attack or "blackmail," prospects for further opening to the North would disappear. Dealing from "strength" in this sense does not mean possessing the capability to launch a successful first strike across the DMZ, but rather the capacity to inflict such grievous damage on the invader that he would be deterred from adventurous undertakings in the first place.

Even if one accepts Soviet and Chinese assertions that the North, too, acts out of a sense of vulnerability rather than from aggressive intent, still, the DPRK's history of threatening behavior and the vituperative harangues launched daily in North Korean media against the government in Seoul, argue that confidence must be built up between the two parties before any variant of the grandiose North Korean proposals for political alignment or military reductions can be seriously contemplated.

Similarly, Soviet proposals for mutually agreed limits on military supplies to both Korean governments are neither productive nor realistic. Soviet experts express concern about the destabilizing effects of eventual ROK military superiority (reversing the North's historical advantage) and, in any case, about unintentional incidents arising from confrontation between such heavily armed adversaries. At some point, the disparity in military strength in the South's favor could become substantial. In the foreseeable future, however, the modernization of the South Korean military is not likely to result in overwhelming ROK superiority, and, in the meantime, the growing parity of forces in the North and South should spur Pyongyang to seek a reduction of tensions that will allow both sides to address the long-run military balance.

Thus, while one can understand the Soviet desire to have at least a tacit understanding on mutual restraint in arms supplies, the concerns — which many Soviets share — that decisions in Pyongyang are not always rational will have to be addressed on their own terms. Placing into the hands of the North Koreans weapons of the sort Moscow has recently provided can only raise tensions; Moscow should urgently review that supply relationship.

Having said that, it is not in the U.S. interest to see South Korea develop a large-scale sophisticated weapons industry — which would only scare the North — or, certainly, a nuclear weapons capability. In past years, the United States has taken steps to head off any inclination in those directions, most recently through the agreement on F-18 assembly. It should continue to do so. As long as the fear of Northern aggression is real, however, the only alternative to such unwelcome choices is for the United States to provide the reassurance it now does through both its deployments and its treaty commitments.

Deployments

Once a relationship of trust has been developed between the two halves of Korea — in economic, political, and human terms — it may be that the nature of the U.S. involvement should change. And if at any time the South Korean people determine that they want the United States to withdraw its forces, of course, this should be done. Otherwise, however, to insist, as North Korea does, that the first step is to cut forces radically, including the removal of the American military presence, is to move in the direction of instability, not stability. There have already been some calls in the U.S. Congress to substantially reduce American forces in Korea. Given growing budgetary pressures and the rapidly changing climate in East-West relations, such proposals may gain more support. Even though some reduction may thus occur within the next several years, without a change in the political climate — and, hence, in the security threat — on the Peninsula, a massive withdrawal would be destabilizing and risk not only damaging the South's more open approach but basic U.S. interests in the region as a whole.

At the same time, two other issues can be addressed — nuclear weapons and the use of Korea as a strategic base.

Though most military planners find it hard to conceive of a scenario on the Korean peninsula in which nuclear weapons could be effectively used, retention of the American nuclear umbrella is likely to prove a necessary minimum in light of the North's current political attitudes and military deployments, as well as its security treaty with the Soviet Union. But if there are nuclear weapons stored in the ROK — and here we will respect the U.S. practice of neither confirming nor denying their presence — it would seem feasible to remove them.

From a military perspective, there would appear to be little advantage to having nuclear weapons on Korean soil. They could as easily be held available in other ways. Moreover, with the rising sense of nationalism in South Korea, it would behoove the United States to act with foresight and imagination to eliminate an issue before it grows to troublesome proportions. An agreement like those recently reached with Spain and the Philippines, which effectively preclude storage of nuclear weapons but preserve the integrity of the American policy to "neither confirm nor deny" the presence of nuclear weapons in transit on ships or planes, could be reached with Seoul as well.

And though nuclear weapons should not be deployed in Korea, in any case, for the reasons cited, it is also worth noting that Soviet experts contend that Moscow's arms supply relationship with Pyongyang is related to "what is happening" south of the DMZ. In the view of those experts, if nuclear weapons were excluded from American deployments in Korea, even prospectively for some future specific date (for example, two years hence), the United States would have the "right" to expect a Soviet response *now*, primarily in the area of weapons provided to the DPRK.

On the issue of strategic basing, even today, though their mission is defense of the ROK, the very presence in Korea of over half of all U.S. ground and air combat forces in the Western Pacific contributes importantly to the sense of regional security. One can imagine that, as an American military commander looks around the Pacific, he must be tempted by the potential advantages of using Korea as a base for long-range weapons, as well.

Such strategic deployments, however, would not only change the character of the U.S. military involvement within South Korea, creating a target for far greater anti-Americanism. It would also draw Korea explicitly into the East-West face-off in a way that could only complicate the security picture on the peninsula. The issue of U.S. forces currently deployed in Korea and whether and how to remove them is troubling enough for the overall American posture in East Asia. Any plan to augment or change the nature or mission of those forces would only serve to complicate the problem.

Despite the opportunity costs involved, the United States should seriously consider indicating now that it will not base in Korea strategic forces, or any forces, that are not related specifically to the defense of the ROK. By doing so it could pre-empt a crisis in U.S.-ROK relations, contribute to peace and stability on the peninsula, and provide some assurance to the Soviet Union that could elicit an appropriate response on Moscow's part (much as Gorbachev is doing in Europe).

As a further symbol of their willingness to reach out, the United States and South Korea could — and should — cut back on the annual Team Spirit exercise, one of the largest joint exercises in the world and one that has often been cited by Pyongyang as an obstacle to North-South dialogue. North Korea's demand for elimination of Team Spirit is unacceptable; it is a legitimate exercise. But it does not have to be maintained at the level that it has been in the recent past. There is nothing sacred about the size and duration of Team Spirit, and indeed the 1990 exercises are being scaled back, if only for budgetary reasons. Again, however, one should emphasize that the problem is not the American and ROK deterrent or exercises, it is the political attitudes in Pyongyang that lie behind the North-South confrontation that make that deterrent — and those exercises — necessary.

It is unlikely that comprehensive arms control agreements in Asia and the Pacific (other than some confidence-building measures) will be feasible except in the context of global accords centered on the face-off in Europe. This, in turn, will likely depend on improvement in the state of political relations between the United States and the Soviet Union. However, both sides need to consider carefully the impact of new deployments in the region on their mutual goal of reducing tensions in Asia generally, and specifically in Korea.

Political ties

Soviet specialists — both official and unofficial — have been dropping broad hints that Moscow favors cross recognition[2] and simultaneous entry of the ROK and DPRK into the United Nations. Seoul and Washington have long advocated such moves. The Soviets add unhappily, however, that Pyongyang is totally opposed out of concern that these steps would lead to the permanent creation of "two Koreas." And although some Soviets have suggested that President Gorbachev might soon try to change Kim Il Sung's mind, this seems unlikely in view of the strong reiteration of Moscow's formal opposition to cross recognition in the communique that "[t]he Soviet Union has no intention of officially recognizing South Korea or of establishing political or diplomatic relations with it." More recent statements by Soviets have reiterated these points.[3] Doubtless these renewed pledges have been the price for North Korean acquiescence in the Kremlin's new policy toward South Korea, something which is of far greater importance to Moscow than the formalities of diplomatic ties.

In any event, with the moves announced by the United States on October 31, 1988, including, as noted, restoration of permission for American diplomats to discuss any topic with North Korean diplomats in a "neutral" setting, Washington has accepted a degree of official contacts with Pyongyang. Some people have advocated that the United States go further, either by sitting down in formal bilateral conversation with the DPRK or even by establishing liaison offices in each other's capital to facilitate communication.

While the U.S. would want to be careful to do nothing that undercuts the position of South Korea and, specifically, would want to stand by its commitment against *negotiating* with North Korea in the absence of the ROK, it is not beyond the realm of possibility to hold serious bilateral discussions. How far this could go beyond the limited exchange of views that has already taken place on six occasions in Beijing as of January 1990 would depend upon what North Korea wanted to discuss and how serious its intention was. Such a development could only come about, however, as the result of a more positive North Korean response to U.S. moves to date and in the context of close consultations among Washington, Seoul and Tokyo.

The establishment of liaison offices, or even "interest sections" in the embassies of friendly countries, does not hold any particular attraction, however, unless Pyongyang allows its allies in Moscow and Beijing to do the same in Seoul. Trying to match the "unofficial" trade offices that the Chinese and Soviets are exchanging with South Korea does not seem realistic given the differences in our systems (though it might be more feasible for Japan).

One could argue that for political reasons the United States should relax trade restrictions with North Korea more than it has, especially since the ROK seems to have encouraged it. In light of the new South Korean policy, the measures adopted by the United States do, in fact, appear quite timid. Given the pattern of terrorist acts by North Korea and the sanctuary given to Japanese terrorists however, the reality is that it would be difficult for Washington to adopt a more forthcoming posture in the absence of a change in North Korean policy and practice. In any case, trade will be limited not only because of current restrictions but also because of what is commercially feasible between the United States and the DPRK.

Conclusion

The relaxation of tensions between the ROK, on the one hand, and China and the Soviet Union, on the other, is only to be welcomed. Though ostensibly grounded solely in trade and other economic relations, it will contribute importantly to development of a whole range of links that will promote understanding between the parties and stability on the peninsula. The key is that both sides want it.

Similarly, a key to future progress more generally on the peninsula will be the extent to which North Korea can be persuaded to take advantage of the new policies adopted by Seoul and its friends to deal on a civil basis, rather than persisting in confrontation. There, one can be hopeful, but thus far, anyway, not optimistic.

Notes

1. An earlier version of this chapter was published in 1989 under the same title, as part of the *Critical Issues* series issued by the Council on Foreign Relations (New York City). The later version that appears here has been revised and updated to the beginning of 1990.
2. That is, for the Soviet Union and China to recognize South Korea, the United States and Japan to recognize North Korea.
3. See, for example, the interview with Nladlen Martynov in *Novoe vremya* (November 27, 1987).

Part V

Working Group on Nuclear and Conventional Arms Reductions

THE WORKING GROUP ON NUCLEAR AND CONVENTIONAL ARMS REDUCTIONS was responsible for exploring ways in which arms reductions and other arms control can contribute to mutual security, in selected problem areas involving nuclear weapons and conventional weapons in Europe. Arms control is a topic within mutual security studies that is already being widely addressed by many other groups of independent specialists. Hence this Working Group chose to select certain problem areas where unusual or especially powerful forms of the mutual security approach deserve exploration.

This Working Group has contributed four papers to this book. The first, joint chapter by three American and three Soviet specialists develops a proposal for a far-reaching reconception of the proper role of strategic nuclear deterrence. P. Terrence Hopmann provides a paper describing a joint research project on arms reductions in Europe, research that is now underway by Soviet and American specialists working together. Aleksandr Konovalov contributes a paper analyzing the requirements for defensively-oriented conventional forces in Europe. Stephen Fought provides a chapter discussing the application of concepts drawn from strategic nuclear arms control to the conventional arena. Biographical sketches of these authors, and a list of the full membership of the Working Group on Nuclear and Conventional Arms Reductions, are given at the back of the book.

— THE EDITORS

19

Fundamental Deterrence and Mutual Security Beyond START

Jan Kalicki, Fred Chernoff and Eric Mlyn (USA)
and Sergei Fedorenko, Andrei Kortunov and
Aleksandr Pisarev (USSR)

Introduction[1]

This paper attempts to explore the implications for strategic forces of the concept of mutual security. In particular it attempts to explore the implications of the principle of "mutual threat reduction." The paper begins from the premise that substantial improvement in mutual security is possible in the strategic realm. That is, the U.S. and USSR are experiencing substantially more hazardous strategic nuclear threats, in both the present situation and under the proposed START regime, than are necessary or justified by national security considerations. A substantially different strategic regime is possible and desirable in which mutual security would be significantly enhanced. We term this different regime "Fundamental Deterrence."

A strategic regime of Fundamental Deterrence is one in which both sides possess highly secure second-strike forces, in quantity sufficient to retaliate amply, as well of course as secure C^3I capabilities.[2] But in this regime neither side possesses forces large or capable enough to threaten, in any significant degree, or in any conceivable scenario, the other side's second-strike forces. Since each side knows that the other is not capable of significantly threatening its forces, each would be much more secure (mutual security). An additional important feature of a regime of Fundamental Deterrence is that forces on both sides are structured such that neither side could move in the future toward altering this situation, except in ways that would be very costly, very time-consuming, and highly visible (thus giving the other side ample opportunity to respond).

Advocacy of Fundamental Deterrence, so conceived, is not *in the first instance* advocacy of numerical reductions in strategic forces, compared to either their present levels or proposed START levels. The first and defining properties of a Fundamental Deterrence regime involve *qualitative* characteristics of the forces and of the relationship between them, not their numbers. However, it analytically turn outs to be the case that — if certain preconditions are met — this regime would require forces much fewer in number than the current or proposed START quantities: under optimal conditions perhaps as few as 600 to 1000 warheads. The motive behind this paper is not one of seeking numerical reductions for the sake of numerical reductions. Rather it is one of seeking *threat* reductions, and specifically, seeking mutual threat reductions for the sake of greater mutual security.

It will be argued that Fundamental Deterrence is the safest realistic posture for the two sides, provided that it can be achieved through a set of stabilizing steps.[3] This chapter examines the nature of Fundamental Deterrence, contrasts it to other possible goals, such as complete nuclear disarmament, and considers a step-by-step path to reach the end-point of Fundamental Deterrence. The chapter also considers possible complications for, and obstacles to, Fundamental Deterrence, such as the role of defensive systems, domestic political factors, and other important foreign policy goals, such as security commitments to allies.

Our proposals are made because we are not satisfied with the current nuclear status quo nor with the thinking that is used to justify it. Since the dawn of the nuclear age, the superpowers have built more nuclear weapons than either side could possibly need. The evolution of the nuclear arms race, which has resulted in massive overkill, has not proceeded according to any sound logic. Instead, incremental decisions, made over decades, have accumulated to the point where the nuclear arsenals of both sides are too large, too threatening, and too destructive.

Though crisis and arms race stability are the most important criteria for assessing changes in the nuclear force structure, other important benefits would accrue for both sides if the changes proposed here were implemented. These include long-term economic savings, a decreased likelihood of unauthorized or accidental use of nuclear weapons, and an easing of the negative psychological effect that large nuclear arsenals have had on the citizens of the U.S. and the USSR, their allies, and others. In stressing crisis stability and arms race stability, we do not at all mean to diminish the importance of these criteria.

The United States and the Soviet Union are now attempting to stabilize and reduce the total number of strategic nuclear delivery systems and warheads. At the same time, qualitative modernization proceeds as old systems are replaced by new ones, featuring greater counterforce potential. We fear that the interaction of these two factors may in effect contribute to a situation of growing strategic *instability*. As the result, the likelihood of nuclear conflict may actually increase even as numerical reductions are being negotiated and carried out. We argue that the unsatisfactory present situation and the possibly even more unsatisfactory situation of the near future require that the Soviet Union and the United States thoroughly redefine their arms control policies, to move away from nuclear war fighting capabilities and toward Fundamental Deterrence.

In principle, arms reductions can achieve several important goals: they can decrease the risk of war by creating greater crisis stability, they can create fiscal savings by slowing down military competition and thus improving arms race stability, they could help to limit potential damage if war would not be deterred, they can reduce the chances of third party nuclear wars by stemming the advance of horizontal proliferation, and they can help to restrain the development and deployment of some destabilizing weapons.[4] Limitations and the reductions in past treaties, unfortunately, did not bring significant progress in achieving these goals. In contrast, those recommended in this chapter are designed to make progress on all five points.

The essential feature of a regime of Fundamental Deterrence is that each side should have strategic nuclear delivery vehicles (SNDVs) only in sufficient quantities to deter any conceivable use of strategic weapons by the other, and properly deployed so that neither side can destroy the bulk of the other side's weapons in any first strike. Each side would have some freedom to choose how to achieve the proper mix of systems (ICBMs, SLBMs and long-range bombers). Each would also have survivable command and control facilities, which would both ensure its ability to order a retaliatory strike and minimize the likelihood of an unauthorized or accidental launch of strategic forces, even during a severe crisis. The two sides would also have secure capital-to-capital communications and take other measures for greater crisis stability.[5]

Development of a Fundamental Deterrence system would require resolving the complex problem of objective asymmetries in the strategic force structure of both sides. The United States has traditionally relied primarily on sea-based nuclear capabilities, while the Soviet Union has preferred to rely mainly on land-based capabilities. It might be difficult for the two superpowers to agree on an identical structure for their strategic forces since their geostrategic positions are so different.

A solution to these problems can be found by mutually shifting to Fundamental Deterrence in two phases. In the first phase, Fundamental Deterrence would encourage both sides to move away from "bean counting" to pursuing mutual security through equivalent, stabilizing *capabilities*. The criteria for planning each side's forces would shift away from the narrow quantitative notion of "parity" embodied in recent strategic arms treaties, and toward a broader, more realistic form of parity. A stable strategic balance in a regime of Fundamental Deterrence would not require that the two sides have weapons that correspond to, or match, one another. Rather, they should have capabilities that, when viewed dynamically (in first strike and retaliatory scenarios) produce similar outcomes. New criteria for measuring the two sides' arsenals should aim to eliminate motivations and capabilities that would give either side an advantage in launching a first strike, and aim to ensure that each side would have strategic forces able to withstand ("ride out") a first strike and to retaliate, inflicting "unacceptable damage."

The two sides will then have equivalence or "parity" in an altered and more reasonable sense. This concept of "parity" is approximately the original meaning of strategic parity, employed in analysis and policy in the 1950s and 1960s. It was only later that the concept became narrowed.[6] Movement toward Fundamental Deterrence would encourage a return to the original and (we argue) more realistic qualitative concept of parity.[7]

The goal of Fundamental Deterrence would require changes in U.S. and Soviet nuclear forces quite unlike any that have resulted from past arms control negotiations or would result from current ones. The impending START treaty will numerically cut forces much more significantly than any previous agreement. But, like its predecessors, it changes neither the strategic thinking of either side nor the options for targeting. The force structures of Fundamental Deterrence change both of these.

Some analysts argue that a posture of Fundamental Deterrence could create more problems than it solves. They suggest that we presently have relatively high nuclear stability and that substantially lower numbers of nuclear weapons could create unacceptable verification problems and less stable force postures.

We disagree. The posture that is outlined in this paper is superior to the current status quo in at least four ways. First, Fundamental Deterrence is designed to render obsolete nuclear war-fighting scenarios that might bring the superpowers closer to nuclear war. As discussed later, Fundamental Deterrence can promise a substantial reduction in the risk of actual war, and a very high degree of crisis stability, by denying both sides the option — and importantly, any appearance of an option — for war-fighting.

Second, lower SNDV levels, when achieved in the manner suggested, would increase security by reducing the perception that either side could launch a successful first strike. Lower warhead levels would also cut deployment and maintenance costs.

Third, Fundamental Deterrence does not preclude, and indeed may require, force modernization that might be needed to truly stabilize the nuclear balance. Present modernization of nuclear forces generally stresses accuracy, thus increasing fears on the other side of a first-strike and pre-emption. Such trends make for a less stable nuclear structure and lead to an acceleration of the arms race. However, movement toward Fundamental Deterrence would make for a more stable structure and a deceleration of the arms race. The deployment of less accurate but survivable warheads, on single-warhead missiles, as proposed in this paper, should be interpreted as much less dangerous by both sides.

Finally, the achievement of such a force posture could create a greatly enhanced political climate for further measures of cooperation between the superpowers. Although the primary roots of the arms race have been political, it should also be recognized that the ever increasing number of nuclear weapons has very often exacerbated these tensions. Thus a reduction in the quantity of nuclear weapons can help ease the political relationship between the two sides.

We should emphasize that we are not proposing these changes in the nuclear force structure independent of important political changes in the relationship between the superpowers, and we recognize the reciprocal relationship that can exist between military and political change. Today, there are solid reasons to expect U.S.-Soviet relations to continue to improve. Such improvements could not only help bring about these important military changes, but will also help create the conditions, such as greater transparency, that will facilitate and increase confidence in the changes that are proposed here. We are not here assuming dramatic breakthroughs in U.S.-Soviet relations. Rather, we assume that the recent trend towards improved political relations, in incremental steps, is sustained. And we assume that the implementation of agreements such as that proposed here will increase confidence and add some additional momentum to the improvement.

The question of zero levels

All arms reductions are not equally helpful or unhelpful for improving security. A reduction of arms does not by itself help to solve any of the problems noted above. Lower arms levels, improperly structured, could increase the risk of war. Fundamental Deterrence, however, constitutes a path and goal for arms reductions that could indeed reduce the chances of war and enhance security.

Some have argued that the end-point of the arms reduction process should go beyond any form of nuclear deterrence and achieve the total abolition of nuclear weapons. But there are important difficulties with this goal. First, nuclear weapons have already been invented. Locking them away is hardly possible, as humanity will forever retain the knowledge to make them. Second, nuclear weapons in U.S.

and Soviet hands have coincided with almost half a century of peace among the great powers. Anyone proposing the abolition of all nuclear weapons must deal with the serious objection that it would remove the deterrent that has prevented war between East and West and has given modern Europe its longest peace. It is important to note, however, that the nuclear balance has not prevented conflict in other parts of the world, and the existing elements of instability do not offer the best possible guarantee that peace among the great powers will continue indefinitely.

In any event, zero nuclear levels could be extremely difficult to achieve because neither Americans nor Soviets would agree to them unless they were certain of the denuclearization of all other states. The number of other proliferators and potential proliferators, the nature of those states' security problems and political systems, the few incentives for some of them to cooperate, and the formidable challenges of verification make abolition a difficult goal. Furthermore, zero levels could undermine security commitments to allies and stimulate a search for alternative, less stable security arrangements, including possibly increased nuclear proliferation. However, we must at the same time acknowledge the moral appeal of the belief that, especially in the long run, the most reliable way to rid humanity of the threat of nuclear suicide lies in the complete elimination of nuclear weapons.

The role of conventional arms and tactical nuclear forces

As strategic nuclear arms are reduced by the U.S. and USSR, other weapons, particularly conventional and tactical nuclear weapons, take on greater importance. The Conventional Armed Forces in Europe (CFE) talks will be especially important in assuring that the response to perceived conventional imbalances will be to reduce conventional weapons to equivalent and stable levels, rather than to build them up on each side in an attempt to overcome real and perceived asymmetries. There is a widespread perception in the West that the Soviets enjoy an overall advantage in conventional forces that needs to be redressed. Regardless of the extent to which this is actually true, the U.S. answer to the perception of imbalance has always been to make a nuclear guarantee to its NATO allies: the "first use" of nuclear weapons if and when necessary to prevent defeat at the conventional level. But movement toward Fundamental Deterrence would be perceived as affecting this guarantee; hence such movement calls for achieving a conventional balance satisfactory to all parties.

Recent progress in the CFE talks bodes well for curtailing this important area of U.S.-Soviet competition, an area that has eluded meaningful arms control measures for over forty years. Both sides seem to be moving toward consensus on the need for defensively oriented rather than offensively oriented conventional forces, at much lower levels. Despite these trends that lead us to be optimistic, the long history of the conventional arms race indicates that the negotiating process to achieve these results is likely to be extremely difficult.[8]

The long-term goal of these nuclear and conventional reductions should be to build confidence that conventional war in Europe between NATO and the WTO can indeed be deterred by conventional rather than nuclear weapons. Within the U.S. at least, one current justification for a large nuclear arsenal is that it has helped guarantee the peace in Europe. However, a much-reduced conventional threat, coupled with important political changes on both sides of the European divide, would significantly curtail the need for nuclear weapons to deter a conventional war. This in turn would increase the firebreak between conventional and nuclear war and thus decrease the chances of inadvertent escalation.

Similar arguments can be made regarding short range nuclear forces (SNF), sometimes referred to as tactical or battlefield nuclear weapons. Our proposal here is for the eventual elimination, under appropriate conditions, of these destabilizing nuclear forces. Thus far, Western states have offered to consider some dual capable systems in negotiations, but they have not agreed to Soviet proposals to add a "Third Zero" to the INF agreement by eliminating SNF.[9] This remains a particularly contentious issue within NATO, though recently the alliance has edged closer, in somewhat equivocal terms, to the view that SNF might be negotiable. In our view, a stable conventional military balance and improved political relations should go hand in hand with progressive elimination of these forces. Ultimately SNF do not have a role in a posture of Fundamental Deterrence. Because war-fighting scenarios cannot be part of a Fundamental Deterrent posture, SNF, which are essentially war-fighting weapons, should be phased out as part of the reductions suggested here. The reduction and eventual elimination of this class of weapons will go a long way toward reducing the chance of nuclear war and thus will make for a more stable international environment.

It is beyond the scope of this paper to propose arms control approaches for conventional and SNF reductions, but several points are worth mentioning. Success in achieving substantial strategic nuclear reductions could facilitate East-West consensus as well as consensus within NATO on SNF and conventional forces. Progress on conventional force reductions would go a long way toward reducing the perceived need for SNF. Conversely, a failure to achieve progress in CFE will likely jeopardize progress, over the long term, for a move toward Fundamental Deterrence. Exactly what progress means in this area is difficult to define, but some criteria that should be applied include: the resulting conventional forces are in a stable balance; neither side feels an increased threat and both sides feel a reduced threat; both sides have adopted a defensively oriented rather than offensively oriented posture; no new arms races result; and nuclear forces are less important as an adjunct to conventional weapons.[10] Both nuclear and conventional reductions must go hand in hand if true mutual security is to be achieved.

Proposal: a three-stage reduction

The *structure* of the U.S. and Soviet nuclear arsenals, after the fifty percent cuts are made that are currently envisaged in START, will be virtually identical to the present structure (although we note that within the START framework, some provisions are made for certain qualitative limits on strategic offensive forces). While still desirable, the reductions under START thus will not necessitate changes in the nature of either side's strategy, targeting or warfighting capabilities.

Because of the magnitude and potential impact of deep reductions, there are sound reasons for making them in stages. Specifically we propose including a transitional second stage before Fundamental Deterrence is fully achieved. There are several good reasons for proceeding in stages. But each stage must itself improve the security of both sides, rather than serve simply as a means to some future improvement.

First, stability in nuclear arms depends on a perception that both sides' deterrent capability is fully adequate. A staged reduction lessens the chance of any dramatic shift in perceived deterrent capabilities and thus lessens the danger of destabilization.

Second, reduction to Fundamental Deterrence will create major changes in the nuclear postures, options and thinking of the U.S. and USSR. A second, intermediate stage provides needed time. The meaning of the changes, its implications, and the advantages for both sides have to be absorbed and reacted upon. The radical new posture will ultimately be beneficial to both sides, but it could be difficult, even dangerous to move to that posture too quickly. Neither the domestic nor the international political environment is currently ripe for such drastic cuts in U.S. and Soviet nuclear arms; a transitional second stage would thus be a useful, integral step in an evolving process of nuclear arms reductions.

Third, the high strategic force levels remaining under START create a certain "stability reserve" with respect to qualitative modernization. Presently, an abrupt qualitative breakthrough in any one part of the triad would hardly upset an overall strategic balance, as a quantitative "margin of safety" would compensate for it. This situation might change when weapons levels significantly decrease. For this reason, the transition to Fundamental Deterrence will require that strong measures be taken to limit or regulate the modernization of strategic forces in certain directions. The problem of regulating modernization is extremely difficult and will require significant changes in the sides' political relations and in international relations as a whole.

Fourth, if each side retains (say) only 600 to 1000 delivery vehicles, redundancy will be practically eliminated. Currently, redundancy plays an important role as insurance in case some component of the strategic nuclear force does not function for technical reasons. A resolution to the problem of loss of redundancy is possible but will require a certain amount of time and imagination.

Fifth, we noted above that movement toward Fundamental Deterrence requires a shift from a narrow quantitative concept of "parity" to a more realistic, qualitative one. It will not be easy to bring about this shift of the criteria of comparison of the two sides' power. Use of a three-stage process would allow success in the intermediate stage to demonstrate to both sides that some shift in criteria are realistic, practical and desirable, and thus increase confidence in shifting them further, as required by full Fundamental Deterrence.

We propose, then, a three-stage reduction. Stage I consists simply of the START regime currently being negotiated; we will assume that the negotiation is successfully completed, along roughly the lines presently being discussed. Stage II is our proposed intermediate stage, which would represent important but partial movement toward Fundamental Deterrence. Stage III represents full Fundamental Deterrence. In this paper we will not discuss Stage I further.

Stage II

Stage II should provide the focal point for post-START consideration of nuclear arms reductions and will stand as the link between previous attempts at primarily quantitative reductions (the SALT and START process) and the qualitative emphasis that becomes crucial as both sides move on toward drastically lower levels of nuclear weapons. At the core of our proposal is the idea that we must move beyond considerations that call for the simple reduction of numbers of weapons, toward the more important considerations concerning the *characteristics* of the weapons that make up the nuclear force structures on each side. It should also be emphasized that although Stage II is a transitional step within this arms reduction plan, it should also be viewed as highly valuable in itself, representing a considerable improvement over the force structures that would be left by the START reductions.

Consideration must be given to both the structure of the two sides' nuclear arsenals and the specific characteristics of the weapons within these arsenals. In terms of the structure, the U.S. and USSR would need to consider the relative emphasis put on different legs of their own triads, and should allow for certain asymmetries that reflect the historical evolution of each side's nuclear arsenals. For example, Stage II reductions might allow for the U.S. to have more of its strategic nuclear forces in the submarine-based leg of its triad while Soviet forces might rest primarily in the land-based leg of its triad.[11] However, these asymmetries must not allow either side to achieve meaningful superiority. An equivalence or "overall symmetry" in capabilities must be maintained.

Although this proposal would lead to mutual reductions in nuclear arsenals, force modernization that could lead to stability should not be precluded. For example, the replacement of MIRVed launchers with single warhead ICBMs would have a stabilizing impact on the arms race; the importance of such moves is not discounted under this proposal.[12] The potential restructuring of the American and Soviet nuclear arsenals would, in the long run, be important for the achievement of stability at reduced numbers.[13]

At the root of concerns over strategic stability is the survivability of strategic weapons for retaliatory purposes. Such concerns have been exacerbated by the increase in counterforce capabilities by the U.S. and USSR. In considering the survivability of strategic weapons, the accuracy of strategic nuclear weapons and the warhead-to-launcher ratio becomes crucial. Stage II reductions should move in the direction of eliminating MIRVed warheads and a hard-target kill capability, which in turn will press the countries to move away from the war-fighting doctrines that make up their deterrent postures. Such steps would enhance stability by reducing the vulnerability of each side's nuclear arsenals and by providing a strong framework for the further quantitative and qualitative reductions that would move toward a posture of Fundamental Deterrence.

Among the specific criteria that we would envisage for Stage II are these:

— move toward elimination (or great reduction) of hard-target kill-capability;[14]

— move toward elimination (or great reduction) of MIRVed warheads;

— more survivable command and control;

— more survivable capital-to-capital communications;

— perhaps some 3,000 warheads on each side (that is, roughly another fifty percent cut).

There have been some attempts, by both American and Soviet specialists, to project what cuts beyond START might look like. A useful U.S. attempt by May, Bing and Steinbruner,[15] examining the stability of post-START force postures (of about 3,000 nuclear warheads), studied three force structures: one emphasized mobility; one emphasized accuracy; and one was simply a proportional reduction of both nuclear arsenals. It is worth making a few observations about this study. First, a purely proportional reduction is exactly what our proposal here is arguing against; such reductions do not take into account the important qualitative criteria that we have discussed above and thus do not adequately insure stability. Second, the force structure that emphasizes counterforce runs *directly* contrary to the goal of making both American and Soviet nuclear arsenals less vulnerable; the adoption of such a posture would clearly be a move in the wrong direction. The force structure that emphasizes mobility is compatible with our proposals here because it can greatly improve the survivability of nuclear forces, though it must be noted that mobility may not be the best or the only way to accomplish such a goal. It becomes clear from these considerations that as we move to these lower levels of weapons, the survivability of forces becomes a more crucial factor for assuring retaliatory capabilities and the essence of deterrence.[16]

However, the May-Bing-Steinbruner approach does not go far enough in outlining the future force structures that would be necessary for the enhancement of strategic stability. By giving specific attention to the characteristics of the weapons within the nuclear arsenals, our Fundamental Deterrence proposal seeks to go further in offering a concrete and specific road map for the achievement of lower numbers in a way that is stabilizing.[17]

Within the framework of our Stage II, preceding Fundamental Deterrence, it is important to find solutions to several problems that otherwise may block progress to the creation of mutual security in the strategic nuclear sphere. These potential problems are: drastically reducing the probability of unintended nuclear conflict; preventing the erosion of deterrence through arms reductions, which could occur because of technological breakthrough in related areas; and curbing other destabilizing developments in the vertical or horizontal arms race.

Unintentional or "inadvertent" nuclear war may result from an accident in any strategic weapons or warning system: from loss of control by the national command over any of the components of the triad. It may also arise in the course of escalation from a non-nuclear conflict to the nuclear level. Although the likelihood of such a development is quite small, it is nevertheless greater than the possibility of a sanctioned nuclear strike. It is therefore essential to minimize this possibility.

To that end, the Soviet Union and the U.S. should create crisis control capacities, for instance to warn and influence the activities of countries involved in regional conflict. The superpowers could renounce options of "launch on warning," which considerably increase the likelihood of nuclear war as a result of technical breakdown or human error. Weapons and warning systems which are not sufficiently reliable must be removed from both sides' arsenals and C^3I systems must be perfected. An important step in this direction would be further sophistication and possible expansion of the system of "hotlines" with a view of encompassing other nuclear powers.[18]

Erosion of deterrence at Stage II could take place if one side achieves a technological breakthrough in anti-submarine warfare or in offensive weapons that could lead toward a first-strike capability, or if one side deploys an effective system of anti-satellite weapons. U.S.-Soviet negotiations should seek to prevent such a destabilizing development.

Finally, a threatening trend, which eventually could undermine East-West deterrence, is nuclear proliferation. The Soviet Union and the U.S. must take measures within the framework of Stage II to strengthen the non-proliferation regime and agree beforehand on steps to be taken in the event of a breakdown in it.

Options for defenses

The military and political changes that we propose suggest that we reconsider the role that defenses should play in strategic deterrence. In contemplating defenses, we need to project our thinking toward a future of nuclear arsenals of greatly reduced numbers and a significantly improved political relationship between the United States and Soviet Union. The change in force structure resulting in far fewer nuclear weapons requires that we pay special attention to the potential vulnerability of the remaining nuclear weapons. With the current levels of overkill on both sides, the issue of vulnerability, while important, is not as pivotal as it would be under a force posture with greatly reduced numbers of nuclear weapons. In addition, the change in the political relationship requires that we re-examine the way that both sides perceive the deployment of defenses. Under some circumstances, some kinds of limited defenses might have a stabilizing impact on strategic deterrence.

We must differentiate between area defense and point defense. It has been widely accepted that large-scale area defense (the protection of populations) is not possible and that the attempt would be dangerously destabilizing.[19] In addition, both sides have already agreed (as codified in the ABM Treaty) that the deployment of territorial defenses against nuclear weapons would be destabilizing. However, the nature of the changes proposed here might lead to reconsideration of the role of defenses for the attainment of strategic stability. With greatly reduced numbers of weapons, it is conceivable that the deployment of a *limited* point defense on both sides could enhance stability by greatly reducing the vulnerability of remaining nuclear forces. Both sides might deem such a step as a desirable element of the transition to a posture of Fundamental Deterrence.

It should be apparent that our proposal here bears no resemblance to the Strategic Defense Initiative announced by President Reagan in March of 1983. We are not proposing any unilateral pursuit of strategic defenses, nor are we suggesting any deployment of defenses meant to protect populations. Instead, our advocacy of reconsidering the role of defense stems from one concern — the survivability of strategic nuclear arsenals. Of course, it is possible that the particular posture of Fundamental Deterrence adopted will be comprised of mobile ICBMs and/or SLBMs. In this case, defenses may not be necessary to assure survivability.

However, if it were decided that silo based ICBMs represented the most feasible force posture for Fundamental Deterrence, the deployment of limited point defenses might indeed be an effective way of ensuring strategic stability. In such an event, these defenses should be deployed in such a way that they could not be readily adapted for population defense.

Limited defense systems might also have a certain value in protecting national command centers and C^3I systems. They might also provide some security in the event of accidents involving third nuclear parties, or conceivably, against minor nuclear powers or some terrorist activities in the future.

In considering strategic defenses, political considerations are just as important as force posture considerations. Because this multi-staged reduction is set within the overall framework of mutual security, any defenses created would necessarily be created by both the U.S. and USSR. Any *unilateral* deployment of defensive systems, whether for point defense or area defense, would very likely be destabilizing, since such deployments could be perceived as threatening, and would thus most likely be met by a build-up of offensive forces by the other side. However, because a new political relationship of mutual security leads each side to view its security as linked to that of the other, defensive deployments within this new context could enhance crisis stability and the chance of avoiding nuclear war. It is this potential change in the political relationship that could suggest that we abandon previous conceptions of the impact that defense can have on the nuclear balance.

There is a danger that, in the event that this multi-staged framework were to break down, the agreements would unravel and an unrestrained defensive competition could break out. Thus it is our view that the pursuit of these far-reaching changes must take place within the context of a much improved political situation that would ensure the cooperation that is essential for the attainment of these overall goals.

Stage III: Fundamental Deterrence

In our proposed third stage, the two sides would make substantial further changes in their strategic arsenals to achieve full Fundamental Deterrence. Naturally these changes would be made by mutual agreement and carried out concurrently; the actions involved are readily verifiable (some requiring on-site inspection).

In a regime of full Fundamental Deterrence, the strategic (and political) situation should be such that neither side has an incentive or capability for a nuclear first strike. To that end, it is necessary to promote "transparency" between the two sides, since stability increases when both sides are open about the sizes and characteristics of their strategic forces and operational plans. Uncertainty regarding future development of strategic forces in the Soviet Union and the United States should be drastically reduced.

The weapons that support Fundamental Deterrence would fulfill two general criteria: they would have to be survivable and they would have to avoid threatening the survivability of the other side's forces. Importantly, nuclear war-fighting strategies would become impossible through employing such weapons. We can identify a number of weapons characteristics that follow from these two general criteria. Single-warhead launchers are highly preferable, to produce a zero, or negative, strategic exchange ratio. They enhance crisis stability because it becomes difficult or impossible to pre-empt or be pre-empted. Mobility may be helpful because it increases survivability; thus SLBMs are preferable and mobile ICBMs also may be.[20] Secure C^3I is crucial to help prevent unauthorized or accidental launch. Finally, area defenses would be prohibited, since they could make a first strike more tempting in a crisis; as noted, limited point defense systems might be allowed if the protection of strategic forces would enhance survivability and stability.

Fundamental Deterrence would require low overall totals of SNDVs. In a bipolar, U.S.-Soviet analysis only, probably not more than 600 to 1000 warheads would be required. (Consideration of the arsenals of other nuclear powers, a topic addressed below, might change this figure.) Achieving stable, mutually secure arsenals at these levels probably could not be produced by cuts alone; certain new single-warhead weapons might be needed. Perhaps even new, small submarines would be desirable, to achieve wide dispersion, and thus high survivability, of the lesser number of SLBMs that would be permitted. Some of these specific programs might prove to be expensive. But the aim here is to offer an overall strategic force posture that would, when taken as a whole and considered in the long-run, offer major security (and also fiscal) advantages.

The third and final stage, in which Fundamental Deterrence was achieved fully, would offer very high levels of both crisis stability and arms race stability, compared to the existing situation, to any situation of the last couple of decades, or to the START regime currently being negotiated. It would offer a high level of crisis stability because both sides would know that both lacked any incentive to engage in attacks — to any significant level — on the other side's strategic forces. A zero or negative exchange ratio would mean that either side would consume as much or more of its own forces in any attack as it could hope to destroy on the other side. No rational leader would decide upon such an action. Instead, a rational leader would tend to do in a crisis just what analysts should recommend: search for acceptable ways to end the crisis without resorting to nuclear war.

Perhaps the most significant feature of this high crisis stability is that the other side would be in a position to clearly anticipate this kind of behavior. Rather than facing pressures to pre-empt, the other side would be able to employ the capital-to-capital communications to address the difficult task of finding a mutually acceptable way out of the crisis. The other side would not have to resort to the use of its strategic forces out of a fear that the first side was about to. Each side, knowing the other's lack of incentives to strike, would be able to have an important measure of confidence in the other side's behavior. It should be stressed that this high level of crisis stability would be intrinsic in the existing strategic situation under Fundamental Deterrence; it would not be dependent upon either side's (necessarily uncertain) estimate of the other's immediate intentions, or the other's political goals, or the other's leadership personalities. And this form of crisis stability, once achieved, could not be quickly or easily lost.

Our proposed third stage, in which Fundamental Deterrence is fully achieved, would also offer a high level of arms race stability. This brings us to one of the most interesting and attractive features of the Fundamental Deterrence concept. Properly designed, a mutual posture of Fundamental Deterrence would be one that would be relatively hard for either side to "break out" of. And any attempt to do so by either side would be very costly and very time-consuming, and would give the other side ample time to respond.

A Fundamental Deterrence regime, properly designed, would have been reached by appropriate stages of reductions and eliminations, not merely of a certain number of weapons, but mainly of strategic capabilities. We emphasize that war-fighting capabilities would not merely have been rejected as a matter of policy; the capabilities themselves would have been eliminated from the force structures on both sides. Weapons suitable for war-fighting would have been destroyed, on a mutually verified basis, much as the INF weapons have now been destroyed. Production lines for the manufacture of such weapons would also have been dismantled, in a similar verified way. Under the Fundamental Deterrence regime, both sides would lack not only the weapons to engage in war-fighting, but also the immediate capacity to manufacture any.

This would be an exceedingly stable situation, compared to the present situation or the situation under the proposed START regime, in which both sides do have production lines, in existence and under construction, for the building of war-fighting weapons. Under those conditions, only a policy decision is required for the weapons actually to be built. Under a Fundamental Deterrence regime, far more would be required, and the other side would know it. If one side decided to "break out" of a Fundamental Deterrence regime it would have to decide to build new production lines. This would be costly and time-consuming. It also would be extremely easy for the other side to observe, and its significance would be unambiguous to the other side. The other side would know how weighty and dangerous that action was, and would have ample time to respond appropriately. Furthermore, because each side would know all this ahead of time, each would have strong political and economic incentives not to reach such a drastic decision, but to maintain the Fundamental Deterrence regime.[21]

If the two sides can agree to maintain the Fundamental Deterrence regime, then their requirements for new generations of modernized strategic weapons would decline dramatically. A full discussion of this question is outside the scope of this paper. But the pace of the arms competition could be expected to slow dramatically, since neither side would have any strategic need for developing new weapons or new types of weapons. This by itself represents an additional form of high arms race stability (and also offers, in the long term, major fiscal savings.)

Difficulties in achieving Fundamental Deterrence

Despite the strategic and security benefits of Fundamental Deterrence, its adoption as a goal and the attempt to arrive at it through staged reductions is likely to encounter serious obstacles arising from other military problems, competing foreign policy aims and political considerations. A balanced advocacy of this posture should acknowledge and discuss those obstacles.

At least three difficulties are worth noting, beyond the issues of strategic defense, conventional arms and short-range nuclear weapons noted above. First, the levels of strategic forces of the U.S. and USSR are much greater than those of other states; thus the two superpowers are perceived as having many options that other states do not. The reductions discussed in the 1970s and 1980s (including START) do not fundamentally threaten this disparity; thus they do not affect the relative relationship of these third parties and the superpowers. However, because Fundamental Deterrence would cause the number of U.S. and Soviet SNDVs to decrease substantially, the proportion of SNDVs that the third parties possess becomes much more relevant. As a result, the third states begin to acquire the ability to make threats of the same order of magnitude as the superpowers.

Over time, this problem should be dealt with by pressing for reductions by other states possessing nuclear weapons. This could be a difficult undertaking, but it would be facilitated by U.S.-Soviet movement toward Fundamental Deterrence. A concerted effort must be made to prevent the alternative — a more unstable strategic environment and increased proliferation. Furthermore, the political acceptability of minimal levels of nuclear weapons under British, French and Chinese control will be increased as both East-West and Sino-Soviet tensions diminish and additional arms control agreements are negotiated.

Second, each side has treaty commitments and thus each must consider not only its own but also its allies' security. The European alliances are predicated on extended nuclear deterrence, which could be undermined by nuclear arms reductions. There would likely be difficulties (especially among some NATO members) in garnering support for deep nuclear reductions, since some states may fear that American extended deterrence would suffer. On the other hand, reductions would be structured to increase stability and reduce the chance of war in Europe. Furthermore, a decisive shift to defensively oriented postures on both sides in Europe could reduce or eliminate the need for extended deterrence. The diminished chance of war clearly benefits Europe, both with respect to the psychological climate under which people live in normal times, and with respect to the danger of any outbreak of war. Thus the proposed nuclear arms reductions, leading to Fundamental Deterrence, would be beneficial for the European allies. We stress that these changes should be made in close consultation with the allies of both sides.

Finally, deep cuts could, under some conditions, stimulate proliferation. Potential proliferators might have the incentive of being able to match the destructiveness of the largest arsenals, which now is impossible for them because each superpower possesses huge strategic arsenals. This problem could be dealt with by carrying out the reductions in a multilateral framework, which would require careful diplomatic effort.[22] Joint U.S.-Soviet cooperation in helping to resolve acute international conflicts and to relieve third parties' security concerns would be indispensable. Furthermore, the U.S. and USSR have long been accused by other states of not fulfilling their obligations to reduce nuclear stockpiles under the Nuclear Non-Proliferation Treaty (NPT) and this accusation might be used as an excuse by others to weaken the non-proliferation regime. Substantial cuts of the kinds we advocate could reduce that pressure, and even strengthen the non-proliferation regime, by showing potential proliferators that the superpowers *are* willingly devaluating the political and military utility of nuclear weapons and honoring their commitments to the NPT.

Conclusions

We have attempted to show that Fundamental Deterrence is, in principle, the safest nuclear posture, and that it could be realized in such a way that each step toward it would move Soviet-American relations and the international security environment onto more secure footing. It is essential to place this proposal within the broader context of the mutual security framework. Some elements of the proposal, taken individually, may or may not appear desirable. Together we believe they provide us with a map toward the achievement of strategic stability within a mutual security framework.

There are of course difficulties with implementing a posture of Fundamental Deterrence. However, we should not compare these difficulties to an "ideal type" — that is, to some imagined nuclear force structure or international political environment that poses no serious complications for superpower or alliance relations. (There may be no possible situation that poses zero complications.) Instead, Fundamental Deterrence should be compared to the current or post-START situations, which pose great risks of a number of different kinds. The current and post-START situations are ones that, to say the very least, are highly imperfect. Fundamental Deterrence is not perfect, and is not without its problems, but it represents a far more rational and stable situation than these.

Eventually, it might be possible to go beyond nuclear deterrence entirely. The complete abolition of nuclear weapons, endorsed by Presidents Mikhail Gorbachev and Ronald Reagan, remains a potential goal, which we believe requires scrupulous consideration. However many serious problems with it, outlined above, would have to be overcome. Regardless of whether one chooses zero levels as an ultimate goal, achieving Fundamental Deterrence, in and of itself, would produce a security environment immeasurably superior to any that has thus far been sought by the two superpowers in strategic arms negotiations.

Notes

1. This paper is, in the truest sense of the word, a collaborative effort. The original outline for the paper was discussed in the fall of 1988 by Soviet and American scholars. The American authors wrote the first draft which was then given to Soviet authors, who drafted material and returned the paper to the American side; this process was repeated a number of times. In addition, numerous joint discussions of the paper were held in Providence, Moscow and Washington, D.C. We wish to acknowledge substantive contributions from Richard Smoke. Some of the Soviet contributions were translated during this collaborative process by Dina Ganz and Tania Lozansky and edited by Heather Hurlburt.

2. "C-cubed-i" is a technical abbreviation for "command, control, communications and intelligence." The term "triad," which will appear below, refers to the three types of strategic nuclear forces: land-based intercontinental ballistic missiles (ICBMs), submarine-launched ballistic missiles (SLBMs), and bomber aircraft.

3. We have chosen to use the term "Fundamental Deterrence," first proposed by our former colleague Dan Caldwell, rather than "Minimum Deterrence" because it is our view that such a posture actually maximizes deterrence and because this paper contemplates measures which go beyond other discussions of Minimum Deterrence. What we propose could be regarded as one version, arguably an especially desirable version, of a *mutual* Minimum Deterrence regime.

4. U.S. and Soviet scholars and policymakers have acknowledged the multiple goals of arms control. Perhaps the most widely cited are those criteria that were proposed by Schelling and Halperin over twenty-five years ago. These include "reducing the likelihood of war, its scope and violence if it occurs and the political and economic costs of being prepared for it." See Thomas C. Schelling and Morton H. Halperin, *Strategy and Arms Control*, rev. ed. (New York: Pergamon Press, 1985), p. 3; and Aleksei Arbatov, "Criteria of Correlations of Strategic Offensive Forces," *IMEMO Yearbook* 1987, pp. 225-237. We have also drawn upon an unpublished paper prepared for the Mutual Security Project, written by Igor Malashenko, entitled "Nuclear Parity: Political-Psychological Aspect."

5. Survivable C^3I on each side also discourages any temptation on the other side toward a "decapitating" nuclear strike.

6. For this valuable point we are indebted to Malashenko, "Nuclear Parity." Malashenko points out that the narrow, quantitative concept of "parity" tends to imply that parity exists only when the two sides' forces "mirror" each other. This misguided desire to "mirror" each other, he argues, has produced on both sides a desire to match the forces of the other and thus has spurred the arms race.

7. The distinction between "quantitative" and "qualitative" notions is not always made in the same way. By "qualitative" here we mean that the focus is on the ability to inflict (retaliatory) damage, viewed from a dynamic perspective. We use "quantitative" to refer to static measures of forces as they are deployed, including characteristics like size, number of warheads, accuracy, etc., which some authors regard as qualitative.

8. These difficulties have been widely acknowledged; see for instance A. Kokoshin, "From the Standpoint of the New Thinking: Three Major Elements in Stability," *Krasnaya zvedza* (September 16, 1988), p. 3, and P. Terrence Hopmann, "Conventional Arms Control and Common Security in Europe," *Arms Control Today* (October 1986), pp. 10-13.

9. For a comprehensive statement that opposes battlefield nuclear weapons, see Leon V. Sigal, "The Case Against Battlefield Nuclear Weapons," *Arms Control Today* (September 1989), pp. 15-20. President Gorbachev's January 15, 1986 offer included these weapons. The Committee of Soviet Scientists for Peace Against the Nuclear Threat also endorsed this step in its report, *Strategic Stability Under the Conditions of Radical Arms Reductions: Report on a Study* (Abridged) (Moscow, April 1987), p. 30. This report argues that tactical nuclear weapons raise the likelihood of nuclear war because they serve as a "bridge" between conventional and nuclear war.

10. These criteria are taken from P. Terrence Hopmann's chapter in this book, "Mutual Security and Arms Reductions in Europe."

11. It should be noted here that there is not yet full agreement among proponents of Fundamental Deterrence (or similar concepts) as to what would make for the most stable force structure. We are in agreement with Richard Garwin who proposes that a particular basing mode should not be forced on either the U.S. or USSR. See "A Blueprint for Radical Weapons Cuts," *Bulletin of the Atomic Scientists* (March 1988), p. 10. For a view that asserts that ICBM deployments would be the most stable for Fundamental Deterrence, see Committee of Soviet Scientists, "Strategic Stability," p. 31. We are skeptical concerning this conclusion.

12. "MIRVed launchers" refers to ICBMs or SLBMs with MIRV warheads. "MIRV" stands for Multiple Independently-targetable Re-entry Vehicles — that is, multiple warheads that can be directed to separate targets.

A posture of Fundamental Deterrence will, in the long run, decrease the amount spent on nuclear weapons by placing severe limits on deployments. However, the modernization of forces necessary for these reductions may actually add to defense spending in the short term, although probably less than would be added by force modernizations under a continuing START-type regime.

13. For example, the U.S. Department of Defense is currently considering a proposal that would replace the MIRVed warheads on the Minuteman III with single warheads, to be dubbed the Minuteman IV. In addition, some have proposed that the Midgetman, a small, single-warhead mobile ICBM currently being developed in the U.S., might be used to replace MIRVed warheads in the U.S. arsenal.

14. This could either be accomplished by substituting warheads or limiting quantitatively their deployment.

15. Michael M. May, George F. Bing and John D. Steinbruner, "Strategic Arsenals After START: The Implications of Deep Cuts," *International Security* 13, no. 1 (Summer 1988), pp. 90-133.

16. A similar point is noted by Committee of Soviet Scientists, "Strategic Stability," p. 28. Proportional reductions in each side's nuclear arsenals may have certain political advantages. That is, at times when the parties to a negotiation cannot agree on the various characteristics of the nuclear arsenals, a fallback position becomes one where each side will make some type of proportional cuts (or perhaps set proportional limits) in its arsenals. Though this type of reduction may lower the number of nuclear weapons within the arsenals, it cannot assure the more stable nuclear postures advocated in this proposal.

17. The results of the May-Bing-Steinbruner study strongly suggest that our proposal would enhance strategic stability. Calculations show that the nuclear force structure that maximizes mobility (and thus survivability) offers the least incentive for a first strike. Furthermore, those force postures that involved proportional cuts and that increased accuracy were found to be less satisfactory from the standpoint of stability. It should be added that these authors do not consider force levels below three thousand warheads and do not seriously consider the role of limited defenses.

18. Specific proposals along these lines have been made by other specialists; for example by William L. Ury and Richard Smoke in *Beyond the Hotline: Controlling a Nuclear Crisis*, A Report to the U.S. Arms Control and Disarmament Agency (Harvard Law School: Nuclear Negotiation Project, 1984).

19. See, for instance, Committee of Soviet Scientists, "Strategic Stability," p. 21. The report seems to rule out only space-based area defense without specifically ruling out point defense. It should be noted here that most who advocate a posture of Fundamental Deterrence (or similar concepts) do rule out an important role for defenses. For example, see Harold A. Feiverson, Richard H. Ullman and Frank von Hippel, "Reducing U.S. and Soviet Nuclear Arsenals," *Bulletin of the Atomic Scientists* (August 1985), p. 148, and Garwin, "A Blueprint for Radical Weapons Cuts," p. 10.

20. Concealability is advantageous, since it helps prevent one's forces from being destroyed in a first strike, as long as it can be achieved consistently with verification needs of a treaty; the latter is important because the entire Fundamental Deterrence regime would depend on the possibility of negotiating treaties. Concealability is inherent in SLBMs and some ICBM basing systems, which have been studied for a number of years.

21. Additional research is needed on the problem of ensuring that military research on both sides is appropriately controlled to permit maintaining a Fundamental Deterrence regime. This problem is complicated, but in our opinion by no means unresolvable. The best means of control may turn out to be firm control over the testing of new weapons, not over laboratory work. The two sides already limit, in important ways, the extent to which laboratory work is allowed to develop into actual weapons.

22. It is beyond the scope of the present paper to detail the mechanisms for achieving multilateral consent to the Fundamental Deterrence regime, which, admittedly, would be complex.

20

Mutual Security and Arms Reductions in Europe

P. TERRENCE HOPMANN

Introduction[1]

Mutual security is a process that seeks to improve the joint security of the United States and Soviet Union, as well as of their allies, across a broad spectrum of political, economic and military relationships. One important element of mutual security between the two alliances involves the reduction and control, not only of nuclear weapons, but also of conventional arms in such a way as to augment simultaneously the security of both East and West. Nowhere is this more important than in Europe, where the Cold War began and where some four and a half million soldiers still face each other in a military confrontation which could, if ignited, explode into nuclear war.

Recently, new negotiations on Conventional Forces in Europe (CFE) have opened in Vienna, and these offer the first hope in many years for significantly reducing this confrontation. A First Phase agreement in these negotiations appears likely to be reached sometime during 1990, which will lead to parity in the major armaments systems that face one another in Europe. However, parity of major force units does not guarantee joint improvements in security. These forces consist of armaments with significant qualitative differences, they operate within the context of very different strategic and tactical doctrines, and they are structured quite differently. Therefore, parity alone cannot remain a sufficient goal for achieving mutual security in Europe. Parity of insecurity is not the long-term answer to the security dilemma in Europe. Rather, what is required is a long-term strategy for reductions that produces joint improvements in actual security. Improved mutual security might or might not be based on a strict parity of specific military units.

Thus what is needed now is an exploration of long-term approaches for achiev-ing major arms reductions in Europe in ways that will succeed in improving mutual security. Such an exploration is a logical next study, to follow the Mutual Security Project between the Center for Foreign Policy Development at Brown University and the Institute for the USA and Canada of the Soviet Academy of Sciences. The two research institutes have agreed to conduct such a study jointly. Later in this chapter I shall explain the research plan. Before doing so it is useful to present, as background, the perspectives and premises upon which this research will be based. This chapter thus begins with an overall assessment of the criteria for improving mutual security in Europe, and a review of the lessons we can learn from previous efforts to negotiate arms reductions in Europe.[2]

Conditions for mutual security in Europe

Virtually all analysts agree that the *probability* of a premeditated war in Europe has been relatively low for many years, and that this probability has dropped much further in the last years of the 1980s. Nevertheless, the *capability* to conduct a major war in this region is still extremely high. An inadvertent outbreak of conflict in Central Europe is still distinctly possible. In that event, the vast military potential could contribute to the rapid escalation of even a limited conflict to the global level, possibly entailing the use of nuclear weapons. Attention must be devoted to this issue, to make such a tragic event as close to impossible as we can attain.

Dramatic political events in 1989, as well as the signing of the Intermediate Nuclear Forces (INF) Treaty in Washington, D.C. and the subsequent ceremony in Moscow marking its entry into force, have also increased the two sides' attention to the state of their conventional and tactical nuclear forces in Europe. On the Eastern side, mounting economic pressures and the need to restructure the domestic economies of the Soviet Union and other Warsaw Pact states have prompted efforts to reduce defense budgets, to enable those countries to reallocate financial and human resources from the military sector to the domestic economy. The West as well has economic and other needs to reduce defense spending if possible. This enhanced perception on both sides of the importance of conventional arms reduc-tions to further mutual interests has accounted in large part for the rapid progress in the Vienna CFE negotiations during their first year. That progress stands in marked contrast to the experience in the previous negotiation in Vienna on Mutual and Balanced Force Reductions (MBFR), which lasted more than fifteen years with no concrete results.[3]

Furthermore, political and economic cooperation in Europe requires reduced military tensions. Strains which emanate from the perceived threat posed by both NATO's and the Warsaw Pact's awesome military capabilities remain an obstacle to other aspects of East-West cooperation in Europe. Thus a reduction in the military confrontation in Europe would seem to be a necessary prerequisite to (and also a possible consequence of) improved political relations between East and West. The burst of reform movements throughout Eastern Europe in 1989 has also produced a highly favorable political climate for dramatic troop reductions. Therefore there is reason to be hopeful that the earlier vicious cycle of arms races and political tensions can be replaced by a benign cycle of reduced military confrontation and enhanced political and economic cooperation.

Several conditions would seem to be essential to reducing the perceived threat of war in Europe within a mutual security framework:

Condition #1: It should be clear that the only possible role for nuclear weapons in Europe (or anywhere) is to deter their use by others. As an adjunct to conventional forces to be used in "war-fighting," they threaten widespread destruction. Rather, nuclear weapons must be used only for Fundamental Deterrence. In such a second-strike-only role, a "reasonable sufficiency" of nuclear forces should be adequate to maintain the basic and robust mutual deterrent relationship intact well into the future.[4]

Condition #2: The major threat of the outbreak of war in Europe is not direct, deliberate aggression, but rather the danger that unanticipated, unsanctioned or accidental events might quickly escalate out of control. Threats to the peace are more likely to arise from political conflicts, perhaps from conflicts within individual countries in Central Europe which spill beyond their borders, than from a planned, surprise "blitzkrieg" style attack. The ability to keep such incidents isolated and limited and to avoid escalation is essential for mutual security in Europe. Thus attention must be given not only to mechanisms for crisis resolution, but also to creating a military situation where escalation *cannot* occur so rapidly that existing crisis resolution facilities might be overwhelmed.

Condition #3: The ability to avoid any resort to the first use of nuclear weapons, for reason of military need, depends upon a broad perception of stability at the conventional level in Central Europe. If conventional deterrence is undermined, then either side may feel it needs to rely upon nuclear weapons to compensate for its perceived conventional inferiority.

Condition #4: Conventional stability in Europe requires at least four components:

— elimination of the capability to launch a surprise attack, and the establishment of sufficient parity in Europe to make any successful execution of a large-scale conventional operation virtually unthinkable;

— lowering the presently high overall quantitative level of the military confrontation in Europe;

— avoidance of conventional arms races that could create new disparities or exacerbate old ones; and

— the adoption of overall military postures in which essentially defensive potentials dominate over offensive potentials.[5]

The more these conditions can be met, the more both sides will perceive a reduced threat and the more they will enjoy mutual security.

Dangers to mutual security in Europe

Presently none of these conditions are fully met. Especially noteworthy are the following problems:

1. Tactical nuclear weapons remain a significant part of the arsenals of both NATO and the Warsaw Pact, and NATO continues to maintain a policy of reliance on possible first use of nuclear weapons. While the Warsaw Pact has pledged not to be the first to introduce nuclear weapons into a conflict in Europe, it has the capability to do so should circumstances warrant.

2. Present defense planning is directed toward the prevention of a major assault, generally under the assumption that the enemy might attack in a "blitzkrieg" type of operation. There are relatively few mechanisms in place to resolve tensions and conflicts in Central Europe, or to engage in rapid consultation in a crisis or after an incident has set off limited fighting. All of these factors make escalation of even relatively minor incidents a distinct and dangerous possibility.

3. There still is considerable disagreement about the degree of disparity of forces between NATO and the Warsaw Pact. Whether the overall balance is one of parity or disparity, however, it is clear that there are a number of significant asymmetries between NATO and the Warsaw Pact in Europe, including asymmetries in doctrine, tactics, and armaments. Many of these asymmetries may contribute to instability in times of crisis. Of these asymmetries, NATO's reliance on possible first use of nuclear weapons to compensate for its perceived inferiority in conventional armaments is potentially the most dangerous. The much closer geographical proximity of Soviet territory to the central front in Europe, compared to U.S. territory, is also a concern that must be addressed.

4. Some specific revisions in doctrine, force structures and armaments threaten to promote a new arms race between NATO and the Warsaw Pact. The proposed deployment by NATO of precision-guided, long-range conven-

tional weapons capable of deep strikes into Eastern Europe and the Soviet
Union, in conjunction with NATO's Follow-On Forces Attack doctrine, is
one element of this arms race. Such a deployment would probably set off a
response in kind by the Warsaw Pact. The offensive military doctrine and
structure of Warsaw Pact forces has led many in NATO to call for a more
offensive (or "counter-offensive") strategy by the Western alliance as well.

All of these elements are potentially dangerous. They highlight the importance
of successful CFE negotiations between NATO and the Warsaw Pact to reduce the
conventional confrontation in Europe. Some valuable lessons may be learned from
the previous stalemated negotiations on conventional force reductions, lessons that
may usefully be applied in the new talks.

Lessons for CFE from the MBFR negotiations

The current negotiations on CFE have followed on the heels of more than fifteen
years of frustrating and largely unproductive negotiations in Vienna known in the
West as MBFR.[6] The CFE negotiation opened in a much more auspicious political
environment than that which characterized most of the MBFR period, and this
undoubtedly accounts in large measure for the much more rapid progress of CFE in
a short period of time. Indeed, the entire approach to the negotiations has changed
from an essentially zero-sum orientation, in which both sides advanced proposals
that would serve their unilateral security interests, to a much more positive-sum
approach, oriented towards achieving joint interests.

In spite of this significant shift in the orientation of the negotiations, any effort
to analyze future directions for conventional arms control in Europe can benefit
from an examination of the fifteen-year MBFR experience, to identify both possible
opportunities that the new negotiations might exploit, as well as possible pitfalls
that should be avoided. Here are some important issues where MBFR offers lessons
that can be usefully applied to the CFE negotiations:

1. Substantially more countries are involved in CFE than were involved in the
   MBFR negotiations. The participation of more countries has both potential
   benefits and costs. For example, there is no doubt that French absence from
   MBFR was a serious problem, especially since France has approximately
   50,000 troops stationed in the Federal Republic of Germany (FRG). Furthermore, a long-term improvement in European security is unlikely to come
   about without the participation of all important states in Europe, obviously
   including France. On the other hand, the quite different perceptions by the
   French government of both the purposes of arms control negotiations and of
   the role of nuclear weapons in the defense of Europe, compared to most of

the NATO allies, might create problems both within the NATO alliance and within the CFE negotiations.

The integration of the French position into NATO will not be the only problem that the Western alliance faces. The expanded geographical scope of CFE will involve the flank states such as Greece and Turkey (with their own regional disputes), and Denmark and Norway with their own special security concerns. In addition, the special position of the Federal Republic of Germany, due to its geographic location and its military centrality to the NATO alliance, will have special influence on the evolution of the NATO position.[7]

Similarly, for the Warsaw Pact the expanded role for some countries could present challenges if their positions on disarmament would differ significantly from those of their allies. In addition, the rapid pace of domestic political change in Eastern Europe, as perestroika and glasnost spread throughout the socialist bloc, will also present challenges to any negotiations on security in Central Europe. With the events of late 1989 having thrown the entire political future of Central and Eastern Europe into some doubt, there is a great deal of uncertainty about the role that the Warsaw Pact will play in these negotiations as a single, unified alliance. On the positive side, it is conceivable that the dramatic changes in the structure of European politics could enable CFE to move well beyond the strictly "bloc to bloc" negotiations which characterized MBFR. This might remove some of the rigidities which were introduced into MBFR by the necessity to maintain bloc unity and discipline.

2. The enlarged geographical scope of reductions in CFE presents both advantages and disadvantages compared to MBFR. On the one hand, the inclusion of all European territory from the Atlantic to the Urals can overcome some of the most fundamental flaws with the MBFR framework as viewed by many in the West, especially by many in the FRG. From the perspective of many West German specialists, it is especially valuable to include significant portions of Soviet territory in the reduction zone for several reasons. First, they argue that it was intrinsically unfair for the major NATO power in Europe, the FRG, to have to reduce its forces since it was located within the MBFR reduction zone, while the major Warsaw Pact country in Europe, the Soviet Union, would only have had to withdraw troops from Eastern Europe, without making any actual reductions, because Soviet territory lay outside the MBFR reduction zone. The inclusion of Soviet territory in CFE will make the reductions seem more symmetrical from a West German vantage point. Second, a major NATO concern since the

beginning of the MBFR talks was that the USSR would only have to withdraw its forces several hundred kilometers into Soviet territory, from which they could be rapidly reintroduced into Central Europe in a crisis, whereas the United States would have to withdraw its troops all the way across the Atlantic Ocean to bases in the United States. Again, reductions on Soviet territory will at least reduce the significance of this important asymmetry.

On the other hand, the larger geographical zone means that problems of verification will be magnified substantially compared to the MBFR negotiations, where they were already a serious obstacle. Not only will a larger geographical area have to be covered by the verification regime — a daunting task in itself — but extensive on-site verification will have to take place on the territory of several countries in both East and West which have resisted such intrusive measures in the past.

3. There can be little doubt that agreement about data on force levels prior to reductions will be even more important in CFE than it was in the case of MBFR, especially if deep reductions are to be made. A Phase One agreement on parity of major armaments systems may be attained without prior agreement on data, since in this case the final outcome of reductions can be verified to assure that agreed levels of parity have been reached by both sides after the reductions have taken place. However a deep reduction agreement in Phase Two will require better initial data in order to determine the starting point from which percentage reductions will be implemented.

Hopefully the new negotiations with a broader geographical focus will enable all parties to present new and more realistic data about forces currently stationed in Europe. These data can best be established through on-site observation of a statistically selected sample of military units throughout the reduction zone. Verification resulting from the 1986 Stockholm accords on Confidence- and Security-Building Measures, as well as from implementation of a Phase One CFE agreement, will also facilitate the establishment of an agreed data base as a foundation for subsequent reductions.

4. Even though a focus on a larger geographical area has important benefits for the CFE negotiations, there were some benefits from MBFR's focus on the more delimited area of Central Europe where the two sides confront one another most directly. Some of the features of the central zone are, therefore, likely to be retained within CFE. The current negotiations find both sides in agreement on a concept of dividing the territory slated for reductions into several zones. NATO proposes to create four zones on each side and the Warsaw Pact three. However both sides are in almost complete agreement

about the scope of the central zone, consisting essentially of the MBFR reduction zone (although the Warsaw Pact has proposed adding Denmark to this zone). Any CFE agreement will undoubtedly have to include special arrangements for this central zone, where military forces and equipment readily capable of offensive operations will be especially provocative and destabilizing.[8]

In summary, the MBFR negotiations were locked in stalemate for over fifteen years in part because of the tremendous complexity introduced in the negotiations by multiple participants (most members of both alliances) and by the multiplicity of issues that are entailed in something as complex as a conventional force reduction in an area as large as the Central European reduction zone. There is a grave danger that the CFE negotiations will be bogged down by the even greater complexity due to the participation of even more actors, to say nothing of the wider scope of the negotiations in terms of both geographical territory and the kinds of forces covered. In order to avoid complete chaos, the negotiations will need to find an integrative framework or formula for guidance. Without such a formula, the negotiations will almost inevitably become lost in a forest of details.[9]

In spite of the many obstacles that could complicate the CFE negotiations, progress through 1989 was impressive, and a First Phase agreement appears to be attainable sometime in 1990. Such an agreement will concentrate on reducing some of the most important disparities in major weapons currently deployed in Europe. While this will be an important first step toward the creation of a more stable balance of forces in Central Europe, it will not guarantee long-term stability. That is likely to depend more upon a restructuring of forces on both sides into more defensive postures, which will likely be a focus of a Second Phase CFE negotiation. It is not too early to begin designing a conceptual framework for a Second Phase negotiation that will advance more directly the goals of mutual security.

A proposed model for conventional arms reduction in Central Europe

A conceptual framework, or model, should produce an outcome that both sides regard as fair, equal and desirable in spite of asymmetries of force structure and in the absence of complete mutual trust. A model should also suggest priorities for the process of mutual reductions. An especially beneficial stability could be attained if the model resulted in the removal of those forces on each side that the other views as most threatening.

It is tempting to try to devise a comprehensive scheme to reduce forces along one carefully planned path to some defined, ideal end-point in the future. But this approach is likely to fail. It is likely to fail not only because of the differences in interests, force structures, weapons, and doctrines between the two sides, but also because of different threat perceptions on the two sides in Europe.

A better model is one that takes an incremental approach. The model that I propose makes small reductions initially, taking into account each side's perception of threat, and then allows each side to evaluate and adjust its objectives before the next reduction. Further steps then follow. The goal of these incremental steps is to achieve significant reductions, in the perceptions of each side, of the *threat* to their security from the other side, not merely numerical reductions for the sake of numerical reductions. Thus the process is one of progressive, mutual threat reduction, and hence progressive improvement in mutual security.

It must be stressed that the model I propose is primarily an analytic device, not necessarily a literal program for the two sides' actual force reductions. The model is intended for the assistance of planners and perhaps of negotiators. In particular, it is aimed at helping planners and analysts on both sides understand what the likely consequences would be of taking this step or that step. As such, it may be able to help guide the complicated planning and analytical process that each side must employ during the negotiations. Nowhere in this paper do I mean to imply that the incremental model discussed here is meant chiefly as a proposal to be carried out literally, step by step, by NATO and the Warsaw Pact.

The conceptual core of the model is suggested by the simple child's game of cutting a cake, sometimes known as "I cut, you choose." Two children who do not completely trust one another try to divide a cake equally. They can succeed if one cuts the cake but the other gets to choose which piece to take first. The child doing the cutting thus has an incentive to divide it equally, so as not to get left with the smaller piece.[10]

Suitably developed, this idea can provide a basis for a useful model. In the proposed model, each side evaluates the relative contribution of all its forces to its overall security needs, and the other then selects a small percentage of those forces to reduce. As explained further below, the first side has an incentive to evaluate its forces fairly, since a failure to do so will hurt only itself. Just as the other child will take a bigger piece of cake if the opportunity is presented to do so, so the other side will select a disproportionally large cut if it is given the opportunity to do so.

After a pause for each side to reevaluate the situation, a second round of cuts are made by the same method; then a third, and so on. The goal of the model is thus to reduce forces in a way that produces approximately equivalent reductions of threat to both sides. The process should, in practice, emphasize reductions on each side of the forces perceived by the other as most provocative.

With this introduction, let me now explain the operation of the model in more detail:

1. As an initial planning step, both sides must first agree on data about the size of all their forces stationed in Europe from the Atlantic to the Urals. These data might consist of divisions or other smaller units for ground forces, including their location by country or military district (in the case of the USSR), their approximate size in manpower, their primary function and/or major armaments, and category of readiness. For air forces, data could include specific combat aircraft and combat helicopters by type and by location. Reductions would take place on a basis of specific units with specific locations.

2. Estimates of the forces from these locations would then be modified, to take into account the unilateral Soviet reductions announced by President Gorbachev in December 1988 and all reductions agreed upon in a First Phase CFE negotiation. These latter reductions will probably result in parity for main battle tanks, armored personnel carriers, artillery, combat aircraft, and combat helicopters. Thus the estimates of the two sides' forces will be approximately symmetrical *overall*.

3. In the proposed model, each side would assign a total of 10,000 points, distributing them across all of its remaining forces. Each side may "weight" its various forces as it wishes in assigning points. Obviously each side will not weight each division or unit equally, since some are more valuable than others. Thus points will be distributed so that some units or systems receive many points and others receive fewer points. Each country assigns weighting points to each of *its own* forces according to the value that *it* believes each element of its force structure contributes to its overall security. Each division, airplane or helicopter may be weighted according to whatever criteria each country feels to be important, perhaps including firepower, defensibility, mobility, preparedness, quality of training, etc.

   It is important to emphasize that this model does not require agreement between the two sides about what criteria are important. Each side uses the criteria that it believes are important in assigning weights to its own forces. All units are assigned value by each side only in comparison to other units on its own side. No comparison is required with forces on the other side. These features of requiring no agreement on criteria and no comparison with the other side are among the greatest advantages of this model.

   Each side will be discouraged from "cheating" in its assignment of its points, because cheating can and usually will backfire. Each side knows that the forces corresponding to a small percentage of the points it has assigned will shortly be removed by *the other* side. And each side has only 10,000 points to assign. Thus if certain forces are overrated, others must be underrated. When the other side selects the forces to be cut, it can take advantage of any distortion, by choosing a larger number of the underrated forces to be eliminated. Thus the process is structured so that misrepresentation will hurt the party which engages in the misrepresentation. If each party is reasonable it will not engage in a self-defeating manipulation of the process.

This kind of miscalculation may be illustrated with a concrete example. To avoid invidious implications, let us call the two sides "Alpha" and "Beta." Suppose that Alpha believes that Beta wants to reduce Alpha's quantity of tanks. To make this difficult for Beta, Alpha might thus overvalue divisions equipped with tanks. Thus tank divisions really worth, say, 150 points each might be overvalued at 200 points each. This might discourage Beta from selecting tank divisions to cut. But Alpha has only 10,000 points total to distribute. Having increased the distribution to tank divisions, it now must decrease the distribution to other things. Suppose Alpha compensates for its overvaluation of tank divisions by reducing the value of motorized infantry divisions. Let us say that these divisions are really worth 150 points each, but now are undervalued at 100 points each. When Beta makes its cuts, it will see that for 200 points it can demand the removal of two of these infantry divisions, or just one tank division. Realizing that the infantry divisions have been undervalued, it might well decide that it preferred to cut the two infantry divisions rather than the one tank division. Thus Beta will be able to take advantage of the distortion made by Alpha, to gain a greater reduction than it otherwise could have gained. Alpha, which should have valued those two infantry divisions at 300 points, has "given them away" for only 200 points, and thus has lost 100 points in real terms.

Something like this will, in principle, always occur in this model. For every distortion, in principle there will be a response available which makes the "dishonest" side worse off than if it had been honest in its evaluation in the first place. It is this aspect of the model where the metaphor of the two children cutting the cake applies and is powerful.

4. The operation of the model can then proceed through a series of many similar steps. For purposes of analysis I believe the best procedure would be as follows: Each side will select two percent of the forces of the other side to be removed every six months over a span of ten years. Two percent of 10,000 being 200, each side will choose forces from the other side worth 200 points to be removed every six months. Over ten years there will be a total of twenty such reduction steps, and hence a total reduction on both sides, at the end of the ten years, of forty percent. Of course this forty percent reduction is a reduction *beyond* the reduced levels agreed to in the First Phase CFE

negotiation. Many other combinations of time span, size of cut and frequency of cut could also be selected without changing the operation of this model in principle.

However for military reasons it is important that each increment be small. It is essential that no one reduction can ever cripple or seriously damage the defensive structure of either side. The purpose of arms reductions, after all, is to make both sides more secure, not less.

It is important to notice that the reductions that each side makes every six months will be of equal *value*, but the actual size or number of *forces* to be eliminated may not be the same. For instance, at step three the two sides might "trade" one tank division for four helicopter brigades. The numbers are different but, by the nature of the model, the two sides would be stating that, in terms of what they value, they see the "trade" as an equal one.

5. For the model to operate correctly it is essential that each side be allowed to reassign its points after each cut. It must be able to do so, to reflect any changes in its own perceptions of its security needs in the light of the reductions now made (or for other reasons). Thus after the first step, Alpha and Beta each have 9800 points left. They then may redistribute those points across their remaining forces in any way they wish. Then another cut of 200 points is made and each side reevaluates its security situation again; and so forth.

This device prevents either side from attempting any systematic "campaign" to remove some key sector of the other side's force structure. If Alpha saw Beta trying to take away something of key importance, Alpha can re-weight its forces, increasing the value of those units it saw Beta trying to remove. Doing so would make it extremely "expensive" for Beta to continue in this way.

Again an example may be helpful. Let us imagine that Alpha sees that, in one step after another, Beta is trying to cut away all of Alpha's tank divisions, thus exposing Alpha to unacceptable risks. Alpha can increase the value of tank divisions in subsequent rounds. Thus the first tank division to be removed might be worth 150 points, but the next worth 160 points, and so forth, until the reduction of tank divisions became prohibitively expensive for Beta. (Alpha would compensate by reducing the value of forces where no reductions had yet been made, thus making these more attractive objects for cuts in subsequent rounds.)

Over a series of twenty small steps, this procedure should produce balanced, safe reductions. In any one stage the cuts might not be perfectly balanced, but cuts at one stage will be so small that an imbalance would not be militarily significant. Adjustment at the next stage will correct it. The process of continuous adjustment thus enables each side to maintain a balanced posture and to avoid any serious gaps in its overall force structure.

6. The precise magnitude of the overall reduction at the end of the time span is somewhat arbitrary. But a forty percent reduction beyond the Phase One CFE level seems to represent the deepest reduction that can presently be envisaged without going below the operational minimum necessary to maintain adequate defenses on both sides. Of course, continued rapid change in political conditions in Europe might make even larger reductions plausible in the future. One of the strengths of this model is that it can be readily adapted to some other overall goal.

7. This model will work best if there is a freeze, during its time span, on the deployment of new forces or the modernization of existing equipment. However even if this were not possible, there would still be strong incentives against such new developments. In this model Alpha can add more forces but cannot exceed 10,000 points, which means that the larger number of forces must be covered by the same number of points. Every cut of 200 points will simply reduce a larger number of actual forces. Also, if some equipment is modernized, Beta can select those units for removal in the next round. Thus Alpha faces the possibility that new weapons would be eliminated almost immediately after their deployment. Of course, Alpha could assign a large number of points to those new units, but again this would require Alpha to undervalue other units. Larger quantities of other units would be cut away in the following rounds than would have been cut in the absence of modernization.

8. This model requires that forces may not be introduced into the reduction zone from outside, for instance from the USSR east of the Urals or from the U.S. or Canada. The model must also restrict the movement of forces from rear areas into the central area surrounding the West German border with East Germany and Czechoslovakia, in order to prevent "stacking" an excessive number of forces in forward areas while forces are pulled away from rear areas. That situation could be dangerous.

At the same time, the model requires that forces not be reduced excessively in the central zone. It is necessary to avoid any potentially destabilizing vacuum in Central Europe, which could also be dangerous. An agreement is thus needed to maintain a certain minimum level of forces in the central zone. That minimum might be, say, thirty percent of the total forces of the entire region from the Atlantic to the Urals. In addition, a ceiling and floor should be placed on forces of countries outside the central zone but stationed within it (e.g., the forces in Germany of the U.S., Britain, Canada and the USSR). These forces might always constitute, for example, at least twenty percent but never more than fifty percent of the total forces of the two blocs in the central zone.

9. This model assumes that adequate verification procedures can be agreed upon to assure that the selected reductions are actually carried out, and that any new forces or armaments introduced into the region at any time are also added to the data base. Here as always, political acceptance of substantial arms reductions depends upon the belief, by both governments and the public, that verification procedures are fully adequate and that appropriate measures will be taken to respond to suspected violations.

   Recent improvements in verification provisions in the INF and other agreements, and the Soviet policy of glasnost suggest that many of the verification problems encountered in previous conventional arms negotiations may now be overcome. Indeed, several NATO states seem currently more likely to raise objections to intrusive verification measures than are members of the Warsaw Pact.

10. A reduction procedure of this kind could be implemented initially between the U.S. and the USSR alone without the participation of the other European states. However there must be a clear commitment to move on to reductions of allied forces soon after initial reductions are undertaken by the two superpowers. Binding commitments to carry out reductions would be required from all states of Europe (and non-European states with forces stationed there, such as Canada).

11. The model should lead to an outcome in which the forces remaining after the reductions are completed are more defensively oriented than the forces existing at the outset. This should be a natural outcome of the selection process by the two sides. In general, each side would be likely to assign the largest number of points to those units it deems most essential to its defense, thus making them most immune to reductions. Neither side is likely to undervaluate its essential defensive forces. Conversely, when making its selections of forces on the other side to remove, each side is likely to pinpoint those forces that it sees as posing the greatest threat, that is, the other side's most offensively oriented forces. There is little incentive to cut the non-threatening, defensive forces of the opponent. Therefore, over a period of time this reduction procedure should naturally lead toward a force structure on both sides where both retain those forces most essential for their defense, while simultaneously reducing the most provocative and offensive forces of

the other. This "built in" tendency toward emphasizing defensive forces is another of the important strengths of this model.

12. A word is needed about nuclear weapons deployed in Europe. In my view, the preferable approach is to include the so-called "tactical nuclear" and dual-capable forces in the model.[11] They would be assigned points and reduced like any other forces. This would have the effect of halting and reversing any competition in tactical nuclear weapons in Europe.

Remaining in the background, of course, would be the very large nuclear forces maintained by both the USSR and the U.S. that are stationed outside Europe but are capable of striking targets in Europe. These background forces would provide, at the nuclear level, what McGeorge Bundy has called "existential deterrence."[12]

To summarize, this model is intended to help find sensible ways of accomplishing large reductions, not only in the quantities of troops and equipment deployed in Europe, but also in the military threats that the existing forces pose. The model should also promote the development of force structures that would be increasingly defensive and less provocative. The resulting military situation in Europe should be, in overall terms, considerably more stable, less dangerous, and less expensive. Thus mutual security in Europe would be much improved. This improved security situation, in turn, would create a context in which political, economic and other cooperation between West and East in Europe can continue to expand.

Exploring the model

Will this model work as well in practice as this analysis suggests that it should? Can it actually provide valuable guidance to planners and negotiators? To answer such questions there is no alternative but to conduct experiments, employing the model in simulations. As with many other simulation exercises, teams who pretend to represent the two sides can "play" this exercise and see how it develops in practice. As noted above, the Center for Foreign Policy Development at Brown University and the Institute for the USA and Canada of the Soviet Academy of Sciences have agreed to investigate the problems of arms reductions in Europe by simulating reductions employing this model.

The model offers a unique and novel approach to overcoming many of the difficulties that have been experienced in negotiating European arms reductions. On the other hand, there are many complications entailed in the model, and there is no guarantee that it will in fact produce the kind of stable, desirable outcome that is hoped for. Therefore we intend to evaluate it through a simulated, but realistic, exercise that will test both the step-by-step process and the military outcomes.

To my knowledge this will be the first such simulated arms control negotiation in which American specialists will play the role of Western negotiators and Soviet specialists will play the role of East-bloc negotiators. This should introduce an element of realism into the simulation which has not been captured by any other simulation effort of this kind to date. At a minimum, joint participation will enable each side to learn more about the real fears, perceptions of threat, and security needs of the other. Furthermore, a process of joint evaluation by Soviet and American specialists should enable us to determine whether both parties believe that the outcome really would make both sides feel more secure — which in the final analysis is the ultimate criterion for mutual security.

Our joint evaluation of this exercise will focus on two principal subjects:

The outcomes. The military balance, resulting at various stages and at the conclusion, will be evaluated to determine whether or not both sides believe that their military security has been improved, compared to the prior situation. Of special interest will be noting the extent to which the remaining forces do or do not become configured in more defensive, less provocative postures than presently exist.

The process. The process of making small, incremental reductions and repeated reassessments of force structures will be evaluated for feasibility. The accompanying process of communication back and forth between the two sides will also be evaluated. These evaluations should give some indication of the value of this model for assisting in actual negotiations for arms reductions in Europe.

On the basis of the evaluation, the experimenters will then decide among three options:

1. Discontinue the experiment. It is conceivable that this model will turn out to be not worth pursuing. But even in this case, we will still have learned a great deal from the simulation exercise. For example, the assignment of points and the selection of units for reductions will reveal valuable information to each side about the other side's perceptions of threat and basic military security needs.[13]

2. Modify and repeat the experiment. The experimenters may discover problems in the model that can be corrected by making modifications in it. If this model attracts interest from official planners in either or both capitals, it might also be useful to repeat the exercise with appropriate officials present as observers.

3. Recommend application in some form to the real negotiations. A successful experiment with this simulation, or the discovery of important results, may attract significant attention from the governments on the two sides, seeking to improve their negotiation process.

In this case the model might, in some suitable fashion, become part of the analytic foundations that help guide negotiations in the Second Phase CFE negotiations. We do not, of course, expect that NATO and Warsaw Pact negotiators will adopt this procedure wholesale, nor that the two sides would carry out literally this way of accomplishing military reductions. For one thing, the abstract nature of the model might make it difficult to "sell" politically on either side, and it would be difficult for the public in any country to understand. For another, it is unlikely for political reasons that NATO and the Warsaw Pact would find it easy to carry out small reductions in forces many times. But there are other, less crude, ways in which this approach could be applied in practical terms.

In essence, experimenting with this model is intended to identify what might be called "equal reductions in units of perceived threat." Application of this model might enable planners to identify ways that seemingly unrelated forces could be eliminated, to achieve equal reductions in the perceived threat, and thus equal security gains for both sides. The *actual* reductions negotiated and decided upon could simply be presented to the public as concrete ad hoc deals.

Experimenting with models like this one has a further possible consequence that could be very valuable to both sides, quite apart from the specific value of any one particular model. The approach leads naturally to the creation of *joint study teams*. A reasonable degree of success in exploring and developing a model like this one could lead the experimenters to offer this suggestion to their governments: a joint analytical team might be created, consisting of specialists from both sides, who could employ procedures like this one to help guide the actual negotiations. Thus the two sides would move toward a new approach to the negotiation process, in which multinational analytical teams work together to produce unofficial joint analyses, which can then be fed into the official negotiations.[14] The analyses would be valuable not only for the substance of what they contained, but perhaps even more, for the fact that they represented what was already a de facto consensus among experts from both sides. Such joint study teams could assist the official negotiators and provide them with the analyses and background necessary for them successfully to negotiate the actual reductions. Having analyses available that already represent a joint-but-unofficial consensus among experts from both sides could be a more productive procedure than other (mostly ad hoc) procedures proposed thus far for negotiating arms reductions in Europe.

Conclusion

The model proposed here is not meant as a literal formula to be carried out mechanically. It is meant as a research tool, but one with immediate practical utility. It is offered as a novel means out of some of the impasses which have frozen

European arms reduction negotiations in futility for some fifteen years. This approach is one way in which specialists can begin to convert abstract, general discussions of the concepts of mutual security into something that is of concrete value for the respective governments.

If an overall framework were agreed upon to help structure future arms reductions in Europe, much of the complexity that has made the issue seem unresolvable might be significantly reduced. Developed in the present context of growing interest in mutual security arrangements for Europe, this framework could help improve future negotiations. Agreement upon various details could be derived from the general framework. Doing this would be more efficient than trying to treat a large number of issues in a step-by-step and ad hoc fashion. Concrete results in achieving further arms reductions in Europe, in turn, could go a long way toward reducing tensions, making any outbreak of war less likely, and controlling escalation should some conflict break out in Europe. In spite of the differences that remain on many issues between the two major blocs, such an agreement could serve the security interests of both the United States and the Soviet Union simultaneously, which is the essence of the mutual security approach.

Notes

1. Although I am solely responsible for the content of this chapter, I have received invaluable comments and suggestions from numerous American and Soviet colleagues who have worked with me on this project in a most constructive and collaborative process. These include, on the American side, Mark Garrison, Richard Smoke, Eric Mlyn, Stephen Fought, and Mark Kramer, and on the Soviet side, Viktor Kremenyuk, Aleksandr Konovalov, Sergei Fedorenko and Aleksei Arbatov.

2. A Memorandum of Agreement to conduct this study was signed by leaders of the Center for Foreign Policy Development at Brown University and the Institute for the USA and Canada of the Soviet Academy of Sciences in November 1989. It is explicitly understood between these institutes that this study represents a further stage of joint research on mutual security, following their initial Mutual Security Project.

   The overall assessment offered in the next section of this chapter is my own, but I believe that in general terms, it broadly reflects a mutual understanding, shared by all or most American and Soviet members of the Nuclear and Conventional Arms Reductions Working Group of the Mutual Security Project. It also reflects discussions held by that Working Group, as well as other research of mine. This assessment is current as of the beginning of 1990.

3. The reduced role of nuclear weapons in Europe after implementation of the INF Treaty has also accentuated concerns in the West about the stability of the conventional balance, since an important component of NATO's Flexible Response strategy has been removed.

4. See the companion chapter in this volume, "Fundamental Deterrence and Mutual Security Beyond START."

5. Further elaboration of these criteria may be found in Andrei Kokoshin, Aleksandr Konovalov, Valeriy Larionov, and Valeriy Mazing, *Problems of Ensuring Stability with Radical Cuts in Armed Forces and Conventional Armaments in Europe* (Moscow: Novosti Press Agency, 1989), p. 5.

6. Even the title of these negotiations was a subject of contention for many years between NATO and the Warsaw Pact, a dispute which reflected the different reduction philosophies of the two sides. Since those differences have largely disappeared in the current negotiations, this chapter will use this familiar and widely used name for these negotiations without necessarily implying the superiority of the Western conception of reductions which lay behind the Western name.

7. For an excellent discussion of the status of the CFE preparatory talks and of some of the difficulties posed for the NATO alliance, see Jonathan Dean, "NATO Disunity Imperils the Conventional Stability Talks," *Arms Control Today* 18, no. 8 (October 1988), pp. 11-18. ("Conventional Stability Talks" was an earlier name for what is now CFE.)

8. Some interesting suggestions for establishing a more defensive posture in this central zone are made in the companion chapter on conventional forces by Aleksandr Konovalov.

9. For a theoretical discussion of the relationship between formulas and details in negotiations, see I. William Zartman and Maureen Berman, eds., *The Practical Negotiator* (New Haven, Connecticut: Yale University Press, 1982).

10. This concept has previously been proposed as a framework for the reduction of strategic arms. For such a proposal see S.H. Salter, "Some Ideas to Help Stop World War III" (Edinburgh, U.K.: University of Edinburgh, February 1984).

11. Naturally this does not include the British and French strategic nuclear forces, which are properly seen as part of the problem of reducing, world-wide, the strategic forces that are global in scope. "Dual capable" forces refers to forces and equipment that can employ either conventional or nuclear weapons.

12. The inclusion of tactical nuclear weapons in this reduction model must be provisional. From an analytical point of view, there are many important reasons to include tactical or "battlefield" nuclear weapons. In contrast to the intermediate and short-range nuclear missiles that were eliminated by the 1987 INF Treaty, the tactical nuclear weapons are so integrated physically and tactically with conventional force in Europe that it is almost impossible to make changes in one without making changes in the other. On the other hand, there is strong opposition in several countries to reducing nuclear weapons in Europe further, and this may require the exclusion of these forces for political reasons. An alternative would be to exempt them from reductions in the early stages, but to allow them to be reduced in later stages, after purely conventional reductions were well under way and were proving successful.

13. It goes without saying that "reveal" here refers to information that will be constructively useful as both sides seek mutual security in the future. I do not refer to the "revelation" of information that is legitimately secret. In this exercise, all assignment of points and selection of units for removal will be done by non-governmental experts, not by government officials; and all information used will be derived from open, unclassified sources.

14. This suggestion is similar to a "new model" for negotiations proposed by Georgiy Arbatov in "Discussion Platform: Glasnost, Talks, and Disarmament," *Pravda* (October 17, 1988), p. 6.

21

The Problems of Developing Stable Non-Offensive Structures for General-Purpose Forces and Conventional Arms In Europe

ALEKSANDR KONOVALOV

The negotiations under way in Vienna on conventional armed forces in Europe have begun a new phase in the resolution of the extremely complex problem of establishing a stable balance of military capabilities on the continent, a balance that would leave both political-military alliances with forces needed only for defense.[1]

In official proposals put forth by the sides present at the talks one can find common reassuring elements. Above all, this applies to the quantitative limits on various types of arms: tanks, armored personnel carriers (APCs and ICVs) and artillery systems. As we know, in the Soviet three-phase plan, outlined by Eduard Shevardnadze in his speech in Vienna in March 1989[2] and later developed by Mikhail Gorbachev during his talks with U.S. Secretary of State James Baker in the Kremlin on May 11, 1989,[3] and in the American counter-proposals formulated by George Bush in his speech at the NATO Council session in Brussels at the end of May 1989,[4] the proposed limits for both sides to reduce their arsenals have coincided in the types of weapons discussed there.

Of course there are still a significant number of differences in the two sides' positions, and the complex unresolved problems substantially outnumber the concrete achievements. Nevertheless, the first steps toward agreement have now been taken. Furthermore, despite the importance of common views on the desired quantitative limits of individual types of arms, the more essential element of progress has been to narrow the gap between the two sides' assessment of the military and political goals that the process of reducing armed forces and conventional arms in Europe should achieve.

This merger has resulted from the intensive political process of the last four years. Back in May 1987 the Political Consultative Committee of the Warsaw Pact put forth a revolutionary idea on how to change the qualitative and quantitative parameters of the armed forces as well as the principles of the military organization of NATO and WTO so as to exclude the possibility not only of a "surprise attack but also of conducting large-scale offensive operations."[5] Throughout the following years this goal has dominated the most important political initiatives and unilateral steps taken by the USSR and its WTO allies.

Characterizing the principles by which the structure, doctrine, and military make-up of the armed forces of the WTO countries, are changing today, Mikhail Gorbachev stressed in his speech at the European Parliament in Strasbourg on July 6, 1989: "This doctrine, both from the standpoint of the quantity of weapons and troops and from the standpoint of their deployment, training, and military activity in general, excludes the physical capability to launch an attack and conduct large-scale offensive operations."[6]

It must be mentioned that this idea also found support among the official documents approved by NATO. In the statement on conventional arms, approved by the Brussels session of the NATO Council (March 1988), the aims of this alliance were formulated as follows:

— the establishment of a reliable and stable balance of conventional forces at reduced levels;

— eliminating imbalances that threaten stability and security;

— eliminating, as a preliminary step, the possibility of a surprise attack and of conducting large-scale offensive operations.[7]

Support for these aims was confirmed once again in the report: "The All-Encompassing Conception of Arms Control and Disarmament," approved by the heads of state of NATO at the fortieth anniversary session of the NATO Council in Brussels, May 1989. Of course, all of this does not mean that NATO has renounced its doctrine of nuclear deterrence; in fact, support for deterrence has also been confirmed in these same documents. However, the overall congruence of declared aims creates the necessary political base on which to rely when devising and implementing practical steps to bolster strategic stability and reduce the level of military confrontation.

Obviously, transforming such new and unusual political ideas into practical recommendations for reducing the quantities of troops and weapons, and for changing the structure and deployment of armed forces as well as the accepted military-strategic conceptions and methods of training and preparing personnel, poses exceptional difficulty and requires answers to very non-traditional questions. For instance, what is an army that is incapable of carrying out a major offensive operation and what do we need such an army for? What will be, in general, the tasks faced by the armed forces once the new concepts of defensive sufficiency have been adopted and implemented? What meaning will the notion of military victory have under these new conditions? The list of similar questions that have yet to be answered goes on and on.

However, despite the novelty of the underlying approach and ideas, the problem of limiting the capabilities for aggression and of reducing offensive capabilities of military arsenals is itself not unprecedented in the international political and negotiating arena. The resolution of July 23, 1932 that completed the first phase of the tasks of the World Conference on Disarmament in Geneva declared "that the fundamental goal will be the reduction of offensive means."[8] It is useful to recall that even if the Soviet Union at that time advocated general and complete disarmament as the most effective way of achieving that goal, it was nevertheless the first country to officially suggest, at the Preparatory Commission in 1928, "the complete liquidation of the most aggressive types of arms."[9] Thus, contemporary ideas have quite deep historical roots.

It should be mentioned that at the time similar ideas were expressed by the American leadership as well. In particular, the U.S. President Roosevelt in his message on problems of disarmament, on May 20, 1933 wrote that "If all the countries agree to completely give up the deployment and employment of arms needed for a successful attack, then the defense would automatically become impregnable and the borders and sovereignty of each country will be guaranteed. The primary goal of the Conference on Disarmament must be the complete elimination of all offensive arms."[10]

The experience of the Geneva Conference on Disarmament (1932-1934) showed, however, that it is extremely difficult to single out the purely offensive elements in the structures of the armed forces of both sides. Nevertheless, in the new political atmosphere, at present, bearing in mind the experience accumulated from past mistakes and lost opportunities, it is quite possible to solve many of the problems that seemed insurmountable in the past.

Is it possible to defend with a sword and to attack with a shield — or what is the absence of capability for surprise attack and a large-scale offensive?

Proposals concerning the reduction of specific types of arms that have been presented by NATO and WTO in the course of the Vienna talks, can hardly be regarded as a final version of military postures that guarantee the realization of ideas of defensive sufficiency. The problems of assigning a strictly defensive orientation to the armed forces and to principles of military organization of the sides still demand a detailed, methodological elaboration.

The basic political goals declared by the sides, as already noted, are to eliminate the possibility of launching a surprise attack (with brief warning), to substantially reduce capabilities for carrying out large-scale offensive operations, and to attain an unquestionable emphasis on both sides of defensive capabilities. It is evident that all of these goals can and must be accomplished at considerably lower levels of military confrontation, which would lead to the strengthening of military-strategic stability.

In the longer term, goals should probably be to find a stable system of military interaction between the sides that ideally would permit the abandonment of the concept of nuclear deterrence by means of greater reliance on non-nuclear means. In the nearer term the goal should be to significantly raise the "nuclear threshold." The new view on the concept of deterrence is already being worked out. A Soviet diplomat, E. T. Agayev, figuratively called it "deterrence of attack." "Uniquely contemporary deterrence," he writes, "is defensive deterrence. And its pre-conditions, even if only intellectual, already exist." The point is to "consciously arrange a stalemated situation for any aggression in peacetime, so as to make any surprise attack objectively impossible."[11]

No doubt, on the way to creating a model to guarantee military security and stability, some intermediate steps are possible. Realistically speaking, we must accept that nuclear weapons and the concept of deterrence connected with them will continue to exist for a long time. However, that should not inhibit us from searching for more stable models of military confrontation, founded on completely different principles from those of an absurd competition in increasing offensive potentials.

Mikhail Gorbachev spoke about this in his speech in Strasbourg: "We are examining the elimination of nuclear arms as a step by step process. And the part of the distance that separates us from the complete destruction of nuclear weapons the Europeans can walk together, without renouncing their respective positions: the USSR remaining true to its nuclear-free ideals, the West — to the concept of minimal deterrence."[12]

And thus, from the political-military point of view the acceptable goal for both sides is to increase military-strategic stability by reducing the offensive capabilities of their military potentials. Of course this requires a clear definition of criteria to evaluate offensive capability. With this in mind, we are especially interested in those structural components of the armed forces and those types of weapons that must be considered first.

It is extremely difficult, if not impossible, to divide components of the armed forces and the types of weapons, into either strictly offensive or defensive. Back in 1932 the famous English expert General J. Fuller noted that "all armaments, by their nature, must be suitable for aggression. Consequently, the problem needs to be resolved in the case of a particular form of aggression. In that respect, some types of weapons possess a considerably greater offensive potential than others."[13] These reflections can also be applied to various types of units and formations.

To answer the question of what elements in the structures of today's armed forces and what type of weapons determine the offensive capabilities of modern armies, it is essential to specify a number of qualitative parameters, the combination of which will permit judgements about capabilities for a successful surprise-attack or a large-scale offensive. Here again, as previously, a short historical excursion into the given problem can prove useful.

In his works of 1923 and 1926, General Fuller formulated seemingly obvious rules of conduct that govern a hypothetical engagement between two unarmed opponents. In order to defeat the enemy one must get close to him, attack him, and finally prevent him from resorting to possible retaliatory actions.

To translate this into language corresponding to the level of development of military technology at that time, we would say that the main qualitative parameters necessary for the successful conduct of offensive military actions are: high mobility, high protection and firepower. Thus, those types of arms in which these parameters are all present would have been considered predominantly offensive.

Despite all the differences in the technological levels of the equipment of armies from the 1920s and 1930s with that of today, similar evaluations have not lost their relevance even today. This confirms once again the accuracy and timeliness of conclusions made long ago by such famous theoreticians of military art as Clausewitz and Jomini. The latter, in particular, remarked that new weapons "reform the practice but not the principle of the conduct of military actions." This basic assumption found confirmation subsequently. During the pre-war period, American theoreticians E. Dupuy and George Eliot wrote: "It can be said with assurance that contemporary weapons and methods have not changed the fundamental principles that served the greatest generals of all times, even though the methods of their employment have significantly changed."[14]

Thus, to guarantee the success of a major offensive it is necessary to have the units and formations, and also the types of weapons, that simultaneously combine:

— high mobility;

— high firepower; and

— relative invulnerability.

These qualities must of course be treated with regard to the modern level of development of military technology. The notion of mobility includes the ability to transport troops and high-firepower weapons quickly and efficiently, as well as the capability of striking deep into the enemy's zone of defense without a preliminary redeployment and concentration of firepower. One must preserve the requisite density of fire on account of the increased range and accuracy of modern weapons (in particular, tactical surface-to-surface missiles and air-to-surface missiles).

High firepower in general can be defined as the ability to quickly and accurately deliver explosive potential sufficient to destroy a hardened target at the given point. This general definition can be applied to the current as well as to the prospective means of attack, irrespective of the physical principles upon which they are based — be it artillery, various types of missiles, or directed energy weapons.

Invulnerability implies a degree of protection of manpower as well as the means of attack used in the offensive operation. It is achieved primarily by a combination of two parameters: maneuverability, and the quality of the means of active and passive defense as they are applied to weapon systems. Thus, if a tank's invulnerability is determined above all by the quality of its armor, that of a plane depends on its speed and ability to use electronic and infrared countermeasures.

Within the structure of a modern army, this combination of qualitative parameters is found in tank and mechanized units, landing assault and airmobile units, paratroopers, and tactical strike aviation, that is, all the branches of the air force that possess aircraft having the capability to attack ground targets. By types of weapons, this above all includes tanks, self-propelled, large-caliber, armored artillery, armored troop carriers and fighting vehicles, surface-to-surface missiles with ranges over fifty kilometers, and attack helicopters and strike aircraft for tactical aviation.

Observe that five out of the six mentioned types of weapons have already been included in one form or another in the proposals made at the Vienna talks.

Considering the intricacy of the problems before the participants in these negotiations, it may be worthwhile to recall to both the positive experiences acquired at the Geneva Conference on Disarmament and also the miscalculations that were made there — especially since today we are already well aware of the scale of the price one has to pay for such mistakes. Thus, in particular, at the

Conference, the sides repeatedly emphasized their basic agreement on the necessity of "limiting large-caliber mobile artillery."[15]

As for tanks, at the plenary session eight delegations including Germany, Italy, and the USSR suggested their complete prohibition, owing to the manifestly offensive character of such type of arms.[16] Later, this proposal was supported in the General Commission by the U.S. and Great Britain, but, after a more detailed working-through of the idea in the ground forces commission, significant disagreements emerged: Great Britain considered all tanks weighing more than twenty-five tons to be offensive, whereas France would apply only to those heavier than seventy tons. "But war," the Soviet specialists A. Kokoshin and V. Zubok observed, "prepared irrefutable counterarguments." Within eight years, in May 1940, German mobile units composed primarily of light tanks, with air support from bombers, circumvented the Maginot Line, broke into France and cornered the Franco-British forces by the sea under Dunkirk.[17]

And so it may be useful to remind the opponents of the idea of a "zero option for tanks," suggested in the recently published works of V. Shlykov,[18] that it wasn't long ago when this type of plan, heretical as it may seem to some today, was the official position of several countries, even if only for a short time. The problem of military aviation was also discussed at the Geneva Conference — of course in correspondence with its level of development at that time, without separating strike aircraft from air-defense interceptors. Nevertheless it was noted in the documents of the air force commission that "the most dangerous aircraft for national defense may be planes with a capacity to strike land targets with any types of arms."[19]

In general, as noted later by the American researcher G. Eliot, "an airplane, in its essence and by virtue of all its features is an offensive weapon. It is wonderfully suited for guaranteeing surprise, and thus secures the superiority of the side that possesses the initiative. It presents an even greater threat when used as part of a plan in which its use in the correct place at the correct time, as accurately calculated by competent staff, can support an attack being carried out by other means and by the delivery of strikes at a time and place unforeseen by the opponent."[20]

Although the mandate of the ongoing Vienna talks includes troops and weapons deployed from the Atlantic to the Urals, it will be relevant to mention here certain judgments reached at the conference in Geneva and outside it, with respect to naval arms. Although at the conference itself the U.S. delegation adhered to the view that "the division into offensive and defensive is inapplicable to naval arms," even then, as later, famous Western specialists, including Americans, expressed more distinct and keen views. For example, the above-mentioned American specialists Dupuy and Eliot wrote: "It is necessary to keep in mind that a fleet is above all an offensive weapon. It acts offensively even while performing a strategically defensive mission."

Moreover, while evaluating the role of naval bases, these authors came to the conclusion that "even if the sole purpose of the naval bases is to safeguard naval operations in a particular area of the ocean, by their essence they can be used for offensive purposes, unlike other stationary ground-based fortifications."[21] These thoughts are worth considering today by the American side when considering the scale and influence of Western naval superiority on the correlation of forces between the Warsaw Pact and NATO. Of course, at today's level of excessive ground forces in both alliances the influence of the naval component on the general balance is relatively small. However, as the ground forces and ground-based weapons are being reduced, the naval factor will steadily grow. This is particularly true if we consider the current and foreseen capabilities of navies to attack targets deep inside the continent from the sea (using on-deck aviation, and highly accurate means of attack capable of long-range operations — for example, sea-launched cruise missiles).

But let us return from the problems of the near future to the problems of today. Having defined the types of units and weapons that warrant first priority when carrying out drastic cuts in the offensive capabilities of the two sides' military potentials, it is useful to conduct a systematization of those instruments that can be used today to attain specific political-military goals. Such a systematization is even more useful because it allows us to present the whole spectrum of available means, not being artificially limited to one, however important and effective it may be.

In particular this pertains to the traditional and — from the standpoint of negotiations — understandable concentration on reductions in and of themselves. Despite the significance of this process, it must not be forgotten that reductions of arms and armies are not the goal of the political process, but simply a means of attaining it, and far from the only means. Furthermore, reductions that are unsound in method will not necessarily strengthen, and in fact may undermine, military strategic stability and decrease the security of both sides. Thus, what are the means that can promote the mutual elimination of the capability for a surprise attack and for large-scale offensive operations? It seems that they can be lumped into six major areas:

1. *Reduction of troops and weapons* remains one of the most effective instruments, especially if the cuts are carried out in the offensive elements of the two sides' forces. Therefore, to strengthen stability, the reduction of troops and weapons must be applied predominantly to the types of units and categories of weapons that were listed earlier.

2. *Disengagement* of the most destabilizing elements in the armed forces of the sides. This implies the creation of zones (above all in regions along the NATO-Warsaw Pact divide in Europe) with low levels of the troops and

weapons that could be used for a large-scale offensive. This removal of destabilizing units and types of arms would not mean the total demilitarization of the border regions. "Military vacuums" as such could easily represent a significant destabilizing and, in some cases, provocative factor. On the contrary, what would be created are zones with a defensively oriented structure of armed forces on both sides. Along with limited numbers of units and weapon systems suited for counteroffensive operations, the zones would be filled with "barrier" or "obstructive" forces, which could be used to defend certain regions but would be organically incapable of large-scale offensive operations.

With both military (including military-geographical) and political factors in mind, such zones could be created not only in Central Europe but also in other regions where the possibility of a surprise attack or large-scale offensive operations is most worrisome. The creation of such zones must be accompanied by a particularly intensive and strict system of verification.

3. *Structural reorganization* of the armed forces toward a defense-oriented posture. For example: reducing the proportion of highly mobile assault units in the armed forces, or changing the structure of these units in a way that would reduce their offensive capability; and reducing the number of tanks or tank battalions in a motorized rifle division. In essence, the main elements of such a structural reorganization are reflected in the unilateral steps that have already been initiated by the USSR and other numbers of the WTO. As has been noted by the Chief of the Soviet General Staff, Army General M. A. Moiseyev, "a large number of tanks (forty percent from motorized rifle divisions and twenty percent from tank divisions) are being removed" from Soviet army divisions on the territory of our allies.[22]

4. *Redeployment* of the most destabilizing units and types of weapons from the NATO-Warsaw Pact front line back into the depth of national territories, at a distance, say, that would exclude a sizable increase of strength within a one-day period. Similar methods are partially related to disengagement, since the organization of zones of reduced concentration of attack units and offensive arms naturally requires their redeployment from these critical regions.

5. *Dismantling the offensive infrastructure*, which implies the elimination from border zones between NATO and the WTO of facilities and equipment that are essential to supply offensive units with ammunition, fuel, mobile bridging equipment, etc.

6. *Organization of a system of confidence-building measures and verification* will include permanent air surveillance of particularly significant sectors and on-site inspections, on both a challenge basis and continually. For example, the headquarters of counteroffensive units located in the border zones of NATO and WTO or other areas subject to mutual verification could have observers from the opposite side, on a permanent basis at the level of a brigade or division.

Obviously, to attain genuinely stable, non-offensive military postures with large reductions in opposing forces, one must use all available means, finding their optimal combination at each phase. The proposed methodological base presents some specific requirements regarding the character of the reductions, which in addition to all the other requirements must conform to accepted strategic and operational-strategic concepts. The problem of retaining a counteroffensive potential will have to be reassessed, along with the concept of "military victory" and the nature of political and military problems, which can be solved through the use of military force — on the strategic, operational and tactical scale.[23]

The question of the size of the counteroffensive potential permitted to each side is especially important, since it is here that the ideas of non-offensive defense clearly contradict traditional military dogma that defense alone is incapable of guaranteeing a military victory. The maximum that one can attain with purely defensive actions is a military stalemate. "In case of war," wrote G. Eliot, "be it offensive or defensive, the desired results may only be obtained with offensive operations. History does not provide us with a single example where a complete victory was achieved purely through the defense."[24]

Obviously, there is logic in these arguments. However, the principles of non-offensive defense do not imply the complete elimination of counteroffensive potential but only the limitation of its operational scale to what is needed to re-establish the national borders in case of an invasion from outside. Accordingly, the notion of military victory is possible only on an operational and tactical scale, but is excluded at the strategic level.

It is interesting to note that a similar remark was made by V. Shlykov in his recent interview in the magazine *Mezhdunarodnaya zhizn*. In particular, he stressed that, in his view, armed forces in contemporary circumstances must be prepared not to rebuff a massive surprise attack but rather to keep any war that breaks out at the lowest possible level. When asked whether that meant the aim of the defensive strategy does not consist of a military victory, he replied: "The goal lies in returning to the status-quo as fast as possible and in depriving the enemy of any incentive to conduct a long-lasting, exhaustive war."[25]

Perhaps the sole point open to criticism is the contrast between (1) returning the situation to the existing status quo and (2) achieving military victory. Of course it is not simple to break away from familiar stereotypes. However, the joint transition to defense-oriented military structures in practice suggests that the re-establishment of the status quo and the cessation of conflict at the lowest possible level in themselves will signify a military victory for the defender. Thus, it is not correct to say that victory is not the goal of a defensive war — it is simply that the whole concept of "victory" has been radically redefined.

Therefore, the following elements become very significant as parameters for future military postures: those that define the scale of reductions, the structure and the deployment of the retained counteroffensive potential, which, on the one hand, would exclude its use in a surprise incursion or in large-scale offensive operations on the territory of states that are neutral or belong to other alliances and, on the other hand, would ensure absolute confidence that there is sufficient force remaining to destroy the enemy forces if they invade the defended territory.

In practical approaches to the reduction of troops and weapons, specifically those that are most offensive in character, it is possible to delineate three main groups of recommendations. The first two assume reductions, either symmetrical or asymmetrical, of agreed upon numbers or percentages of specified types of units and weapons, the third calls for the acceptance of common ceilings for specified unit and weapon types which the sides pledge to reach during the arms reductions process.[26]

The disadvantage of the first two methods is that they require a detailed comparison of the current potentials of general-purpose forces. This is a very difficult and time-consuming problem. A rigorous comparison of the military potential of the opposing sides requires, in addition to the quantitative and qualitative analysis of the armed forces and arms, consideration of parameters that cannot be measured numerically.

In this respect, the method of common ceilings is significantly simpler, especially if NATO and WTO agree upon numerically equal levels and there is no need for compensating the quantitative superiority of one side with the qualitative superiority of the other through the use of various parameter comparison scales.

In essence, this approach was already accepted by the two sides at the Vienna talks with regard to tanks, infantry combat vehicles, and artillery and later to aircraft and helicopters.

At the same time, the drawback of the third method is that equal numbers of troops and specific weapons do not mean equality of the combat capability of the parties. It is apparent, however, that the most acceptable method is still that of setting general and identical ceilings, with the support of a range of other political-military instruments mentioned above that can compensate for the deficiencies of the method. The ceilings must be established for key elements that define offensive capabilities. They should be set at such low levels that even with the inherent inequality and asymmetries that will emerge in the offensive capabilities, neither side will have the potential to launch a surprise attack or a large-scale offensive.

A possible stable configuration of WTO-NATO general purpose forces after radical reductions from the Atlantic to the Urals

Let us take a look at how this approach could be transformed into a military structure of opposing forces in a critical region of Central Europe.

The line of direct contact between the WTO and NATO in this region extends for 780 km. According to the proposal of former State Secretary of the Ministry of Defense of the FRG, A. von Bulow, it can be divided into thirteen defensive sectors each with a frontage of 60 km.[27] The entire border strip is designated as a special zone with a depth of 150 km. This creates thirteen defensive sectors of 60 x 150 km in frontage and depth respectively. Inside the 150 km zone it is advisable to create three subzones each 50 km deep.

Now we can suggest the composition of exclusively defensive and counter-offensive forces for each of the thirteen defensive zones. The numerical ceilings and space concentrations will primarily concern the counteroffensive potential. Each of the thirteen basic defensive sectors can contain one motorized rifle or tank division or an equivalent force. The diagrams show a scheme with nine motorized rifle or four tank divisions.

The first subzone (0-50 km from the border) of each defensive sector can have up to one tank or motorized rifle battalion from its division force; the second (50-100 km) — up to one tank regiment or motorized rifle regiment and the third (100-150 km) — the remaining divisional units.

In the second subzone the deployment of a certain agreed upon number of tactical non-nuclear surface-to-surface missiles with a range of up to fifty kilometers and MLRSs (Mulitiple Launch Rocket Systems) can be permitted. In the third subzone — a strictly limited number of large-caliber (over 100 mm) armored self-propelled artillery and armored attack helicopters would be allowed. Also allowed in this third subzone would be mobile bridging equipment within the limits of regular divisional (tank or motorized rifle) level. The number of infantry fighting vehicles should be limited in the 150 km zone to the number of these vehicles in nine motorized rifle divisions and four tank divisions.

The limited number of highly mobile counteroffensive units permitted for deployment in the border zone completely changes the issue of their movement within the zone and of the allowable limits of concentration of these units. Within the parameters of the suggested scheme, the following principles can be used to determine the limits of concentration.

The standard area unit could be a strip equal in its dimensions to two subzone elements, i.e., a rectangle 120 km wide and 50 km deep. The formula for the maximum concentration of counteroffensive troops and weapons could be as follows. At any given moment this control strip could be placed in any point of a subzone so as to permit their borders to overlap, and at that time this control strip should not contain more than three units having counteroffensive capability and of the type permitted within this subzone, e.g., the first — up to three battalions; the second — up to three regiments; the third — up to three motorized rifle or tank divisions.

Within the described thirteen Central European border sectors there could be deployed defensive forces not structurally related to the counteroffensive potential as realized by the motorized rifle or tank division; these units could be established under different organizational and mobilization principles (for instance territorial forces), with substantially different training principles and with significantly less stringent numerical limits. These "barrier" units would not be armed with tanks, APCs, self-propelled large-caliber armored artillery, etc.

The first subzone would deploy barrier forces of "light infantry." These would be permitted to be armed with small arms, both stationary and mobile Guided Anti-Tank Weapons (ATGWs), towed anti-tank guns (up to 120 mm), stationary air defense systems and C^3I systems.[28]

The role of the last category of military equipment under these new conditions would be greatly increased. Receiving constant, adequate information about the military activity of the opposite side in the region of direct contact, and proper safe communications with one's own units is one of the necessities of insuring stability. Therefore, in the border areas it is not only counterproductive to limit these systems, but would serve a useful purpose to forbid, near the border, the deployment and use of Electronic Counter Measures (ECM) equipment for the purpose of disrupting the communications and monitoring systems of the opposing side.

In all of the following calculations the author, at this stage of the study, has almost not touched on the issue of how many tanks exist in any particular East European country or in the military districts of the USSR at the present time. This work proposes their reduction to levels significantly below the present levels of NATO or the WTO.

The suggested structure for counteroffensive potentials in the Central European zone can be supplemented by subregional and general European ceilings, in particular, a limitation on tank forces. In the border strip (780 x 150 km) the tank force could be defined as follows:

4 tank divisions x 300 machines = 1,200 tanks.

The tanks in motorized rifle divisions must be reduced to give the divisions a more defensive structure, e.g., down to 140 machines. Then 9 motorized rifle divisions x 140 machines = 1,260 tanks.

$$\Sigma = 1,200 + 1,260 = 2,460 \text{ tanks}$$

This would require each side in the Central European border zone of 780 x 150 km not to climb above a 2,500 tank limit. Another 3,000 machines could be deployed by each side in a rear area of the Central European zone.

In the Warsaw Pact, this would include: East Czechoslovakia, Hungary, Poland, and the military districts of the Baltic, Byelorussia, Carpathians, Moscow, Volga-Urals. In NATO, it would be: the remaining territory of the Federal Republic of Germany, Denmark, Great Britain, the Netherlands, Belgium, France and Luxembourg. This condition could be reinforced by placing limitations of the maximum concentrations of tanks and tank units in the specified zones. The "zonal approach" to the problem of reduction in armed forces and conventional arms is used by Soviet specialists from the Institute of World Economy and International Relations.[29]

With some modifications to these methods, an approach could be developed to create more stable military structures on the southern and northern flanks of NATO and WTO. The southern region poses the most difficult geostrategic situation. The USSR and the WTO countries have common borders with NATO countries in the Transcaucasus, a land border between the USSR and Turkey, and in the Balkans, between Bulgaria, Greece and Turkey.

Considering the fact that the USSR shares an even longer border with Iran, with whom it has had an agreement from 1921, and the difficult terrain, a zonal approach similar to one in Central Europe would prove more troublesome and may not even be useful. Still, it is possible to isolate a 360 km-long corridor within the Transcaucasus military district which borders on Turkey.

It seems feasible in this region to establish something similar to the first subzone of Central Europe. This would include a depth of fifty kilometers and a limit of no more than six tank and motorized rifle battalions deployed simultaneously and a space concentration limit as given earlier with a total limit on tanks not to exceed 150 in the subzone. In total: the mobile counteroffensive forces of the USSR and Turkey in this region could be limited to a total of 5 motorized rifle divisions and one tank division, or:

$$(5 \times 140) + (1 \times 300) = 700 + 300 = 1,000 \text{ tanks}$$

Accounting for the extended border with Iran, the Transcaucasus military district would be permitted an additional counteroffensive potential equal to one tank or two motorized rifle divisions, or roughly another 300 tanks which would be deployed at a great distance from the Turkish border. Turkey in turn could balance this with additional equipment in its southern Asian territory. From this we get a total of 1,300 tanks within the Transcaucasus military district.

On the southern flank of the WTO, Bulgaria shares borders with Greece and Turkey. The land border stretches for approximately 500 km. For geostrategic reasons the zonal approach in this area (primarily Bulgarian-Greek border) would be difficult to implement. It would be worthwhile to isolate the northern territory of Greece and the western part of Turkey with the permissible limit on tanks at 1,000 and the geographical breakdown as follows: 650 tanks in northern Greece, and 350 in western Turkey. This tank potential would be balanced by the tank potential of Bulgaria (1,000 tanks).

Greece's remaining tank potential would be balanced by Romania (550 vehicles), while the Turkish potential (excluding that which was allotted previously for Soviet and Bulgarian borders) would allow for another 1,000 tanks to be balanced by the tank potential of the Odessa military district (another 1,000 tanks). Thus, the tank forces on the southern flank for both sides (Bulgarian, Romanian, the Soviet military districts of the Transcaucasus and Odessa, and Greece and Turkey) would be as follows:

$$\Sigma_{WTO} = N_{TC} + N_O + N_B + N_R$$

Where:

N_{TC} - number of tanks in the Transcaucasus military district

N_O - number of tanks in the Odessa military district

N_B - number of tanks in Bulgaria

N_R - number of tanks in Romania

$$\Sigma_{WTO} = 1,300 + 1,000 + 550 + 1,000 = 3,850 \text{ tanks}$$

$$\Sigma_{NATO} = N_G + N_T$$

N_G - number of tanks in Greece, 650 + 550 = 1,200

(N. Greece) (S. Greece)

N_T - number of tanks in Turkey, 1,000 + 350 + 300 + 1,000 = 2,650

(Sov. Border) (Bulgar Border) (Ctrl. Asia)

$$\Sigma_{NATO} = 1,200 + 2,650 = 3,850 \text{ tanks}$$

Under this scheme both sides are left with "southern rear areas." On the NATO side these are Spain, Portugal and Italy; for the WTO, Kiev and North Caucasus military districts. At this point it would be appropriate to introduce a certain asymmetry to the NATO-WTO balance, taking into consideration the significant imbalance on the northern flank, where as stated by the West German expert A. von Bulow, 115 Norwegian tanks confront 2,300 tanks deployed on the territory of the Leningrad military district.[30] Of course, it should be recognized that the USSR has taken some unilateral steps to reduce its military potential in the northwestern part of the country. As stated on March 20, 1989 by Eduard Shevardnadze at a Moscow meeting with the Minister of Foreign Affairs of Finland P. Paasilo, in recent years the USSR has removed from the northwestern part of the country a total of 700 tanks and at present there are no large tank formations deployed in the area.[31]

The presence in a future defensive structure of regional imbalances on the flanks does not, in my opinion, signify a rejection of equal, overall, European ceilings for NATO and WTO.

In regards to this issue I would like to suggest the following distribution of tanks. The Kiev and North Caucasus military districts would have 1,500 tanks and Spain, Portugal and Italy, 2,050 tanks. In turn, the Leningrad military district would have 650 tanks and Norway, 100.

This gives a total ceiling on tanks for Europe as follows:

$$\Sigma_{WTO} = 2{,}500 + 3{,}000 + 3{,}850 + 1{,}500 + 650 = 11{,}500$$

$$\Sigma_{NATO} = 2{,}500 + 3{,}000 + 3{,}850 + 2{,}050 + 100 = 11{,}500$$

A similar approach could be used for other elements of the counteroffensive land forces, infantry fighting vehicles, APCs and large-caliber self-propelled (SP) artillery.

The distribution of tanks among the European states and Soviet European military districts is shown in Table 1.

This concrete scheme was worked out in 1989, before dramatic internal changes occurred in the countries of Eastern Europe. In this regard the question arises about how realistic it is today to consider a model of arranging defensive military structures for NATO and the Warsaw Pact along the borders of the FRG, GDR, and Czechoslovakia. First of all, the proposed scheme implies the preservation of a significantly smaller quantity of offensive weapons and types of units needed for a large-scale offensive than at present in the designated Central European region. In any case, such changes would serve the interests of all countries.

We should bear in mind that the problem of eliminating offensive weapons, as proposed in the above-mentioned cable from President Roosevelt in 1933, has not in any way lost its urgency at the present time. The mutual elimination, particularly by the most powerful countries, of capabilities for a surprise attack and large-scale offensive will be the basis for safeguarding military-strategic parity, irrespective of the continued existence of one or another military alliance.

As far as the near future of NATO and the Warsaw Pact is concerned, the USSR has supported the dissolution of the two alliances on a mutual basis; but it nonetheless appears that, in the current situation of fundamental changes in the East European countries, the interests of all states would be served by the preservation of these alliances and the restructuring of them away from being political-military organizations to political-military ones, and perhaps eventually to being purely political organizations. The mechanisms and structures of the alliances can be used as an internal means of stabilizing the political situation in Europe and the world as a whole.

Possible ways to stabilize the balance in tactical aviation of the European continent

Theoretically, the reduction of offensive capability in the combat potential of tactical aviation is more difficult than the establishment of non-offensive structures for the land forces. The difficulty has many explanations. Primarily, the inherent high mobility of aviation makes it difficult to confine it to a given region. This difficulty, however, can be overcome if the deployment data of all units of land-based tactical aviation is available and inspection of air bases is permitted.

A frequent objection in the West to the inclusion of tactical aviation in the category of offensive weapons is that aircraft cannot seize and hold territory, which, it is claimed, is the normal goal of aggression. This is an obvious fact; however, it should be noted that, with the proper use of tactical aviation, it is possible to seize and hold territory using substantially fewer tanks and motorized rifle units.

Also, recent experience shows that the seizure of territory is not always an immediate goal of aggression. There are situations where the destruction or severe damage of vitally important targets of the opposing side is the goal of an aggressor's political and military policy. These are the tactics which the United States used against Libya. In this case, tactical aviation becomes the most effective means of aggression.

Tactical aviation can obviously be divided into a defensive type (air defense interceptors) and an offensive type (fighter-bombers, attack aircraft) which due to their guidance equipment and armaments are suited for ground attack.

This distinction is often difficult to make because (particularly in NATO) aircraft and their crews are equipped and trained to carry out both missions. In the Soviet Union and other WTO states the same tactical aircraft are used with modifications for interception and ground attack missions.

At the same time, there is a serious difference between NATO and the WTO regarding tactical aviation. The readjustment of aircraft and the replacement or retraining of crews from interceptor to ground attack missions in the WTO would be a long process requiring the utilization of special facilities, at best a few months. The same conversion by NATO can be done at the air base and requires a few hours (replacement of electronic guidance modules and hook-up of air-to-surface missiles); furthermore, no replacement crew is required.

There also exists a historical difference in the philosophy of tactical aviation between NATO and WTO. The West traditionally prefers heavy multifunctional and more expensive aircraft; where the USSR has for a long time preferred relatively simpler, specialized types of aircraft.

All of these differences demonstrate the difficulty involved in the problem. Yet they also highlight the fact that without its resolution it would be difficult, perhaps impossible, to speak of stable non-offensive military postures. Therefore, as a first step towards a resolution of this problem, let us examine some suggested methodologies. These could be used as a foundation for the development of a mutual understanding of the problem between NATO and WTO.

The most easily acceptable and presentable is the method of common ceilings. To account for the quantitative and structural asymmetries in the tactical aviation of the sides, it is logical, in my opinion, to use two parameters:

— quantity of the aircraft;

— the total combat payload, deliverable at a certain range.

The second parameter is of vital importance for determining the realistic combat capability of tactical aviation and its role in the development of large-scale offensives. Logically it corresponds to parameters such as the throw weight of an ICBM or SLBM, whose fifty percent reduction is envisaged by the future agreement on a reduction of strategic offensive nuclear weapons. This parameter in strategic missiles disturbed the U.S. and it is understandable that the Soviet side feels the same in regard to this parameter in tactical aviation. The necessity of limiting the combat payload of tactical aviation is mentioned in the proposals developed by the American expert R. Hatchett.[32]

Of course, the payload of an aircraft is intimately tied to its operating range, and depends on its in-flight refueling capability and flight path. A flight through organized air defenses with its requisite maneuvering and low-level flight will require increased fuel consumption and lower the operating range of the aircraft. It is, however, preferable to determine the operating range by a generally accepted formula which does not factor in the in-flight refueling capability of the aircraft. The range is, in this case, determined by the optimal flight path under a given combat payload.

In this case, a reduction in the offensive capabilities of tactical aviation could consist of the following phases:

1. Determination of strike aircraft within tactical aviation, i.e., the aircraft with ground attack capability. The multi-purpose aircraft that can be readjusted for ground attack mission by replacement of guidance systems and on-board weapons at their permanent bases would also be categorized as strike aircraft.

   Those aircraft which perform interception missions and require extensive modification at special facilities in order to be readjusted for ground attack would be considered interceptors. In the first phase the mutually acceptable limit for tactical strike aviation would be set a "M" aircraft.

2. The agreed upon number of ground attack aircraft would establish a basis for similar to the following: if the allowable number of land-based strike aircraft of each side does not exceed "M," then the allowable number of interceptors for the opposite side is not to exceed "KM," where "K" is the coefficient of interceptors permitted for side A per one strike aircraft for side B.

   For example, if the agreed limit for strike aircraft, after reductions, is 1,000 per side and K = 2, then the allowable interceptor limit is 2,000 (2,000 = 2 x 1,000). If one of the sides reduces its strike aircraft to below the set limit, then the opposite side must also reduce its interceptors.

Both of these phases could be supplemented by determinations of the total combat payload of all 3,000 tactical aircraft, i.e., both sides would be restricted to 3,000 tactical aircraft with a combat load not to exceed "L" thousand tons delivered within an operational range of 1,000 km. This criteria could be divided into two parts; total combat payload delivered within a range of 500 km ($L_{0.5}$) and 1,000 km (L_1) could be compared.

The above rule for the reduction of tactical aviation and its structural changes would, in general, look as follows:

Each side would be allowed to deploy up to "M" strike aircraft, no more than "KM" interceptors without ground attack capability, and the total combat payload delivered within an operational range of 500 km would not exceed $L_{0.5}$ thousand tons, for those with an operational range of 1,000 km it would not exceed L_1 thousand tons.

These conditions could be supplemented by a number of strategic interceptors, which would be determined on the basis of quantity of strategic bombers permitted to be deployed after the fifty percent reductions in strategic nuclear weapons, i.e.,

$$S_{si} = K_{sb} M_{sb}$$

Where:

S_{si} — number of strategic interceptors of one side

K_{sb} — agreed upon number of strategic interceptors per one strategic bomber

M_{sb} — number of strategic bombers left with the other side, after the reduction

This approach does not yet include the Soviet medium-range bombers based in Europe, Soviet land-based naval aviation aircraft and the carrier-based aircraft of the Western countries. Although the carrier-based aircraft are not officially included in the mandate of the Vienna talks, they exist within the NATO-WTO balance in Europe and they have serious influence on the southern and northern flanks. It is relevant to note that the U.S. and its West European allies have roughly 900 carrier-based aircraft, which does not include reconnaissance or ECM aircraft.

The USSR has 52 light, short-range aircraft with combat payload, in my opinion, not exceeding 95 tons.

The combat payload of the 900 aircraft of the NATO countries, delivered within a range of 1,000 km, is approximately 3,200 tons.

The total combat payload of U.S. and West European carrier-based aircraft and the medium-range bomber force of the USAF and France (100 FB-IIIs and Mirage IVs), as I see it, is comparable to the total combat load of all Soviet medium-range bombers and all aircraft of the land-based naval aviation (Tu-16, Tu-22, Tu-22-M).

Of course this approach may produce an objection from the West: not all carrier aircraft should be included in the European balance equation because many aircraft are used for defending the carrier group and not for attacking ground targets, etc. Soviet naval aviation and medium-range bombers, however, are also not all based in Europe and ground-based naval aircraft with their guidance, navigation systems and on-board weapons cannot attack ground targets. Thus, there is sufficient reason to schedule the problem of Soviet naval aviation and medium-range bomber force for a later phase of the reduction and structural changes of tactical aviation.

The quantitative restrictions on tactical aviation can be supplemented by strict on-site inspections of air bases and by placing a ban on permanent deployment of strike aircraft at air bases near the NATO-WTO border, primarily in Central Europe.

Considering the exceptional cost and complexity of modern aircraft, it would be possible to agree not to destroy a percentage of the reduced tactical aircraft but to place them in storage where they would be kept in a partially disassembled state (sealed equipment, removed engines, removed wings, removed landing gear, etc.) under strict mutual control.

New types of weapons, qualitative improvements in arms and stability

The problem of improvement in conventional weapons has a definite influence on the actual combat capability of the forces, on the evolution of operational-strategic and operational-tactical concepts, which dictate their use in the event of an armed conflict.

The massive application of the latest technological advances in the military sphere could bring about a radical shift in offensive capabilities even without a major numerical increase in the armed forces or armaments.

Qualitative improvements of conventional arms create a number of problems. One problem is the development of stable, non-offensive military structures of both sides. Another problem would be the negotiating on limiting and reducing armed forces and conventional arms in Europe. Even an ideally calculated model[33] can be destabilized by a major, one-sided development in the qualitative character and parameters of weapon systems; this increases with the massive infusion of the new types of weapons.

With the present rate of scientific-technological progress, the negotiations on limiting and reducing conventional weapons are always oriented toward the solution of current problems, and at times the solution of yesterday's problems. The mandate for negotiations in Vienna was developed with the present state of the armed forces and arms in mind and the current understanding of the factors determining the offensive capabilities of the sides' combat potential. The time frame of the negotiation process is such that during it the growth of qualitative improvements in conventional arms and their massive distribution could create new, more serious problems for the stability of Europe than a mere numerical imbalance.

From this standpoint, the qualitative factors of weapons become necessary for a proper analysis of the present conventional balance in Europe. This has even more importance in any evaluation of the future condition.

At the same time, the complexity of qualitative problems (especially as they are not yet well understood) makes them politically unappealing. Furthermore, efforts to compensate the technical inferiority of one side by awarding it numerical superiority could greatly drag out the negotiations, and even drive them into a dead end.

Therefore, in my opinion, the present task is to consider, within the future organizations of non-offensive military postures, all political and military-technical mechanisms which could minimize the possibility of upsetting the military-strategic balance that could be reached as a result of substantial reductions, structural reorganization of the armed forces and arms and the reorganization of the process of military build-up.

The more basic point is this. The modern development of equipment and technology, and the comprehension of new political realities, brings us to the necessity of deciding the fundamental problem of separating the scientific-technical progress *in general* from the current automatic process of its implementation in the sphere of the military. And if the process of acquiring new knowledge and the scientific technological progress must develop completely freely, then their military exploitation can and must be limited in correspondence with the principles of consolidating stability. That is, the *application* of any innovation to the military sphere must be evaluated with regard to how it will influence the offensive capabilities of the side which will acquire it and how that will be taken by the opposite side.

We can suggest a theoretical definition of a certain absolutely stable political-military situation, the attainment of which is our ideal.

Introducing this definition will help us evaluate in every concrete case the extent of a possible impact on the stability of the military-strategic equilibrium by a sudden change in qualitative characteristics of existing systems of arms or the arrival of new ones. The value criteria will be extremely simple. The introduction of qualitative changes into the systems of weapons and military technology is permissible only if they offset the existing equilibrium in the direction of making the situation still more stable.

An absolutely stable military-strategic situation is one where, first of all, neither of the sides possess the capability to complete a military aggression with any rational results, and secondly, where each of the sides is convinced of the absence of such a capability on the other side. The latter part of the definition concerns not only the real correlation of power and intentions of the other side but also with an extremely important question of the forming perception within the country the security of its defenses. Forming this perception is of no less importance than the symmetry in combat capabilities of the armed forces of the sides.

In the documents of the League of Nations one can find such evaluations of the perception of military security of a country. "Security is comprised of the absence of any threat of aggression, but there are two ways of judging the absence of that threat. It may be acquired from the objective view of whether the threat exists or from the subjective view, depending on whether the country feels that it is safe. In today's conditions it is not very important that the other countries think of themselves as not being threatened in any way. What matters is that the country itself feels the same."[34]

Taking these evaluations into consideration, we can derive definite conclusions about the character of impacts made on the military-strategic stability by changes in qualitative characteristics of the systems of arms, which could occur in the very near future.

There is a substantial danger to the military-strategic stability in the area of general purpose forces and conventional arms in the possibility of a broad implementation by NATO of the officially accepted FOFA concept and the development of weapon systems within the framework of this concept.[35] Officially FOFA is designed for a scenario in which the WTO launches a large-scale offensive into

Western Europe. In this scenario the WTO assault echelon would require reinforcements from the second echelon and reserve forces. The success of this offensive would depend on the ability to efficiently concentrate and utilize the armor and motorized rifle divisions of the second echelon.

The weapon systems which are to be developed within the framework of the concept are to prevent the concentration and movement to the battle areas of WTO's second echelon forces. This is to be achieved by the destruction of these units at their concentration points, away from the battle zone (up to 400 km or even greater). In this way, FOFA is presented as an exclusively defensive concept. But it is impossible to overlook the fact that given a different hypothetical situation, one in which the roles of aggressor and defender are reversed, these long-range, smart weapons (reconnaissance strike complexes, RSC) substantially enhance the offensive capabilities of their owner.

In the first place, if one side deploys weapon systems which enable it to automatically locate and destroy targets deep in the interior (400 km plus), away from the line of contact, then it is able to concentrate massive firepower without the preliminary concentration of the weapons that produce this firepower. This increases the chances for a successful surprise attack, primarily by the disruption of the opposing sides' C^3I systems.

Furthermore, the development and deployment of these types of weapon systems is contrary to the desire and aim of the reorganization of the military structure into a defensive posture. It is also contrary to achieving a higher level of openness through confidence-building measures which is of prime importance in the areas near the lines of direct contact between NATO and WTO. The normal and natural reaction of the opposite side to the appearance of weapons capable of locating and hitting targets at ranges exceeding 400 km would be a higher level of secrecy in its military activity near the border, greater uncertainty and unpredictability and an overall decrease in the military-strategic stability.

Of course there exist a number of efficient countermeasures against long-range enhanced-accuracy weapons. Still, the competition between these types of weapons and countermeasures against them would most likely be counterproductive to a stable balance.

In the negotiations in Vienna it is reasonable, in my opinion, to avoid a detailed discussion of the comparative, qualitative characteristics of weapon systems. However, it is necessary to predetermine the limits on the qualitative improvements of conventional weapons in the agreements, which the sides will be reaching.

In the long run one could form a list of the qualitative parameters of weapon systems and military technology, abrupt changes in which would not be permissible without previous mutual agreements. In particular, these limits can include the banning of the deployment of any new systems which can quickly and accurately deliver energy potential sufficient to destroy hardened targets deep in the other side's territory without looking at their physical nature (regular artillery, smart missiles or directed energy weapons).

In practice these limits could include the total rejection of surface-to-surface missiles with a range above fifty kilometers. It is the tactical missiles that are to be fitted with artificial intelligence modules which (along with guidance and data transmission systems) will be capable of seeking and destroying mobile and stationary targets.

This limit could be supplemented by forbidding the deployment of such missiles in areas closer than fifty kilometers to the borders of NATO and WTO. It is also possible to set limits on range of similar air-to-surface missiles on strike aircraft, in conjunction with the previously mentioned limits on the basing of aircraft with these weapons.

Perhaps it is already expedient to especially select a complex of measures for exploiting the means of electronic warfare (EW). In front of our eyes EW is turning from combat actions into a means of combat. It is becoming an essential part of combat, a relatively independent, specific form of armed struggle. The questions of inputting C^3I means into strategic stability deserves our particular attention. These means increase the offensive as well as defensive potentials of the sides.

The issue of openness and the predictability of the actions of the opposite side in the sphere of military affairs is of prime importance in ensuring stability. This raises questions of the admissibility of systems with technology of the Stealth class. This issue touches upon weapon systems in all areas — air, land and sea based. In general, the inability to detect and intercept an attacking system creates a situation in which finding stability becomes enormously harder. The deployment of undetectable, offensive weapons virtually guarantees the escalation of any conflict. Such a deployment also forces the other side to make a military response in its own deployments, thus perpetuating the arms race, even in an atmosphere of low overall political tension.

Only taking into consideration the perspective of perfecting the quality of the weapon systems, the character of perception of its deployment by the other side and its responding reaction can one come up with variants of truly stable non-offensive structures. We must also apply these to the whole process of military deployments. Only these variants will guarantee the elimination of not only intentions and motives for using military power, but also physical capabilities to carry out a surprise aggression and a large-scale offensive.

Table I

THE PROPOSED SCHEME OF THE DISTRIBUTION OF TANKS BETWEEN THE COUNTRIES OF NATO AND WTO IN EUROPE

WTO		NATO	
THE CENTRAL ZONE OF IMMEDIATE CONTACT 780 x 150 KM			
East Germany, Czechoslovakia	1,500	West Germany	2,500
THE CENTRAL BASE ZONE			
East Czechoslovakia, Poland and the Military Districts of the USSR: Byelorussia, PriBaltic, PriCarpathian, Moscow, Volga-Urals	3,000	Western West Germany, Denmark, Great Britain, Belgium, Luxembourg and France	3,000
THE SOUTHERN ZONE OF IMMEDIATE CONTACT			
Soviet Military Districts:			
Transcaucasus	1,300	Northern Greece	650
Odessa	1,000	Southern Greece	550
Bulgaria	1,000	Turkey	1,000
Romania	550	Border w/USSR	1,300
		Border w/Bulgaria	350
		Central part of Territory	1,300
Total	**3,850**	**Total**	**3,850**
SOUTHERN BASE ZONE			
Kiev, Northcaucasus Military Districts	1,500	Spain	2,050
NORTHERN FLANK			
Leningrad Military District	650	Norway	100
Total	**11,500**	**Total**	**11,500**

COMPOSITION OF COUNTEROFFENSIVE AND BARRIER FORCES IN THE CONTACT ZONE FOR NATO AND WTO IN CENTRAL EUROPE (FOR ONE SIDE)

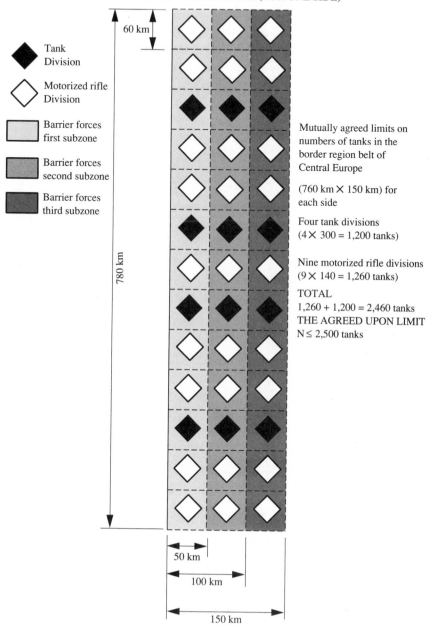

Tank Division

Motorized rifle Division

Barrier forces first subzone

Barrier forces second subzone

Barrier forces third subzone

60 km

780 km

50 km

100 km

150 km

Mutually agreed limits on numbers of tanks in the border region belt of Central Europe

(760 km × 150 km) for each side

Four tank divisions
(4 × 300 = 1,200 tanks)

Nine motorized rifle divisions
(9 × 140 = 1,260 tanks)

TOTAL
1,260 + 1,200 = 2,460 tanks
THE AGREED UPON LIMIT
N ≤ 2,500 tanks

Table 2

POSSIBLE STRUCTURE OF ONE DEFENSIVE SECTOR
IN CENTRAL EUROPE

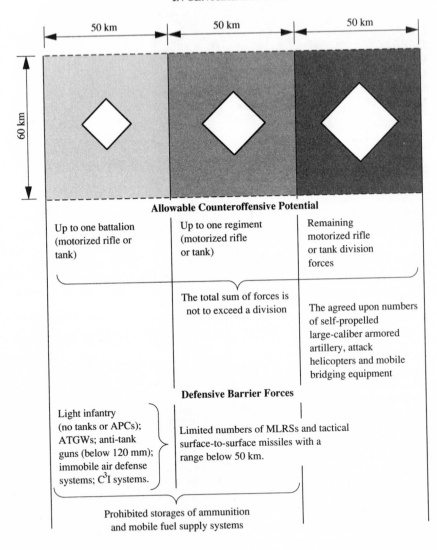

Allowable Counteroffensive Potential

Up to one battalion (motorized rifle or tank)	Up to one regiment (motorized rifle or tank)	Remaining motorized rifle or tank division forces
	The total sum of forces is not to exceed a division	The agreed upon numbers of self-propelled large-caliber armored artillery, attack helicopters and mobile bridging equipment

Defensive Barrier Forces

Light infantry (no tanks or APCs); ATGWs; anti-tank guns (below 120 mm); immobile air defense systems; C^{3}I systems.

Limited numbers of MLRSs and tactical surface-to-surface missiles with a range below 50 km.

Prohibited storages of ammunition and mobile fuel supply systems

Table 3

Notes

1. An extract from this chapter is being published in Ander Boserup and Robert Nield, eds., *The Foundations of Defensive Deterrence* (London: Macmillan Press, 1990). Some material in this chapter also draws from several earlier publications by the author.
2. *Pravda* (March 7, 1989).
3. *Pravda* (May 12, 1989).
4. *Pravda* (May 30, 1989).
5. *Pravda* (May 30, 1987).
6. *Pravda* (July 7, 1989).
7. "Conventional Arms Control: The Way Ahead," Statement issued under the authority of the Heads of States and Governments participating in the Meeting of the North Atlantic Council in Brussels, March 2-3, 1988, *Atlantic News*, no. 1988 (March 4, 1988), pp. 5-9.
8. League of Nations, *Conference for the Reduction and Limitation of Armaments: Conference Documents* 1 (Geneva, December 1932), p. 268.
9. League of Nations, *Records of the Conference for the Reduction and Limitation of Armaments; Series A: Verbatim Records of Plenary Meetings* 1 (Geneva, February 2-July 23, 1932), p. 86.
10. U.S. Department of State, Press Releases, Weekly no. 190, p. 352.
11. Ye. T. Agaev, "A Model of Strategic Stability," *Mezhdunarodnaya zhizn*, no. 4 (1989), pp. 103-111.
12. *Pravda* (July 7, 1989).
13. J.F.C. Fuller, "What is an Aggressive Weapon?" *English Review* 54 (1932), p. 601.
14. R. Ernest Dupuy and George Fielding Eliot, *If War Comes* (New York: Macmillan Company, 1937), p. 37.
15. League of Nations, *Records of the Conference for the Reduction and Limitation of Armaments; Series B: Minutes of the General Commission* 1 (Geneva, February 9-July 23, 1932), 154.
16. League of Nations, *Records of the Conference for the Reduction and Limitation of Armaments; Series B*, p.58.
17. V. Zubok and A. Kokoshin, "Lost Opportunities of 1932?" *Mezhdunarodnaya zhizn*, no. 1 (1989), pp. 132.
18. V. Shlykov, "And Our Tanks Are Fast," *Mezhdunarodnaya zhizn*, no. 9 (1988), pp. 117-129; "Strong Armor," *Mezhdunarodnaya zhizn* (1989), pp. 39-52.
19. League of Nations, *Conference Documents*, p. 246.
20. George Fielding Eliot, "The Offensive Still Gives Victory," *Foreign Affairs* 17 (1938), p. 57.
21. Dupuy and Eliot, *If War Comes*, p. 160.
22. M. Moiseyev, "Soviet Military Doctrine: Implementation of its Defensive Orientation," *Pravda* (March 13, 1989).
23. See A. Kokoshin and V. Larionov, *Confrontation of General Purpose Forces within the Context of Strategic Stability, World Economy and International Relations*, no. 6 (1988), pp. 23-31.
24. Eliot, "The Offensive Still Gives Victory," p. 59.
25. V.V. Shlykov, "Who's Devising Military Strategy?" *Mezhdunarodnaya zhizn*, no. 4 (1989), p. 26.
26. The latter method is used, for example, in the works of a well-known West German expert A. von Muller. He proposed to set in the future military posture on the European continent numerical ceilings for the basic categories of the sides' weapons (10,000 tanks on each side

with a space density of 500 tanks per 100 sq. km; 500 strike aircraft; 500 attack helicopters, etc.) See A. von Muller, *Towards Conventional Stability in Europe*, Commissioned Paper for 38th Pugwash Conference on Science and World Affairs, Dagomys, USSR, August 29-September 3, 1988.

27. A. von Bulow, *Conventional Stability NATO-WTO: An Overall Concept*, Hearings before the U.S. Congress, House of Representatives Armed Services Committee, Washington, D.C., October 7, 1988.

28. To a great degree, this idea has a solution: in the machine gun/artillery divisions which are being formed in the USSR, these make up a third type of division in addition to the two main types (motorized rifle and tank), whose structure significantly changes with the elimination of a tank regiment from their Table of Organization.

29. O. Amirov, N. Kishilov, V. Makarevsky, and Yu. Usachev, "Problems of Reducing Military Confrontation, Disarmament and Security," *IMEMO Yearbook* 1987, pp. 450-454.

30. A. von Bulow, *Conventional Stability NATO-WTO*, p. 39

31. *Pravda* (March 29, 1989).

32. R. Hatchett, *Restructuring Air Force for Non-Provocative Defense in Non-Provocative Defense as a Principle of Arms Reduction* (Amsterdam: Free University Press, 1989), pp. 177-188.

33. I.e., a mutually acceptable, contemporary military organization of armed forces and arms of the sides in Europe, with significant and stabilizing reductions in troops and arms.

34. League of Nations, Committee on Arbitration and Security, memorandum on Arbitration, Security and Articles of Covenant (Geneva, 1927), p. 15.

35. FOFA stands for Follow-on-Forces-Attack, a NATO doctrine for conducting certain kinds of attacks deep into Warsaw Pact territory.

22

Translating the Lessons and Methods of Nuclear Arms Control to the Conventional Arena

STEPHEN FOUGHT

Let us begin with an understatement: conventional arms control is *vastly* more complicated than strategic (nuclear) arms control. Then, let us remember that strategic arms control has been somewhat unsuccessful — largely due to its complexity. The topic of conventional arms control, therefore, is not flush with optimism; but there are some intriguing possibilities. This chapter attempts to explore some of the ways we can extrapolate the lessons of these earlier negotiations to help make real progress toward mutual security.[1]

Some specialists may take issue with the term "somewhat unsuccessful" with regard to strategic arms control offered in the preceding paragraph. After all, the superpowers have sequentially placed ceilings on arms production (SALT I), captured and capped certain advanced technologies (MIRV's and MIRV launchers in SALT II), and now look to reduce total inventories (START, not yet completed).

By the same token, certain confidence-building measures (CBMs) have been developed which probably have contributed to an air of cooperation between the competitors (the "hot line," non-interference with national technical means of verification, etc.). Further, some agreements have been reached which shape the bounds of the arms competition, leading to greater predictability (SALT I, especially the ABM Treaty, Outer Space Treaty, Nuclear Non-Proliferation Treaty, etc.).[2]

Thus there may be more grounds for optimism than what my opening salvo suggests — if what has been accomplished in strategic nuclear arms control can be translated to the conventional arena. But, it is translation of these concepts which may prove to be the most significant obstacle; or, more directly, the differences between conventional and strategic nuclear armaments may be so great that direct translation of concepts is not possible.

The strategic concepts in question are ones of symmetry (based on specific counting rules), segmentation (accounting for weapons systems individually rather than in the aggregate), delineation of weapons by categories (strategic versus theater and offense versus defense) and relative indifference to geographic location or operational doctrine strategy. Although there have been considerable difficulties in overcoming these obstacles in the strategic arena, they have been overcome, gradually, over a period of more than twenty difficult years of negotiations.[3] It remains to be seen whether they can be overcome in the conventional arena.

To take an example from the strategic arena: once the U.S. had decided to base its strategic security on "essential equivalence" or "rough parity," rather than "clear superiority," the negotiation process narrowed to creating a "counting" regime to judge the strategic balance.[4] Then, since "counting" essentially revolves around determining what constitutes a "1" (what would be counted) and what constitutes a "0" (what would be ignored), the arms negotiations could focus on specific physical entities such as ballistic missiles, warheads, bombers, or submarines.

However, it should be recalled that in SALT I a "1" was determined to be a ballistic missile launcher (all launchers were single warhead at that time), and afterwards both the U.S. and Soviets circumvented the launcher constraints by placing multiple independent re-entry vehicles (MIRV's) on their launchers. SALT II of course counted re-entry vehicles and MIRVed launchers as "1's" (with a complicated array of sublimits), but excluded cruise missiles because of verification problems. And, as we know, cruise missiles quickly became the weapon of choice for the military communities on both sides.

These kinds of counting difficulties and associated methods of circumvention are magnified in the case of conventional arms. For instance, the basic unit of count might be the soldier; then one must ask if a soldier is a man with a gun or a cook who knows how to shoot. Additionally, since the Western nations have habitually required more support personnel than the Warsaw Pact, any manpower-based counting scheme will be disadvantageous to the West. By the same token, since the East has lower technologies in conventional armaments, any equipment based comparisons could be unacceptably favorable to the West.

Beyond these general categorical differences, any counting comparisons in the conventional arena probably need to incorporate the multiple roles of conventional armaments. For instance, a tank has both an offensive and a defensive capability. Indeed, many army specialists point out that the best anti-tank weapon is another tank. This, of course, brings another dimension into the analysis. A static comparison of, say, tanks, is meaningless because several other weapons exist to counter tank (or armored) forces. This suggests that if a static method of comparison is to be used, then it should be asymmetric. Helicopters, anti-tank missiles, and even simple mines should be included in the count against tanks as these systems essentially negate tank, or armor, capability. Unfortunately such systems as helicopters have missions well beyond their anti-tank capabilities. Thus an asymmetric analysis would have to count helicopters under the headings of anti-tank, tactical airlift, close air support, air assault, command and control aircraft, and evacuation. The same multiple counting requirement exists for other multi-function equipment.

As if this were not complicated enough, static comparisons (whether symmetric or asymmetric) suffer from their own unique shortcomings. In the strategic nuclear arena, where "utility" of nuclear weapons beyond simple deterrence is questionable, it makes some sense to compare nuclear warheads and/or delivery systems in an aggregate (static and symmetric) manner. However, both the relative utility and specific mission of conventional forces change dramatically as the battlefield changes. For instance, as the battle progresses, artillery may be used for defense suppression (in the offensive mode) or interrupting the offensive charge (in the defensive mode).

It is also well understood that the role of airpower can change significantly even on a day to day basis. In the initial phases of a defensive battle, airpower might be allocated as primarily defensive in both counterair and close air support roles (both of these missions are conducted, roughly, over one's own troops or territory). However, as the battlefield changes, either by a deep enemy offensive thrust or one's own counterattack, airpower might shift to offensive counterair or interdiction (each of these are conducted forward of one's own troops and, possibly, over enemy territory). However, the same aircraft can be used in each of these missions. In fact, multipurpose aircraft (F-16, F-15, etc.) have been purchased by the Western alliance to provide exactly this flexibility. Naval aviation, by the same token, can be used for air defense (mainly at sea), for power projection (against sea or land targets) and for offensive action against other air forces.

By the same token, many conventional weapons have a nuclear capability. Both NATO and Warsaw Pact artillery pieces are well known to have both capabilities. Thus there is no distinction between conventional and nuclear artillery as nearly any artillery piece can fire both types of projectiles. Dual capable aircraft present a similar obstacle. Naval vessels compound the issue even further as many of these ships possess both a nuclear and conventional capability at the same time.

For at least the reasons cited in the previous three paragraphs, a dynamic analysis of conventional forces seems more appropriate than a static analysis. However, a dynamic analysis quickly reveals the fact that conventional weapons, and again unlike nuclear weapons, possess a synergism when capabilities are combined. For instance, armored forces, when considered in isolation, do not actually present a significant offensive capability. However, when they are combined with artillery, infantry, and air power, the resulting package packs a significant offensive punch. By the same token, light infantry by itself is no real matter of concern, but light infantry which is air mobile offers a capability for both surprise and maneuver (both critical elements of an offense). In fact nearly all categories of conventional forces, when considered in isolation, are less threatening than the combination. Thus it may be impossible, or more correctly possible but meaningless, to consider conventional arms control on a weapon-by-weapon basis. Conventional weapons, because of their synergistic effects, are properly considered in the aggregate.

Conventional forces, especially naval forces but certainly other mobile forces as well, also have roles and missions in a wide range of theaters. In this regard the U.S. will argue that its naval forces (and its ground and air forces based in the continental U.S. or outside the NATO area) should be excluded from a NATO analysis. The Soviets, on the other hand, can be expected to argue that these non-European based U.S. forces must be included because they can be applied to the NATO force balance — that indeed is precisely the U.S. commitment to NATO. However, restricting these U.S. forces would have a dramatic impact on U.S. security outside of the NATO area. In this regard, the U.S. habitually obligates all of its non-European based, conventional forces to multiple theaters (i.e., even those forces committed to NATO reinforcement have commitments to other regions of the world). Done largely as a cost saving measure, this approach nonetheless induces a risk that the U.S. would have to commit these forces at two places simultaneously. Similar arguments exist for Soviet forces associated with border security and civil administration within the Warsaw Pact countries or for Soviet forces assigned to the eastern border, or for Soviet military advisors overseas. Thus what may seem to be a reasonable assumption from an analytical basis, that is restricting the analysis of the conventional force balance to the NATO theater, may so simplify the problem that it loses the sophistication of how conventional forces fit into the global security equation.

Conventional forces are also inherently dependent upon logistics (current stocks, resupply and production from the industrial base, etc.). Thus, unlike nuclear weapons, an army division might be used in one phase of the battle, be withdrawn to replenish its combat power, then reapplied in another area. Stockpiles of ammunition, potential reinforcement from reserve units, and strategic mobility assets therefore become a part of the force balance problem. The same logic applies to tactical mobility capabilities such as bridging equipment, theater (tactical) airlift (aircraft and helicopters) and even road networks.

Beyond these fairly easily understood difficulties (!), NATO and the Warsaw Pact presently possess completely different doctrine, tactics, and tables of organization and equipment for conventional forces. Concerning organizational differences, if one observes that NATO only has a capability to generate a total of, say, sixty divisions, while the Warsaw Pact has over one hundred divisions on active duty and can eventually generate over three hundred divisions, one must conclude that the Warsaw Pact has an insurmountable advantage. However, this simplistic approach misses the fact that NATO divisions are considerably larger, are probably better trained, and certainly have more modern equipment. It also mistakenly counts Soviet divisions in military areas which are not applicable to European security problems (Soviet forces in the Far East for instance).

Concerning doctrine and tactics, NATO is committed to Flexible Response. Flexible Response is a political-military concept which forms the basis for NATO strategy and was formalized in a Military Committee decision document in 1967 (MC 14/3). Flexible Response replaced an earlier concept of a conventional "tripwire" which, if "tripped," would spawn a wholesale nuclear response (Massive Retaliation). Under both Massive Retaliation and Flexible Response, NATO essentially conceded conventional superiority to the Warsaw Pact and therefore depended on the threat of nuclear first use to deter Warsaw Pact aggression. The difference between the two concepts is, at the core, how much time would be spent attempting to repel a conventional attack before nuclear use.[5]

The Flexible Response concept is based upon providing NATO additional time to conclude that a Warsaw Pact attack was intentional (i.e., not an ambiguous border crossing). Flexible Response, as it stands today, consists of this: first, NATO formally declares that it will not be the first to use force. But second, if force is used, NATO reserves the right to respond at any level, including the nuclear level, in its own defense. Many specialists concede that there are no clear alternatives to Flexible Response.[6] Still, the most debatable feature of Flexible Response is the requirement for nuclear first use; however, this requirement is driven by the perceived conventional force imbalance. Therefore, rather than initiating a futile search for options to the basic strategy of Flexible Response, it might be more appropriate to examine alternatives for compensating for the conventional imbalance.

Toward that end, we should examine the sub-elements of Flexible Response to see what options are available. Flexible Response is based on: forward defense (a linear defense at the inter-German border); rapid reinforcement (from European and U.S. reserves); and incalculability (an assured response, but one which depends on a nuclear first use option of uncertain timing and extent). We will consider each sub-element in turn.

On the first point, a forward (linear) defense is both a political requirement (imposed by the Germans as a condition of their entry into NATO), and a military requirement as NATO lacks depth for anything other than a defense stabilized fairly far forward. However, NATO could improve its linear defensive position by incorporating permanently prepared defenses along the Inter German Border (IGB). Politically, this has proved impossible because it implies the permanent division of Germany and, in fact, of Europe — something which is unacceptable to NATO. Beyond this the physical space which would be used for prepared defenses is valuable land and the Germans are naturally reluctant to sacrifice this land on a permanent basis.

Second, rapid reinforcement from the U.S. and European reserves is required because any other approach would dictate large standing armies in Europe. This is impossible from both a fiscal and demographic standpoint. Neither the U.S. nor its European allies can (or would) afford such armies, nor do they possess the requisite population base of 18-24 year old males. Hence a strategy which depends upon reserves and reinforcement seems necessary and should actually be less threatening to the Warsaw Pact on a day-to-day basis.

Finally, given a historic inferiority in conventional forces, NATO's dependence upon the threat to use nuclear weapons seems inevitable. "Incalculability" is a term used to express the idea that a potential aggressor should be able to calculate that NATO will respond to an attack, however the aggressor should *not* be able to calculate with any degree of accuracy what that response will be. If one allows the aggressor to calculate the response, then a potential aggressor could also calculate cost versus benefit and, possibly, contemplate an attack with limited aims. NATO wishes to present a situation where little (if anything) can be gained and, potentially, everything is to be lost. To create this situation, NATO depends upon a credible threat of nuclear first use.

However, it would be incorrect to conclude that there are no options to change these three elements of Flexible Response. In fact, NATO has recently accepted a fairly significant change in the basic concept of a linear defense. NATO is now seeking a capability to disrupt Warsaw Pact forces before they could be applied to the battlefield, thus relieving the stress on the linear defense.

As a preliminary to this change in NATO military doctrine, the U.S. Army and Air Force developed a joint doctrine labeled Air-Land Battle. Air-Land Battle stresses attacking deep targets, disrupting forces before they can be applied, "taking the battle to the enemy," and counterattack by combined air and ground forces.

Air-Land Battle therefore seems ideal for NATO's conventional force balance predicament. Further, since Air-Land Battle had been accepted by the U.S. Army and Air Force, there was an obvious question in NATO circles concerning whether the U.S. would automatically apply this doctrine in Europe.

The central concern in NATO's questioning was that Air-Land Battle clearly establishes a supremacy of the offense over the defense, even if for defensive purposes. Such a possibility struck at the very heart of the NATO charter and the alliance's declared war termination objective of restoring NATO territory with a minimum amount of damage. Nowhere in NATO circles do we find any intention of gaining territory as a result of a European conflict. Nor do we find a military capability to seize territory. Air-Land Battle threatened to violate this crucial premise. In turn, General Rogers (U.S. Army), then the Supreme Allied Commander in Europe (SACEUR), had to find an explanation how this particular U.S. Army and Air Force joint doctrine was not, and would never be, a part of NATO doctrine.

The net result was a rough partitioning of Air-Land Battle into two parts, an air component and a land component. The land component was refuted by General Rogers and NATO. However, the air component, which became known as the Follow-on-Forces-Attack (FOFA), was accepted by NATO. This doctrine (FOFA), which was precipitated by NATO's perception of a serious imbalance in conventional forces, requires NATO air forces to project power into Warsaw Pact rear areas to disrupt forces before they can be applied along the front lines. Thus under a FOFA doctrine, NATO's "linear defense" would have a "defense in depth" quality to it. Perhaps unfortunately, the depth would be acquired on the East side of the battlefield, thus raising the specter of an offensive capability in an alliance whose declaratory policy is defensive.

A similar dichotomy has been recognized by the Warsaw Pact. Here, it is clear that the Warsaw Pact, like NATO, has a declaratory objective of defense. However, Soviet (and Soviet allied) forces have long been operationally committed to offense. Offense is seen as the best battlefield use of force. Defense is a circumstance which may be forced upon a battlefield commander, but it is a condition which is only to be maintained until sufficient firepower is available to regain the offense. According to Soviet literature, this approach is the product of an analysis of Soviet-German battles during the Second World War and is deemed to be the most appropriate use of force to repel an invading army. This, in turn, dictates a capability to mass forces, an absolute requirement for superiority across the battlefield and considerable integration of forces (combined arms approach, operational maneuver groups, etc.). Unfortunately, these Soviet doctrinal requirements for offensive capability and numerical superiority, in spite of the declaratory objective of defense, have produced a force structure which is also capable of immediate offense.

Thus we may be in a position where both NATO and the Warsaw Pact have declaratory doctrines of "defense," yet each has an operational capability of offense. This is certainly true of the Warsaw Pact forces; indeed the Soviets have recently raised this problem in their own analysis of their forces. Whether or not it is true of the NATO forces probably depends upon how far this alliance goes toward a FOFA concept. Nonetheless, a rather frightening dynamic may be in place. As the Warsaw Pact increases its conventional capability, NATO will be pressed to increase FOFA and as FOFA is improved, the Soviets, given their doctrinal requirements, will increase their conventional forces.

Thus a structural dynamic may be emerging that will create ever-increasing levels of offensive forces in the name of defense. This is a self-fulfilling prophecy, which may well be "an accident looking for a place to happen." If we wish to defuse this dynamic, we may have to attack the structure — the military doctrines.

Fortunately, this is precisely the approach now recommended by the Soviets as a part of their "new thinking" on security and arms control. From a military-technical perspective, Soviet specialists have argued that their analysis of Soviet defensive requirements may have been based on either the incorrect battles from World War II, or on the correct battles but without sufficient analytic scope. Soviet public statements on these conclusions began several years ago with some interesting discussions of a "defensive-defense" doctrine. Under this doctrine, NATO and the Warsaw Pact would deploy forces that were capable of defense, and only defense; offense, therefore, would be impossible from a military-technical perspective. If this could be accomplished, we would have succeeded in aligning declaratory policy and operational capability.

However, more recent Soviet statements have suggested an intermediate doctrinal proposal which revolves around a prolonged period of defense followed, if necessary, by a period of counteroffensive. This latter proposal seems to aim to reduce the immediate threat of offense, but still gives some weight to the earlier conclusion that offense (counterattack) is a necessary capability to regain potentially lost territory.

It would be pure conjecture to assert that the Soviets have abandoned their search for a "defensive-defense" in favor of the intermediate objective of a delayed offense. After all, a "defensive-defense" position would seem to meet the declaratory objectives of all the participants. Nonetheless, we have not yet seen, in either U.S. or Soviet specialist circles, a rigorous military-technical analysis which proves that a "defensive-defense" can be created. Lacking such an analysis, it may prove useful to more closely examine the intermediate position. But in doing so, we should not foreclose the option to go further.

In this regard, the Soviets may have concluded that a period of "defense," possibly to consolidate forces for the counteroffensive, might meet their objectives equally as well as their existing doctrine. Such a posture would certainly be less expensive to maintain, and is undoubtedly less threatening, than their previous doctrine of an immediate offensive capability. It would also provide an impetus for progress in conventional arms control which does not exist under the older doctrine and would allow the specialists to later examine the objective of "defensive-defense." Operationally, this "new thinking" appears to be the stimulus for changes not only in military training but in restructuring of Soviet Army divisions; thus it would be difficult to conclude that the Soviet proposals are simple rhetoric.

This intermediate approach is clearly less ambitious than the initial proposal. It may also be more realistic. Specifically, if one seeks to construct a force balance from which offense is completely impossible (the first approach), then one is actually seeking to provide a military-technical solution to war initiation. This seems highly unlikely to succeed as the causes of war are not military-technical, but political. A military-technical analysis may well contribute to a war initiation decision,[7] but it is unlikely to be the sole cause. However, if one seeks to eliminate or reduce the military stimulus to the war initiation decision, then one might seek to delay the potential use of offense. Here war (offense) would still be possible, but since it is delayed considerably, it would better allow for crisis management and (hopefully) war prevention.

Taking this latter approach (i.e., seeking to construct a force balance which is only capable of delayed offense/counter-offense), also has the advantage of allowing us to focus on specific types of forces rather than forcing us to try to construct new forces which are only capable of defense. Specifically, armored forces (tanks in particular but including armored personnel carriers), artillery (especially that which is mechanized), helicopters and certain types of long-range (fixed wing) aviation stand out as particularly interesting. In spite of their individual capabilities for both defense and offense, when considered in the aggregate these types of weapons present the most threatening combination of offensive capabilities. Thus, if one only seeks to delay the offense (not to prohibit it all together), one might focus on reducing these combined forces to some non-threatening level.

An informed reader will note that these are exactly the categories of forces being considered at the current Conventional Forces in Europe (CFE) negotiations in Vienna. At the time of this writing, a framework for a CFE Phase One level of forces is being constructed, with each of these categories given a ceiling well below what exists now in the Warsaw Pact but nearly approximating what exists in NATO.

Both superpowers have declared their intention to follow the CFE Phase One force reductions with further reductions, although the specific level is as yet undecided.

Still, several obstacles remain even in concluding the CFE Phase One agreement. First, although the level of "tanks" has been decided, it is unclear what constitutes a "tank." Does a "tank" have treads or tracks, does it have a gun (how large, and how many), and how much armor does a vehicle have to have before it is called a "tank" without regard to its specific offensive capability? The same difficulties apply for mechanized artillery and armored personnel carriers. Second, the Soviets believe that naval aviation (especially naval aviation which is ground based, as is the case for several European nations) should be included in the aircraft totals. Finally, the issue of how to account for dual capable aircraft (conventional and nuclear capable) remains largely unresolved. However, the negotiators are gradually making progress toward establishing these definitions.

Still, a caution is in order. Focusing on these forces, and only these forces, would constitute a potentially grievous error. First, an analytical diversion to constructing rigorous definitions or absolute counts may miss the point of trying to reduce the offensive synergism of these forces. However, establishing these reduced levels of forces, especially if the ceilings are further reduced, may render void any necessity to make these definitions precise.

Second, depending on operational doctrine and geographical differences, certain of these types of forces might logically be excluded from the analysis. For instance, given the close physical proximity of Soviet forces to the European theater, Soviet ammunition and equipment stockpiles probably should enter the equation; however, U.S. forward position equipment (for which there are no forward forces) might not. Similar arguments can be made for naval forces, and for forces stationed in areas outside of NATO. By the same token, Soviet forces in the Far East, even if they possess these categories of equipment, should probably be excluded from the European force balance.

Still, in spite of the cautions raised in the last two paragraphs, it seems a reasonable approach to focus on the most threatening types of forces as a logical first step in solving the security problem in Europe. But one should not stop at simply reducing the level of these forces immediately available to the front lines. This approach only focuses on reducing the day-to-day military-technical contribution to the war initiation decision (i.e., the "bolt out of the blue" attack or the World War II scenario); we need to look to reducing that contribution in a crisis situation.

Fortunately, there is already an organizational framework for this additional consideration — the Helsinki (or Helsinki/Stockholm/CSCE) procedures. This little touted but very successful set of negotiations has produced some interesting CBMs — such as ceilings for and notification of military exercises, and procedures for monitoring/inspecting these exercises. Although one might cynically conclude that such monitoring might be disallowed in a time of crisis, one should note that for one side to suddenly stop allowing such monitoring provides a great deal of information in and of itself. These sorts of CBMs are probably exactly what is needed to provide the military-technical information as a part of crisis management.

Now, if one combines the principles of Helsinki with the precedents established by the INF Treaty (asymmetric reductions, on-site and intrusive verification, elimination of the most modern weapons systems, and "zero" as the preferred level for verification), then a reasonable regime is established for concluding a conventional arms control agreement in Europe. Such an agreement could proceed along the lines proposed by the current CFE discussions and incorporate the CSCE concepts for verification, monitoring, and decision making in a crisis. Having taken this combined approach, we would be working toward preventing the "surprise" war (World War II) by lowering force levels and capability (in CFE) and for preventing the "accidental" or unintended war (World War I) through the framework of CSCE.

More specifically, the current CFE Phase One force levels would correct the imbalances in the most threatening (offensive) forces which now drive the dynamic derived earlier — thus destroying NATO's rationale for FOFA and eliminating whatever dynamic exists for a Warsaw Pact reaction. Further, if the Soviets are successful in incorporating their declaratory doctrine of "defense sufficiency" (or delayed offense/counteroffense) into their operational doctrine and force structure, one might then contemplate going significantly below the CFE Phase One levels — thus delaying offense even further. In the interim, it should be obvious that the Helsinki/INF ideas present excellent guidance for both verification and crisis management — both essential political ingredients which must be satisfied before greater reductions can be achieved.[8]

Still, even if we are successful at reaching the CFE Phase One force levels we will have fairly large quantities of forces opposing each other in Europe, maintained at fairly high costs to both sides. In fact, although the Warsaw Pact would make great reductions in the CFE scheme, the NATO reductions are far less significant and the cost to NATO of verification might actually exceed any cost savings associated with reductions. This follows simply because the Warsaw Pact has greater numbers of forces at the beginning and parity is achieved by it reducing more. Until we attempt to go below the levels proposed by CFE Phase One, most of the force structure changes simply represent a threat reduction to NATO and a cost savings to the Warsaw Pact.

CFE Phase One does not require NATO to revise its doctrine, as it makes only small changes to NATO force structure, yet NATO will see the threat diminish

328 *Nuclear Arms Control and the Conventional Arena*

considerably. After Phase One the Warsaw Pact will have relieved its economic burden somewhat. But since the Pact has much less of an economic base in absolute terms, the Pact's remaining cost would still be a greater relative burden than NATO's burden is. It would be logical to conclude that, even if only for economic reasons, both NATO and the Warsaw Pact should then be interested in further force reductions if their security needs could be met at lower levels of forces. Thankfully, as discussed earlier, there is a political commitment to proceed with further reductions.

It is in going beyond these CFE Phase One force levels that the concepts of "mutual security" derived in this volume become especially important. It is then, and perhaps only then, that the superpowers are going to be forced to entertain real mutual threat reduction. Consequently, it may be necessary to develop new security (and military) doctrines based on mutual, rather than unilateral, security.

This brings to the forefront an issue which has not arisen in prior arms control discussions. Previous arms control discussions have been based on the assumption that equal, and nearly mirror image, levels and types of forces somehow constitute an equal level of security. This may be a good assumption for either conventional or nuclear forces when the force levels under consideration are quite large. But since military force requirements are based on many different things, and these factors are different between the superpowers (and their alliances), this may not be a good assumption when we turn to major reductions, as we will in going beyond CFE Phase One.

In fact, is it not ludicrous to assume that mirror image forces would provide for mutual security when the two countries involved have different geo-strategic positions, different ideological backgrounds, wholly different bases for their alliance structures, vastly different military doctrines and strategies, nearly unrelated concepts of military operations, and significantly different levels of sophistication and design in their specific military equipments? In such a situation the prudent analyst would ask that the mirror image concept be proved rather than assumed. I believe the proper assumption is that some collection of asymmetries will have to exist.

Some specific examples might be useful. From a geo-strategic perspective, one might equate Soviet proximity to the European theater with the U.S. ability to reinforce. The U.S. would be unlikely to accept any parity in overall forces without considering its reinforcement problem. Thus, U.S. naval forces might be considered in the same equation as the Soviet network of ground transportation. Along these same lines, U.S. equipment (stationed forward) might be equated to Soviet personnel (similarly stationed forward). In support of these conceptual asymmetries, I suggest that U.S./NATO equipment might remain in Europe, but the personnel would depart (leaving only headquarters infrastructure). However, Soviet equipment would depart the theater (to some sort of deep reserve status or even, ideally, destroyed), whereas their troops might stay behind (as light infantry perhaps). U.S. naval forces, which would be especially useful in balancing the Soviet road network in the case of reinforcement, would not be physically limited. However, their deployment areas might be somehow constrained so as not to present an immediate threat to Soviet security.

Asymmetries on a global scale must also be entertained. One might consider here that, given continued Sino-Soviet difficulties, the U.S. might not require any offset for Soviet troops stationed in the Far East as these Soviet capabilities counter a threat which does not present itself to the U.S. Similarly, the Soviets might not need any offset for U.S. deployments in Korea or the Philippines. These same sorts of conceptual and physical asymmetries certainly exist in other regions as well.

The point of these examples is that mutual security, and the mutually beneficial exchange (threat reduction) may turn out to require a complex web of asymmetries. That web might be difficult to construct, but nonetheless be a necessary condition to proceed below the force levels envisioned by CFE Phase One. The conclusion I draw is that conventional force reductions, beyond the CFE Phase One level, will have to incorporate significant asymmetries (in fact a collection of asymmetries), whose net effect is mutual security.[9]

Unfortunately, little research has been done to investigate what asymmetries might be appropriate in the conventional arena. Here, the mutual security approach might prove especially fruitful. I suggest it would be productive to begin such research with an examination of the concept of "stability," which seems to be a common objective in both nuclear and conventional arms control. Since it seems clear that asymmetries in forces will be a requirement for mutual security, the question for research is whether a common definition of stability is required. Or, do the required asymmetries in forces also dictate a difference in concepts of stability?

"Stability," as normally used in the nuclear arena but is broadly applicable to the conventional problem as well, involves two concepts: eliminating an incentive to "go first" by precluding a large or permanent advantage associated with a first strike (crisis stability); and eliminating the requirements to produce more armaments by greatly reducing or eliminating any advantage of a first strike (arms race stability). Such definitions are inherently military-technical considerations of stability and, as such, are generally devoid of the political circumstances that would be associated with any first strike.

Indeed, in the West, one of the most common discussions when reviewing these sorts of analysis occurs when the briefing officer begins with "Suppose the Soviets launch a first strike" and someone from the audience asks "Why did they do it?" The analyst answers, "It doesn't matter. Suppose the Soviets....." My point is that it does matter. No political leader has ever gone to war, especially when the stakes are as high as they are today, on the basis of purely a military-technical calculation. Our current definitions and calculations of stability miss this point completely.

A better definition of stability would include a measure of whether or not military-political options, short of war or short of total (nuclear) war, were available. That is, "stability" would be a measure of each side's ability to preserve its own (perhaps independent) security strategy. Thus, since security strategies are different, one should also expect the concept of stability to be different among the participants.

Having established that requiring a common definition of stability may actually be an obstacle to arms control rather than a necessary condition, the question remains how to accommodate this difference in the actual negotiations. Toward that end, consider the research model proposed by P. Terrence Hopmann in this volume. As the participants proceed through the series of conventional arms reductions in this simulation, they will be preserving what they understand to be their own military security strategies while eliminating (in an asymmetric fashion), the threats to those strategies.

Hopmann's research, using this new definition of stability, may allow us to explore what asymmetries in definitions of stability and resulting force structure might be necessary to achieve mutual security. Other models or methods of analysis might, of course, be used to extract the same information. The point is that we need to better understand how force reduction can be accomplished, while at the same time allowing different perceptions of the world to remain operative.

This theme may be stated in a different way. As one contemplates going to significantly lower levels of conventional forces in Europe, the specific, and differing,*political* requirements of these forces will have to be reflected to the force structures. "Stability" in its correct sense must measure our ability to avoid both a surprise and an unintended war. Hence it must reflect the political factors which lead to war, and thus we will need to go beyond the military-technical measurements we now use. It seems fruitless to insist that common, agreed upon, measures of stability be used. Instead, we should strive for a situation where we are confident that the other side is not going to war and we, as a consequence, have no requirement to prepare an offensive posture in response or, in the worse case, pre-empt.

Such a situation can be reached. However, it cannot be reached if we predicate our thinking on mirror image forces, nor upon producing mirror image strategies. Instead it must be predicated upon constructing an environment of mutual (cooperative) security in a manner where each side can preserve those aspects of its security strategy which it deems most valuable and also eliminate from the other side what it believes presents the greatest risk.

Let me conclude this paper with a few final remarks. We must realize that the conventional arms control problem is more complicated than it has ever been in the past. No longer can we calculate military power on such simple bases as coal, iron and steel production or the number of men who can be placed under arms. Even more recent methods of calculating conventional force effectiveness have been blurred by advances in technology, sometimes making even the distinction between conventional and nuclear weapons vague. Given this, the lessons and principles we have derived in the strategic nuclear arms control regime, which has been the base case for most analysis, may not be directly translatable to the conventional arena. Or they may be translatable only if we are willing to continue to maintain very large levels of conventional forces.

However some excellent prospects are on the horizon. First, there is an obvious, and important, call to examine military doctrines and operational strategies as a preliminary step to changing the security arrangements in Europe. This is a necessary first step as both NATO and the Warsaw Pact have declaratory defensive objectives, yet each can be argued to have (or to be approaching) offensive capabilities. Second, using the precedents established through Helsinki and INF, there is an intellectual and practical framework developing for cooperation and an eventual environment of mutual security. Third, for whatever reasons, the CFE Phase One levels of forces appear to be politically attainable, setting the stage for future cooperation and, quite possibly, significant further reductions.

Still it may not be possible, and hence not a feasible negotiating objective, to try to create a situation that reliably prevents war on a purely military-technical basis. Instead, one should seek to reduce or possibly eliminate the military-technical factors which contribute to the political decision for war initiation by focusing on both the surprise and accidental or unintended war scenarios. One can never prevent, after all, the war which is initiated intentionally.

Towards these ends, as I have argued here, major reductions beyond the CFE level will have to accommodate the many and vast differences between the alliances. I believe the best approach to this objective is to define a goal of mutual security. But we should conclude that it will have to be based on a wide range of agreed asymmetries. We should not undertake an impractical, unwise, and probably impossible effort to achieve mirror image forces, concepts or strategies.

Notes

1. The views presented in this paper are those of the author. They do not represent the views of the U.S. Naval War College or any other organization.

2. The basic SALT I document limited ballistic missile launchers, thus providing some sort of later ceiling on warheads. The Anti-Ballistic Missile (ABM) Treaty, also a part of SALT I, limited defense against ballistic missiles in conjunction with limiting the offensive competition. The Outer Space Treaty prohibited weapons of mass destruction (nuclear weapons) in space, thereby eliminating that part of the arms race from further consideration. The Non-Proliferation Treaty sought to limit the spread of nuclear weapons to those already possessing them, thereby limiting the number of nations which would have to be involved in nuclear arms reductions.

3. For example, it was nearly impossible to agree whether the long-range INF missiles, Pershing II and Ground Launched Cruise Missiles (GLCM) were strategic or theater weapons; the solution was to eliminate them completely under the INF Treaty. Additionally, given the bi-lateral nature of strategic nuclear negotiations (SALT and START), the French and British nuclear forces, and the Soviet forces dedicated to countering the Chinese threat, presented a considerable obstacle. A compromise position was that the French and British weapons would not have to be considered in preliminary reductions (down to a certain level); however, at some later point, these weapons would have to be accounted for in the negotiations. Concerning the Soviet weapons facing China, the U.S. and Soviet negotiators discussed a compromise where the U.S. reserved the right to match these Soviet weapons (numerically) on a global basis, but did not have a right to place these weapons in the European theater — thus creating a "balance" in both the regional and global contexts. This compromise, since it was discussed in the context of the long-range INF missiles, was not formally agreed upon since the missiles were eventually eliminated. The offensive-defensive relationship of nuclear weapons was circumvented by prohibiting strategic defenses through the SALT I/ABM Treaty; however, it remains to be seen if this distinction will hold given advances in ballistic missile defense technology.

4. During the post-World War II period, the U.S. had sought, and actually maintained, a position of clear (numerical and technological) superiority over the Soviets in the area of strategic nuclear weapons. By the mid-1960s, especially given the Soviets' progress in intercontinental ballistic missiles, U.S. security specialists began to question whether this superiority could be maintained or, even if it could be maintained, how one might measure superiority or what consequence it might have with respect to security. The Soviets may have conducted a similar debate. President Nixon, along with his national security adviser Henry Kissinger, abandoned the concept of superiority in favor of "essential equivalence," or sometimes called "rough parity," in conjunction with their objective to place some sort of mutual ceilings on strategic nuclear arms production. Again, given that the Soviets entered into the SALT negotiations, the Soviets probably reached similar conclusions. The point for our discussions of conventional arms reductions is that abandoning superiority may be a logical precursor to placing ceilings on arms productions or deployments. However, it still remains to be determined how one calculates equality or, if equality is reached, how that contributes to security.

5. The stimulus for a change from Massive Retaliation to Flexible Response was two-fold. First, there was a Western perception that Soviet nuclear forces had, or would have soon, reached a level where the U.S. could not avoid a nuclear response from the Soviets. This caused both European and U.S. specialists to question the credibility of a U.S. nuclear response. Second, there was a growing feeling in the U.S./NATO intelligence communities

that the Soviet conventional threat had been overestimated; raising the possibility that NATO could accomplish some greater degree of deterrence with conventional forces.

6. Without seeming trivial, some of the options to Flexible Response might be labeled Rigid Response, Puny Response, Inappropriate Response, or No Response — none of which seem interesting. Flexible Response seems to capture the military flexibility required to support a political commitment to defense. The only questionable feature of Flexible Response seems to be the requirement for nuclear first use. However, this requirement is driven by the perceived conventional force imbalance. The proper place to begin the analysis, therefore, might be at confirming and/or correcting this imbalance.

7. Probably the best example of the military-technical analysis driving the war initiation decision was World War I. Without going deeply into the wide range of studies of that war, we can summarize Ole Holsti's argument that the stimulus was a crisis where the leaders of all nations felt, simultaneously, the same things: that they were losing control of the situation; that other leaders were gaining control and had more options; and, finally, that the only option available was to prepare for war (and, eventually to go to war). This thesis clearly establishes the circumstances where the military-technical evaluation can overcome the political leaders' ability to preserve options short of war; thus preventing this circumstance is important. If we accept this thesis, then crisis management (or providing clear and accurate information to political leaders) is an essential ingredient to European security.

8. See in this connection the companion papers in this book by Aleksandr Konovalov and P. Terrence Hopmann.

9. This idea of a collection of asymmetries leading to a mutually satisfactory outcome (mutual security) is reminiscent of Adam Smith's classic economic model of a mutually beneficial exchange where the buyer and seller have different assessments of value yet each achieves a satisfactory outcome. Here, since "mutual security" (and whatever constitutes mutual threat reduction) probably has to be derived from differing perceptions of security and threat, one might use a free market model as a basis for analysis. The project proposed by P. Terrence Hopmann is based on this concept and is described in this volume.

Part VI

Working Group on Future Scenarios and Conclusion

THE WORKING GROUP ON FUTURE SCENARIOS was responsible for an overall assessment of the future prospects for the development of mutual security, and for assessments of public opinion in the Soviet Union and the United States regarding possible scenarios for the evolution of the foreign policy of each nation.

The Working Group has contributed three chapters to this book. Two of them represent the assessments of public opinion. Andrei Melvil and Aleksandr Nikitin analyze Soviet public opinion, and Mark Lindeman analyzes American public opinion. The final, joint, chapter is contributed by Howard Swearer and Sergei Plekhanov. This chapter, the last in the book, represents a summing up of the prospects for mutual security.

— THE EDITORS

23

The End of the Consensus That Never Was: The Future of Soviet-American Relations as Viewed by the Soviet Public

ANDREI MELVIL AND ALEKSANDR NIKITIN

Introduction

What impact are perestroika and glasnost beginning to have on Soviet public attitudes about foreign policy, and especially about policy toward the United States? What spectrum of opinion is forming among the Soviet people on key questions of international politics, security, and Soviet-American relations?

These questions are of great importance for several reasons. One is that the development of an entire spectrum of views, rather than adherence to a single viewpoint, serves as an indicator of the progress of reform and transformation in Soviet society. Another, obviously, is that as Soviet society becomes more democratized, public opinion will come to play an increasing role in influencing the formulation of Soviet foreign policy. For decades, opinion polls on foreign policy issues were not conducted in the USSR. It was assumed that there was silent, virtually unanimous consent for the government's foreign and national security policies. There was no open, systematic consideration of alternative views, in spite of it being generally known that some differences in viewpoint existed in fact.

This paper summarizes some of the earliest research done within the USSR on newly emerging public attitudes about foreign policy, especially toward the United States. To some extent this research employed, as a model, some prior research carried out in the United States by the Center for Foreign Policy Development at Brown University and the Public Agenda Foundation in New York City. Specialists at Brown University were consulted during early stages of the Soviet research project.[1]

The Soviet project, like the American one, was carried out in two stages. A first stage was required to create a basic framework of concepts and to identify potential new tendencies. The Soviet research project studied, at this stage, the opinions of foreign policy specialists. The second stage then employed the concepts that had been developed to ask questions of the public. Due to the limits on space and the desirability of giving emphasis to the opinion of the public, this chapter will summarize the first stage of research only briefly.[2]

The first stage: research on specialists' opinion

In the spring of 1988, an extensive questionnaire of approximately 170 questions was developed, exploring different possible viewpoints on the nature and dynamics of Soviet-American relations, international security, trends in world development, and the foreign policy goals and interests of the USSR. The questionnaire was then answered by 120 Soviet specialists in international relations, including academic specialists, diplomats, journalists, and representatives of various social organizations. In choosing our respondents, we emphasized two criteria: their professional competence, and their diversity of policy viewpoints.[3]

The results of this initial stage of research allowed us to draw some important conclusions. First, the results demonstrated that there has been a *major erosion of the entire set of traditional viewpoints associated with the old thinking*. There were many and clear disagreements with traditional ideological formulas. These disagreements included a refusal by the majority to agree that "the opposition of socialism and capitalism is a fundamental contradiction of the epoch," which was the very prism of all thinking for decades.[4] Almost 80% disagreed that the main goal of Soviet foreign policy should be premised on the "class struggle" and aimed at the spreading of socialism worldwide. Instead, 77% said the chief goal should be the prevention of nuclear war. More than 90% said that questions of human rights is *not* "a zone beyond criticism," including criticism from other countries.

Similarly, we found among these specialists a general *departure from the ideologized perception of Soviet-American relations* and of international relations in general. Asked whether Soviet-American relations would always be defined chiefly by political and ideological rivalry, 43% said no, and only 34% said yes. A full 50% predict a reduction, at least, in the salience of ideological differences. Asked about Soviet aid to the Third World, only 24% supported directing it by ideological criteria, and 35% supported giving it to those most in need. A larger number, 38%, supported a reduction in aid in order to turn all resources toward the domestic progress of perestroika.

Another notable result was *an erosion of "superpower" psychology.* Forty-three percent foresee Soviet-American relations occupying a less prominent place in future world politics (35% do not); and 59% said the USSR and U.S. should not have any special rights among nations.

These specialists tend to *de-emphasize military aspects of security.* Only 17% said that the most effective means for achieving Soviet security are military-technical, while 52% saw political means as most effective. Forty-two percent advocated the attainment of Soviet security on the basis of agreements with the United States, suggesting that the emphasis on mutual security in Soviet "new thinking" is being widely accepted by specialists. Fifty percent of the respondents saw parity as a more secure and preferable state of the nuclear balance, but nearly as many said that "the USSR has no need for as many [nuclear] weapons as the U.S." Defensively oriented conventional postures were endorsed by 30%, even as a strategy for the Soviet Union to carry out unilaterally. A deliberate attack on the USSR by the United States was assessed as either "unlikely" or "very unlikely" by 82%. However 43% agreed that in general terms an "American threat" does exist and two-thirds of this group sees it as including a military threat. We assess these numbers as relatively low, when it is recalled that for decades the existence of a serious "American threat" was part of the core of Soviet political culture and thinking. In spite of President Gorbachev's proposal that nuclear weapons be abolished by the year 2000, only 10% of the respondents thought this possible.

Analysis of the specialists' responses

To create the framework for our next stage — research on public opinion — we analyzed the results of the first stage in a particular fashion. All the responses to all the questions were statistically analyzed to identify "clusters" of viewpoints. That is, we sought to identify a limited number of alternative, main tendencies. This form of statistical research is called "cluster analysis."

This analysis yielded six major clusters. We gave names to these six alternative viewpoints, and might briefly describe them as follows:[5]

1. *An "ideological" scenario.* This is the traditional Soviet ideological view-point. Class and ideological factors and conflict are, and will continue to be, the defining features of Soviet-American relations. The rivalry between the two sides is rooted in profound contradictions between their social systems, and can only end with the victory of one side. However, most proponents of this view expect the victory to be political and ideological, not military, and they foresee a preservation of approximate military parity between the two

sides. The main reason for the arms race is the constant American effort to achieve military superiority, and the important role of the military-industrial complex in American society. Soviet and American rivalry for the allegiance of Third World countries will continue sharply.[6]

2. A *"superpower" scenario.* This viewpoint focuses not on ideology but on the state interests of the USSR, and also of the United States. These two nations are superpowers unlike any other on Earth, and will de facto have special rights and powers, even well into the future. Since the foreign policy of the USSR should be guided not by ideology but by "realpolitik," the USSR should limit its aid to socialist and developing countries and focus its resources on consolidating its national strength. Then it should engage in economic and scientific-technical competition in global markets, for its own national advantage. Tension in Soviet-American relations can be reduced by reaching practical agreements of benefit to both, and by at least partial de-ideologization of relations. The growth of the USSR's national power will guarantee Soviet security in the event that security agreements with the United States prove unsuccessful.

3. A *"competitive coexistence" scenario.* This viewpoint focuses on the imperative of preventing a global nuclear war, and advances this as the most important goal for Soviet foreign policy. To this end, the USSR should focus on reaching agreements with the United States to reduce the nuclear threat. The security of the USSR will be guaranteed in the form of mutual security with the United States, strictly verified by national means. Reductions in military forces will be achieved step by step, maintaining at least approximate parity at each step (although it probably is unrealistic to expect nuclear weapons to be entirely abolished even by 2010.) An ideologically based competition in the non-military spheres of Soviet-American relations will continue, although with some moderation as a by-product of the military reductions.[7]

4. A scenario of *"general normalization."* This viewpoint suggests a sweeping change in Soviet-American relations, developing over time. Tensions will reduce greatly. Both sides will understand that the balance between elements of competition and elements of cooperation is shifting steadily toward cooperation. Ideological competition will cease to be important in Soviet-American relations, and the two sides will work to resolve, step by step, all problems between them. Progress, achieved in stages, in military affairs (arms reductions) will assist in improving relations in economic, political and other spheres; and vice-versa. Friction between them in the Third World will

diminish greatly, and by 2010 the two sides can achieve radical reductions (though perhaps not the complete abolition) of nuclear weapons.[8]

5. *A scenario of complete restructuring of international relations.* In this viewpoint, entirely new principles of international relations and international security will be developed. A global transformation will occur, in which not only the USSR and the U.S. but all nations will cease relating among each other in terms of threat, and instead will jointly address common global problems. Both Soviet and American interests will be subordinated to those of the world community; political and ideological conflict will yield to the recognition of global interdependence. Mutual security between East and West will merely be part of, and partially a result of, the development of common security for all the world's nations.[9]

6. *A scenario of the USSR focusing on domestic problems.* This scenario gives unconditional priority to the interests of domestic development. The USSR would reduce its aid to the socialist and developing countries, reduce or end all foreign commitments, cease to act abroad on ideological motives, focus all resources on domestic needs, and adopt the slogan that socialism is best advanced by force of example. The American threat will continue, but the USSR will retain and improve its defensive potential sufficiently to guarantee its security unilaterally and to continue its own development peacefully. Relations with the United States will become relatively unimportant. Nuclear weapons will remain, but the USSR will not require parity with the United States and can retain merely a reasonable sufficiency of nuclear forces.[10]

It should be emphasized that in our research project, none of these possibilities was considered "correct" or "incorrect." Determining their correctness was not our research goal. Rather our goal was to identify broad alternatives, each of which would be regarded as "correct" by its own adherents. Evidently there is no homogeneity, but rather great diversity, in the views of these 120 specialists in international affairs.[11]

Several areas should be mentioned where there was agreement among a majority of them, whatever their other disagreements. A majority agreed that common and parallel interests will increasingly arise between the USSR and the U.S., such as resolving such common problems as problems of ecology, energy and terrorism. A majority agreed that the Soviet understanding of what socialism means should be brought up to date to incorporate common interests and values of all of humanity. A majority agreed that an exact correlation of Soviet and American military capabilities is not and will not be decisive for their security; in other words exact parity is not necessary for the military balance. A majority believe that arms reductions will remain the single most important area for Soviet-American cooperation. A majority are convinced that the progressive success of perestroika in the USSR will evoke a largely positive response in the United States and hence an improvement in Soviet-American relations. A majority believe that further developing economic, scientific-technical and cultural ties with the U.S. are important, independent of the ups and downs of their political relations.

The second stage: research on public opinion

In the second stage of our research, we employed these six "future scenarios" to improve our questionnaire. Some questions were removed; some new ones added; some were reworded. Having identified some major, basic tendencies, we were able to identify issues and problems more clearly, and ask questions that would get more nearly to the heart of peoples' attitudes. We also were able to simplify the questionnaire, in the sense of removing some technical ideas and jargon that, as we discovered, do not reveal important, underlying issues. Some simplification of the questionnaire was necessary before employing it with the general public.

We then took our improved questionnaire to the Soviet public. Specifically, we asked many hundreds of Soviet citizens to answer the questions it poses. Rather than relying on responses being mailed back, we took the questionnaire to citizens in their homes. The research was conducted in two cities in the European portion of the Russian Republic. In what follows, we shall refer to "Soviet public opinion," while noting now that the sample was not drawn from all parts of the USSR.[12]

Before reporting the results let us offer one preliminary observation, which we believe is significant not only regarding research on Soviet public opinion but also public opinion research in other countries. In the course of our work we discovered that it made a great difference whether questions were worded using the phrases of official rhetoric, or using other phrases and terms. When we worded questions using the phrases of official rhetoric, large majorities would respond by agreeing with that rhetoric. When we asked the *identical questions* using other language, we often received different responses.

The interpretation of this result is clear. When people hear the phrases they have already heard many times from the government, it is natural that they respond with agreement. Clearly, they are not actually thinking through the meaning of the question in their own minds, or not entirely. On the other hand, when they are asked a question that does not use official phrases, they have no choice but to think about the question itself. They must think through its meaning in their own minds. Of course, in some cases it is not possible to ask a question without using the standard terms for it, or words that resemble the official phrases sufficiently that nearly anyone will be reminded of the official phrase. In what follows we present our results, insofar as possible, reflecting people's conclusions when they seemed to be considering questions in their own minds and not repeating official slogans.

The decline of ideology

Various evidence suggests a decline in the importance of ideological considerations in Soviet public opinion. For example an overwhelming majority of the citizens (77%) disagreed with the statement that the main goal of Soviet foreign policy should be the spread of socialism throughout the world. Only 14% of the public supported this statement. We also put the question more concretely by asking which should receive priority in Soviet aid to foreign countries — support for socialism abroad or support for the general interests of humanity (such as ecological interests or humanitarian concerns like hunger). Only 9% of the public agreed that support for socialism should always receive priority, while 71% supported giving priority to the interests of humanity. In a different version of the question, 46% said the USSR should help, insofar as possible, all needy countries while only 12% said that help should be restricted to needy countries that are pro-socialist and anti-capitalist.

The decline of ideological motives was also revealed in other ways. A 57% majority rejected the idea that any cooperation between the socialist and capitalist camps can only be temporary and limited; only 24% agreed. Asked whether the intensity of the ideological conflict between the two camps will increase, continue the same, or decline, only 7% predict an increase, 20% responded that it will remain the same, and an absolute majority of 55% think that it will decline.

For many years, official Soviet rhetoric declared that questions of human rights in the USSR are strictly an internal matter, and not something that may be an object of criticism or discussion from abroad. Yet our survey found that today this view is shared by only about one-third of the population. The other two-thirds support the position that human rights questions cannot be "off limits" to foreign criticism, because human rights are universal concepts that transcend national frontiers.

We asked this question: "At present there are a number of rules affecting the import into the USSR of books, videos, and other forms of information. Assuming that pornography and propaganda for war and racism are excluded, do you think all the other restrictions should be left in place as they are now, or strengthened, or reduced, or abolished?" Only 8% responded that the general restrictions should strengthened and only 19% that they should be left in place as they are now; 25% answered that they should be reduced and 36% said they should be removed completely.

Other data were also consistent with our conclusion that the importance of ideology as a criterion or motive in Soviet foreign relations has declined significantly among the Soviet public.

The nuclear threat

We asked a number of questions regarding perceptions about the danger of nuclear war. Perhaps the most dramatic response concerned the possibility of victory. We asked the question "If a nuclear war occurs, who will be the winner?" and received these responses from the public:

U.S.	2%
USSR	5%
neither	87%

In other words, nearly nine citizens out of ten regard a nuclear war as unwinnable.

The Soviet public evidently feels secure from surprise attack. Seventy percent responded that the United States cannot launch a surprise nuclear attack upon the USSR, and only 16% said that it can. The public also sees no need for Soviet nuclear superiority. Only 8% advocated it, compared to an overwhelming 74% who called for parity between the two sides' nuclear arms. However the public feels that that parity need not be exact. Asked to agree or disagree that "the U.S. and USSR have so many nuclear weapons that an exact parity is not that important," 71% agreed and only 17% disagreed.[13]

The citizens also place much more faith, at this point, in the power of international agreements to improve Soviet security than in further unilateral efforts. Observe these results:

Question: What is most important for the security of the USSR?

1) Strengthening its own defense	10%
2) Bilateral agreements	17%
3) Multilateral international agreements	64%

We interpret the emphasis on multilateral agreements here as reflecting a belief that international treaties mean more if they are made in the context of international law and with the participation of the international community as a whole.

All this does not mean that the Soviet people have become simple-minded optimists. More than one-quarter of the respondents fear that a process of arms reductions will work asymmetrically: it will eventually make the USSR more vulnerable than it makes the United States. Concerns are also aroused when citizens are asked whether the USSR should scrap all its offensive weapons and maintain only a defensive arsenal. In spite of the fact that this idea has been part of official doctrine for several years, it enjoys the support of only about half the citizens we surveyed. (By contrast, it was supported by more than 90% of the specialists we had surveyed.)[14]

We also asked about nuclear weapons themselves. There is no doubt that the Soviet people regard them as an absolute evil, and a grave danger to the whole of mankind. Even the most casual observer of Soviet public opinion observes that much. At the same time, our research found strong evidence that Soviet citizens are accepting the idea that under present circumstances, they may be a necessary evil — to ward off the far greater evil of nuclear war. Not surprisingly, we found that 59% of the citizens agree that the existence of the Soviet nuclear arsenal is instrumental in maintaining peace. Very surprisingly, we found that 30% of them believe that the existence of the Western nuclear arsenal also is instrumental in maintaining peace. There is only one reasonable interpretation for this result. The 30% have come to accept the idea of a balance of mutual deterrence. They have accepted the idea that the two nuclear arsenals balance each other and make it irrational for anyone to consider using the weapons.

Soviet public opinion also holds a complicated attitude about the abolition of nuclear weapons. (Incidentally the same complication is found also in Western public opinion.) On the one hand, nearly all citizens desire a nuclear-free world. Our research found that 91% believe that nuclear weapons should not exist. But when specifically asked about whether it is possible to abolish the weapons, only about 60% say yes. About one-third say it is not possible (the remainder being unsure). Even among those who think that it is possible, a mere 16% believe that it can be done by the year 2000, which is an official proposal of the Soviet government.[15]

The American threat

We asked citizens how they saw the threat from the United States. The fact that the Soviet public feels relatively secure from any direct, surprise American attack has already been shown. Nearly half of the public (46%) still believes that, in general, there is an American threat; but almost as many (41%) now believe there is not.

More revealing than this is the fact that two-thirds of those who do believe in an American threat cannot say what the threat is:

Question: If you believe there is an American threat, in what spheres of life does it manifest itself?

```
1) economics . . . . . . . . . . . . . . . 4%
2) science & technology . . . . . . . . 2%
3) military . . . . . . . . . . . . . . 23%
4) ideology . . . . . . . . . . . . . . . 3%
5) culture . . . . . . . . . . . . . . 0%-1%
6) cannot say . . . . . . . . . . . . . 67%
```

There are several remarkable things about these responses. Of course, one remarkable thing is how few believe there is an ideological threat, or an economic or technological threat. The number of people saying that the threat is military is more remarkable for how low it is than for how high it is. But the most remarkable thing of all is how many people cannot specify what they think the threat is, *even after they are offered five possible answers.*

We believe that the correct interpretation of this result is that "the American threat" has become psychological. In their emotions, people feel some kind of vague threat, but in their minds they cannot actually find anything specific. The threat no longer exists in the realm of external reality, but it continues to have an internal, psychological existence. To some considerable extent, people still feel an "image of an enemy." But it is only an image; it is intangible.

Responses to questions about the American people and the American government are consistent with this interpretation. Soviet citizens agree almost unanimously (95%) that the American people want to reduce the danger of nuclear war. This is not surprising because for decades, official rhetoric has drawn a firm distinction between the "good" American people and the "bad" American government. But the answer to the next question is more surprising:

Question: The American government, as well as the Soviet government, wants to reduce the danger of nuclear war.

> Agree: 60%
> Disagree: 20%

The other 20% were unsure. In other words, among the Soviet people willing to make a judgment, a three-to-one ratio believes that the United States government does want to diminish the danger of war. This is not the judgment of a people who actually fear a military enemy.

Soviet-American relations in the future

Responses to a number of our questions all point to a conclusion that the Soviet people both desire and anticipate a continuing improvement in Soviet-American relations. More than 80% of the respondents favored the further development of trade, other economic contacts, and scientific and cultural relations with the United States, "regardless of the political situation between the two countries." More than 80% also agree that progress in Soviet-American relations cannot be limited to one specific area (such as the military) but must incorporate all areas — arms reductions, and also economics, science, technology, economics, culture, etc. Perhaps more significant, nearly 90% percent believe that "common problems facing the U.S. and USSR will force both sides to cooperate."

Taken together, these data probably signal the arrival of a new mass perception of priorities in Soviet-American relations. Contrary to the recent past, when the main emphasis in at least the Soviet official position was on progress in arms reductions, the Soviet people today support simultaneous cooperation between the USSR and the U.S. in all directions.

A majority of Soviet citizens apparently are also willing to give up the special privileges of being a "superpower" along with the United States. While more than 50% believe that relations between the USSR and the U.S. will continue to shape international politics, 68% endorse the idea that the two countries should have only the same rights and privileges in the international arena as any other countries.

The scenarios of Soviet-American relations and characteristic individual types

Naturally we researched the responses of the citizens surveyed to the six future scenarios for Soviet-American relations. As we anticipated, a simple breakdown of peoples' preferences is not very meaningful with a sample of this kind. Partly this is because, as mentioned earlier, one individual may want to endorse more than one scenario. A more subtle and more important reason is that the scenarios require discussion before they can be used very meaningfully. To respond intelligently, people must understand some complicated things. They must understand the practical implications of each scenario; they must understand what the USSR would gain and what it would have to give up in each case; and they must understand that certain combinations of policies are possible and other combinations are impossible. Understanding all this, without discussions, is too much to ask of ordinary people, particularly people who are not used to public opinion surveys on great issues of policy, and not used to public debate of policy alternatives.[16]

Therefore we approached the public response to the six scenarios in a different way. Naturally we recorded their preferences. We also compared their preferences with their responses to other questions. We also made cross comparisons among their other answers, such as their opinions about security and their opinions about Soviet-American relations. In addition, we held some discussions with groups of citizens. We also evaluated our results in the light of other research that we and others have done.

Our most significant conclusion, after the completion of all these things, proved to be the illumination of several characteristic "types" of individuals. Specifically, we were able to identify five types of people or five typical "mentalities." Of course only a few individuals fit each type perfectly. But we found that people of each type tend, on the whole, to give similar answers to certain questions. Indeed once their attitude on some questions was identified, we could predict with a fair degree of confidence how they would answer other questions. We also believe that these five types can be found throughout many parts of the USSR. We will conclude this chapter by discussing these five types of "political consciousness" with respect to Soviet foreign affairs.

The traditional ideological type

In a political culture that traditionally has been highly ideological, it is not surprising to find a well-defined type of ideological mentality. While ideological perspectives are found among others also, in this type they are paramount. Ideology acts as a lens through which all issues of politics, economy and culture are perceived.

What are the attributes of this type? Perhaps most important, this mentality relies heavily on stereotypes. Ideas like "American imperialism," "world socialism," "parity," "the American threat" and other, easily recognized newspaper clichés produce an immediate and nearly automatic response. Like a conditioned reflex, they lead to a predictable reaction.

More of this type (62%) believe that an American threat exists than does the general population. Two-thirds of this type believe that the ideological conflict between socialism and capitalism is the main reason for the arms race. Nearly a third of them do not believe that having normal relations with the United States would have any value for the USSR. Among this type we find the highest percentage of people who believe that the main goal for Soviet foreign policy should be the promotion of socialism around the world, and also the greatest support for directing Soviet foreign aid by ideological criteria.

The ideological mentality may generate curious contradictions, because it is dependent upon a blind acceptance of official rhetoric and newspaper clichés. Currently one such cliché is that common problems will force the USSR and the U.S. to cooperate. Accepting this cliché like any other, the ideological type endorses this idea (even more than other types), apparently not noticing that it contradicts viewing the United States as an enemy. Then, having pledged their support for the cliché, they make another 180-degree turn and support — much more than people generally — the idea that any cooperation with the capitalist states must be temporary, unstable and limited. Here is a second example: the ideological type accepts the concept of "reasonable sufficiency" in weapons because it is part of today's official rhetoric. But it turns out that these people define, in their own minds, "reasonable sufficiency" as meaning that the USSR must have exactly as many weapons as the United States does and not one rocket less. (Of course the concept actually means that the USSR should have only those weapons it needs for its own security, and never mind how many the Americans have.)

The ideological mentality is also a very skeptical mentality. This type has less confidence than people generally in arms reductions, or in the positive impact of perestroika on Soviet-American relations. We suspect there may be an overall constellation of skepticism — doubt about the future of Soviet-American relations, doubt about the impact on it of perestroika, and for that matter doubt about perestroika itself.

About one-third of the citizens we surveyed supported, at least partially, the "ideological" scenario for the future of Soviet-American relations. But a majority rejected it.

Let us mention that we believe this type should actually be called the *traditional ideological* type, because it is our observation that, in their own way, many supporters of glasnost, perestroika and the new political thinking are just as ideological. The only difference is that the contents of their slogans has switched.

The isolationists

In the current domestic situation of the USSR, when many problems are being exposed that were neglected for a long time, it is natural for there to be a new focus of attention on internal development. The extreme or "pure" form of that focus is our scenario called "the USSR focusing on domestic problems." More than one-fifth of the citizens surveyed supported this scenario. We will call them isolationists.

What is the underlying attitudes of this type? Is it isolationism in the traditional geopolitical sense? Is it a form of nationalism? How does this type see the problem of security?

One major feature of this mentality is a desire to remove the USSR from any network of interdependence with the rest of the world. In comparison with people generally, this type believes the least in global interdependence, in the interests of humanity as a whole, or that common Soviet-American problems compel cooperation.

This is a defensive mentality. Most supporters of this scenario believe in unilateral means to achieve Soviet security. They prefer a build-up of military strength and technology over political negotiation as a path to security. More than people generally, they see the threat to the USSR as military, and they tend to mistrust arms reductions and reliance on only defensive weapons. In a sense they are oriented toward what is concrete: they focus on the military threat, not an ideological one, and they believe in military power, not negotiations. This type will insist on military parity with the West at any cost.

Analysis of their responses shows that this type does not adopt its position from feelings of simple weakness as a result of a disastrous situation at home. The stance is not despair before the multitude of domestic problems, but a desire for isolation in a position of strength. In essence, they believe that the numerous internal problems can be solved only behind strong walls. It would not be much exaggeration to call this a Fortress Russia mentality.

Not surprisingly, this type emphasizes the sovereignty of the state. A much higher percentage of this group than of the whole public believes that Soviet human rights questions are a strictly internal matter, which other countries should not meddle in, and believe that information and publications from the West should continue to be restricted. But the psychological stance is not so much fear of ideological subversion, as it is the desire for strong walls for the fortress in every sense.

At a time of nationalist upheavals within the USSR, it would be logical to ask whether this type identifies with the Soviet Union or with its own Republic or ethnic group. At this stage we cannot answer this definitively because our research was conducted in the Russian Republic. However our study of responses to dozens of questions, and the cross comparison of these responses, convinces us that this mentality is focusing on the wall — both existing and desired — between the USSR and the rest of the world. This group wishes to be safe behind the wall of the state. For a multinational state like the USSR, this is a significant observation.

The anti-nuclear type

This type responds strongly to the scenario that we call "Competitive Coexistence." These are worried people who feel keenly the threat of a worldwide nuclear holocaust that could destroy human civilization.

It is this group, much more than others, who see Western as well as Soviet nuclear weapons as preserving the peace — in other words, who accept the idea of a mutual deterrent balance. However exact parity is not necessary since both sides already have far too many weapons.

For this type, preserving mutual deterrence is merely a first step. In this view the urgent next step is to reduce nuclear arms by means of negotiations with the West. This type is more optimistic than people generally about the feasibility of these negotiations, and also more optimistic about the possibility of abolishing nuclear weapons completely, perhaps even by the year 2000. For this group the prevention of nuclear war should be, of course, the chief goal of Soviet foreign policy.

For Soviets it follows logically (although it might seem strange to Westerners) that this type also believes, more than the public generally, that "peace is impossible so long as American imperialism exists." The reason why these people support this idea is not because they ideologically reject the West's social system (as the traditional ideological type does), but because they are fearful of another great nation — *any* other great nation — that possesses huge quantities of nuclear weapons.

There is also a paradox in this mentality, which agrees that rivalry between the USSR and the West will continue, even following great reductions in nuclear arms. This type does *not* believe this from a desire to take revenge in other areas, for having been forced — under the threat of worldwide disaster — to make great compromises on nuclear weapons. As a matter of fact, these people would like to see more comprehensive cooperation with the West in all fields, if they thought it was possible. But this is a pessimistic mentality. They do not think it is possible. They see the elements of conflict in Soviet-American relations as too strong. The reason they believe that great nuclear reductions can be achieved is that they see the threat of global catastrophe as being the one thing so powerful that it can force the two sides to make compromises and reach agreements. No other factor is strong enough to do so, so agreements in other areas will not be successfully reached.[17]

The conciliatory type

Approximately three-fifths of the citizens gave their support to the scenario of "general normalization" of relations with the United States.[18] We will give the name "conciliatory" to this type. However this does not mean that these people want the USSR to make one-sided concessions to the West; it means that they believe both sides should be conciliatory toward each other. What are the attributes of this mentality?

First, it is an "America-centered" mentality, or to be exact, one that sees Soviet-American relations as the centerpiece of world politics, compared to which all other matters are subordinate. These people, more than the population generally, believe that Soviet-American relations will never become secondary (surpassed, for instance, by North-South problems, or Soviet-European relations or Soviet-Japanese relations.) From this viewpoint it follows that security depends on nuclear parity between the two sides, and follows also that American as well as Soviet weapons help prevent war by balancing each other. It also follows consistently that bilateral negotiations and agreements are more important than multilateral ones, and that the superpower arsenals are the decisive question for world peace. This viewpoint does not assign great importance to regional conflicts elsewhere on Earth, to terrorism, or to other possible threats to security and peace.

This mentality is a Western-oriented one and is "liberal." It rejects the idea that there might be any danger to the Soviet Union from "creeping Westernism." People holding this viewpoint desire an open Soviet society with no barriers to information or publications from the West, and they hope for cooperation with the West in economics, culture, and all spheres of life.

In our assessment, these foreign policy attitudes are a reaction against the Cold War — in a sense a simple reaction. This viewpoint does not conceive any brand new ideas. It takes the old categories and reverses them: minuses are switched into plusses and plusses are switched into minuses. It is important to observe this when comparing this type with the next one. The next one also favors good relations with the West, but in a different way.

The global type

In citizens' responses to our "future scenarios," the fifth scenario of a complete restructuring of international relations was the most popular of all. A full 79% of the people surveyed gave their partial or complete support to this scenario, with 40% giving it complete support.[19] These people endorse a future in which security and peace is achieved by creating an entirely new kind of global system.

When people who give the greatest emphasis to this scenario are asked about Soviet-American relations, their typical response is to perceive the question in a global context. They feel that questions of bilateral relations should be resolved according to the interests of the whole of humanity. They reject the idea of "superpower" privileges or that East-West relations are the central international issue. They say that Soviet-American relations are already starting to be of secondary importance on the world scene. People holding this viewpoint reject the idea that the U.S.-Soviet balance in nuclear weapons can be a foundation for peace. They desire multilateral, not bilateral, treaties.

This type also rejects the significance of ideology and of ideological conflict — at any rate the traditional ideological conflict between socialism and capitalism.[20] Naturally their perception of any American threat is minimal. Those holding this viewpoint also have a much more negative view of nuclear weapons than most people. They usually do not accept that even Soviet nuclear weapons help preserve the peace, and they strongly desire complete world-wide nuclear disarmament and a nuclear-free world.

We must add a note of caution in interpreting these results. Many of these themes are part of the "new thinking" and the new official rhetoric. In the last several years these ideas have received great publicity in newspapers and elsewhere. It is not easy to tell how many of the citizens we surveyed may merely be expressing their agreement with the official slogans (as many Soviet citizens have always expressed agreement with the official slogans, whatever they may be at any one time.) The importance of this possibility is demonstrated by an analysis of the responses of this type to other questions. Many who endorse the global slogans also do *not* give much support to concrete policies for coping with global issues, for instance the possibility of directing Soviet foreign aid to all needy countries. Also, many who endorse the global viewpoint also respond positively to the idea that the USSR should concentrate all resources on solving its internal problems, *rather than* pursuing international goals.[21]

We will not analyze these results further here. Rather we wish to emphasize, in conclusion, the tremendous diversity in Soviet public opinion that our results reveal. These five viewpoints all differ greatly. They lead to very different policy conclusions. Yet not one of them can be dismissed as bizarre or unimportant. Each one is supported by large numbers of people.

At the present time, the Soviet Union is passing through a period of both profound and extremely rapid change. The debate, and sometimes the clash, of ideas is more intense than at any time since the period around 1917. As glasnost and democratization advance, debate about foreign policy and national security will no longer be excluded. Thus it will become more and more important to understand the true opinions of the public.

Notes

1. The research in the United States is reported in this book in the chapter by Mark Lindeman, and is referred to there as the "Futures" study. That research is described in greater detail in a book to be published shortly in the United States.

2. A more complete report of the first stage of our research may be obtained by contacting the authors at the Soviet Peace Committee, Moscow.

3. Two hundred questionnaires were distributed, and 120 completed ones were returned. The sample, then, is a self-selected one in a sense. For example, individuals who place no value on this kind of research presumably did not return the questionnaire. The list of respondents did not include a significant number of military officers. The respondents were 80% male and had a median time employed in professions involving international affairs of fifteen years. The breakdown of their ages was as follows: 20-29, 8%; 30-39, 49%; 40-49, 20%; 50-59, 13%; 60 or older, 10%. While this group is relatively young, it must be recalled that it is this group that will be moving into positions of responsibility and influence over the next decade or so.

   The limitations of the sample are less important than they may appear, because in this first stage we were not primarily interested in the exact distribution of responses. Rather we were mainly interested in identifying chief tendencies and in discovering whether various answers tended to cluster together. Certain other basic conclusions, discussed next, can also be validly drawn from such a sample.

   We acknowledge with thanks the great assistance in this work of colleagues at the Institute for Sociological Research of the Soviet Academy of Sciences, and especially the assistance of V. Marinov.

4. A majority of 74% disagreed with the statement that "collaboration between capitalism and socialism can only be temporary and limited." Only 20% agreed that "as long as American imperialism exists, a lasting peace is impossible." Fully 64% disagreed.

5. These six viewpoints, or scenarios, played approximately the same role in our public opinion research that the four "Futures" played in the project conducted by the Center for Foreign

Policy Development at Brown University and the Public Agenda Foundation of New York. There are important similarities but also important differences between the four American scenarios and the six Soviet ones. Naturally we do not mean to imply that the viewpoint of every individual would be exactly captured by any one of these six scenarios. The six represent merely broad viewpoints; many nuances are possible within each one.

6. This scenario corresponds approximately to the Future in the American research project called "The U.S. Gains the Upper Hand" — in reverse, of course.

7. This scenario corresponds exactly with the Future developed in the American research project called "Eliminate the Nuclear Threat; Compete Otherwise."

8. This scenario corresponds fairly closely with the Future developed in the American research project called "Cooperative Problem Solving."

9. This scenario might be seen as an application, to the global level, of the spirit of perestroika within the USSR. It visualizes a thorough global restructuring or "perestroika for the world."

10. This scenario corresponds closely with the Future developed in the American research project called "Defend Only North America."

11. The significance of the relative popularity of these six alternatives among the respondents should not be exaggerated. The cluster analysis technique makes it difficult to determine this accurately. Some individuals may not agree with any of the six; some may agree with portions of more than one. Nonetheless, for the record, our analysis indicates this breakdown among the respondents:

#1. Ideological	13%
#2. Superpower	14%
#3. Competitive Coexistence	35%
#4. Complex Normalization	28%
#5. Restructuring	50%
#6. Soviet domestic focus	20%

    The total adds up to much more than 100% because, as noted, some people support more than one alternative. Due to limitations of space, we will not discuss here a further complication: these "future scenarios" can be understood both as what one expects (prediction) and as what one wishes (preference).

12. A systematic survey of public opinion, on issues of foreign policy, had scarcely ever been conducted before in the USSR; and to our knowledge, had *never* before been conducted employing a large number of detailed questions. Hence this research was necessarily carried out on a somewhat experimental basis. It was not feasible, and was not to be expected, that early, ground-breaking research could, at the very first blow so to speak, meet the highest standards of statistical sampling techniques. For example the limitation to the Russian Republic, and to its European portion, means that the results do not necessarily reflect accurately opinion throughout all the republics of the USSR. It should also be kept in mind that this research was conducted in 1988, and much has changed since, both in the USSR and in the world.

    The report offered here of our public opinion research is necessarily simplified, for reasons of space. Also this book is not primarily about public opinion, and a more elaborate and complete presentation of our work would not be appropriate here. A more complete report of the second, public opinion, stage of our research may be obtained by contacting the authors at the Soviet Peace Committee, Moscow.

13. This was one of the questions where the divergence was striking when the question was reformulated using official phrases for exact parity.

14. Here is an example of a response to official rhetoric that is the opposite of the one discussed earlier. When the official rhetoric is contrary to the traditional attitudes of centuries, there is a tendency for citizens to respond with traditional attitudes.

15. It would not be correct to say that the public attitude contains a logical contradiction or inconsistency. It is not illogical to wish that a nuclear-free world were possible, while believing that, realistically, it is not.

16. This research was conducted in 1988, only about three years from the very beginning of glasnost.

17. Discussions in depth with people holding this viewpoint revealed that the majority of those who hold it feel that it is self-contradictory and unstable. In a sense it is illogical that the two sides would make extremely important agreements in one area and not be able to reach agreements at all in other areas. Many people of the third type saw their viewpoint as actually being a limited or truncated version of the next, fourth viewpoint. But they held to their view nonetheless because they regard it as the realistic one. They pointed out that something like this is, in fact, what the two sides have achieved so far — major agreements in military areas and very little else.

18. Observe that here, as before, the total percentage of supporters of all scenarios will come to much more than 100% because some individuals endorse more than one scenario. Whether they do so, while appreciating possible conflicts among the scenarios they are endorsing remains an open question.

19. As noted in the previous footnote, in this method the total number of supporters can come to much more than 100%.

20. However such people may find themselves in an "ideological" conflict with those who do not share their views; and in a sense this fifth type could be seen as itself a new ideology.

21. Such data are reasons for caution, but not for dismissing entirely the support that these people give to the global viewpoint. For example, some may not have understood the practical contradictions implicit in these questions and would answer differently if they had. And some may have meant, by their responses, to say that the USSR should *temporarily* focus on internal problems until they are solved, and then turn to global needs and global restructuring.

24

Mutual Security and
U.S. Public Opinion

MARK LINDEMAN

Why we consider the "public opinion problem" [1]

Many American specialists on U.S.-Soviet relations have voiced concern about the American public's role in the foreign policy-making process — especially concern that the public may impede the pursuit of a coherent policy. This concern is held by scholars and policymakers across the ideological spectrum, and is rooted in the fact that "mainstream" public opinion itself straddles much of that spectrum. Thus observers who favor a skeptical response to recent Soviet initiatives fear that the public will fall prey to "Gorby fever" and support irresponsible proposals for, e.g., too drastic military cuts. In contrast, those who hope for warmer U.S.-Soviet relations on a basis of mutual accommodation worry that the public is prone to reflexive anti-communism or even "Rambomania," tendencies which might make closer relations almost impossible to sustain. And "moderates" worry that these competing values will cause the U.S. to veer back and forth between logically and politically contradictory policies, harming U.S. interests. Each group has reasons for its concerns.

With respect to mutual security, the "public opinion problem" in the United States is neatly posed by the history of detente. In the early 1970s, American leaders apparently felt compelled to oversell the merits of detente in order to build public support for it. Later, the angry public response to Soviet actions around the world, culminating in the 1979 invasion of Afghanistan, was intensified by a bitter sense that the Soviets had taken advantage of U.S. good will and trustfulness in order to betray us. While the invasion of Afghanistan would have posed a difficult challenge for U.S. policymakers in any case, the public outrage put enormous pressures on the Carter administration, and contributed to Carter's defeat by the conservative Ronald Reagan. Here again, observers at various points on the spectrum will interpret the rise and fall of detente quite differently. Yet probably all would agree that this is a case of a failure to integrate policy and public opinion — a failure which leaves a somewhat embarrassing legacy of policy reversals for present policymakers to contend with.

While the "public opinion problem" is considered in many discussions of U.S.-Soviet relations, it is often treated as an extraneous variable. Specialists typically discuss the "objective" merits of various hypothetical developments in U.S.-Soviet relations, and only then consider whether public views pose an insuperable obstacle to such developments. I consider this approach valuable but inadequate. An issue as fundamental as U.S. policy toward the Soviet Union cannot be settled by government fiat, no matter how enlightened: it will have to address public concerns at every step along the way.

Does careful attention to public views entail an abdication of leadership, drifting with the winds of the polls? I think not. I believe that behind the ephemeral shifts and contradictions of public opinion lies a core of consensual values which can motivate a pragmatic and sustainable policy.[2] I also believe that in the long run, both American democratic ideals and the U.S. national interest are better served by a clear articulation of the costs and risks of various policy options than by simplistic proposals that obscure these trade-offs. I assume, then, that policymakers are constrained by public opinion as well as having some power to shape it;[3] and that policymakers are best able to govern when they respect, rather than insult, citizens' intelligence.

In this chapter, I will focus on the core public values that are likely to shape the debate on policy toward the Soviet Union. These values are not, as some suspect, mutually contradictory, although they do require difficult trade-offs in practice. Then I will consider the implications of these values for variants of mutual (and unilateral) security. This strategy may seem a bit circuitous, but attempts to move directly to the "relevant opinion data," while slighting core values, often misrepresent actual public thinking.

Beyond "contradiction" in public opinion

Opinion surveys conducted over the past five years document both strong U.S. public support for cooperation with the USSR on the one hand, and continued suspicion of the USSR on the other. Some observers are tempted to conclude that public opinion is simply contradictory and is best disregarded. Their reaction exemplifies a common weakness in expert discussions of public opinion: the public is held in contempt for not giving sophisticated responses to basically simplistic questions. Very few Western scholars and policymakers believe either that the USSR can be trusted in every respect or that all forms of U.S.-Soviet cooperation are impossible. Likewise, very few American citizens hold these extreme beliefs, a fact which reflects public thoughtfulness, not inconsistency.

However, public views on concrete policies often can seem flatly contradictory. For instance, in the Americans Talk Security (ATS) surveys conducted between November 1987 and November 1988, over 85% approved of negotiating a freeze on nuclear weapons, yet 53% approved of "moderniz[ing] our nuclear arsenal before we even consider a freeze."[4] Similar results crop up throughout the ATS surveys and other work: as many as 50% or more of a survey group can be induced to endorse two apparently contradictory results.

The cause is easy to understand. When non-experts are asked to take a stand on a particular policy issue, rarely have they had an opportunity to consider the issue's impact on *all* their various values, weigh the pros and cons, and come to a measured conclusion. (Incidentally, even if survey respondents did go through such a process, most questions do not either provoke or reward the effort: there is no room, for instance, to explain *under what circumstances* respondents would support cooperation, or *to what extent* they would support modernization.) So respondents typically react to the one or two most prominent values highlighted in the question. For instance, in the example cited above, few Americans have the knowledge to judge whether the U.S. nuclear arsenal requires "modernization." About all that can be said, on the basis of these two findings, is that the public supports both initiatives to end the arms race and efforts to maintain a strong defense. Survey results like these must be read with the hidden *ceteris paribus* in mind, and considered more as value statements than as specific policy guidance.

Does this mean that public opinion bears at best a metaphorical relationship to actual policy issues? On the contrary, I believe that public value judgments are extremely relevant to policy, although not on the level usually explored by opinion surveys. My analysis hinges on the distinction, first made by Daniel Yankelovich, between "public choices" and "expert choices." As Richard Smoke has summarized the concept:

> Experts identify the limits of policy feasibility. This done, the public — not experts — chooses the ends to be sought, within those limits. The experts, working with the public's representatives, then translate goals and purposes into means and strategies.[5]

In other words, broad value choices are legitimately in the public domain; the public can reach meaningful decisions on fundamental goals, without mastering the narrower issues that require expertise. However, for the public to make real choices — as opposed to vague expressions of utopian desires — it needs guidance about the "limits of the possible" and the areas in which its values conflict. Regrettably, most surveys on security issues have tried to "water down" the expert choices (that is, the specific means and strategies) for public consumption, while they have done little to clarify the fundamental public choices on priorities.

It will not do, then, simply to compile a list of public responses to various survey questions on policy, concluding that Americans do or do not support "cooperation," or "a hard line," or "arms control," or "aid to freedom fighters" or what have you. Analysts must get behind the survey responses to the *value assumptions* that determine them. Again, merely listing the main values of the American public will not clearly illuminate the path to honoring them all equally and simultaneously: there are difficult trade-offs among values, which both leaders and the public must struggle to come to grips with. Still, the analysis is a valuable one. Contradicting a contemptuous view of an ignorant and capricious public, it suggests that the public *does* recognize the real trade-offs and, given some opportunity to do so, will attempt to confront these trade-offs — and will respect American leaders who do the same.

There are many published analyses of American public opinion on Soviet-American relations. Hence I shall review here only briefly some of the most important features of that opinion. Then I shall turn to the analysis of American public opinion for mutual security specifically. The analysis in this chapter draws heavily on a study designed specifically to illuminate public choices. The Center for Foreign Policy Development and the New York-based Public Agenda Foundation conducted, between 1985 and 1988, a project on "The Public, the Soviets, and Nuclear Arms," centered on a framework of four alternative "Futures" for U.S.-Soviet relations. The Futures, which span the spectrum of American opinion, comprise not only long-term goals but also policy imperatives with their attendant costs and risks.[6] The project's opinion study, conducted in February 1988, brought together over nine hundred people in five cities to discuss these Futures for hours at a time, forcing them to grapple with the trade-offs among them.[7] Because the Futures incorporate four radically different approaches to national security, including mutual security, the project's findings have a direct bearing on the present topic. These results are buttressed by a variety of findings taken from more traditional surveys taken before, during, and after the Futures project work.

A survey of key public values on national security

What, then, are the key public values, held by most Americans across the ideological spectrum, which pertain to their views on national security? I make no real effort to rank them, since people may put different weight on values at one time than they do at another. (A trivial example: resisting Soviet expansion will seem more important when the Soviets are perceived as aggressively testing the U.S. than when they are not.) However, there are obvious trade-offs among many of these values, and one can at least suggest what they might be. Here I will express the values as ends, but with some attention to the *fears* and *means* implied by each.

Physical survival

It goes almost without saying that Americans value their own physical security and that of their country. Americans have rarely had to fear a direct invasion by another country, and hardly anyone fears one now. Thus this fear most often now is manifested as *fear of nuclear war*.[8] Without belaboring the point here, we can point out that the public recognizes several different threats of nuclear war: the possibility of a Soviet "bolt out of the blue," the chance of a superpower crisis spinning out of control, the risk of an accidental war, and the risk of another country or a terrorist organization using a nuclear weapon against the U.S.

Survey data consistently show that a "bolt from the blue" is considered very unlikely.[9] The public does not discount the Soviet threat, but it perceives this threat — where U.S. survival is concerned — as created not so much by Soviet aggressive intent as by the inherent dangers of the conflictive relationship between the two countries.[10] Most Americans would probably respond sympathetically to Henry Kissinger's declaration: "The superpowers often behave like two heavily armed blind men feeling their way around a room, each believing himself in danger from the other whom he assumes to have perfect vision. . . . Of course, over time, two blind men can do enormous damage to each other, not to speak of the room."

Preventing "encirclement"

While most Americans are reasonably confident that U.S. borders are secure, most also feel that the unchecked expansion of the Soviet Union (or any other nation) would pose a direct threat to America's security. The specific rationale for this perception is not entirely clear. Many experts would cite the possible loss of American access to raw materials and markets, an argument that the general public will generally assent to when it is invoked, for instance, to support U.S. involvement in the Middle East. But rarely do members of the general public volunteer this rationale themselves. A more common rationale seems to be that the U.S. and USSR stand in a somewhat fragile balance, and any U.S. failure to resist Soviet expansion might undermine the balance and lead in the long run to the overthrow of the U.S. itself. Thus, in the Futures survey, a 55% plurality agreed (with 34% disagreeing) that a convincing argument against pursuing military isolationism was that "our allies may make concessions to the Soviets and eventually leave us alone in a world filled with enemies."

That the reasoning is more impressionistic than literal is suggested by the public's skepticism about aid to the Nicaraguan Contras: the Reagan administration never managed to convince a majority of the public that the establishment of a communist government on the Central American mainland posed a clear and present danger to U.S. security.11 Yet most Americans believe that the threat of Soviet expansion is real — a conviction that straddles the uneasy line between "realpolitik" and ideological belief. Robert W. Tucker has written that "even if the loss of areas deemed vital to security would not render America physically insecure, the result might still be expected to threaten the integrity of our institutions and seriously impair the quality of our domestic life." Most Americans agree, not reflectively but almost intuitively.

On the other hand, most Americans have now abandoned the idea that the Soviet Union poses the greatest threat to U.S. security. In the 1988 Americans Talk Security polling, the public "consistently indicated that international drug trafficking, terrorism, and the spread of nuclear weapons to Third World countries were greater threats to our country than the threat of Soviet expansionism."[12] If the perceived Soviet threat continues to decline, the U.S. public will gradually redirect its concerns toward other adversaries.

Prosperity

This value is manifested in several ways. As noted above, the public generally believes that Soviet expansion could undermine U.S. trade as well as physical security. On the other hand, it fears that excessive military spending will distract the U.S. from other pressing problems, such as the deficit, the homelessness, and the war on drugs. In the Futures study, where participants were asked to assess the likelihood of fourteen distinct threats to U.S. security, two threats in this category were in the front rank: 74% thought it very or fairly likely that "we will seriously damage our economy by spending too much money to defend other countries," and 72% that "we will neglect problems here in the U.S. because we spend so much on what seems like a never-ending arms race."

Predictably, these concerns are borne out in a general desire to curtail defense spending. Even in the November 1987 ATS poll, 48% believed that the U.S. was spending too much on defense (as opposed to 15% "too little" and 34% "about the right amount"). And in a May 1989 study, 52% approved of "dramatically reduc[ing] military spending, recognizing that the current levels of military spending no longer make sense in a world where the Soviet threat has diminished and economic competition has increased."[13] But other surveys find that, even with the rapid changes in Eastern Europe, the public is reluctant to hurry toward any radical military retrenchment.[14]

Addressing global problems

A few years ago it would have seemed oddly visionary to include this in a list of core values of the American public, but our Futures research suggests that it can no longer be omitted. In February 1988, 74% of the participants thought it very or fairly likely that "mistrust and hostility will keep us from working with the Soviets on the real problems facing us like terrorism and the spread of nuclear weapons"; 83% agreed that a convincing argument for cooperative problem solving was that "the spread of nuclear weapons, pollution, and AIDS are the *real* problems facing us and the Soviets." Americans might not all know what "nuclear proliferation" means, and they might not be able to explain just what the "greenhouse effect" is and what it has to do with acid rain or the ozone layer; but they need no reminder that the world is becoming a more dangerous place in many ways. The public is concerned about a large range of global problems: some created or exacerbated by a small number of countries (e.g., proliferation), others by almost all countries (e.g., environmental hazards), and some largely independent of national policy (e.g., AIDS).[15]

These problems pose a potential dilemma for the American public, because it still does not want to "lower America's guard" in order to cooperate with the USSR on these issues. Despite the strong support for cooperative problem solving in principle, we discovered substantial doubt about whether the Soviet Union would cooperate in good faith.[16] This pattern continues in more recent surveys: although the public believes that other threats to U.S. security are becoming more serious than the Soviet threat, it is not yet convinced that the U.S. can safely redirect many resources from countering the Soviets to other concerns. The prevailing public attitude seems to be, "Let's cooperate where we can do so safely, but let's keep our powder dry, too."

Defense of democracy

No discussion of U.S. attitudes toward the Soviet threat would be complete without underscoring the strong American belief that the U.S. has a vital role as leader of the free world. While most participants in the Futures study rejected seeking overall dominance over the Soviet Union, a 55% majority agreed (with 33% disagreeing) that a convincing argument for this Future was that "the U.S. has an obligation to oppose Soviet and communist expansion and defend freedom around the world."

How does this imperative translate into actual policy? The answer is fuzzy at best. In the Futures study, a 64%-31% majority agreed in principle that "we should provide aid to anti-communist groups and governments," although support dropped to 39% when it was added that this might entail aid to "dictators and others who do not believe in democracy." Support also dropped, to 46%, when *military* aid was specified, and to 44% if the aid would increase the risk of U.S. troop involvement. Other data from the ATS surveys confirm that Americans are reluctant to contemplate almost any further use of U.S. troops; yet they have positive views of many past interventions, including the U.S. invasions of Grenada and Panama, and presumably would again offer *post facto* support for a short and successful intervention. Thus Americans appear to be especially confused about the trade-offs between defending democracy and protecting U.S. interests, when these two are in conflict.

The question must be asked whether the profound public dislike of communism precludes mutual security arrangements with the Soviet Union as long as that country remains under communist rule. Apparently most Americans believe that the geopolitical rivalry between the superpowers is grounded in real and lasting ideological differences, and therefore tend to be pessimistic about the chances of reducing the threat. Yet few Americans are opposed on principle to bargaining with the Soviet Union, if the Soviets prove that they can be trusted — or at least if they can be "kept honest" with respect to a particular agreement.

Americans typically pride themselves on being able to rise above ideology and to work out pragmatic compromises; most would be willing to do so with the Soviet Union. Where the public is concerned, substantial progress in mutual security (at least with respect to threat reduction) probably depends less on further Soviet democratization *per se* than on a general perception that Soviet leaders are dealing honestly with the U.S. The growth of trust in a broader sense probably does depend on considerable Soviet democratization. Also, democratization might be prerequisite for Soviet acceptance of the sorts of verification provisions that the U.S. public and experts alike will want, to feel certain that the USSR is complying with its agreements. Still, this public opinion "linkage" may be weaker than policymakers often assume.

Implications for mutual security

So far I have listed five broad categories of public values: physical survival; preventing "encirclement"; prosperity; addressing global problems; and defense of democracy. I want to examine more specifically how these public values pertain to possible public attitudes concerning mutual security. There is no clear consensus on any one view of mutual security; rather, various core values lend support for various perspectives. Different ways of identifying these are possible; here I shall use the three-way typology offered by Richard Smoke in his chapter in this book.

I. Technical mutual security, in which the U.S. and USSR engage in quite limited cooperation to reduce the risk of accidental war (for instance, the establishment of "hot lines" and some degree of unilateral restraint in "hot spots") in the context of an otherwise competitive relationship, has strong support among the American public. To be sure, technical mutual security is few Americans' first choice in principle: most would prefer at least some degree of nuclear arms reductions, if these could be reliably verified. But many are skeptical about the prudence of arms control. For instance, in the Futures study, a 47%-37% plurality agreed that a convincing argument against pursuing nuclear risk reduction was that "the Soviets can't be trusted and will cheat on arms control treaties." This distrust may take considerable time and effort to overcome.

In the Futures study, two of the four Futures involve only technical mutual security efforts: the confrontational "U.S. Gains the Upper Hand," and the military isolationist "Defend Only North America." These Futures were favored by only 12% and 4% of the public respectively. However, close analysis of the results suggests that these figures understate the popularity of a cautious approach to mutual security. Many participants who questioned the viability of arms control and broader cooperative regimes nonetheless preferred them over a quest for U.S. superiority (which 75% of all participants characterized as "a formula for an endless arms race") and over a retreat from most military commitments abroad. If participants had been presented with *five* Futures, including a new variant in which the U.S. competed with the USSR around the world, with little or no progress on arms control, but also without any effort to gain military superiority, it is plausible that one, plus "U.S. Gains the Upper Hand," would have together gained 35%-40% support. Since public views on other policy questions have shifted surprisingly little in the past two years, we should assume that many Americans continue to prefer technical mutual security to its alternatives.

A supporter of technical-only mutual security is likely to believe that the threat posed to U.S. interests by the Soviet Union is great and enduring, and will therefore emphasize the priority of ensuring physical survival, preventing encirclement, and defending democracy. Supporters of this path accept some risks of economic damage and harm from global problems: in the Futures study, supporters of "U.S. Gains the Upper Hand" considered these threats as likely as did supporters of any other Future. But these risks are seen as a necessary evil in the face of the overriding imperative of countering the Soviet threat. (Supporters of this view tend to discount the risk of an inadvertent war between the superpowers: if nuclear war begins, they believe, it will probably be because of a Soviet attempt to gain advantage.) While the public overall does not support necessity for U.S. military superiority, it does endorse spending on defense whatever is needed to assure U.S. safety, despite the cost.[17]

II. Threat-reduction mutual security, is partly represented in the Futures study by the Future called "Eliminate the Nuclear Threat; Compete Otherwise."[18] The public was generally supportive of this Future, but with several important reservations.

First, the most popular argument *against* this Future, which a 53%-33% majority found convincing, was that it would leave the USSR with a large advantage in conventional forces. The public split evenly, 47%-47%, on the proposal that the two sides should agree on drastic cuts in nuclear weapons *"even if that means* leaving [the USSR] with the largest army in the world." But a 74%-20% majority endorsed drastic nuclear cuts if the U.S. also simultaneously increased its conventional strength to match that of the Soviets. These findings suggest that further progress on conventional arms control will be needed to ease public (as well as expert) concerns about nuclear reductions.[19]

Second, a 47% plurality were concerned that the Soviet Union could not be trusted to abide by its treaties. Verification and compliance will continue to be major public concerns, and potential political footballs, for the foreseeable future in the United States.[20] The public will not follow the nuances of the technical debates on verification; it simply wants to feel very sure both that the USSR will keep its word, *and* that if it doesn't, the U.S. will unilaterally discover the violation in time to prevent serious harm to U.S. interests.

Third, and perhaps most important, a large minority question whether it is possible to isolate the nuclear threat from the rest of the U.S.-Soviet relationship. Thirty-eight percent agreed that a convincing argument against this Future was that "it's just not realistic to think that we can compete with the Soviets in the Third World while, at the same time, cooperate with them to eliminate the risk of nuclear war"; another 17% were not sure. Meanwhile, fully 73% agreed that a convincing argument for a Future of "Cooperative Problem Solving" was that unless the superpowers changed their relationship, "even the most comprehensive arms agreements won't make [them] safe," and that such a change is "the *only* way we'll be able to end the arms race." Thus the public is skeptical that the superpowers can "get nuclear weapons off the playing field" without fundamentally changing the competitive game itself.

Many experts believe the failure of the detente of the 1970s proves that attempts to isolate security issues, particularly arms control treaties, from broader currents in U.S.-Soviet relations are indeed unrealistic. The case is probably still unproven: during the 1970s, no consistent effort was made to isolate arms control from the broader relationship. If a series of American presidents had gone before the public to ask that it weigh the merits of arms control agreements on their own terms, *not* as part of an overall improvement in relations, might arms control have been more successful? There ultimately is no answer. However, most observers would probably agree that in the absence of fundamental change in U.S.-Soviet relations, truly drastic cuts in conventional and nuclear forces are unlikely, if only because of the likelihood of domestic opposition in both countries blocking such agreements.

It should be noted, however, that "fundamental change" in this sense does not necessarily require any great degree of closeness between the two countries. It does not require large exchange programs, extensive cooperation on common problems, or any particular ideological "meeting of minds." It does require substantial initiatives by both sides (unilateral, parallel, and bilateral) to reduce mutual risk to each other's interests. At present the U.S. public has no clear vision of what this "peace without friendship" might resemble, but our analysis of the public's values suggests that Americans would accept and even embrace the development, even if it is less than their fondest hopes.

III. Supportive mutual security, which entails the near elimination of competition and cooperation between the U.S. and USSR on a broad range of issues, is in principle the most popular Future among the U.S. public. A full 46% chose "Cooperative Problem Solving" as their preferred Future in the Futures study.[21] It should not be thought that public support for cooperation with the Soviets reflects an ephemeral euphoria about Gorbachev's reforms. Indeed, such support predates Gorbachev's rise to power. For instance, in another study conducted in 1984, during the listless tenure of Konstantin Chernenko, a 55%-40% majority supported "expand[ing] trade with the Soviets and mak[ing] other cooperative gestures, even if that makes them stronger and more secure."[22] Just how far the public would have wanted cooperation to go then, or would like it to go now, is a difficult question, but the openness to such cooperation is clearly not new.

On the other hand, we have already noted the broad public skepticism about Soviet motives and honesty, and the general unwillingness to take great risks in cooperating with the Soviets. To cite another figure from the Futures study, a 53%-27% majority agreed (with 21% unsure) that "no matter what they say, the Soviets really want every country in the world to be communist and they will never stop trying to reach that goal." Thus, while Americans would like to cooperate with the Soviets on global problems, they are not at all convinced that broad cooperation is desirable *if* it means acquiescing in a greater risk of encirclement or abandoning the defense of democracy.

The prospects for supportive mutual security, then, depend largely on American perceptions of Soviet motives around the world. If the U.S. public becomes convinced that the USSR is limiting its interference in other nations' affairs, pressure will grow on the U.S. government to expand cooperation with the Soviets.[23] If, on the contrary, the public decides that the USSR is exploiting U.S. warmth while it continues an aggressive role around the world, the backlash will likely block progress not only on supportive measures, but on threat reduction as well.

Conclusion

In sum, this survey of relevant U.S. public opinion does not reveal a ground swell of public insistence on mutual security measures, but it does reveal a very warm interest in exploring such measures. Most Americans believe that the threat of Soviet aggression and communist expansion is rapidly being eclipsed by a broad array of other threats to U.S. security; at the same time, they remain wary about taking the Soviets' good intentions for granted. The public's attitude might be summarized as follows: it would be a shame if we let the differences between the U.S. and USSR keep us from winding down the most dangerous aspects of our rivalry and working together on common problems; but it would be an even greater mistake if the U.S. let down its guard too soon and the USSR took advantage of us.

While this conclusion might seem pessimistic for advocates of extensive mutual security policies, it still allows for large mutual security initiatives. On balance, the American public does not insist upon any particular Soviet concessions, such as some specific degree of democratization, a great increase in mutual warmth, or a particular disposition of troops in Central Europe, as prerequisites for progress on mutual security. The public simply asks U.S. policymakers to work for explicit or tacit agreements that reduce the risk to both countries, and with which compliance can be unilaterally confirmed. These are criteria whose good sense expert observers can readily concede. The American public does not want to trust Gorbachev immediately, but it does want to put him to the test. The public's message is, "Proceed with caution" — not "Wait and see." Since an extensive mutual security regime must evolve over time in any case, the public's attitudes offer an open door for well-considered mutual security initiatives. The public is in no position to formulate specific mutual security proposals, but it can be expected to respond warmly to them, as long as they are seen as fair and safe for the U.S.

This discussion has not unearthed any startling new consensus on the ideal direction of U.S.-Soviet relations: in public opinion, as in expert discourse, we find that every policy option has distinct benefits, costs, and risks. I would like to suggest, in closing, that this very finding should give great comfort to American specialists across the ideological spectrum who may be inclined to fear the impact of uninformed public opinion. While there is no neat public consensus on what the U.S. should do next, there is ample basis for such a consensus backing a measured policy: one which would actively explore opportunities for U.S.-Soviet cooperation and mutual security efforts without making any dangerous concessions. A stable and sensible U.S. policy with solid public backing may be closer at hand than some people have thought.

Notes

1. Soviet readers are reminded that extensive public opinion surveys are conducted in the United States constantly, not only on foreign affairs, but also on an immense range of other political questions. So much data, even about foreign affairs alone, is collected that the *analysis* of the results is a recognized field of specialization and may occupy some experts nearly full time. A full assessment of American public opinion on foreign policy might require a book as long as this one.

   Due to the limitations of space, I have chosen to emphasize in this chapter a single study, called the "Futures" study, conducted jointly by the Center for Foreign Policy Development at Brown University and the Public Agenda Foundation of New York, as stated later in the text. Other data are introduced, sometimes in footnotes, when it may be helpful. Some of the methods of the "Futures" study were later employed in the Soviet research project that is discussed in the chapter by Andrei Melvil and Aleksandr Nikitin in this book.

   I gratefully acknowledge comments on earlier drafts of this chapter from Eric Mlyn of the Center for Foreign Policy Development and Paul Joseph of Tufts University.

2. For an analysis which argues, on the contrary, that "an overarching public opinion consensus on foreign policy is not possible," see Ronald H. Hinckley, "Public Attitudes Towards Key Foreign Policy Events," *Journal of Conflict Resolution* 32, no. 2 (June 1988). (This statement is found on p. 305.) My difference with Hinckley is largely one of emphasis: while recognizing the perduring disagreements he cites, I believe that they do not prevent substantial agreement on many key policies.

3. These constraints are difficult to specify, as Bernard C. Cohen demonstrates in *The Public's Impact on Foreign Policy* (Lanham, MD: University Press of America, 1973). They include active (or anticipated) opposition to policy initiatives, a simple lack of support when a leader seeks a "popular mandate" for a new policy, and variously focused or diffuse pressures for policy changes — in other words, both limitations and imperatives.

4. Possibly the latter question was interpreted by many of those polled as referring to a *unilateral* freeze, which might account for much of the difference. If so, the question illustrates the difficulty of wording a question to measure what one wants it to measure.

5. Richard Smoke, "Four Futures: Alternatives for Public Debate and Policy Development" (Center for Foreign Policy Development and the Public Agenda Foundation, 1987), p. 5.

6. Throughout this chapter, the word "Future" is capitalized when it refers to this work, to remind the reader of its specialized meaning.

7. The results are reported at length in "U.S.-Soviet Relations in the Year 2010: Americans Look to the Future," available from the Center and Public Agenda. Many of the results are summarized in Daniel Yankelovich and Richard Smoke, "America's 'New Thinking'," *Foreign Affairs* 67 (Fall 1988), pp. 1-17.

8. In the October 1987 ATS survey, 30% said they considered it very or fairly likely that the U.S. would get into a nuclear war within the next ten years — down from an apparent peak

of 47% in a Gallup poll in June 1981, but still a substantial number. And 44% considered nuclear war at least fairly likely in the next twenty-five years.

9. For instance, in the Futures study, only 15% considered a Soviet "bolt from the blue" or invasion of Europe the most likely way a nuclear war might start. (52% thought escalation of a war in the Third World, drawing in the superpowers, was most likely.)

10. As emphasized elsewhere, the public does take seriously a Soviet threat to other key values, and this threat is perceived as largely due to Soviet aggressive attentions.

11. The public was of several minds about aid to the Contras in Nicaragua. For instance, an ABC News/*Washington Post* poll taken in March 1986 showed that, by 62% to 28%, Americans agreed that the U.S. should not "be involved in trying to overthrow the government in Nicaragua." A Yankelovich Clancy Shulman poll taken the following month showed 58% support, against 29% opposition, for "aid[ing] the rebels in Nicaragua in order to prevent communist influence from spreading to other countries in Central America." Contra aid, then, was more popular than its opponents have claimed, but less popular than its advocates wished.

12. John Marttila, "American Public Opinion: Evolving Definitions of National Security," in Edward Hamilton, ed., *America's Global Interests: A New Agenda* (New York: W. W. Norton Company, 1989), p. 265. For instance, drug trafficking was cited as an "extremely serious" or "very serious" threat by 86% of respondents in the August 1988 poll, while 50% considered an increase in Soviet military power extremely or very serious.

13. The study was conducted by Greenberg-Lake: The Analysis Group for the World Policy Institute, "Defining American Priorities," p. 31. The response to this (somewhat loaded) question, like any such result, must be taken in context: in the same survey, 70% approved of "maintain[ing] our military troop levels in Europe and South Korea to defend against communist aggression."

14. A November 1989 poll conducted by Louis Harris & Associates, Inc. for *Business Week* asked, "With the changes in Eastern Europe, should the United States sharply cut its military spending, or not?" A 66% majority said it should not, while 29% said it should. In the same poll, the public split evenly, 48%-48%, on whether the U.S. should withdraw its troops from Europe if the Soviet Union withdrew its troops.

15. Of course, both environmental hazards and the spread of AIDS are, to varying degrees, affected by national policies.

16. In the Futures study, 55% agreed that "the Soviets truly want to work with us to solve common problems," but 24% disagreed and 21% were not sure. And a 42%-39% plurality agreed that a convincing argument *against* pursuing cooperation is that "the Soviets will trick us, pretend to cooperate, then turn on us as they've done in the past."

17. In ATS #3 (March 1988), a 60% majority agreed that the U.S. should "spend whatever is needed for military defense rather than only what we can afford," with 38% disagreeing. A larger (67%) majority agreed that "we have to maintain our military strength no matter what the costs."

18. Here the paraphrase of "threat-reduction mutual security" obscures the richness of Richard Smoke's typology. It would be more accurate to say that this category allows for substantial variation in the degree of cooperation and competition, from "arms control only" through a very broad settlement of the political competition internationally. Thus this Future is representative, but not definitive.

19. It is important to note that these results come from a time prior to the Soviet announcement of certain unilateral Soviet reductions in conventional forces in Europe.

20. Interestingly, in ATS #3, a 54%-39% majority said the U.S. Senate should require President Reagan to certify that the Soviet Union was adhering to all past arms control agreements

before the INF Treaty could take effect. In contrast, a 52%-37% majority *rejected* the idea of requiring the Soviet Union to remove its restrictions on Jewish emigration before allowing the treaty to take effect.

21. One distinctive element of supportive mutual security, active mutual support against internal political unrest, is at best implicit in this Future, but the Future's emphasis on other common problems (in Richard Smoke's nomenclature, "extraneous-origin dangers") is typical of the category. The broad citizen exchanges envisaged by this Future would help to create the sense of "common stake" that typifies this conception of mutual security.

22. *Voter Options on Nuclear Arms Policy, a Briefing Book for the 1984 Elections* (New York: Public Agenda Foundation in collaboration with the Center for Foreign Policy Development, 1984).

23. As I write in January 1990, so far this transformation has not occurred. One reason is suggested by the findings of the November 1989 *Business Week*/Harris poll: by 64% to 26%, respondents agreed that "faced with the opening up of so many communist-controlled countries, the rulers of the Soviet Union will allow reforms and democratization to go only so far before they crack down." The continuation of reforms and upheavals in both Eastern Europe and the USSR since then may actually have intensified public fears of an eventual reversal — a "Soviet Tiananmen Square."

25

Conclusion: Mutual Security
and the Future

SERGEI PLEKHANOV (USSR) AND
HOWARD SWEARER (USA)

The idea of mutual or common security is not entirely new. It has been discussed for some years; and in fact, the recognition of mutual vulnerability, and of each side's dependence on the other's behavior to achieve the level of security it wants, has grown steadily over the past two decades. This recognition, not always clearly articulated, has been manifested in a number of agreements, such as SALT I, the INF Treaty, the Incidents at Sea Agreement, and the Nuclear Risk Reduction Centers. In all of these instances, as well as others, each nation sought to increase its own security through cooperative agreements with the other. Moreover, John F. Kennedy's explicit recognition of Nikita Khruschev's political interests — and Khruschev's recognition of Kennedy's interests — helped defuse the Cuban Missile Crisis. Thus, there is an important continuity with past experience and achievements.

Nonetheless, the concept of mutual security has not been deeply plumbed for its value as a guide to making security policy and it has often been used more as a slogan than a serious tool of analysis. By attempting to apply mutual security to concrete situations and issues, the Mutual Security Project has attempted to test its power in U.S.-Soviet relations.

The significance of this joint project goes beyond the findings of the Working Groups dealing with the U.S. and Soviet interests in such geographical areas as Eastern Europe, the Persian Gulf, and the North Pacific, and on issues of arms control. More broadly, its overarching purpose was to examine the substantive meanings and practical consequences of the concept of mutual security and how it might be applied. That is, major issues which have been in conflict between the two powers were addressed in concrete terms, by means of a systematic application of the mutual security concept. Mutual security provided a useful tool to promote constructive dialogue as well as a perspective to address major international issues. It also led to policy recommendations that might not have come about without the mutual security approach.

As Richard Smoke has written, it must be stressed that mutual security focuses on security — the national security of the involved parties. It seeks ways to enhance security for both sides. Mutual security may involve cooperative actions, but it does not seek cooperation as a goal in itself, nor as a means to increase cultural interactions or scientific knowledge. Such cooperative endeavors may be worthy in their own right, but they are not the main business of mutual security. Moreover, mutual security can also be furthered through unilateral and parallel actions. Nor is mutual security about creating friendships. Heightening cooperative relationships, improving understanding, and muting competitive elements may well be important by-products of successful mutual security, but they are not its primary purpose.

Mutual security is not the same as common sense, because there are many issues which, on the surface, may not *appear* to involve the interests of both sides. But if the national security concerns of both sides are not explicitly explored in the policy-making process, the effectiveness of policy may be limited by unanticipated responses. Consider, for example, Henry Kissinger's statement, on the decision to deploy MIRVed missiles, that "I wish I had thought through the implications of a MIRVed world more thoughtfully in 1969 and 1970 than I did. What conclusions I would then have come to I don't know." Properly executed, the mutual security process should entail a tough-minded joint investigation of each side's fundamental national security interests and of means by which perceived threats might be reduced.

The basic idea of mutual security is to seek ways for each side to improve its security by taking steps, separately or jointly, which will improve both sides' security. In other words, increased security for one side should not be sought — and in fact, cannot be achieved — at the price of diminished security for the other. Mutual security does not replace, rather it supplements, efforts to achieve the goal of national security by unilateral measures. This approach provides an opportunity for a concerted effort to ameliorate "the security dilemma." The security dilemma is the interaction cycle set in motion when what one side does unilaterally to improve its security is viewed by the other as so threatening that it feels obliged to take additional steps to improve its security, which threatens the first side and so on. At the very least, mutual security calls on both sides to recognize the existence of the security dilemma. Mutual security does not entail weakness or surrender. Its imperative is to explore both sides' interests, and to take advantage of mutually advantageous options. But that does not mean one side has to take actions which worked against its own priorities.

During the time span of this project, the nature of the U.S.-Soviet relationship underwent a dramatic transformation. At the outset, none of those involved could have anticipated the rapidity and scope of the changes which were to take place in the subsequent eighteen months. In fact, skepticism was expressed in some quarters about the practicality and utility of a project in which American and Soviet analysts would attempt jointly to apply the concept of mutual security to areas of tension and disagreement between the two countries. To some people at the beginning, the project seemed either too idealistic and naive, or simply too "academic."

As it turned out, by the time of the concluding conference in November 1989, the unfolding of events had put the project in the mainstream of security thinking. A month before the concluding conference, Secretary of State Baker referred to "our mission to press the search for mutual advantage . . .," and the opening of the conference coincided with the opening of the Berlin Wall. The evolution of the geo-political environment gave a timeliness to this exploration of mutual security, and a sense of urgency, direction — and adventure — to the participants. Not only did the changing environment and atmosphere provide more scope and opportunities for thinking along the lines of mutual security, it became evident that policymakers in both countries were, in effect, beginning to grapple with mutual security ideas, even if not always in a self-conscious manner. A fundamental purpose of the project was to raise the level of consciousness about the nature and possibilities of a more elaborated and formalized mutual security process.

The project engaged a wide range of people from both countries with a variety of backgrounds. During recent years, the policy-making process in the Soviet Union has become more open and the number of participants in it has been broadened and diversified. This opening up has led to new opportunities for fruitful discussions among a variety of specialists from both countries. And it is reasonable to expect that these unofficial deliberations may help to inform official policy making, especially since there are lines of communication between political leaders and the extended policy community in both countries. Well before the striking developments occurred in Eastern Europe in late 1989, project participants discussed the situation there and how the security interests of the two nations might be assessed in a mutual security framework. Whether or not these exchanges of views contributed to the climate in which policies were decided is impossible to trace; but it is noteworthy that the ensuing course of events was not inconsistent with them.

The two chapters on public opinion in the U.S. and the USSR explore the constraints on policymakers created by public attitudes and values. The influence of public opinion on policy making in these two countries is far from symmetrical today. However, public opinion in the Soviet Union is evolving, with encouragement from above, and is becoming a more important consideration in policy making. The public deliberations of the Congress of Peoples' Deputies highlight the growing diversity and growing role of public opinion in the USSR.

Political leaders in the U.S. and increasingly in the USSR need both to take into account public opinion and to keep the public informed about national security considerations and potential directions in foreign and defense policies. As the messianic quality in the U.S.-Soviet relationship has diminished, leaders have sought new ways to define the nature of this relationship and to explain it to their citizens. Although without necessarily using the precise terminology, ingredients of mutual security have gradually become a part of the public discourse in both countries. As the doctrines of containment, class struggle, and detente appear to have lost their utility as concepts both to guide foreign policy and to explain foreign policy to publics, mutual security, in one permutation or another, has demonstrated its usefulness in the public discourse between political leadership and the public. This is true in both countries, because mutual security plays to the near-universal desire to maintain security while seeking ways jointly to improve East-West relations.

Three principal factors have multiplied the possibilities for more fruitful applications of mutual security than normally existed in the past. The first is the potential for catastrophe resulting from weapons of mass destruction — especially, but not necessarily limited to, nuclear weapons. This danger is now widely recognized by leaders and publics alike. The second is the sweeping changes in Soviet domestic and foreign policy, and the Western reaction to these changes, including the decline of ideological intensity in the East-West relationship. Third — and directly related to the second — is the rapidity and scope of the alteration of the international landscape now underway which, while hopeful in many respects, also contains potentials for dangerous instability. To understand the meanings and implications of these events, and to avoid serious misunderstandings among the major participants, requires in-depth, sustained, and structured interaction between the American and Soviet policy communities. Perhaps more importantly, however, the interaction needs to be geared to the joint development of alternatives to cope with rapidly changing events. Naturally no one concept, including mutual security, is always the best one with which to address every international issue. But mutual security is usually helpful for seeing new options because it requires both sides to address problems from more points of view than just their own.

It became evident as the project proceeded that a mutual security approach cannot be applied uniformly everywhere. It needs to be tailored to the circumstances of each situation. Moreover, some areas and issues are more conducive to this approach than are others. For example, strategic and conventional forces and Eastern Europe were riper for a broad application of mutual security thinking than were the North Pacific and the Persian Gulf — perhaps because the two powers feel their vital interests are more directly and dangerously involved in the former than in the latter. However, even in the North Pacific and the Persian Gulf, the Working Groups believed mutual security provided a beneficial perspective for identifying issues and anticipating potential future difficulties. As one of the participants observed, "even if in some future situation one of the two powers decided that it had to act unilaterally, there would be greater understanding of the circumstances and motivations on the part of the other and less likelihood of misunderstanding."

It bears stressing, as several of this book's authors have pointed out, that mutual security must never be allowed to become an excuse for, or degenerate into, some sort of superpower condominium. In fact, much of the potential of mutual security can be achieved only by the superpowers coordinating their policy with other states. And progress in mutual security should, in fact, contribute to a useful redefinition of the global role of a superpower and the development of a more stable and benign international order.

Nowhere is the need to consult and draw other nations into the process more apparent than in the case of Eastern Europe, and especially in the German issue. As discussed in the chapter on the German Question by Francis Meehan, the extremely complex issue of the relationship of the GDR and the FRG cries out for the closest East-West consultations and coordination, involving the Four Powers as well as the two German states. The German Question is central to issues of arms and force reductions and postures in Europe, as well as to the future shape and character of Europe. Of course, economic and other considerations are also at stake, but security issues are at the heart of the German Question. Actions by one side or the other seeking to gain unilateral advantage could lead to dangerous instability and tensions, in both the short and long term. Moreover, East and West, working in concert — and with the two Germanies — would help to ensure a more stable transition to whatever future arrangements are put in place and to strengthen the mutual security of Europe and the international community.

The experience of the participants in this project has persuaded them of the value of working closely together on the concept of mutual security and its application to particular situations. We are also convinced of the desirability of instituting a more formal and comprehensive process through which representatives of both countries may regularly consider together national security issues on a mutual security basis. *In fact, one of the major conclusions and recommendations of this study is that the two countries establish joint analytical teams to conduct mutual security studies and talks on an on-going basis.* As has been argued repeatedly in many contexts in this volume, to be effective a mutual security approach should be regarded not as a one-shot elixir but as a purposeful, on-going process through which the security of both sides is strengthened and their relations are made more predictable and stable.

Rapid and far-reaching changes in the U.S.-Soviet relationship have occurred and the conditions under which these relations are being conducted are being dramatically altered. New possibilities — and potential dangers — are being opened up. The two sides should plan and think together carefully about where the relationship is headed — and where we would like it to head. After forty years of Cold War and antagonism — and, during the last twenty-five years, relative stability and predictability — dramatic shifts in ways of thinking and conducting foreign policy are indicated. Unsuspected events and forces will continue to influence strongly the relationship well beyond the control of any planning or consultative process. However, a well-designed process may help to anticipate them and to accommodate them with less danger and less misunderstanding.

It is a fact that in recent months and years, events have outrun expectations and, at times, even the ability to analyze carefully the future consequences. It is particularly at such times, when historic changes are taking place, that an established mutual security process could have great value to policymakers in helping them to comprehend more fully what perceived national security interests are involved on both sides.

What is suggested is not a confidence-building measure, although it could have that effect. Nor would it be a joint planning enterprise working on the day-to-day issues which necessarily preoccupy the time of policymakers, although it should assist these officials in the conduct of their affairs. It would not replace national security and foreign policy planning, but it would help inform it. Rather, we visualize a mechanism through which an effort is made jointly to maximize the reduction of threats in the unfolding relationship between the two countries.

This procedure is not a negotiation in which hard bargaining takes place, as each side seeks to advance its position, ending in a compromise. It does not replace negotiations, but it may help to facilitate them by providing a solid preparatory groundwork. The mutual security process does not guarantee agreement, but it does encourage each party to think through carefully the difficult trade-offs in a particular situation and their longer term consequences. If successful, it should result in longer range thinking and better mutual understanding. It may also suggest new avenues for actions and negotiations; and lead to innovative means for developing a common base of understanding for negotiation, as is suggested by P. Terrence Hopmann's chapter.

It would be premature to suggest with any specificity how such a mechanism should be organized or how it should operate. Moreover, to propose a specific mechanism might blunt the force of this recommendation by fostering debate on details rather than on the merits of the approach. Certainly the participants should be respected, experienced, and knowledgeable and have access to governmental policymakers. But they should be sufficiently removed from national policy making that they have sufficient freedom to express views and search for new ideas and concepts without the danger of committing their governments. What developed over time in this project was a cyclical process of jointly identifying and diagnosing problems affecting each side's security, and exploring opportunities for dealing with them in ways that would improve both sides' sense of security. The charge should be sufficiently broad to give the body latitude to range broadly over the terrain of mutual security; but not so sweeping as to encourage consideration of foreign policy goals of all kinds. Participants should draw on the expertise of government officials, scholars, and others.

"Planning" frequently implies setting a goal and then figuring out what steps need to be taken to achieve it. Such is implied by statements urging the development of blueprints or road maps for the future of longer range U.S.-Soviet relations. Such exercises have heuristic value, but the unpredictable and complex realities of international relations do not readily lend themselves to such map making — at least with any specificity or lasting value. Of course, general goals can and should be established to guide policies. During the Cold War, for the U.S., containment served as a general doctrine, and for the USSR, class struggle (tempered somewhat in the later period by peaceful coexistence).

The detente of the 1970s saw the first attempt to define common goals for both sides. In a document called "The Basic Principles of Relations Between the USA and the USSR," signed at the end of the Nixon-Brezhnev summit in Moscow in May 1972, the two governments registered their consensus on a set of ideas to guide their behavior in the future. They proclaimed that differences in ideology should not prevent them from developing normal relations; pledged to conduct their policies so that military confrontations are voided; recognized that efforts to obtain unilateral advantage at the expense of each other would damage their relations; and spoke of the special responsibility of the U.S. and the USSR to prevent dangerous international conflicts.

Of course, the detente proved to be short-lived, and by the late seventies the Basic Principles would be recalled, if ever, mostly to charge the other side with violating them; or to ridicule the very idea that anybody could seriously put trust in such a code of conduct. However, the document was never more than a statement of intentions, which was to be developed into a regime. The building process was soon aborted. But that fact in itself does not discredit the original intentions. There is, of course, the charge that the intentions expressed were never sincere, that the signers did not actually believe in the principles, but merely paid them lip service. But even if one accepts this charge, that is a judgment on the signers, not on what they signed. The intention of elaborating common goals and the ideas of the 1972 document are hardly disputable. No wonder that in the mid-1980s, when Mikhail Gorbachev and Ronald Reagan joined in an effort to resume the normalization of U.S.-Soviet relations, they acted very much in the spirit of the 1972 document.

The current phase of U.S.-Soviet relations makes possible a more advanced and specific set of guidelines. The 1972 formula recognized equal rights of the two countries to security, but it lacked explicit recognition of interdependence between the two countries in security matters. Ironically, it has taken another round of Cold War tensions to make manifest the fact that security of each side is in certain respects a necessary condition for the other side's security.

A process of mutual threat reduction could also help people recognize the reality of tremendous redundancy in the numbers and destructive power of weapons accumulated by the superpowers and other participants in the global arms race. The inertia of arms competition has been curbed somewhat by economic constraints and the increased fear of nuclear war. But any serious attempt to scale down the arms race needs a conceptual framework embracing realistic security requirements and realistic ways to meet them.

The mutual security concept helps deepen understanding of the need to demilitarize U.S.-Soviet and East-West relations — that is to reduce drastically the importance of their military component. De-ideologization of the relationship should be pursued hand-in-hand with demilitarization, since the ideological and military dimensions have become mutually reinforcing. A major impetus to de-ideologization has been given by the reform processes in the USSR and Eastern Europe, reflecting an intention to base the legitimacy of sociopolitical systems on a broader set of interests and values ("universal human values"), transcending narrower class and political interests. Claims to universality have traditionally characterized the American creed, but the need to reduce the influence of ideology is quite pressing for U.S. foreign policy, as well.

Demilitarization and de-ideologization of U.S.-Soviet relations would make the two sides less fixated on each other in their security outlooks, and more prepared to view their interests in a broader international context. The need for multi-lateralism in approaching international issues was recognized decades ago: indeed, it forms the basis of modern international law and the United Nations system. But in a world sharply divided militarily, ideologically, and economically, multi-lateralism suffered as a serious policy. Now that the Cold War appears to be receding into history, conditions seem more ripe for a strong multilateral approach for building mutual security in East-West relations, as well as for other world issues.

There has been considerable progress in the past three years in tackling the traditional agenda of U.S.-Soviet relations: arms control, regional issues, human rights, and economic cooperation. For example, by 1989 both President Bush and President Gorbachev supported the goal of a more integrated Europe, whole and free in a "common European home."

The new, post-Cold War agenda in U.S.-Soviet relations will have to respond to new concerns as well. The mutual security approach, which grew out of work on the traditional agenda, is also exceptionally well suited for addressing the newer issues. The global environment, terrorism, AIDS, and other issues know no boundaries; economic cooperation is based on the idea of mutual benefit, and it is to be hoped that on both sides there is now enough maturity not to welcome each other's domestic predicaments as something that "weakens the enemy."

Guided by the mutual security concept as a compass, the U.S. and the USSR might undertake a purposeful exploration of their future relations. Alexander George offers the apt metaphor of the expedition by Lewis and Clark in exploring the American West in 1804-06. They had a definite final goal in mind, namely to reach the Pacific Ocean; and they knew they had to travel in a westerly direction to achieve this objective. However they did not lay out a specific route in advance and they did not know at what exact location they would reach the Pacific Coast. They charted their course as they went along, taking into account their past experience and the terrain ahead. Similarly, we urge a commitment to exploring purposefully and jointly opportunities to strengthen each country's national security through the strategy of mutual security. This exploration would seek to put in place individual "building blocks," each useful in its own right, but also adding to a foundation for additional constructive actions.

Appendices

The Contributors

Richard Smoke is Research Director of the Center for Foreign Policy Development at Brown University, and also professor of political science at Brown University. A specialist on security and peace in international relations, he is the author or co-author of several books on these topics, including two textbooks widely used in American universities. He has long been interested in the subject of mutual or common security. In the summer of 1982 he created (with others) an independent research center called "Peace and Common Security"; and was the first executive director of that center, before going to Brown.

Andrei Kortunov is Head of the Department of General Problems of American Foreign Policy, at the Institute for the United States and Canada of the Soviet Academy of Sciences. He is a specialist not only on American foreign and military policy but also on problems of international security generally. Among his books are, most recently, *Reasonable Sufficiency* (1989, co-author) and *America as We See It* (1989, co-author).

*

Mikhail Bezrukov is a research fellow at the Institute for the USA and Canada. His specialty is international security affairs. He is a contributor to *Typological Studies of Social and Political Processes in the U.S.* (1989).

Aleksis Bogaturov is a senior research associate in the Institute for the USA and Canada. He specializes in the international affairs of the Far East and in the foreign policies of Japan and the United States. He is author of *The Struggle of Japanese Diplomacy for Energy Resources* (1988), and several articles on the Asia-Pacific region.

Fred Chernoff is an assistant professor of political science at Colgate University, and has previously taught at Wesleyan and Brown universities. He has held research positions at the Rand Corporation, International Institute for Strategic Studies, London, and the Center for Foreign Policy Development at Brown. He has contributed to various journals of international studies, including *International Affairs, The Journal of Conflict Resolution, International Relations,* and is co-editor, with Bruce Russett, of *Arms Control and the Arms Race.*

Yuriy Davydov is Head of Department at the Institute for the USA and Canada and holds the academic rank of Professor. He has written widely on international relations, with a specialty in European affairs. His books include, most recently, *The USA and the European Process* (co-author, 1989) and *The USA and European Problems of Detente* (editor, 1986).

Sergei Fedorenko is a senior research fellow at the Institute for the USA and Canada. He specializes in international security affairs and military affairs. His books include *U.S.-USSR Strategic Power* (1990), *Military Force and American Foreign Policy* (1990), and *The Scientific-Technological Factor in the Military Policy of the United States* (1989).

Stephen Fought is the director of the Defense Analysis course at the U.S. Naval War College. He has published a text and several articles on the Strategic Defense Initiative, and is a contributing author to the *Encyclopedia Britannica*. He is a lieutenant colonel of the U.S. Air Force, retired, and he lectures internationally for the United States Information Agency on these topics.

Alexander George is Graham H. Stuart Professor of International Relations at Stanford University. He is the author of many well-known books in the fields of international relations, American foreign policy, and U.S.-Soviet relations. He also is co-author, with his wife Juliette George, of *Woodrow Wilson and Colonel House*, widely regarded as a classic study of the role of personality in politics.

Petr Gladkov is Head of Section at the Institute for the USA and Canada. He is a specialist in the political history and social psychology of the United States. He is a co-author of *The American Model on the Scales of History* (1984), and a contributor to *The Glasnost Papers* (Boulder, CO: Westview Press, 1990) and other books.

Jo-Anne Hart is an assistant professor of political science at Brown University and a research associate at the Center for Foreign Policy Development. She specializes in superpower relations and arms control in the Middle East. Currently she is completing a book about U.S. national security doctrines and their relation to the Middle East and American policies in the Middle East.

P. Terrence Hopmann is a professor of political science at Brown University, where he also serves as director of the International Relations Program and as a research associate at the Center for Foreign Policy Development. He is co-author of *Unity and Disintegration in International Alliances* (1973 and 1984), and co-editor of *Rethinking the Nuclear Weapons Dilemma in Europe* (1988). His major research interests have focused on theories of international negotiations and on arms control negotiations, especially on arms control in Europe.

Jan Kalicki is Senior Adviser of the Center for Foreign Policy Development, adjunct professor of political science at Brown University, and Senior Vice President of Shearson Lehman Hutton, Inc. He has served as the chief foreign policy adviser to Senator Edward Kennedy, as well as a member of the Policy Planning Staff in the U.S. Department of State and of the U.S. Arms Control and Disarmament Agency. His previous teaching positions include appointments at Georgetown, Harvard and Princeton universities.

Aleksandr Konovalov is a senior research fellow at the Institute for the USA and Canada. He is a specialist on the security and military dimensions of Soviet-American relations. He is a contributor to *Conventional Arms Control and East-West Security* (Durham, N.C.: Duke University Press, 1989), and his books include *The Military-Technological Policy of the United States in the 1980s* (co-editor, 1989) and *Non-Provocative Defense as a Principle of Arms Reductions* (1989).

Mikhail Kozhokin is a research fellow in the Department of European Problems (of the USA), of the Institute for the USA and Canada. He specializes in both contemporary and historical issues in the relations between the United States and Europe.

Mark Kramer is a research fellow at the Center for Foreign Policy Development. He is also an adjunct research fellow at the Center for Science and International Affairs at Harvard University. He teaches international relations at Brown University, and previously taught in the Government department at Harvard University.

Viktor Kremenyuk is a deputy director of the Institute for the USA and Canada and holds the academic rank of Professor. His specializations include the theory of conflict resolution, the problems of developing countries, and the history of the United States. His books include *Washington's Policy Against the Revolution in Iran* (1984), *The USA and Conflicts in Asian Countries in the 1970s* (1979), and *American Policy in Developing Countries: Problems of Conflicts* (1976).

Mark Lindeman is a research associate at the Center for Foreign Policy Development. He is the author of *The U.S., the Soviets, and Nuclear Arms: Choices for the Twenty-first Century,* a college-level text on alternative futures for U.S. foreign policy. He received his B.A. degree from Brown University in 1987.

William Luers was a career diplomat for thirty years and served as U.S. ambassador to Venezuela, 1978-82, and to Czechoslovakia, 1983-86. Much of his career was dedicated to dealing with and writing about the Soviet Union, where he served in the U.S. Embassy. Since his retirement from the U.S. State Department in 1986, he has been the president of The Metropolitan Museum of Art in New York.

Vladimir Lukin has just been appointed Chief of the Center for Analysis and Forecasts, attached to the Supreme Soviet. Formerly he was Chief of Department for Regional, Political and Economic Questions for the Pacific Ocean and Southeast Asian Countries of the Soviet Ministry of Foreign Affairs. He is the author of several books and holds the academic rank of Professor.

Francis Meehan was a U.S. foreign service officer from 1951 until his retirement in 1989. He was U.S. ambassador to Czechoslovakia, 1979-80, Poland, 1980-83, and the GDR, 1985-88, and earlier served in Moscow, Berlin, Budapest, Bonn and Vienna. In 1983-85 he was research professor at Georgetown University.

Andrei Melvil is Deputy Chairman of the Soviet Peace Committee and holds the academic rank of Professor. He specializes in political psychology and political philosophy and is editor of *The Glasnost Papers* (Boulder, CO: Westview Press, 1990). His other books include *Contradictions of Contemporary American Capitalism and the Conflict of Ideas in the United States* (1984) and *The Social Philosophy of American Conservatism* (1980).

Eric Mlyn is a research associate at the Center for Foreign Policy Development and an adjunct lecturer in international relations at Brown University. He is also a Ph.D. candidate in the political science department of the University of Minnesota, where he is writing his dissertation on the history of U.S. nuclear weapons policy. His chief research interests are U.S. foreign and national security policy.

Aleksandr Nikitin is Director of the Scientific International Center of the Soviet Peace Committee. His specializations include political psychology and political philosophy. He is author of *The Evolution of American Globalism: Ideological Discussions about the Role of* *the United States in the World* (1987), and a contributor to *Public Consciousness and American Foreign Policy* (1987) among other books.

Mikhail Nossov is Head of Section at the Institute for the USA and Canada. He specializes in the problems of the Asia-Pacific region. His recent books include *Relations Between Japan and China* (1989), and *U.S. Policy Toward the Pacific* (co-author, 1989).

Aleksandr Pisarev is a research fellow at the Institute for the USA and Canada. He specializes in international security and in European affairs. He is co-author of *The USA and the European Process* (1989) and a contributor to *The USA and European Problems of Detente* (1986).

Sergei Plekhanov is a deputy director of the Institute for the USA and Canada. He specializes in the political system and the history of the United States. His recent books include *America as We See It* (co-author, 1989), *Soviet-American Relations in the Modern World* (co-author, 1986), and *Right Extremism and American Foreign Policy* (1986).

Konstantine Pleshakov is a senior research associate at the Institute for the USA and Canada. He specializes in the North Pacific region, and in processes of mutual perception in international relations. He is the author of several articles on mutual perceptions, images and stereotypes in Soviet-American relations.

Alan Romberg is Senior Fellow for Asia at the Council on Foreign Relations in New York City, and the author of numerous articles on Asian and Pacific affairs. Formerly a career Foreign Service officer, he served as Senior Deputy Assistant Secretary of State for Public Affairs and Deputy Spokesman of the Department, 1981-85. He was director of the Department's Office of Japanese Affairs, 1978-80.

Harold Saunders, Visiting Fellow at The Brookings Institution, served on the U.S. National Security Council staff 1961-74, and in the U.S. State Department 1974-81. He was Assistant Secretary of State for Near Eastern and South Asian Affairs 1978-81, and is the author of *The Other Walls: The Politics of the Arab-Israeli Peace Process* (1985). He participated in the disengagement negotiations 1973-75, and helped draft the Camp David Accords and the Egyptian-Israeli Peace Treaty.

Andrei Shumikhin is Head of the Department of Regional Problems at the Institute for the USA and Canada. He has a particular interest in the problems of the Middle East and has written widely on that subject. His books include *Soviet-American Relations in the Middle East at the Height of the New Thinking* (Moscow, 1990); and he is author of a report of the Institute of East-West Security Studies (New York City), "Soviet Policy Toward Arms Transfers in the Middle East."

Howard Swearer is the director of the Institute for International Studies at Brown University. He is President Emeritus of Brown University and Carleton College. Earlier he served as program officer in charge of European and International Studies at the Ford Foundation.

Donald Zagoria has for thirty-five years been a student of international politics with a particular focus on the Soviet Union, China, and the Pacific region. He is the author of two books and more than 150 articles on these subjects. He is a professor of government at Hunter College and a research fellow at the Harriman Institute for Advanced Study of the Soviet Union at Columbia University.

Members of the Working Groups

Joint Project on Mutual Security of the Center for Foreign Policy Development at Brown University and the Institute for the USA and Canada (ISKAN) of the Soviet Academy of Sciences:

Working Group on Principles and Criteria

Alexander George, Co-Chair, *Stanford University*
Michael Mandelbaum, *Council on Foreign Relations*
Richard Smoke, Convenor, *Brown Center*

Viktor Kremenyuk, Co-Chair, *ISKAN*
Andrei Kortunov, *ISKAN*
Sergei Plekhanov, *ISKAN*
Pavel Podlesniy, *ISKAN*
Sergei Rogov, *ISKAN*

Working Group on Europe

William Luers, Co-Chair, *President, Metropolitan Museum, former Ambassador*
Mark Garrison, Convenor, *Brown Center*
Mark Kramer, *Brown Center*
Michael Mandelbaum, *Council on Foreign Relations*
Francis Meehan, *former Ambassador*

Yuriy Davydov, Co-Chair, *ISKAN*
Vladimir Baranovskiy, *Institute for World Economy and International Affairs*
Mikhail Bezrukov, *ISKAN*
Vyacheslav Dashichev, *Economics of the World Socialist System*
German Gvintsadze, *Ministry of Foreign Affairs*
Mikhail Kozhokin, *ISKAN*
Viktor Shein, *European Studies Institute*
Vladimir Shustov, *Ministry of Foreign Affairs*
Anatoliy Utkin, *ISKAN*

Consulted

Condoleezza Rice, *Senior Director for Soviet and European Affairs, NSC*
Thomas Simons, Jr., *former Deputy Assistant Secretary of State*

Aleksandr Bessmertnykh, *First Deputy Foreign Minister*
Rafael Fyodorov, *First Deputy Chief International Department, CPSU Central Committee*
Georgiy Shakhnazarov, *Assistant to the General Secretary*

Working Group on the Persian Gulf

Harold Saunders, Co-Chair, *The Brookings Institution*
Helena Cobban, *The Brookings Institution*
Jo-Anne Hart, Convenor, *Brown Center*
Judith Kipper, *The Brookings Institution*
William Quandt, *The Brookings Institution*
Philip Stewart, *Ohio State University*

Andrei Shumikhin, Co-Chair, *ISKAN*
Oleg Darkovskiy, *Soviet Embassy, Washington*
Igor Khripunov, *Soviet Embassy, Washington*
Dmitriy Olshanskiy, *Institute of Marxism-Leninism*
Sergei Rogov, *ISKAN*
Aleksandr Zotov, *Central Committee of the CPSU*

Working Group on the North Pacific

Amos Jordan, Co-Chair, *Center for Strategic and International Studies*
A. Doak Barnett, *Johns Hopkins University*
Coit Blacker, *University of Southern California*
William Gleysteen, *Japan Society*
Richard Holbrooke, *Shearson Lehman Hutton, Inc.*
Jan Kalicki, Convenor, *Brown Center*
Mark Kramer, *Brown Center*
Alan Romberg, *Council on Foreign Relations*
Robert Scalapino, *Institute of East Asian Studies University of California, Berkeley*
John Vessey, *former Chairman, Joint Chiefs of Staff*
Donald Zagoria, *City University of New York*

Mikhail Nossov, Co-Chair, *ISKAN*
Vladimir Lukin, *Ministry of Foreign Affairs*
Yevgeniy Mironenkov, *ISKAN*
Aleksandr Nagorniy, *ISKAN*
Aleksandr Panov, *Ministry of Foreign Affairs*
Boris Zanegin, *ISKAN*

Consulted

Desaix Anderson, *U.S. Department of State*
Donald Gregg, *Office of the Vice President*
J. Stapleton Roy, *U.S. Department of State*

Working Group on Nuclear and Conventional Arms Reductions

Lt. Col. Stephen Fought, Co-Chair, *Naval War College*
Fred Chernoff, *Brown Center*
Lynn Davis, *Foreign Policy Institute, SAIS*
P. Terrence Hopmann, *Brown Center*
Jan Kalicki, *Brown Center*
Eric Mlyn, *Brown Center*
Richard Smoke, Convenor, *Brown Center*

Aleksandr Konovalov, Co-Chair, *ISKAN*
Aleksei Arbatov, *Institute for World Economy and International Affairs*
Grigoriy Berdennikov, *Ministry of Foreign Affairs*
Sergei Fedorenko, *ISKAN*
Andrei Kokoshin, *ISKAN*
General Valeriy Larionov, *ISKAN*

Working Group on Future Scenarios

Howard Swearer, Co-Chair, *Institute for International Studies*
Mark Garrison, *Brown Center*
Alexander George, *Stanford University*
Amos Jordan, *Center for Strategic and International Studies*
Jan Kalicki, Convenor, *Brown Center*
Mark Kramer, *Brown Center*
Mark Lindeman, *Brown Center*
Philip Stewart, *Ohio State University*

Andrei Melvil, Co-Chair, *ISKAN*
Stanislav Kondrashov, *Izvestiya*
Andrei Kortunov, *ISKAN*
Vladimir Marinov, *Institute of Sociological Research*
Aleksandr Nikitin, *ISKAN*
Pavel Podlesniy, *ISKAN*
Nikolai Shishlin, *Central Committee of the CPSU*

The American side of these Working Groups employed the device of having both a "chair" and a "convenor." The chair was a senior person who oversaw the work. The convenor was a member of the staff of the Center for Foreign Policy Development.

Chronology of Major Meetings

Joint Project on Mutual Security of the Center for Foreign Policy Development at Brown University and the Institute for the USA and Canada of the Soviet Academy of Sciences:

July 1987   Initial discussions and formal agreement to create the project. Moscow.

Jan. 1988   Planning meeting held by directors of the two institutes. Providence.

July 1988   *Opening Conference* in Moscow, hosted by the Institute for the USA and Canada.
All working groups held their first meetings.

Sept. 1988   Nuclear and Conventional Arms Reductions Working Group meeting. Providence.

Oct. 1988   Persian Gulf Working Group meeting. Washington, D.C.

Nov. 1988   North Pacific Working Group meeting. Washington, D.C.
Planning meeting held by the directors of the two institutes. Moscow.

Dec. 1988   Principles and Criteria Working Group meeting. Providence.
Future Scenarios Working Group meeting. Providence.
Planning meeting held by the directors of the two institutes. Providence.
Directors of the Center for Foreign Policy Development briefed the "transition team" working for incoming President Bush on the project. Washington, D.C.

Feb. 1989   Future Scenarios Working Group meeting. Providence.

Mar. 1989   European Working Group meeting. Moscow.

May 1989   Persian Gulf Working Group meeting. Washington, D.C.
European Working Group meeting. Providence.
Nuclear and Conventional Arms Reductions Working Group meeting. Providence.

Aug. 1989   Persian Gulf Working Group meeting. Washington, D.C.

Nov. 1989   *Closing Conference* in Providence (first two days) and in Washington, D.C. (next three days), hosted by the Center for Foreign Policy Development. All Working Groups held meetings, and briefings were conducted in Washington, D.C. for the policy community, including Administration officials.

Several of the Working Groups plan to continue in independent existence, despite the end of the formal project. This list does not include the many meetings at which people from only one side were present, and does not include numerous meetings held by individual members of the Working Groups while they were traveling in the other country.

The Center for Foreign Policy Development

The Center for Foreign Policy Development is a non-profit organization established in January 1981 to engage in research on U.S. policy toward the Soviet Union and on related nuclear weapons issues. The Center is affiliated with Brown University, one of the leading private (that is, not governmentally-supported) universities in the United States. The Center's mandate is to bring together scholars, practitioners and the public in a search for policy choices that can lead to consensus on the best ways to reduce the risk of nuclear war while defending basic American values and interests.

The Center engages in a variety of research projects on U.S.-Soviet relations and nuclear issues. In addition, it publishes research reports, briefing papers and a newsletter, and sponsors conferences, lectures and courses. The Director of the Center is Mark Garrison; its Research Director is Richard Smoke; its Associate Director is Alan Sherr. The professional staff of the Center includes ten full-time researchers, plus an additional half-dozen who conduct research at the Center on a part-time basis, and an equal number of junior research assistants. This does not count administrative and support staff. In addition, the Center often secures the participation in its projects of senior specialists from other organizations.

Major projects of the Center prior to the Mutual Security Project included these:

1983-85: *Voter Options on Nuclear Arms Policy.* This joint project with the Public Agenda Foundation of New York City researched the spectrum of American perceptions and opinion, primarily regarding nuclear weapons issues, and developed four basic options reflecting that spectrum.

1985-88: *The Public, the Soviets and Nuclear Arms.* Also conducted jointly with the Public Agenda Foundation, this project developed basic options for U.S. policy toward the USSR. The project was overseen by a nonpartisan National Council of one hundred leading Americans. Using research on public values as the starting point, researchers tested and refined options through discussions with experts, community leaders, and representative groups drawn from the public. The final options were then presented in campaigns in selected cities using specially prepared video and print materials, and communicated to political leaders through a series of briefings. An article entitled "America's 'New Thinking'," published in the Fall 1988 issue of *Foreign Affairs* presents some of the results of this project; and a book is forthcoming.

Current projects of the Center for Foreign Policy Development include these:

— The Center is examining ways to conduct further research on *East-West mutual security*. One project being launched is described by P. Terrence Hopmann in this volume.

— A project on *Soviet Foreign Economic Policy and International Security* is exploring relationships between U.S. security interests and Soviet economic policy. Joint commercial ventures have been chosen as a case study to examine Soviet policy and U.S. options. The project includes five parts. First, researchers are publishing a series of briefing papers on topics such as financing of joint ventures in the USSR and Soviet laws governing such ventures. Second, books are being published to expand the base of theoretical and practical research on the relationship between perestroika and U.S. interests. Third, researchers are collaborating with scholars of the Moscow Institute of Economy and Management, under the Moscow City Council, on the practical prospects for joint ventures. Fourth, an extensive data base on joint ventures and related issues is being developed and will be made available to researchers in the U.S. and abroad. Fifth, a "mini-course" on Soviet political economy is being offered to U.S. policymakers and business people.

— A project entitled *The U.S. and the USSR: Choices for the 21st Century* is developing curricular materials for use at the secondary, college, and adult education levels. Preliminary research has shown that the "options" approach, developed in the projects described above with the Public Agenda Foundation, can be a powerful tool for educating people about the complexity of East-West relations and nuclear weapons issues.

The Institute for the USA
and Canada

The Institute for the USA and Canada is a non-profit, non-governmental research institute, one of more than two hundred research institutes within the Soviet Academy of Sciences. The Institute is the Academy's institute for scholarly and scientific study of the society, politics, economy and other affairs of the United States and Canada. Increasingly often in the West, as well as in the Soviet Union, the Institute is referred to as ISKAN, which are the initials of its formal name in Russian.

The Institute for the USA and Canada was founded in 1968. Its Director is Academician Georgiy A. Arbatov. "Academician" is the highest scholarly and scientific rank possible in the USSR. Academician Arbatov is also a People's Deputy in the Supreme Soviet of the USSR. The Deputy Directors of the Institute are Andrei Kokoshin, Viktor Kremenyuk, Sergei Plekhanov, and Anatoliy Porokhovsky.

The Institute conducts social science research on contemporary and historical politics of the United States, its social structure and economy, American law, and American domestic affairs. It makes a particular study of the policies, both domestic and foreign, of the U.S. government, with a special focus on American foreign policy toward the Soviet Union. The Institute's research staff are sometimes called "Americanologists," just as Western specialists on the Soviet Union are called "Sovietologists."

The Institute also draws upon its research to prepare analyses, upon request, of American foreign policy and U.S.-Soviet relations for departments of the Soviet government, for organs of the Party, and for other public bodies. Numerous research projects are under way at all times. The Institute publishes its own monthly magazine entitled "U.S.A.- Economy, Politics, Ideology," which is also translated into several foreign languages including English.

The Institute for the USA and Canada includes seventeen departments and a total professional staff of about 300 scholars. This does not include clerical and support staff. The main departments are as follows (each title except the last referring to the United States): Internal Political and Social Problems, General Economic Problems, Agriculture, Management, General Problems of Foreign Policy, Regional Problems of Foreign Policy, European Problems, Military-Political Problems; and Canada.

The Institute maintains numerous contacts with scholars and foreign policy specialists throughout the United States and Canada; and also with other specialists around the world who study the United States or Soviet-American relations. The Institute has always sought ways to improve understanding and communications between the United States and the Soviet Union.

Index

Anti-Ballistic Missile (ABM) Treaty, 260, 317

Accord on Civilian Air Traffic Safety in the Pacific, 198

Afghanistan: Geneva Accords on, 205; and Iran, 185; Najibullah government, 180; Soviet invasion of, 5, 28, 179, 184, 356; Soviet withdrawal from, xxi, 180, 204, 215; and superpower competition, 175

Agayev, E.T., 299

Agreement on Prevention of Nuclear War, 38

AIDS (Acquired Immune Deficiency Syndrome), xviii, 6, 362, 379

Air-Land Battle, 322-23

"All-Encompassing Conception of Arms Control and Disarmament," 289

Americans Talk Security (ATS) public opinion poll, 358, 361, 363

Arbatov, Georgiy, viii

Arms control, 22, 31-32, 364, 365-66, 371, 379: agreements, 215; chapters on, 249-68, 269-87, 288-316, 317-33; Geneva arms control negotiations, 28; historical perspective on, 12-14; and improvement of superpower relations, 174; and mutual security, ix; negotiations, 218, 219; role of in North Pacific, 198-99, 243

Arms race, 4, 250, 253, 258, 271, 311, 361, 378; in Asia-Pacific region, 202, 204; reasons for, 340; renewal of, 272; stability of, 262, 263, 329

Association of Southeast Asian Nations, 215, 218, 219, 226

Asian Development Bank, 219

Austrian State Treaty, 140

Azerbaijan, 186

Baker, James, 40, 174, 288, 373

Bali Treaty, 219

"Balkanization," 127, 132, 133, 139

Bank for Reconstruction and Development, 145

Basic Principles Agreement, 21, 33-39, 378

Berlin crisis, 20

Berlin Wall, opening of, 373

"Beyond containment," 3, 28, 40, 153

Bing, George F., 259

Bismarck, Otto von, 141, 228

Bogomolov, Oleg, 121

Brezhnev Doctrine, 5, 34, 121, 134

Brezhnev, Leonid: and Basic Principles Agreement, 33, 38; "Brezhnev Doctrine," 34; compared to Gorbachev, 174; policy in Asia, 215; and superpower parity, 23, 26, 27

Bulgaria, 118

Bundy, McGeorge, 283

Bureaucratic interests, 50

Bush, George: and arms talks, 288; moving "beyond containment," 3, 28, 40, 153; and China, 216; and Japan, 208; and Kampuchea, 206; and release of Iranian assets, 184; and "whole and free" Europe, 161

C^3I (command, control, communications and intelligence), 249, 258, 259, 261, 262, 300, 310, 311

Cambodia, 175, 195: Heng-Samrin, 206; Hun Sen, 218; resolution of conflict in, 202, 206, 217-18, 225; Son Sann, 206; withdrawal of Vietnamese troops, 204

Canada, x, 281, 282

Capitalism, xx, 25, 154, 338, 343, 348, 352

Carter, Jimmy, 12, 26, 34, 174, 357

396

Center for Foreign Policy Development, ix, 270, 283, 338, 359
CENTO (Central Treaty Organization, "Baghdad Pact"), 179
Central America, 28, 175, 177, 361
Central Command (CENTCOM), U.S., 178, 179
CFE. *See* Conventional Forces in Europe talks
Chemical weapons, 35, 188, 214
Chernenko, Konstantin, 366
Chernobyl, xix
China, People's Republic of: and India, 214-15; and international cooperation, 220; and Korea, 196, 222, 224, 227, 232, 233; opposition to reform in, 219; and the Soviet Union, 5, 12, 203-4, 214-15, 237, 264; and the U.S., 27, 216-17, 220
Class struggle, 25, 338, 375, 377
Clausewitz, Karl von, 172
Cold War, xv, xxii: end of, 4, 115-16, 166, 175, 379; intense competition of, 9, 19; legacy of, 16, 158-59, 179; origins of, 120; public opinion of, 351-52; revival of, 20; "second" Cold War, 20, 22, 28; superpower doctrine during, 377
Collective security, xiv, 5, 60
"Common European home," 116, 153, 155-58, 160, 161, 166, 379
Common Market, 167. *See also* Economy: world
Common security, 8, 59, 60, 83, 84, 204, 371
Common Security, viii, 59, 60
Communications, 180, 251, 258, 263
Communism, 363
Communist Party: of the Soviet Union, 46, 47-48, 50, 51, 135; in Eastern Europe, 128, 129, 130, 135
Comprehensive security, 24, 25, 56, 57
Comprehensive System of International Security (CSIS), 56
Condominium, 52, 53, 75, 176, 183, 375
Conference on Security and Cooperation in Europe, 117, 147-48, 153, 155, 198, 327

Confidence-building measures: confidence- and security-building measures (CSBMs), 78; confidence building, xxi, 35; in Europe, 297, 310, 317, 326; in Korea, 227; in North Pacific, 198, 202, 219; in Persian Gulf, 188; Stockholm Accords on Confidence- and Security-Building Measures, 147-48, 275, 327
Congress of Peoples' Deputies, 374
Containment, 12, 13, 204, 372, 377
Contras, Nicaraguan, 361
Conventional Forces in Europe (CFE) talks, 146-47, 254-56, 294, 298, 308, 310, 327: lessons from MBFR, 273-76; Phase One, 269, 275, 325-26, 327-28, 331; Phase Two, 275, 276, 285; Soviet three-phase plan, 288
Cooperative security. *See* Mutual security: cooperative
Council of Europe, 122, 155
Council for Mutual Economic Assistance (CEMA), 129, 131, 133, 146, 156
Counterforce, 251, 258
"Counting" in arms negotiations, 251, 318
Crisis avoidance, 20, 25, 139
Crisis management, 20, 139, 223, 259, 262, 325
CSCE. *See* Conference on Security and Cooperation in Europe
Cuban missile crisis, 13, 19, 20, 371
Czechoslovakia: civil unrest in (1953), 144-45; and Germany, 143, 167; reforms in (1988-1989), 118; Soviet invasion of (1968), 120, 131, 138; Soviet troop withdrawal from, 147

"Decoupling," 18, 22
Defense sufficiency, 290, 291, 327
"Defensive defense," 218, 324, 325. *See also* Defensively oriented postures, Non-offensive postures
Defensively oriented postures, 81, 96, 98, 265, 296: and arms control, 282-83; defensive deployments, 261; defensive orientations, 90-91, 291; defensive postures, 276; defensive potentials, 272

De-ideologization. *See* Ideology: de-ideologization

Delors, Jacques, 168

Demilitarized Zone (DMZ), 218, 233-36, 239, 240, 242

Democratization: of Eastern Europe, 130-32; elements of, 45-48; and mutual democratic security, 52-54; upsurge of, 155; of South Korea, 235; of the Soviet Union, 337, 363

Deng Xiaoping, 216

Denmark, 276

Detente, 12, 374; and Basic Principles Agreement, 32-33, 34; in Korea, 196, 217, 229; lessons of, 19-27, 37; and public opinion, 356-57

Deterrence, nuclear, 7, 11, 289, 291: and European alliances, 265; and force survivability, 259; minimum deterrence, 91, 291; problems of, 29; public opinion of, 345, 350; role of, 89-90, 271; role of defenses in, 260; stabilizing influence of, 4, 146, 153, 254; *See also* Fundamental Deterrence

"Differentiation," 123

Disarmament, xxii, 132, 250, 274, 290, 352; World Conference on (Geneva), 290, 293-94

Domestic conditions, xx, 23, 141, 240: in the Soviet Union (chapter on), 42-58

"Double zero" option, 13

Drug traffic, 6, 212, 361

Dupuy, R. Ernest, 292, 294

Economy: East European, reform of, 124, 128-132, 133, 139-40, 144-46, 270; and East-West relations, 16, 87, 140, 148; economic security, 56, 84; market, 130, 132, 135, 146, 219; Soviet, 16, 146, 157, 208-9, 215, 270; world, 15-17, 43, 54, 56, 240

Eisenhower Doctrine, 178

Electronic Counter Measures (ECM), 293, 300, 307: electronic warfare, 311

Eliot, George Fielding, 292, 294, 297

Environment: agreement on protection of, 209; ecological organizations, 46; ecological security, 56, 84; environmental controls, 145; greenhouse effect, 5, 362; ozone layer, 5; pollution, 5, 145, 212, 362; problems of, xviii, xxi, 154, 202, 379

Escalation, inadvertent, 24, 30, 79, 88, 138, 259, 271, 272

Ethnic issues, 127, 228, 350

"Europe, United," 158

European Community (EC), 139, 146, 156, 168: and Germany, 143, 167, 169; "1992," 125, 158, 167

European Free Trade Association (EFTA), 168

"Evil empire," xxi, xxii, 30, 43

Exchanges, scientific and/or cultural, 35, 87, 184, 209, 217

F-15 (aircraft), 319

F-16 (aircraft), 197, 238, 319

F-18 (aircraft), 238, 241

Falkland Islands, xix

First strike, nuclear, 61, 240, 252, 253, 259, 261, 329-30

First use, nuclear, 66, 254, 271, 272, 321

Flexible Response, 321-22

Follow-On Forces Attack (FOFA), 273, 309-10, 323, 327

Forward defense, 214, 321

Four Powers, 163-64, 170, 375

"Four Tigers," 5

France, 264, 273-74

Fuller, General J.F.C., 292

Fundamental Deterrence, 91, 271: chapter on, 249-68. *See also* Deterrence, nuclear: minimum

Game theory, 61-62

Gandhi, Rajiv, 214-15

George, Alexander, 379

German Question, 133, 141-43, 375: chapters on, 161-65, 166-70; and Korean parallel, 224, 228; and Warsaw Treaty Organization, 132, 156

Germany, 52, 322: German Democratic Republic (East), 118, 138, 145, 281, 375; Federal Republic of (West), 142,

273-74, 281, 375; reunification of, 141, 142, 143, 159, 162, 166, 168, 169. *See also* German Question

Glasnost, 46, 51, 54, 337: and Eastern Europe, 123, 128, 274; and erosion of enemy image, xxi, 31, 47; "openness," 25

Global problems, xxi, 5, 43: and need for cooperative efforts, 24, 154; and public opinion, 362, 364;

Global security. *See* Common security

Gorbachev, Mikhail S., viii, 4, 21, 22, 23, 26, 27, 28, 30, 31, 35, 36, 48, 50, 55, 121, 122, 123, 129, 137, 144, 153, 161, 174, 184, 203, 206, 212, 243, 266, 288-89, 291, 366, 367, 378

"Grand deal," 140

Great Britain, 264

Greenhouse effect. *See* Environment

Grenada, xix, 363

Guided Anti-Tank Weapons, 300

Hard-target kill capability, 258

Hatchett, Ronald L., 305

Helsinki process, 154, 170, 205, 213, 326-27, 331. *See also* Conference on Security and Cooperation in Europe

Hitler, Adolf, 7, 142, 228

Hobbes, Thomas, xiv

Hoffman, Stanley, 12

Hotlines, 78, 208, 259, 317, 364

Human interests: human rights, 35, 36, 174, 338; interests, common, 226, 343; values, common, 121, 130, 378

Hungary: civil unrest in (1956), 138, 145; reforms in (1988-1989), 118; Soviet invasion of (1956), 120, 121, 131; Soviet troop withdrawal from, 147

Ideology, 30, 210, 339-40, 348-49; de-emphasis of in East-West relations, 338, 343, 352, 374; de-ideologization, 23, 378, 379

"Image of the enemy," x, 7, 42-43, 224, 346: erosion of, xxi, xxii, 47, 129, 153; strengthening of, 24, 30-31

"Incalculability," 322

Incidents at Sea Agreement, 35, 39, 40, 198, 220, 371

Institute for the USA and Canada, ix, 270, 283

Institute of World Economy and International Relations, 301

Interdependence, 23, 56, 63, 87, 158, 201: and mutual security, 10-18, 86; recognition of, xx, 339, 378

Intermediate-range Nuclear Forces (INF) Treaty, 13, 215, 255, 371: and Basic Principles Agreement, 35; and conventional arms talks, 270, 282, 327; and cooperation, 40, 331

International Atomic Energy Association (IAEA), 197

International Monetary Fund (IMF), 145

Iran, 179, 186-87: Iran-Iraq War, 182, 183, 184, 189; Joint Soviet-Iranian Communique, 184; and the Soviet Union, 184-85; and the United States, 183-84

Islamic movements, 184, 186

Isolationism, xiv, xviii, xxiii, 26, 349

Israel: Arab-Israeli conflict, 175; Egypt's attack on (1973), 38

Japan, 196, 213, 220, 222, 224, 232: and the Soviet Union, 207-8, 214, 216-17, 220, 351

Jiang Zemin, 216

Joint ventures, 54, 125, 209, 215

Jomini, Henri, 292

Kampuchea. *See* Cambodia

Kennedy, John F., 371

Khmer Rouges, 218

Khrushchev, Nikita, 371

Kim Chong Il, 237

Kim Il Sung, 237, 238, 243

Kissinger, Henry, 12, 120, 360, 372: Nixon and, 22, 26, 33, 34

Kohl, Helmut, 142, 167

Kokoshin, A., 294

Korea, 202, 213, 217, 220, 233-45, 329: conflict, 197, 206, 213, 217, 220, (chapter on) 222-32; Korean War, 223, 233, 234; and parallel to German Question, 224, 228; People's Democratic

Republic of (North), 195-206, 217-18, 225; Republic of (South), 195-206, 215; reunification of, 229, 230, 236; and the Soviet Union, 225, 237-39; and the United States, 234-35

"Launch-on-warning," 29, 259
"Launch-under-attack," 29
Law, international, 55, 155, 344
League of Nations, xv, 309
Lebensraum, xix
Legislature, Soviet, 44, 46, 49, 210
Legitimacy, 120, 121, 145
Lenin, V.I., xvii, 43
Leninism, 43, 130
Lewis and Clark Expedition (1804-1806), 379
Linear defense, 321-22, 323

Maginot Line, 294
Malykhin, V., 48
Marshall Plan, 124
Marx, Karl, xvii, 43
Marxism, 43, 130
Massive Retaliation, 321
May, Michael M., 258, 259
Media, role of, 44, 51-52, 125
MiG-23 (aircraft), 238
MiG-29 (aircraft), 197, 238
Military exercises, 197, 203, 220, 230-31
Missiles, defense against, 260-61
Mitterand, Francois, 168
Mitterand Plan, 168
Modrow, Hans, 143
Moiseyev, General M.A., 296
Multipolarity, xv, 29, 212, 213
MIRVs (Multiple Independently-targetable Re-entry Vehicles), 258, 317, 318, 372
Multiple Launch Rocket Systems (MLRS), 299
Mutual advantage, viii, 33
Mutual security, 3, 6-9, 24, 31, 39, 45, 52, 59, 60, 62, 72, 155, 174, 187, 329, 359: cooperative, 6, 330; defined, vii, 6, 59-60; "democratic," 52-54; enabling conditions, 98-99; joint study for, ix, 9, 94-95, 270, 285, 371; long-term sense, x-xii; multilateral vs. bilateral, 52-53; supportive conception of, 88, 89, 92, 93, 366-67; technical conception of, 88, 89, 92, 93, 364; threat reduction conception of, 88, 89, 92, 93, 365-66; transition to, 45-58, 130-35; and trust 92, 97; "victory" defined under, vii, 298. *See also* Common security
Mutual threat reduction, 30, 33, 81, 190, 277: and the arms race, 378; and defensive defense, 218; and mutual security, 8-9, 40, 249; need for, x, xii
Mutual and Balanced Force Reductions (MBFR) negotiations, 28, 35, 270, 273-76

National interest, 44, 52, 176-77, 185, 187, 205
National security, xiii-xviii, 3, 6, 10-11, 35, 73, 75, 99, 161, 372, 376: League of Nations definition of, 309; redefinition of, 213; as "unilateral" or mutual security, 6-7, 24, 62, 69-71, 72, 73, 80, 88, 100, 328
Nationalism: East European, 127, 130, 139; German, 142; Korean, 234, 242; in the Soviet Union, 350
NATO (North Atlantic Treaty Organization), 4, 132, 138, 147, 159, 255, (chapters on) 269-333: nuclear first-use policy, 254; future of, 28, 143-44, 156; Council, 288, 289
Negative-sum game, 62, 63, 77, 97
Negotiation, 11, 94, 244, chapters on, 269-316
New political thinking, xvi, xix, xxi-xxii, 22, 23, 45, 48, 153, 159, 174, 178, 200, 210, 213, 324, 325, 339, 352
Nixon, Richard, 174: and arms control, 12; and Basic Principles Agreement, 33, 34, 37; and U.S.-Soviet relations, 22, 26, 32
Nonaggression pact, 206
Non-aligned movement, xv

Non-offensive postures, 297, 305, 308. *See also* "Defensive defense," Defensively oriented postures

Non-Proliferation Treaty, 5, 74, 143, 197, 265, 317

Norms, explicit, 22, 53. *See also* Basic Principles Agreement

Nuclear free zone, 225, 232

Nuclear power plants, xix, 6: nuclear energy, 35

Nuclear Risk Reduction Centers, 35, 40, 78, 371

Nuclear waste, 6

Nuclear weapons: ICBMs (Intercontinental Ballistic Missiles), 251, 258, 260, 261, 262, 305; in Korea, 241-42; "nuclear threat," 344-45; SLBMs (submarine-launched ballistic missiles), 251, 260, 262, 305; strategic, 91, 146, 202, 212, 249-54, 257; strategic nuclear delivery vehicles (SNDVs), 251, 252, 262, 264; tactical, 202, 255-56, 272, 283; testing, 35; three-stage reduction of, 256-64; triad, 256, 257, 259; umbrella, 197, 241. See also Proliferation, nuclear

Offensively oriented postures, 30, 96, 254, 255, 272, 282

Oil, 178, 181, 220: embargo, 179; prices, 180, 185, 190

Olympics, Seoul (1988), 238

On-site inspection, 31, 261, 275, 327

"Openness." *See* Glasnost

Outer Space Treaty, 317

"Owls," 78

Ozone layer. *See* Environment

Paasilo, P., 303

Pacific Economic Cooperation Council (PECC), 219

Palme, Olaf, viii, 59

Palme Commission, viii, 59

Palme Report, 59, 60, 60-61

Panama invasion (1989), 178, 363

Paris Club, 145

Parity: conventional, 271, 303; strategic, 23, 24, 252, 257, 269

Peaceful coexistence, 25, 33-36, 377

Peredyshka, 93

Perestroika, xvi, xxi, xxiii, 45-52, 54, 337, 342, 349: and the Asia-Pacific region, 200; and Eastern Europe, 123, 128, 131, 134, 135; global, 55, 56; in Korea, 217

Persian Gulf: chapter on, 173-91

Phillipines, 329

Poland: crises in, 120, 138, 145; and Germany, 143, 167; reforms in (1988-1989), 118; Soviet troop withdrawal, 147

Political Consultative Committee, 156, 289

Pollution. *See* Environment

Popular Fronts, 131

Positive-sum game, 62, 77, 97, 273

Proliferation, nuclear, 5, 251, 254, 265, 361: desirability of preventing, 220, 260, 264

Public opinion, 38, 205, (chapters on) 337-55, 356-70: influence on policy, 45, 374; Japanese, 208; Soviet, 47, 51-52

Public Agenda Foundation, 338, 359

"Public, the Soviets, and Nuclear Arms, The" (project), 359

Rafsanjani, Hashemi 184

Reagan, Ronald, 13, 28, 266, 361, 378: and Gorbachev, 21, 35; and Strategic Defense Initiative, 260

"Realpolitik," 340, 361

"Reasonable sufficiency," 271, 290, 291, 348

Report of the Commission on Disarmament and Security Issues. See Palme Report

Reykjavik Summit, 13

Roberts, U.S.S. (warship), 183

Rogers, General Bernard William, 323

Roh Tae Woo, 234, 236

Romania, 138, 145

Roosevelt, Franklin D., 290, 303

SA-3 (surface-to-air missile), 238

SA-5 (surface-to-air missile), 197, 239

SALT I (Strategic Arms Limitation Treaty I), 12, 40, 257, 317, 318, 371

SALT II (Strategic Arms Limitation Treaty II), 13, 34, 317, 318

Schlesinger, James, 13

Scowcroft, Brent, 216

Security dilemma, 24, 30, 76, 269, 372-73

Shevardnadze, Eduard, 55, 207, 288, 303

Shlykov, V., 294, 297

Shultz, George, 35-36

Sihanouk, Prince Norodom, 206, 218

Social Darwinism, 10

Socialism, xx, 16, 50, 121, 274, 341: capitalism, end of dispute with, 154, 166, 338, 352; in China, 216; in Eastern Europe, 128, 130, 134, 136; in Korea, 234; world socialism, 343, 348

Sovereignty, xvii, 33, 350

Spinoza, Baruch, xvi

SS-20 (missile), 28, 215

Stability, 17, 152, 160; concept of, 329-30; and Fundamental Deterrence, 259, 263, 265; political, 31-32; strategic, 32, 250-51, 271

Stalin, Joseph, 116, 120, 144, 217, 219

Standing Consultative Commission (SCC), 39

Stealth technology, 311

START (Strategic Arms Reductions Talks), 13, 249, 256-58: and Fundamental Deterrence, 252, 262-66; and improvement of U.S.-Soviet relations, 35, 214

Steinbruner, John D., 258, 259

Strategic Defense Initiative (SDI), 14, 28, 29, 260

Su-25 (aircraft), 197, 238

Summits: Malta (1989), 3, 122; Nixon-Brezhnev (1972), 377; Reagan-Gorbachev (1985), 35; Reagan-Gorbachev (1988), 35

Supreme Soviet, 45, 49, 50, 131

Tactical aviation, 304, 305, 306

Taiwan, 228

Team Spirit (exercise), 225, 227, 243

Technology, 29, 49, 128, 188, 215, 308: arms control, 14, 159

Tension reduction, 196, 210, 239, 243-44, 286, 340

Terrorism, xviii, 6, 154, 188, 361, 379: in Korea, 223, 233, 235, 244; U.S.-Soviet cooperation against, 24, 341

Thailand, 219

Third World, xxi, 5, 29, 38, 49, 361: U.S.-Soviet competition in, 24, 25-26, 28, 34, 81, 178, 179, 340, 365

"Third Zero," 255

Tiananmen Square, 216

"Tin Shield" (system), 238

Trade restrictions, 244

Transaction costs, 64, 67

"Transparency," 79, 189, 198, 215, 253, 261

Tripartite Declaration, 178

Truman Doctrine, 178

Tucker, Robert W., 361

Unilateral approach to security, 6, 7, 24, 31, 72, 73: unilateral security, 62, 70-71, 80, 88, 100, 273, 341

United Nations, xv-xvi, xxi, 182, 230: Charter, 182; General Assembly, 236; Korean entry into, 218, 243; Security Council, 218

Verification, 73, 92, 252, 275, 327, 365: necessity of, 282, 296, 297

Vienna Congress (1815), xv, 141

Vietnam: Haiphong Harbor, U.S. bombing of, 34; Vietnam syndrome, 28; U.S. involvement in, 12, 206

Virginia conference (1988), meeting of the International Research and Exchanges Board and the Soviet Academy of Sciences, 119

Vance, Cyrus, 13

Von Bulow, A., 299, 303

Walesa, Lech, 122

War fighting, 271: capabilities, 251, 256, 263; scenarios, 252, 255, 262

War of 1812, xi

Warsaw Pact, 4, 28, 131-32, 138, 255: chapters on, 269-87, 317-33; efforts to undermine, 159; preservation of, 121-22, 135, 156

Weapons, modernization of, 238, 256, 258, 281, 358

World community, 341

World order, 26

World War I, xv, 127, 327

World War II, xvii, 156, 169, 170: influence on modern Soviet military strategy, 323, 324

Yalta conference, 116: "Yalta II," 120, 125

Yankelovich, Daniel, 358

"Zero option," 13, 294

Zero-sum game, 61-63, 77, 169, 175, 176, 181, 187, 273

"Zonal approach," 301

Zubok, V., 294